MONOGRAPHS OF THE
SOCIETY FOR RESEARCH IN
CHILD DEVELOPMENT

Serial No. 240, Vol. 59, Nos. 2–3, 1994

THE DEVELOPMENT OF EMOTION REGULATION: BIOLOGICAL AND BEHAVIORAL CONSIDERATIONS

EDITED BY

Nathan A. Fox

WITH COMMENTARY BY

Joseph J. Campos et al.

MONOGRAPHS OF THE SOCIETY FOR RESEARCH IN CHILD DEVELOPMENT
Serial No. 240, Vol. 59, Nos. 2–3, 1994

CONTENTS

ABSTRACT

Fox, Nathan A. (Ed.). The Development of Emotion Regulation: Biological and Behavioral Considerations. With Commentary by Joseph J. Campos et al. *Monographs of the Society for Research in Child Development,* 1994, **59**(2–3, Serial No. 240).

Research on the development of emotions and their functional characteristics as regulators of behavior has grown dramatically over the past 10 years. There is currently renewed emphasis on the importance of emotion regulation and dysregulation for our understanding of normal development and the development of psychopathology. The 11 essays that constitute this *Monograph* survey theoretical, conceptual, and methodological issues involved in the study of emotion regulation, placing particular emphasis on the role that physiological systems play in the regulation of emotion and on the interface of a biological and a behavioral perspective.

The *Monograph* is divided into three parts. Part 1 contains essays on the definitional issues involved in the study of emotion regulation. Kagan and Thompson attempt to define exactly what phenomenon it is that we are interested in studying. Kagan argues for a descriptive approach to studying emotional behavior, one in which psychological labels are put aside until there is a clear understanding of the behavioral pattern. Thompson provides a thorough review of the possible topics to be studied under the rubric of *emotion regulation* and emphasizes the importance of context for studying these phenomena. Both authors provide guidelines for approaching the study of emotional behaviors during development. Calkins outlines the influence that individual differences in emotion expression have on emotion regulation. She addresses the role of temperament and temperament/environment interactions and their effect on the development of emotion regulation. Cole, Michel, and Teti deal with the role that emotion regulation plays in developmental psychopathology, outlining the manner in which the development of emotion regulation may become dysfunctional and lead to problem outcomes. Their essay serves as a bridge between traditional developmental work on emotion and research in developmental psychopathology.

The four essays in Part 2 focus on three different physiological systems—the neuroendocrine (Stansbury and Gunnar), autonomic nervous (Porges, Doussard-Roosevelt, and Maiti), and central nervous (Dawson and Fox) systems. These essays share common approaches to the study of emotion regulation, even though each system presents novel and potentially nonoverlapping information about the behaviors in question. The reader is provided with the background necessary to understand each complex physiological system and hence to evaluate the research that is being undertaken in that area.

The three essays in Part 3 consider the role of relationships as regulators of emotional behavior. Both Hofer and Field write from the perspective of developmental psychobiology, presenting evidence of the effect that relationships have on physiological systems that are important for growth and development. Cassidy discusses current attachment theory and the role that working models of attachment play in the regulation of emotion.

Taken together, these 11 essays offer a particular perspective toward emotional development and emotion regulation. This perspective reflects a functionalist view of emotions and provides evidence for the role that emotions play as regulators even as they themselves are being regulated during behavioral interaction.

PREFACE

This *Monograph* contains a series of essays that were first presented as papers at a conference on the development of emotion regulation that was held in Washington, DC, in March 1991. Two forces motivated the organization of this conference. The first was the great interest prevailing at that time in redefining our conceptual understanding of emotions and emotional development. Researchers were clearly beginning to articulate a functionalist perspective toward emotions and emotional development, and this position was likely to have a significant effect on developmental research in this area.

The second motivating force was the set of advances in the field's understanding of the biological bases of emotion and emotional development. Work on a number of different physiological systems, including the neuroendocrine, the autonomic nervous, and the central nervous systems, had in the previous decade begun to produce interesting patterns of findings that could assist in understanding emotional behavior. The conclusion being reached by increasing numbers of investigators was that emotions could no longer be thought of as static, discrete behaviors but instead must be viewed as regulating behavior—just as these emotions themselves are regulated. Psychophysiological and psychobiological data seemed to fit well within this scheme since physiological change was both an end result and a driving force in emotion regulation.

The meeting represented an attempt to define these phenomena and the various methods of approach to their study and to present the most recent psychological and psychophysiological work related to emotion regulation. The essays in this *Monograph* are refined presentations of those original conference presentations. Their aim is to provide the reader with an overview of the nature of the problem, the methods for its study, the physiological systems that are involved, and the work from psychobiology that can inform our understanding of the development of emotion regulation.

The conference was sponsored by the John D. and Catherine T. MacArthur Foundation Early Childhood Network and by the Center for Educa-

NATHAN A. FOX, ED.

tional Research and Development at the University of Maryland. I would like to thank Robert Emde from the MacArthur Foundation and John Guthrie from the Center for Educational Research and Development for their support of the meeting.

N.A.F.

PART 1:
DEFINITIONS AND CONCEPTS OF
EMOTION REGULATION

In his essay in this volume on the nature of emotion and emotion regulation, Jerome Kagan writes that a major difference between biologists and social scientists is that the latter prefer to begin their inquiry with a priori, idealized concepts, whose referents they then try to find in observations, while the former start with robust phenomena and invent constructs a posteriori. The study of emotion and emotion regulation has not been immune to the social science approach. There have been numerous writings that have suggested the importance of emotion regulation in developing social relationships and in understanding atypical development. Until recently, however, there has been less empirical work done on exactly how these processes occur and how they are influenced by individual differences in constitution and variations in environment. It is, however, safe to say that there is general agreement that the regulation of emotions is a significant developmental objective for the child and that exactly how this is accomplished is of considerable interest to both the clinical and the developmental psychology communities.

Perhaps one reason for the dearth of research in this area has been the lack of precision as to exactly what phenomenon was under study. In its simplest form, emotion regulation has been viewed as reflecting the child's ability to modulate the expression of negative emotions. As such, the infant's ability to regulate his or her distress is seen as evidence for emotion regulation. In the more complex instance, emotion regulation has been viewed as affecting the development of complex social relationships; furthermore, the quality of social relationships has been implicated as having a regulatory effect on the individual expression of emotions. For the psychologist interested in studying emotion regulation, there is thus a broad set of areas from which to choose, all of which seem to come under the general heading of *emotion regulation.* There may be nothing wrong with this situation—if, in fact, there are a certain number of assumptions that are agreed on by investigators studying different aspects of the same phenomenon. Among the assumptions that seem most important to be shared among researchers are the method of approach to the study of emotion regulation and the agreement on the factors to be included in describing the model used for investigating the phenomena.

Many of the problems in the study of emotion and emotion-related phenomena, such as temperament or mood, arise from a lack of agreement as to the method of study. The issue is easily illustrated in the study of infant temperament. For quite some time, individual differences in infant temperament were known to exist, having been evinced in descriptions given by parents or clinicians of infants' behavior. Questionnaire studies, and the factors derived from the data thus obtained, produced a range of traits or characteristics that we think of today as composing the classic infant temperaments (e.g., rhythmicity, mood). More recently, variations in infant behavior style were studied either in the laboratory or in the home context, focusing on observations of behaviors that constitute the corpus of material used to construct temperamental traits. These observational studies produced descriptions of temperamental types that had not been previously described with questionnaire methods; moreover, observed behavior often did not correspond to parents' reports. This is not to imply that questionnaire data do not provide important information regarding parents' perceptions of their infant's behavior. Indeed, dissociations between parents' perceptions and observed behavior may in themselves be of interest in the study of social development. Nevertheless, given the wide range of circumstances in which emotion regulation may be studied, it seems critical that there be some agreement as to the approach utilized in investigating the phenomenon. The variety of contexts in which emotion regulation occurs necessitates multimethod approaches even if there is lack of convergence among the different indices that are collected.

A second issue that has slowed progress in this domain has been the view that emotions serve only to disorganize or interfere with analytic or cognitive processing. In this view, emotions represent the "psychological underground," the "Sturm und Drang" that disrupts productive, rational thought. In some sense, emotion states were viewed as noise in the system and therefore to be controlled in experiments of higher-order cognition. This position is embodied in research on emotion regulation that viewed the goal of regulation as the diminution of negative affect and distress. As infants grow older, their distress response to novelty diminishes, paving the way for them to utilize sophisticated cognitive coping skills in response to stressful challenge. More recently, however, the study of emotions and emotion regulation has been approached from a functionalist perspective. Emotions are viewed as organizing behavior and as serving specific functions for various types of environmental demands. These emotions are not only responses to be regulated but also themselves regulators of environmental interaction. The goal of emotion regulation is not simply the modulation of negative affect but also the regulation of distress by the activation of other emotions. This bidirectional influence may be accomplished by maintaining or enhancing emotional arousal as well as diminishing it.

This view of the organizing function of emotions provides a framework for studying the contexts within which particular responses are adaptive or maladaptive. It also allows us to examine how emotions either interfere with or facilitate the achievement of particular developmental tasks. In this sense, a functionalist study of emotions and emotion regulation provides a link to the study of developmental psychopathology or, at the very least, the conditions that place a child at risk for such behavior problems. It also provides the frame for examining the role of emotions across a wide variety of contexts, including dyadic interaction and family interaction processes. Emotion regulation, then, may serve to organize cognitive processes for the individual, or it may allow the individual to adjust to the complexities of a particular situation. These functions serve to build social relationships as they are modified by the interactions that take place within those relationship experiences.

The role of experience and context is thus an additional important aspect that must be incorporated within the model or approach adopted in common by investigators of emotion regulation. Patterns that might in one instance be viewed as dysregulated may be functional responses to a harsh or chaotic environment. Thus, the context (e.g., the caretaking environment) should be seen as playing an integral part in shaping the strategies and patterns of the emotion response that the child develops as he or she meets different developmental challenges.

Definition, method of approach to its study, and the boundaries of the phenomenon investigated are all issues that are raised in the first part of this *Monograph*. This group of essays tackles the difficult task of presenting the areas of study, the nature of the questions to be asked, the notion of a common approach, and the factors that make up a model with which we may interpret the data.

Jerome Kagan addresses the issue of the use of language in the psychological study of emotions and the problem of definition of psychological concepts prior to empirical description of those states. He raises an important challenge for a theory of discrete emotions and thereby sets the stage for the introduction of new approaches to an understanding of the role of multiple response measures and multiple functions of emotion. Kagan provides examples from his own work on the construct of behavioral inhibition in terms of its reliance on multiple measurement and empirical definition.

Ross A. Thompson takes on the task of providing a taxonomy and understanding of the role of emotions as both regulating and being regulated. In his wide-ranging essay, Thompson provides a logical classification

system for understanding the issues in research on emotion regulation. He
touches on aspects of both the regulating function of emotions and the
manner in which emotional behaviors regulate interactions. In all, his essay
is a touchstone for researchers engaged in work in this area.

Susan D. Calkins discusses the role of context and social interaction
as they both are regulated and regulate individual differences in infant
emotionality. Emotion regulation does not develop solely as a function of
the input that caregivers provide during socialization but is a product of
the disposition of individual children to express certain emotions with
greater or less frequency. Calkins's essay describes the multiple pathways
by which adaptive and maladaptive emotion regulation may occur as a function of the interplay of context and infant individuality.

Pamela M. Cole, Margaret K. Michel, and Laureen O'Donnell Teti an-
chor their discussion of emotion and emotion-regulating functions within
a clinical/developmental framework. They describe the issues involved in
understanding process and individual differences in emotion regulation.
They underscore the meaning of emotion regulation within clinical psychology and its importance within developmental psychopathology. They also
provide illustrative data on the different consequences that emotion dysregulation has for child behavior.

Together, the four essays that make up this first part provide the foundation and framework for the empirical data that follow in subsequent
parts. They present the scientific issues that must be faced, the necessary
definitional clarity, and the theoretical factors that make up a shared model
on the basis of which productive investigation into the multiple facets of
emotion regulation may take place.

N.A.F.

ON THE NATURE OF EMOTION

Jerome Kagan

The reasons why particular phenomena dominate serious inquiry during a historical era are not easily specified. When the phenomenon is a part of human nature, however, philosophical assumptions about the relative significance of action, emotion, and ideation always become relevant. These three qualities, like the Greek quartet of earth, air, water, and fire, seem so distinctive to all observers that they remain the most attractive way to parse the human psyche. Although future theory will replace this trio as surely as post-Renaissance science replaced the Greek elements, at the moment we still must reason around the current categories.

The Greek view of human functioning held that each person possessed a different balance of the four humors—blood, phlegm, and yellow and black bile—and that the relation among all four determined a person's mood, thought, and behavior. This holistic conception of human functioning assumed a reciprocity among physiological and psychological processes. The Greek ideal of paideia, defined as the passionate perfection of a talent, combined emotion, thought, and action.

However, the divorce of biological from psychological events, essential to Christian philosophy, was followed in the West by a competition for priority among the separate components. The rationality central to cognitive functioning was preeminent during the Enlightenment; affects reigned during the nineteenth century, and during the first half of this century action moved to the center of inquiry owing, in part, to the philosophy of pragmatism and the premises of behaviorism. At present, cognitive pro-

Preparation of this essay was supported in part by grants from the John D. and Catherine T. MacArthur Foundation and the Leon Lowenstein Foundation. I thank Nancy Snidman, Doreen Arcus, and J. Steven Reznick for their loyalty and wisdom in our collaboration.

cesses have returned, after two centuries, to center stage, but this time closely allied with the neurosciences. There are, however, early signs of a renewal of interest in both human emotion and temperament, linked to the hope that, by bringing biology back into psychology, the Greek vision will be revived, albeit with greater sophistication. There are at least three bases for the expanded curiosity about human emotions.

The first, and perhaps most significant, originates in physiological research on the relation of neural activity in selected limbic sites to changes in mood and behavior. The empirical work of Adamec and Stark-Adamec (1986), Davis, Hitchcock, and Rosen (1987), and Mishkin and Aggleton (1981), among many others, has taught us that the amygdala, hippocampus, and hypothalamus, together with their projections to the frontal cortex and motor and autonomic systems, participate in the states that philosophers, psychiatrists, and psychologists have called *passion, surprise, fear, sadness, joy, anger, disgust,* and, at a more abstract level, *pleasure* and *displeasure.* When these structures are compromised, through surgery or chemicals, the action sequences normally linked to these states are either absent or seriously different from their usual form.

A second development derives from the psychological studies of human affects. One line of inquiry, which can be traced to Paul Ekman (1980) and Carroll Izard (1977), focuses on the universality of a small number of discrete affect states, each associated with a facial expression. A second psychological theme originated in the theoretical essays of John Bowlby (1969/1982) on the emotional attachments of children to their caretakers.

The third development is the revival, after a century of neglect, of inquiry into temperamental types. The investigators in this domain regard variation in chronic mood and receptivity to acute affect states as due, in part, to inherited variations in the susceptibility to specific profiles of physiological arousal (Kagan, Reznick, & Snidman, 1988). This essay considers the concept of affect and its relation to temperament by arguing that some children are born with a biological preparedness to experience fear of the unfamiliar more easily and more intensely than others.

THE CONCEPT OF AFFECT

I approach the idea of affect in a nonpragmatic, Baconian frame that resists positing an a priori, closed set of abstract, discrete emotion categories. One reason to maintain an attitude of skepticism toward current practice is that most of the popular affect categories used in scientific discourse are obvious derivatives of the language that people use to name their subjectively experienced states. The histories of physics, chemistry, and biology teach us that the first terms used to label natural phenomena, which also came from folk language, were replaced eventually with technical words that were not part of everyday speech but described nature more accurately. The remark to a friend, "I feel sick," communicates a state that is sufficiently accurate for harmonious social interaction. But it is far less useful to a biologist who wants to understand the specific etiology of an illness and its natural course. Emotion terms like *angry, surprised,* or *happy* are adequate for ordinary conversation, but each hides too much variety to be useful for a synthetic theory of emotion. In addition, affects for which names are not available are ignored, for example, the emotion generated in a person who has returned after many years to a favorite New England forest on a clear day in early October as the maples are turning crimson. Put plainly, popular English words for affects are too general and do not accommodate sufficiently to their immediate, contextual origins.

Families of Affects

Most commentators agree that emotions are patterns composed of some (or all) of the following components: (1) a precipitating event in a context is accompanied by (2) changes in motor behavior, especially face and posture, as well as central and peripheral physiology, and both are (3) evaluated cognitively and (4) may lead to a change in subjectively experienced feelings. This broad definition implies that it may be profitable to assume distinctive families of affect states, analogous to animal families in phylogeny. Each member of a particular family is defined by a combination of incentive, physiology, cognitive structure, and motor actions. Although some affect states are associated with distinctive facial expressions that often function as information signals to conspecifics, others are not as clearly linked to unambiguous changes in the face; guilt over lying, anxiety over anticipation of criticism, sexual arousal, and pride while being praised are some examples. Postures and facial expressions can be part of an affective process, but they are probably neither origins nor necessary components of an affect. This strong claim rests on the assumption that elimination of the motor outputs to the facial muscles while watching a comedy might be accompanied by a slightly different state, but not by complete absence of any affective experience.

It may be useful, therefore, to regard each distinct trio of biology, cognition, and motor response, linked to a class of incentive, as an emotion. Consider, as an example, the family of affects that are called *fear-anxiety.* One member of this family is provoked by an unfamiliar event that cannot be assimilated immediately; for example, a mother leaves her 1-year-old in an unfamiliar room. This incentive produces in the child (*a*) activation of sites in the hippocampus and amygdala, together with projections to the striatum, cingulate, central gray, hypothalamus, cortex, and sympathetic nervous system, (*b*) a state of uncertainty, and (*c*) a display of immobility, escape behavior, and/or distress. This combination of events, popularly called *separation anxiety*, is one of the states in the fear-anxiety family.

However, there is a related trio composed of a different state of the amygdala, a cognitive anticipation of criticism, and a disposition to become quiet when a person believes that his or her behavior is being evaluated by someone in a position of authority. This profile of events defines an affect that one might call *anxiety over evaluation*. A third trio, provoked by the sight of a grizzly bear, is characterized by a somewhat different state of the amygdala in conjunction with an inference of physical danger and the disposition to flee. This combination defines an affect that we might call *anxiety over possible harm*. The distinctions among these three affect states are not trivial, even though theorists might regard them as components of the larger family of fear-anxiety.

I recognize that this view is more complex and contextually constrained than current assumptions. But the history of biology reveals that initial conceptions are often too symmetrical, too simple, and too abstract and, as a result, have to be replaced. That is one reason why our current under-standing of the structure and functions of living cells was not invented earlier by a creative biologist sitting at her desk. The reflective human mind does not like, and, therefore, is unlikely to generate, without a rich set of empirical data, a priori categories that are as asymmetrical, complex, and contextually constrained as those that are likely to characterize human emotions.

ARE THERE UNITARY EMOTIONS?

Although some essays on emotion states imply that every distinct incentive produces one dominant emotion, it is likely that many situations produce blends or multiple emotions. Consider a person, S, who is waiting in line to buy a ticket to a movie and who is pushed unexpectedly by O. An observer sees the following sequence: S swears at O, then withdraws a few inches and, seconds later, scans the faces of the other people standing in the line. What affect state (or states) should we ascribe to S? The answer will depend on our purpose. If we wish to study the relation between the incentive of being pushed and S's emotion, we will probably focus on his swearing and conclude that he is angry. If we wish to understand the relation between S's anticipation of being harmed by O and S's affect, we will focus on his bodily withdrawal and infer that he is fearful. And, if we wish to comprehend the relation between S's recognition that he lost control of his behavior in a public place and his subsequent glances at the faces in the crowd, we will conclude that he is feeling embarrassed. Further, it is reasonable to claim that a combination of the three states named above might create a state different from each of them and, therefore, require a distinct name. All these solutions are valid, depending on the purpose of the analysis. Zoologists classify cows as mammals, economists categorize them as commodities, and some cultures regard these animals as sacred symbols.

Provisional acceptance of the argument that single, unified affect states do not occur all the time implies that we should question the validity of our current terms. It would be more profitable if research on affect began with phenomena, like the hypothetical sequence between S and O described above, and determined the complex relations among the incentives and changes in cognition, action, and physiology. When a particular and reliable cluster emerged, investigators would name it. When scientists implement this Baconian strategy, they are apt to discover new categories as well as subtypes within the broad states called *anxiety, anger,* and *sadness.*

AWARENESS

It will be necessary to differentiate between those affect states in which the changes in physiology are experienced consciously and those in which the same physiological events occur without conscious awareness. In the former, the individual is likely to impose a subjective interpretation on the experienced state. The subsequent affective state will have a special quality, and, as a result, behaviors and thoughts might be generated that would not have occurred had the physiological changes remained undetected. Thus, a person who detects a rise in heart rate and increased muscle tension in an unfamiliar social situation will try to interpret that information and, as a result, be in an altered state.

At a minimum, we need a special term, or a suffix to append to an affect construct, that specifies whether an emotion state is a product of conscious awareness of changes in feeling tone and intention. This distinction is similar to the difference between a disease state and a patient's recognition that she is ill (e.g., the difference between an undetected tumor and knowledge that one has cancer). Some adults with a fear of snakes, spiders, blood, or mutilation show a rise in cortisol, skin conductance, and conscious fear on the presentation of pictures of these feared objects. However, there was no relation between the intensity of the fear experienced consciously, as reported to an experimenter, and the magnitude of change in these biological variables (Fredrikson, Sundin, & Frankenhaeuser, 1985). Similarly, there was no relation between the intensity of affect reported by adults as they tried to solve difficult intellectual tasks and magnitude of change in heart rate, blood pressure, and catecholamines (Mills, Berry, Dimsdale, Nelesen, & Ziegler, 1993).

The distinction between more and less conscious states requires differentiating between an affective state in the subjective frame of the person and one in the frame of an observer (or observers). Freud, like Einstein, sought unity and parsimony and wanted all discussion of affects to be in the observer's frame, that is, focused on events in the mind/brain of a person whose characteristics were independent of how they were assessed. However, an equally large number of scientists side with Bohr, who argued that the source of evidence for a scientific construct participates in its meaning.

The conceptual distinction can be put in concrete terms. Consider a compulsive adult who consistently cleans her kitchen a dozen times a day. When asked why, she says it gives her pleasure to know that the room is always spotless, adding that she experiences displeasure whenever she sees any dirt. The psychologist, by contrast, assumes that she is anxious and experiences displeasure each time she scrubs the floor. The psychologist's use of the word *anxious* is in the observer frame and is intended to imply both a physiological state and a hypothetical set of structures that were acquired over time and of which the patient might be unaware. The patient intends only to label her conscious feelings. The distinction between the frame of the agent and that of the observer is important because a large number of psychologists study affects by using questionnaires that ask individuals about the frequency and intensity of their subjective states of anxiety, depression, and anger. Some of these scientists assume, incorrectly, that the meaning of an affect term understood on the basis of self-report evidence is similar to, or even identical with, the meaning understood by psychologists who use behavioral observations or physiological data as evidence for inferring similar states.

NEURAL CIRCUITS AND EMOTION

Recent research by physiologists (see esp. LeDoux, 1986, 1989) suggests that at least four different neural circuits can participate in the affective state that is popularly called *fear*. The most basic circuit, which can be triggered by novel events, innate releasers, and conditioned stimuli, involves connections among the thalamus, hippocampus, basal and lateral amygdala, and sensory cortex (the hippocampus also sends projections to the amygdala, and the amygdala projects reciprocally to the thalamus and cortex). Arousal of this circuit represents a state of surprise and alert preparedness for a subsequent state. For example, when an unexpected sound occurs in a quiet room in which a person is reading, after being processed by the cochlea and the colliculus, the auditory signal arrives at the medial geniculate of the thalamus. Three separate circuits leave the thalamus simultaneously—one to the hippocampus to evaluate the familiarity (or unfamiliarity) of the sound in that particular context, one to the amygdala to prepare for motor and autonomic reactions, and one to the sensory cortex to perform a detailed analysis of the sound. The result of the cortical analysis is relayed back to the hippocampus and amygdala to supplement the message that arrived about 50 msec earlier.

If the result of the cortical processing is the perception of an airplane overhead, there will be no further affective consequences. If the source of the sound remains unclear and assimilation is not possible, a second circuit will be aroused. This circuit involves reciprocal projections from the amygdala and hippocampus to the frontal and association cortex, where further evaluation of the information occurs. If assimilation is still not possible, the resulting state might be called *uncertainty*, to be contrasted with the first state, *alert preparedness*.

A third circuit adds motor and visceral reactions. The motor circuits involve projections from the basal area of the amygdala to the corpus striatum and from the central nucleus of the amygdala to the cingulate, central gray and skeletal muscles, hypothalamus (especially the lateral and ventromedial hypothalamus), autonomic nervous system, pituitary, medulla, and locus ceruleus. Activation of these circuits is accompanied by changes in motor tension, posture, speech, heart rate, blood pressure, respiration, norepinephrine, and cortisol secretion. The state resulting from activation of some or all of these circuits might be called *fear of unfamiliarity*.

The motor and autonomic changes in the body engage a fourth circuit that involves afferent feedback from the peripheral target sites to the nucleus tractus solitarius and the parabrachial nucleus in the medulla and pons. These sites project to the central nucleus of the amygdala, which in turn sends projections to the prefrontal cortex. It is presumed that the prefrontal cortex mediates a subjective appreciation and interpretation of the changes in bodily tone. This state is *conscious fear*. The conscious perception of the changes in bodily arousal can, of course, alter the person's emotion state.

I do not suggest that these four circuits can be separated easily, only that it is not necessary that all circuits be activated when a particular incentive occurs. An unexpected sound in a quiet room might arouse only the first circuit, without producing activation of motor or autonomic components. But the state of alerting is an affect state, different from the one that would be generated if the reader in the quiet room reacted to the sound with a 10-beat increase in heart rate because of a guess that there might be a dangerous animal in the room.

In young infants, the first three circuits can occur without the fourth.

Consider a 4-month-old infant listening to a series of taped sentences spoken by a female voice in the absence of any visual support for that voice. The first sentence usually provokes an alert state, but the sound elicits neither a wary face nor crying. However, after the second or third sentence, the faces of some infants become wary, presumably following the recognition of a discrepancy (a human voice without a face) that could not be assimilated. On the next trial, these infants are likely to cry.

THREE USES OF AFFECT CONCEPTS

A major difference between biologists and social scientists is that the former prefer to start with robust phenomena and invent constructs a posteriori after functional relations have been discovered. Psychologists prefer to begin their inquiry the other way round, with a priori, idealized concepts, whose referents they then try to find in observations. Thus, it is profitable to ask what the reliable phenomena are that we wish to explain with affect concepts.

First, there are the acute changes in physiology, cognition, and action that occur in response to novelty, challenge, loss, attack, or frustration. These changes are sudden, are often temporary, and approach the meaning of the discrete emotions posited by Ekman and Izard.

A second set of phenomena refers to the longer-lasting affect states created by experiences repeated over years. These are chronic moods that can result, for example, from membership in a particular ethnic group, a decade of academic failure, or repeated social rejection. These chronic moods bias a person to react to incentives in particular ways. Folk theory, as well as research reports, makes the distinction between acute states and chronic moods. When we say, "Paul is angry because he was pushed," we understand that Paul's state is different from the one implied by the sentence, "Paul is angry because of his chronic life of poverty," even though the word *angry* is used in both sentences. Because the physiological states and cognitions are probably different in the acute and chronic states, it seems reasonable to apply different names to them.

Finally, there is individual variation in the biologically based biases to react to certain events with particular responses. These inherited biases are called *temperaments*. Neither folk belief nor contemporary theory makes a distinction between chronic emotional moods and temperamental biases, even though nineteenth-century writers did.

For the family of affects called *fear* or *anxiety*, I believe that it will be useful to employ at least three different terms for three states that are members of this affect family. A similar conclusion holds for all other affect families. Concrete examples of the three states follow:

1. A person given a challenging problem displays increases in heart rate, blood pressure, and pupillary dilation as well as a decrease in smiling and a loss in the accuracy of recall memory. Most scientists would call these temporary changes in reaction to challenge an instance of *acute anxiety*. They might write, "When adults are in a challenging situation and have no coping response, they become anxious."

2. A person who grew up in poverty and left school early because of failure to learn to read does not persist when cognitive tasks are presented, shows self-effacing behavior and reluctance to persist with challenge, but does not show any change in physiological functioning in most test situations. Investigators are likely to regard this profile as indicative of *chronic anxiety*, implying that the stable profile is a result of a prolonged history of failure. These scientists would write, "Adults who have consistently failed to meet standards for intellectual mastery become anxious."

3. A person who had been a temperamentally irritable, easily aroused infant and a fearful child shows a rise and stabilization of heart rate and blood pressure together with an increase in catecholamines in unfamiliar social situations. Psychologists are apt to call this person *temperamentally anxious* and write, "Temperamentally inhibited adults become anxious in unfamiliar, challenging situations," implying that such persons began life with a distinct physiology and, as a result of experience, became vulnerable to uncertainty.

Because the sources of evidence for the term *anxious* are different in these three instances, the theoretical meaning of *anxiety* is not the same. The use of *anxious* in the first instance implies a quantitative dimension, characteristic of all individuals, somewhat like the fever of patients with an influenza infection, that can change over a short period of time. By contrast, the term *anxious* in the second instance implies a stable, acquired quality, like the behavioral profile of a pet cat compared with one who has always roamed the street. The term *anxious* in the third instance implies a qualitative category that is genetic in origin, analogous to a specific strain of dog, monkey, or bird.

The history of biology indicates the utility of distinguishing between an abstract quantitative dimension that is shared by all species, on the one hand, and qualitatively different processes in different species, on the other. All animal species can be placed on a continuum of basal metabolic rate (BMR). But the physiological bases for a low BMR in hibernating bears are not identical to those found in sea turtles. That is one reason why these animals belong to very different taxonomic categories. Similarly, the processes activated when a temperamentally inhibited child faces a challenge may not be identical to those provoked in a child who is not a member of this temperamental category. We now consider the idea of temperament in more detail.

TEMPERAMENT

The word *temperament* is used by some, but not all, scientists to refer to psychological qualities that display considerable variation among infants and young children and, in addition, have a relatively, but not indefinitely, stable physiological basis that derives from the individual's genetic constitution. It is also understood that the inherited physiological processes can mediate different phenotypic displays as the child grows and that experience always influences the form of the behavioral display. The temperamental qualities investigated most often by psychologists, pediatricians, and psychiatrists, which are also obvious to parents, include irritability, a happy mood, ease of being soothed, motor activity, sociability, attentiveness, adaptability, approach to or avoidance of novelty, ease as well as intensity of arousal in reaction to stimulation, and regulation of arousal states (Bates, 1989; Buss & Plomin, 1984; Carey & McDevitt, 1978; Goldsmith & Rothbart, 1990; Rothbart & Derryberry, 1982; Sameroff, Seifer, & Elias, 1982; Thomas & Chess, 1977). It is not clear at the moment how many more temperamental qualities will be discovered—more, I suspect, than the list given above, but fewer, one hopes, than 100. One can only wait for history's answer.

Nancy Snidman, Doreen Arcus, Steven Reznick, Cynthia Garcia-Coll, and I, together with many students, have been studying two members from this much larger set of temperamental qualities. Initially, the primary behavioral referents for these two categories were the response profiles of 1–2-year-old children in unfamiliar situations with unfamiliar people and events. Some children consistently become quiet, vigilant, restrained, and avoidant while they assess the situation and their resources before acting. We call such children *inhibited*. Those in the complementary group, who act with spontaneity in the same situations, are called *uninhibited*. The situations that best reveal these two temperamental qualities in 1–2-year-olds are encounters with unfamiliar events, objects, contexts, and people. Only a small proportion of children are consistently shy with unfamiliar people and fearful or avoidant of unfamiliar objects (or conversely social and spontaneous), regardless of the context (Kagan et al., 1988).

The terms *inhibited* and *uninhibited* refer to two classes of children who share a distinct genotype (representing the potential to develop one or the other of the temperamental categories) and an environmental history that determines whether the biological potential will be actualized as one or the other temperamental category. This conceptual stance is common in medicine. Children born with a chromosomal anomaly are not assigned to a disease category if they fail to show any distinctive biological or behavioral features. The diagnostic category is applied only when there is both a genetic anomaly and some phenotypic signs, as in Down syndrome. So, too, with temperament. A child classed as inhibited (or uninhibited) is one who was born with a particular physiological profile and, in addition, showed the appropriate behavioral indices of avoidance of (or approach to) unfamiliarity between 1 and 2 years of age. Either quality alone does not determine assignment to the category.

We have discovered that about 40% of healthy, Caucasian, middle-class 1-year-old children from intact families bring one or the other of these two temperamental biases to unfamiliar situations; about 15% are inhibited in the second year, and about 25% are uninhibited. These proportions might be somewhat different in other ethnic groups. Further, a variety of psychological stressors associated with economic disadvantage, divorce, or abuse could be correlated with an apparently similar display of fearful or fearless behavior, but these profiles would be due primarily to experience, not temperament. There is modest but significant preservation of the two temperamental categories from 21 or 31 months through 8 years of age (Kagan et al., 1988). Unpublished data gathered by Carl Schwartz in our laboratory indicate preservation of these two categories through early adolescence.

We have also discovered two distinct behavioral profiles displayed by 16-week-old infants in response to visual, auditory, and olfactory stimuli that predict inhibited or uninhibited behavior in the second year (Kagan & Snidman, 1991a, 1991b). One group, about 20% of healthy, Caucasian samples, is characterized by extreme degrees of motor activity, combined with fretting or crying, in response to the presentation of colorful, moving objects, human speech, and dilute butyl alcohol (presented to the infant's nostrils on a cotton swab). These infants flex and extend their arms and legs with vigor on about one-third of the trials and occasionally arch their backs in response to the stimulation. In addition, on some trials, these infants cry during their bursts of vigorous motor activity. About two-thirds of these infants, whom we call *high reactive*, show extreme levels of fear in response to a variety of unfamiliar events in the laboratory at 14 and 21 months; less than 10% are minimally fearful. Thus, about 15% are both high reactive as young infants and inhibited in the second year.

A contrast group of infants displays low levels of motor activity combined with little or no fretting. These *low reactive* infants constitute about 40% of the same population. Two-thirds of this group are minimally fearful, while 10% show high levels of fear in the second year. Thus, 25% of large samples of infants are low reactive at 4 months and uninhibited in the second year. Display of vigorous motor activity combined with minimal crying or low motor activity combined with frequent crying—the two other combinations—predict intermediate levels of fear and are correlated with different autonomic and affective reactions.

The high, compared with the low, reactive 4-month-old infants have higher heart rates prior to birth (measured several weeks antepartum) as well as at 2 weeks of age while sleeping and held in an erect posture. The high reactive infants also show larger magnitudes of cardiac acceleration in response to selected events at 14 and 21 months. For example, high reactive infants show larger accelerations of heart rate in response to a sour taste at 14 months and to a rotating wheel that produced a loud, unpleasant noise at 21 months of age (Snidman & Kagan, in press).

One interpretation of this corpus of evidence rests on the assumption that high reactive infants inherit a low threshold of excitability in the amygdala and the many circuits discussed earlier, especially projections to the hypothalamus, sympathetic nervous system, and motor systems served by the ventral striatum and central grey. The low reactive infants inherit a high threshold in the amygdala and its circuits. But we suspect that the neurochemical bases for these two categories are qualitatively different. Although future research will have to evaluate the fruitfulness of that suggestion, recent work supports these ideas (Adamec, 1991; Adamec & Stark-Adamec, 1986).

Adamec and Stark-Adamec (1986) found that about 15% of house cats (*Felis catus*) show a behavioral pattern resembling that of the inhibited child. These cats withdraw when confronted with novelty, are slow to explore unfamiliar events, and do not attack rats, although they will attack mice. By contrast, the larger group of cats that attacks rats does not show defensive or avoidant behavior in response to novelty. The defensive-fearful cats display their salient trait as early as the second month of life—comparable to about 12–14 months in humans—and retain this behavior through adulthood. Exposure to subdued rats while hungry—an event mimicked in life when the adult cat brings injured prey to offspring when they are hungry—will decrease the long-term preservation of the defensiveness. However, exposing defensive kittens to live prey early in life—or not exposing them to any prey at all—increases the likelihood that they will remain defensive throughout life.

Adamec (1991) has measured activity in the amygdala and hypothalamus and found that sites in the basal area of the amygdala are more reactive to threatening stimuli in defensive, compared with nondefensive, cats. Further, the projections from the amygdala to the ventromedial hypothalamus (VMH) are more excitable in the defensive animals; electrical stimulation of the amygdala produces greater output voltages in the VMH of defensive, compared with nondefensive, cats. The enhanced responsiveness of the basal amygdala in defensive cats occurs specifically in response to events that should be perceived as threatening (e.g., the howling sound of an adult cat), not in response to the sound of a cat purring or of ordinary noise. It is important to note that the reactivity of the circuit from the amygdala to the VMH is independent of the reactivity of the amygdala, suggesting that inhibited children may differ in both the threshold of the amygdala's responsiveness to unfamiliar events and the excitability of projections from the amygdala to the hypothalamus.

Unpublished research by Fox suggests that high reactive infants, who become inhibited in the second year, have greater activation of the EEG (desynchronization of frequencies from 7 to 12 Hz) in the right frontal pole, while low reactive, positive affect infants, who become uninhibited, have greater activation in the left frontal pole. In collaborative and independent work, both Fox and Davidson have found that greater activation in the right frontal area is predictive of fearfulness in infants and dysphoric affect in adults (Davidson, Ekman, Saron, Senulis, & Friesen, 1990; Davidson & Fox, 1982, 1989; Fox & Davidson, 1987, 1988; see also Fox, in this volume). Further, more children than adults (a ratio of approximately two to one) show left rather than right frontal activation.

These findings are in accord with a right-left asymmetry in forehead temperature. The arterioles under the surface of the forehead are under sympathetic control. Constriction of these arterioles, mediated by alpha adrenergic receptors, reduces blood flow to the skin and, as a consequence, produces surface cooling. A surprising fact discovered during the last 20 years provides a theoretical basis for expecting a difference between inhibited and uninhibited children in lateral asymmetry of facial temperatures. It appears that discharge of the sympathetic nervous system is greater on the right than on the left side of the body. For example, stimulation of the right stellate ganglion in dogs leads to a tachycardia that is absent following stimulation of the left stellate ganglion (Randall & Priola, 1965). Further, the anatomical connections between the amygdala and hypothalamus, on the one hand, and the sympathetic ganglia that they influence, on the other, appear to be stronger on the ipsilateral than on the contralateral side (Saper, Loewy, Swanson, & Cowan, 1976). Finally, extensive reviews by Cutting (1990) and Silberman and Weingartner (1986) suggest a functional association between asymmetry of activity in those brain areas that influence the sympathetic nervous system and individual variation in behavior or physiology that is assumed to accompany states of anxiety or fear.

However, it will be recalled that left-sided activation of the EEG in the frontal area is more frequent than activation on the right side, suggesting that reciprocal neural activity between the amygdala and the frontal pole, which would desynchronize alpha activity, is greater on the left side. Thus, the dominance of left over right frontal activity in most individuals implies a restraint on right-sided sympathetic activity by the left hemisphere. These facts suggest the following argument and prediction:

(1) If inhibited children are more likely to have right-sided activation of the frontal pole and uninhibited children greater activity on the left side, (2) if this asymmetry is associated with asymmetry in sympathetic activity

through reciprocal connections with the amygdala, and (3) if sympathetic activity constricts the arterioles of the forehead, it follows that inhibited, compared with uninhibited, children should have cooler temperatures on the right than on the left side of the face and/or show greater cooling on the right side following the imposition of mild stress. By contrast, uninhibited children should have a cooler temperature on the left side.

In two independent samples of 21-month-old children ($N = 300$), we have found that significantly more subjects are cooler on the left than on the right side (37% vs. 20%, respectively), in accord with the data on asymmetry of EEG activation (Kagan, 1994). Further, high smiling, uninhibited children were more likely than low smiling, inhibited children to have a cooler temperature on the left side of the face (a difference of 0.15°C–0.40°C). This relation was stronger for girls than for boys.

The corpus of data summarized implies that the two temperamental groups differ in the ease, and perhaps frequency, with which they experience the affect families that we call *joy* or *happiness*, on the one hand, and *anxiety*, *fear*, or *uncertainty*, on the other. Contemporary research implies that the pleasant affect states are mediated more completely by the left hemisphere whereas the dysphoric states are mediated more completely by the right hemisphere (Cutting, 1990). It is of interest, therefore, that as early as 2 months of age infants who became high reactive at 4 months showed significantly less smiling in laboratory episodes than low reactive infants. The former group retained their dysphoric mood in laboratory assessments through 21 months of age. Further, youths who had been classified at 21 or 31 months as extremely inhibited smiled and talked less often in a test situation with an adult examiner at 13 years of age than did youths who had been classified earlier as uninhibited—the differences in mood were retained for over 11 years.

Although high reactive infants, a majority of whom become inhibited children, seem especially vulnerable to the affect state of fear in response to unfamiliar events, it is less clear that this state is identical to the state experienced by uninhibited children who expect to be punished by their parents, rejected by their peers, or attacked by a bully. I have suggested that the emotion states generated by these latter incentives are different from the state of fear induced by the presence of a stranger in inhibited children. However, I remain open to evidence demonstrating that the differences among these states in different temperamental groups are quantitative rather than qualitative.

The current preference for a continuum of anxiety on which all children can be placed is driven by a deeply held premise among many developmental psychologists (but not necessarily by comparative psychologists) that most of the variation in behavior and mood is the product of social experiences that strengthened or weakened particular dispositions. This hypothesis remains unusually resistant to criticism for two reasons. First, it is always possible to invent an explanation of behavioral and affective variation using the principles of conditioning or observational learning. Second, this premise is serving the praiseworthy desire of many social scientists to minimize biological differences among children from different ethnic or racial groups in order to defend a policy of early intervention in the lives of young children living in impoverished or stressful circumstances, even though acceptance of the idea of temperament is not inconsistent with interventions motivated by benevolent, egalitarian principles.

AFFECT, TEMPERAMENT, AND DEVELOPING BEHAVIOR

Environmental events mediate the relation between high reactivity in infancy and avoidant, fearful behavior in 2-year-old inhibited children. One possible script makes the following, and one would hope reasonable, claims. High reactive infants inherit a low threshold of reactivity in the amygdala and its multiple circuits, which leads to vigorous motor activity and frequent crying in response to new events at 4 months of age. But, when these children are 1 year old and mature enough to recognize a variety of discrepancies and to modulate their behavior, they begin to freeze, fret, or withdraw from unfamiliar people and situations. These signs of caution are biologically prepared reactions to discrepancy.

Now the social environment begins to assume importance. The probability that timidity and avoidance will become a preserved habit depends on how the parents (and the staff at a day-care center) react to the child's inhibition. If caretaking adults accept these avoidant behaviors, which is a common reaction in contemporary, middle-class families who are reluctant to stress anxious children, the inhibition will become more entrenched—as classical learning theory would predict. If, on the other hand, adult caretakers gently encourage the child to approach unfamiliar targets and/or prepare the child for an imminent source of novelty, it is more likely that an inhibited style will not become strong. Stated succinctly, the development of a stable inhibited behavioral style requires a combination of a low threshold of reactivity in the limbic sites—the temperamental component—and a social environment that either encourages or fails to discourage timidity.

The development and maintenance of a stable, uninhibited profile are based on a different set of processes, rather than on complementary mechanisms. The occurrence of low reactivity in infancy and uninhibited behavior in the second year is twice as common as the high reactive–inhibited combination. An infant born with a high threshold of reactivity in the amygdala and its circuits is likely to become an uninhibited child, unless special experiences create uncertainty and fear. This prediction assumes that most parents in contemporary America (although not in all cultures) will not try to extinguish sociable, outgoing behavior. Over two-thirds of low reactive infants are minimally fearful in the second year. The events that make some low reactive children avoidant include chronic stressors, like marital quarreling, divorce, the death of a parent, or abuse. Interviews with parents of low reactive children who became timid support this suggestion.

There is, of course, at least one other mechanism that influences the long-term stability of a temperamental style. After age 6 or 7 years, when most children become keenly aware of their personal characteristics and how they will be evaluated by peers, some children consciously attempt to change their behavioral reactions to unfamiliarity. Some inhibited children have told their mothers that they were "trying not to be afraid." These attempts are often successful. Thus, there is ample opportunity for the phenotype to change during the opening years of life; that capacity continues to be vital throughout adolescence and adulthood.

THE REGULATION OF EMOTION

The acquisition of coping strategies by inhibited children leads naturally to a discussion of the concept of emotion regulation, which has an evaluative component because regulation is usually treated, implicitly, as desirable. There is no disagreement over the fact that children differ in the degree to which emotions like anger, fear, and sadness are controlled and the display of associated behavior suppressed. The scientific problem is our current inability to separate, in measurement, the intensity of the emotion experienced by the child from the effectiveness of the regulatory effort. Put simply, if one child screams for 10 min in response to the presence of a masked adult while another stops after a few seconds of fretting (or does not cry at all), it is not possible to determine whether the second child is better able to regulate fear or whether she was simply less fearful in the first place.

A related problem is ascertaining the source of the variation in regulation. Some children are socialized by parents to control behavioral displays of frustration, fear, or anger. If the socialization regimen is successful, the child will appear to be well regulated. Other children will appear well regulated because they have a less reactive central and autonomic nervous system and, as a result, experience a less intense feeling state. It is simply easier for these children to control emotion displays. These are two very different types of children, even though both will appear to observers to be effective regulators of emotion. Thus, the problem with the term *regulation* resembles the puzzle of interpreting quality of performance on a cognitive test. Is poor performance due to insufficient competence or insufficient motivation? If all the scientist knows is the performance score, it is not possible to answer that question.

Regulation has a special quality during infancy, compared with adolescence, because the infant is not mature enough to impose restraint volitionally. Rothbart regards ease of arousal and self-regulation as the two primary temperamental qualities of infancy. However, infants differ in the form of the reaction emitted when they become highly aroused. Some thrash, some vocalize, some turn away, and some cry. Consider a concrete experimental situation. Four-month-old infants are watching a colorful mobile being moved back and forth in front of their eyes. Some infants are minimally aroused; they simply look at the stimulus with attentiveness. It is potentially incorrect to conclude that these infants are regulating affect well and more accurate to infer that they are not aroused by this event. Among the remaining infants who become aroused—thrashing their limbs and vocalizing—some will continue to attend to the display, while others will turn away to avoid looking at the exciting stimulus. Others will suck their hand, and still others will cry. Each of these reactions can be regarded as regulatory attempts to deal with the event. It is not obvious which reaction is more adaptive; further, at this early age, each response is likely to be, in part, a temperamental bias. For these reasons, I believe that it is useful to treat emotion regulation in infants as different from the similarly named process in older children.

In sum, both temperament and experience contribute to the child's reaction to an acute emotion state. But, until psychologists are able to assess regulation independent of intensity of arousal, the characteristics that we quantify will reflect ease of arousal, intensity of arousal, and form of regulation—all three are confounded in the film record of a child's behavior.

SUMMARY

This essay has tried to make three points. First, humans are capable of a large number of affect states (the exact number is not yet known), each marked by a distinct profile of physiology, cognition, and behavior, and each requiring a distinct name. Second, a distinction should be made among acute emotions, chronic moods, and temperamental vulnerabilities to a particular emotion state. Finally, research on human affects will profit from a return to, and a reinterpretation of, Freud's suggestion of unconscious affect states. Such inquiry would provide a corrective to the current reliance on the verbal reports of phenomenal states on questionnaires or in interviews as either the only, or the primary, index of an emotion. Continued use of this strategy will limit analyses to a small number of heterogeneous states that happen to have a popular English name and will retard discovery of the larger number of affect states that are of significance for human function. Discovery of these states will require use of new sources of evidence to supplement popular ones, including facial and postural expressions, muscle tension, EEG, vagal tone, heart-rate changes, blood pressure, GSR, facial temperature, and blood or saliva indexes of norepinephrine, opioids, and cortisol.

When the cosmologist James Peebles was asked to guess the exact numerical answers to a series of astronomical puzzles, like the age of the universe or of a distant star, he replied, "If someone gave me on a tablet of clay the answer and the numbers, I would be disappointed. I would throw it away because the great discoveries are not going to be a final number, but the method you come to apply to learn that number."

EMOTION REGULATION:
A THEME IN SEARCH OF DEFINITION

Ross A. Thompson

Interest in emotion regulation has burgeoned in recent years because it builds on several recent trends in the study of emotional development (Thompson, 1993). First, after more than a decade of research emphasizing the growth of discrete emotions and their consequences for sociopersonality functioning, researchers have realized that the specific emotion indexes only part of the rich individual variability that exists in emotional behavior. In addition, individuals display variations in the intensity, persistence, modulation, onset and rise time, range, and lability of and recovery from emotional responses. These "emotion dynamics" (Thompson, 1990) constitute significant response parameters that are influenced by emotion regulation processes. In a sense, while the discrete emotion may "play the tune" of a person's emotional response, these emotion regulation processes significantly influence its quality, intensity, timing, and dynamic features and thus significantly color emotion experience.

Second, emergent views of emotion underscore its biologically adaptive and psychologically constructive features in contrast with earlier portrayals of emotion, which emphasized its disorganizing, irrational, or stressful side (e.g., Barrett & Campos, 1987; Malatesta, 1990). Emotional arousal has, of course, the capacity to either enhance or undermine effective functioning, and emotion regulation processes are important as they enlist emotion to support adaptive, organized behavioral strategies. Emotion regulation is relevant, for example, to effective social strategies with peers (e.g., Rubin & Rose-Krasnor, 1986), successful cognitive performance in tasks involving

I am grateful to Alice Ganzel, Megan Gunnar, and Kathy Stansbury for helpful, critical readings of an earlier draft of this essay and to Pamela Cole for stimulating exchanges about these issues.

delay, inhibition, or the pursuit of long-term goals (e.g., Mischel & Mischel, 1983), and the management of stressful experiences at home (Cummings, Pellegrini, Notarius, & Cummings, 1989). In a sense, students of emotional development have moved beyond the realization that discrete emotions are biologically adaptive to the awareness that emotional responses must also be flexible (rather than stereotypical), situationally responsive (rather than rigid), and performance enhancing (rather than over- or underarousing) and must change quickly and effectively in order to adapt to changing conditions if they are to support organized, constructive functioning in higher organisms. This is where emotion regulation processes often enter in.

Third, newer portrayals of emotional development also emphasize the socialization of emotion as a significant constituent of emotional development. Through processes ranging from selective reinforcement and modeling of expressions of emotion to emotion-focused discourse, the social context not only fosters greater "emotional competence" (Saarni, 1990) in developing individuals but also channels emotional behavior in directions that meet the expectations of the "emotion culture" (Gordon, 1989) in which those individuals develop. As a consequence, emotion experience derives from an interaction between biologically based emotive processes and the socialized monitoring, evaluative, and regulatory processes by which emotion experience is interpreted and managed in culture-specific ways. Moreover, as developing individuals become more skilled at regulating arousal, emotion and its expression can become better integrated into the child's growing repertoire of strategic behavior in social contexts. Emotion regulation is central both to the socialization process and to its developmental outcomes.

Finally, emotions theory is currently also concerned with individual differences in personality and social functioning and the central role that emotive processes play in these differences. Whether the focus is on individual differences in infant-mother attachment and the emotional biases that they reflect (Malatesta, 1990; Thompson, 1991; see also Cassidy, in this volume), variations in behavioral inhibition and their origins in the self-regulation of emotion (see Fox, in this volume; Kagan, in this volume), or the interpretive processes underlying the emotional reactions of aggressive children to their peers (Dodge, 1991a), researchers are exploring aspects of emotion regulation and dysregulation that guide social and personality processes. The common theme underlying these studies is how emotional arousal comes to *mean* different things to different individuals (e.g., why anger is empowering to some people, disorganizing for others, and to be denied or avoided for others), and emotion regulation is a significant component of these individual differences.

These current trends in theory and research on emotional development have provided an auspicious beginning to the study of emotion regulation. But, as so often happens with auspicious beginnings, recent enthusiasm for the study of emotion regulation has outpaced attention to some basic definitional and conceptual issues. This is because many researchers share a common intuitive understanding of what is meant by *emotion regulation* or of the distinguishing features of the "optimal" self-management of emotion, but these implicit formulations have tended to obscure the heterogeneity of emotion regulation processes, the complexity of their development, their links to significant social relationships and to the "emotion culture" that we share, and the challenges of identifying the origins and correlates of these regulatory processes. My purpose in this essay is to highlight these complexities by (re)considering the following questions: How should we define *emotion regulation?* What is regulated in the regulation of emotion? How do emotion regulation strategies fit into the complex fabric of social interaction? What are the predictable correlates of individual differences in emotion regulation? In a sense, my goal is to "unpack" the concept of emotion regulation to better elucidate its component processes.

DEFINING *EMOTION REGULATION*

The power of our shared, implicit notions of what constitutes emotion regulation is reflected, perhaps, in how frequently papers on emotion regulation (including my own) lack a clear definition of this phenomenon. Yet behind this apparent consensual understanding is considerable diversity in the underlying portrayals of emotion regulation provided by different researchers and theorists. Does emotion regulation pertain exclusively to the inhibition of emotional reactions, for example, or does it also include the maintenance or enhancement of emotional behavior? Is emotion regulation primarily an issue of emotion *self*-management, or is the management of emotional reactions by others also included? Does emotion regulation primarily influence the discrete emotion that one experiences, or rather its quality (e.g., its intensity, speed of onset, or persistence)? Is emotion regulation primarily concerned with the management of expressions of emotion or the underlying arousal processes leading to those expressions—or both?

There is surprising diversity in the ways that different researchers answer these questions in their implicit formulations of emotion regulation. My own answers are indicated in the following definition:

Emotion regulation consists of the extrinsic and intrinsic processes responsible for monitoring, evaluating, and modifying emotional reactions, especially their intensive and temporal features, to accomplish one's goals.

Included in this definition are several characterizations of emotion regulation processes.

First, consistent with Masters (1991), emotion regulation can involve maintaining and enhancing emotional arousal as well as inhibiting or subduing it. It is natural that theorists emphasize emotion inhibition in a culture that, like ours, values this characteristic: in everyday circumstances, emotion regulation skills are most often enlisted to dampen emotional arousal (especially negative emotion). But, even in our culture, strategies of emotion management are often used to maintain or enhance emotional arousal, such as when children intensify their anger to stand up to a bully who is also feared (see Miller & Sperry, 1987), or when they "feel sorry for themselves" when unjustly treated, or when adults ruminate on feelings of guilt, anger, or shame in response to social injustice. And children and adults frequently enlist strategies to heighten positive arousal (e.g., by reenacting pleasant or humorous experiences), sometimes to manage negative affect. In these and other instances, the enhancement of emotional arousal (not just its display) serves important strategic purposes, and this becomes the goal of the emotion regulation process.

Second, emotion regulation encompasses not only acquired strategies of emotion *self*-management but also the variety of external influences by means of which emotion is regulated. This is because a considerable amount of emotion regulation occurs through the interventions of others. In infancy, for example, caregivers devote considerable effort to monitoring, interpreting, and modulating the arousal states of young offspring—in other words, regulating their emotions. As offspring mature, parents use direct interventions as well as indirect strategies (e.g., coaching response alternatives) not only to maintain emotional well-being in their children but also to socialize emotional behavior so that it accords with cultural expectations concerning feelings and their expression (Saarni, 1990). Moreover, parent-offspring relationships and other significant social ties affect the demands for emotion regulation and the efficacy of strategies for managing arousal that children acquire in the context of these close relationships. And, as adults, we frequently manage the emotions of others by extending a sympathetic ear or using humor in a frustrating situation. Taken together, therefore, the development of the skills required to manage one's own emotion occurs in a social context (both proximate and cultural) that significantly shapes children's management of arousal through external regulatory influences.

Third, although emotion regulation sometimes affects the discrete emotion experienced by an individual (e.g., the arousal of guilt or shame rather than anger when unfairly accused), more commonly it affects the intensive and temporal features of that emotion. In other words, aspects of emotion management subdue (or enhance) the intensity of experienced emotion, retard (or speed) its onset or recovery, limit (or enhance) its persistence over time, reduce (or increase) emotion range or lability, and affect other qualitative features of emotional responding. Because of this, new strategies for the study of emotion regulation are required that are sensitive to these intensive and temporal features of emotional responding, even when the discrete emotion itself is unaffected. Several new methodological approaches meant to accomplish this are outlined at the conclusion of this essay.

Finally, emotion regulation must be regarded functionally, that is, in terms of the regulator's goals for a particular situation. These goals may be diverse and changing, and, as I argue later, they include far more than simply maintaining a positive disposition in oneself or another. Indeed, an understanding of individual differences as well as developmental changes in emotion regulation may hinge on an appreciation of the goals for managing emotion that are motivating regulatory efforts, and this makes goal attainment a central definitional feature of emotion regulation. To be sure, historically there have been important problems with functionalist approaches like this one to psychological processes (circular reasoning among them: theorists can easily infer goals that are consistent with their behavioral analysis), but these problems should instill caution rather than avoidance of such an approach to the study of emotion regulation. Indeed, contemporary interest in emotion regulation is consistent with emergent functionalist approaches to emotional development that are currently enlivening emotions research (e.g., Barrett & Campos, 1987).

This is an inclusive definition of *emotion regulation,* and among the many issues not addressed here are distinguishing (if necessary) emotion regulation from related processes like defense mechanisms and display rules, articulating the relations between the self-regulation of emotion and the development of other self-regulatory capacities, and clarifying the inferential, interpretive, and social-cognitive constituents of the self-regulation of emotion. Necessary also are process models that distinguish operationally such other elements of emotion regulation as situation appraisal, goal selection, strategy choice, and outcome monitoring (cf. Garber, Braafladt, & Zeman, 1991). These are formidable challenges, but recognizing them as such steers us away from prematurely assuming that either clear or consensual definitions of *emotion regulation* currently exist. Most developmental researchers (myself included) may "know" emotion regulation when they see it, but considerably more is required if we are to develop a clear and comprehensive definition of this phenomenon.

WHAT IS REGULATED?

Perhaps the most central definitional quandary for the study of emotion regulation concerns the issue of *what* is regulated when we consider the management of emotion.[1] Because emotion is a multifaceted phenomenon (involving physiological arousal, neurological activation, cognitive appraisal, attention processes, and response tendencies), there are diverse avenues toward the management of emotion, and consideration of these avenues reveals that the term *emotion regulation* does not refer to a unitary phenomenon but is rather a broad conceptual rubric encompassing a range of loosely related processes.

Neurophysiological Constituents

At the core of these processes are the systems of nervous system organization that have evolved to regulate arousal (including emotional arousal) through the interplay of excitatory and inhibitory mechanisms. Many of these systems are functionally immature at birth, and their progressive maturation and consolidation not only foster greater behavioral and emotional self-control in the early years of life but also permit greater susceptibility to extrinsic regulatory influences and allow for the enlistment of emotion in aid of strategic behavioral processes. Moreover, individual differences in the reactivity of some of these systems reflect both biologically and experientially based processes that can influence personality and social functioning. Thus, one answer to the question, What is regulated? concerns the control of underlying arousal processes through maturing systems of neurophysiological regulation.

Any explication of these maturing neurophysiological systems must be both complex and incomplete, partly because the subcortical and cortical systems affecting emotional arousal are mutually interconnected and are intimately linked with other neurophysiological systems, including those governing cognition and vegetative regulation, in ways that researchers are just beginning to understand (see, e.g., Fox & Fitzgerald, 1990). Current advances in research in the neurosciences, and in developmental neurophysiology especially, will, one hopes, contribute to a clearer future picture of these regulatory processes. However, early developmental changes in emotion regulation can be linked to at least two neurophysiological advances in the first year of life that provide a foundation for more complex regulatory processes with growing maturity.

[1] I am grateful to Stephen Porges for having raised this provocative question during the working meeting on emotion regulation on which this *Monograph* is based.

First, the diffuse excitatory processes underlying organismic arousal decline in lability throughout the first year. This is partly due to postnatal changes in the functioning of the hypothalamic-pituitary-adrenocortical system that governs reactions to stress and uncertainty (as discussed in Gunnar, 1986, and Stansbury and Gunnar, in this volume) and maturational changes in parasympathetic regulation as indexed by vagal tone (Izard et al., 1991; Porges, 1991; Porges, Doussard-Roosevelt, and Maiti, in this volume). As a consequence, organismic arousal gradually becomes more graded as well as emotionally and motivationally more complex with increasing age. The declining lability of organismic arousal during the early postnatal months also aids caregivers' efforts to manage the emotion of offspring as well as enhancing the effects of other emergent, internal controls on emotion.

Second, cortical inhibitory controls over arousal emerge gradually during infancy, although some do not become fully functional until long after birth. By about 2–4 months, for example, the growth of rudimentary forebrain inhibitory centers, changes in the organization of attention processes, and other neurophysiological advances are manifested in behavioral state changes (e.g., the emergence of more sustained attention and more regular sleep-wake patterns, greater regularity and control of behavioral state, the progressive disappearance of neonatal reflexes) as well as emotional changes (e.g., an increase in exogenous smiling and a capacity for laughter) and growing awareness of and emotional responsiveness to contingent stimulation (Emde, Gaensbauer, & Harmon, 1976; Rothbart, Ziaie, & O'Boyle, 1992; Watson & Ramey, 1972). According to Dawson (in this volume) and others (e.g., Fox, 1991, in this volume), by about 9–10 months maturation of the frontal lobe and its links to response inhibition (cf. Diamond, 1988) fosters the capacity for arousal management and efforts to cope with emotionally arousing events (see also Tucker & Frederick, 1989). These changes may also underlie the growing vitality and complexity of emotional behavior, such as the enhanced speed and intensity of emotional reactions (Thompson, 1990), the use of emotional behaviors to share and affect the attention and affective states of others (e.g., Scaife & Bruner, 1975; Stern, 1985), and the growth of emotional blends and other complex affective states.

Other cortical processes are also implicated in the growth of emotion regulation capacities, and the end of the first year is not the terminus of the neurophysiological changes that influence emotion regulation capacities (cf. Kinsbourne & Bemporad, 1984). There remains, therefore, a considerable research agenda ahead of us if we are to elucidate the neurophysiological substrates of emotion management capacities during the early years of life.

Individual differences in nervous system reactivity related to these arousal regulatory processes have also generated considerable recent interest. Consistent with the views of some temperament formulations that portray individual differences in temperament in terms of variations in emotionality and self-regulation (e.g., Rothbart & Derryberry, 1981), findings from several researchers suggest that differences in various neurophysiological systems mediating emotion emerge early and are related to broader features of social and personality functioning. In his longitudinal study of behaviorally inhibited and uninhibited young children, for example, Kagan and his colleagues have argued that inhibited children have a generally lower threshold of reactivity in limbic structures mediating fear and defense and that these differences can be found in both physiological and behavioral measures through early childhood (see, e.g., Kagan, Reznick, & Snidman, 1988; Kagan & Snidman, 1991b; and, more generally, Kagan, in this volume). Fox and Calkins have compared groups of infants who differed on similar indices of behavioral inhibition early in infancy and found predictable later differences on measures of emotion regulation and attachment (see Calkins & Fox, 1992; Fox & Calkins, 1993; and, more generally, Calkins, in this volume; Fox, in this volume).

Taken together, these findings suggest that early emerging individual differences in physiological reactivity and regulation are related to variations in emotionality and emotion regulation. These differences are not immutable, however; both Kagan and Fox point out that they can be modified by caregivers' socialization efforts as well as other experiences that alter organismic reactions to stress and challenge (cf. Dienstbier, 1989). Consequently, not only confirming the neurophysiological bases for these individual differences in emotional reactivity and emotion management but also denoting sources of continuity and change in functioning remains a significant future research task.

In sum, capacities for emotion regulation and self-management are based, in part, on neurophysiological constituents that unfold during the first year and provide the basis for more complex forms of emotion management in later years. What is regulated is, in part, the neurophysiological processes underlying emotional arousal and its management.

Attention Processes

Another way that emotion can be regulated is by managing the intake of emotionally arousing information. Attention processes assume an emotionally regulating function from very early in life. According to Rothbart (Rothbart, Posner, & Boylan, 1990; Rothbart et al., 1992), maturational changes in the neurophysiological organization of visual control between 3 and 6 months of age permit the infant to shift attention between stimulus events voluntarily, in contrast with the "obligatory attention" observed at younger ages. Not only does this enable the infant to disengage visually from emotionally arousing events (which becomes more commonly observed at this time, e.g., during episodes of mother-infant play; Gianino & Tronick, 1988), but it also enables parents to use visual distraction as an emotion regulation strategy with very young offspring. Consistent with this view is Rothbart's report of an association between individual differences in visual disengagement and soothability in young infants together with a general increase in soothability between 3 and 6 months of age (see Rothbart et al., 1992).

With increasing age, the regulation of emotion through the management of attention processes becomes more complex. The redirection of attention is commonly enlisted by caregivers as a means of regulating emotion in children, for example, during threatening or stressful events, when caregivers may focus attention on positive features of the experience, distract the child during the event itself, or limit the child's knowledge of potentially upsetting information (Miller & Green, 1985). With the assistance of caregivers, young children can also sometimes regulate their emotions themselves, using such attention management strategies as covering their eyes or ears in emotionally arousing situations, removing emotionally evocative stimuli, or leaving the situation altogether (e.g., Altschuler & Ruble, 1989). Indeed, such approaches to the self-regulation of emotion are among the earliest strategies observed in young children: attention-based strategies have been observed in 4- and 5-year-olds in the presence of adults arguing (Cummings, 1987), and such strategies can be understood and articulated by even younger children (e.g., one 28-month-old was reported as saying, "I scared of the shark. Close my eyes"; Bretherton, Fritz, Zahn-Waxler, & Ridgeway, 1986). In situations involving delayed rewards, redirection of attention away from the reward while awaiting permitted access is a behavioral strategy commonly observed in children between the ages of 2 and 6 years (Mischel & Mischel, 1983; Vaughn, Kopp, Krakow, Johnson, & Schwartz, 1986).

As children acquire more complex, psychologically oriented concepts of emotion, their strategies for the self-regulation of emotion increasingly involve the *internal* redirection of attention, for example, thinking pleasant thoughts during a distressing or frightening experience or self-coaching that focuses on positive outcomes (e.g., Band & Weisz, 1988). Even young children are aware that the intensity of emotion experience tends to wane over time as people cease to think about emotionally arousing events (Harris, Guz, Lipian, & Man-Shu, 1985) and that "behavioral distraction"—such as doing something else that takes your mind off emotionally arousing circumstances—can help you manage your emotions (Altschuler & Ruble, 1989). In one study, 8- and 13-year-olds in an English boarding school knew, for example, that thinking about positive aspects of the situation could help alleviate feelings of loneliness when away from home (Harris & Lipian, 1989), and, according to American children of the same ages, internal distraction helps while waiting during a delay task (Mischel & Mischel, 1983). Knowledge of these internal attention management strategies provides a very effective means of regulating one's own emotions because they can be used in situations where escape or avoidance of emotionally arousing stimuli is impossible. In these situations, what is regulated is the focus of attention and the intake of information that affects one's emotional condition.

Construals of Emotionally Arousing Events

At other times, emotion is regulated through other components of information processing. Rather than restricting the intake of emotionally arousing information, individuals emotionally self-regulate by altering their interpretations or construals of this information. This is classically illustrated by defense mechanisms that reduce anxiety and other negative emotions through denial, projection, rationalization, repression, etc., with the result that construals of reality are altered and emotion is thereby managed (cf. Case, Hayward, Lewis, & Hurst, 1988). Other examples are children who reinterpret the outcomes of scary stories in more emotionally satisfying ways (e.g., "He didn't *really* die; he just got frightened and ran away") or who think "it's just pretend" when listening to a sad account (cf. Meerum Terwogt, Schene, & Harris, 1986).

Like most of the avenues to emotion regulation discussed in this essay, children's construals of emotionally arousing situations are often the target of extrinsic regulatory efforts, especially when offspring encounter potentially stressful or challenging experiences (Miller & Green, 1985). Before intrusive medical examinations, for example, parents may liken the procedures to "tickling," or they may exaggerate their delight during a carnival ride when the child appears frightened or look positive when children are approached by unfamiliar but harmless adults. Such strategies are potentially risky if they present children with a construction of current experience that is significantly different from the child's own or if they regularly contribute to the development of dysfunctional inferential biases (as may happen with the offspring of parents with affective disorders; see Cicchetti, Ganiban, & Barnett, 1991; Zahn-Waxler & Kochanska, 1990). But they provide a significant means for emotional arousal to be externally managed by altering the child's construction of the event when emotionally arousing experiences are unavoidable.

Children also create their own interpretive constructions of emotionally arousing experiences, of course, and these constructions commonly focus on the achievement or frustration of personal goals and inferences concerning the causes of success or failure that can have powerful emotional conse-

quences (e.g., Graham & Weiner, 1986; Stein & Levine, 1989; Stein & Trabasso, 1989; Thompson, 1987a, 1989). Not surprisingly, kindergartners are
aware that goal substitution is a reasonable response to feelings of sadness
or anger that have been evoked by the frustration of their initial goals,
probably because goal substitution has consequences for emotion management (Stein & Trabasso, 1989). For example, a child who learns that a
parent does not have time for a bedtime story might decide that playing a
game or listening to music is just as good, and this reinterpretation of the
event can help regulate feelings of sadness or dismay. Altering one's causal
attributions for emotionally arousing events is another way that reconstruals
can have emotionally regulatory consequences (e.g., "Tommy probably
didn't *mean* to knock over my tower"), and this strategy is often used by
adults, although there have been no studies of children's understanding of
this approach to the management of their emotion experiences. In sum,
when these kinds of internal or extrinsic regulatory strategies are employed,
what is regulated is one's interpretations of emotionally meaningful information.

Encoding of Internal Emotion Cues

Another answer to the question, What is regulated? is that individuals
commonly manage their encoding of internal cues of emotional arousal
when they regulate emotion. In other words, emotional arousal is managed
not only by reinterpreting the circumstances eliciting emotion but also by
reinterpreting the internal indicators of emotional arousal, such as rapid
heart rate, increased breathing rate (or shortness of breath), perspiration,
and other concomitants of emotional arousal. One manner of managing
stage fright, for example, is to regard these physiological cues as the ordinary accompaniment to appearing before an audience rather than as signals
of impending dysfunction. Similarly, children who can more easily channel
emotional arousal into adaptive social functioning have perhaps learned to
regard their internal cues of arousal as facilitating (e.g., empowering) their
goals, while children who are more easily undermined by heightened emotion may perceive these internal cues of arousal as reflections of their incompetence or inadequacy. At present, however, we have little knowledge of
how children understand these internal cues of emotional arousal or their
management. Nor do we know how parents influence these constructions
of offspring.

Access to Coping Resources

Emotion regulation also occurs by enhancing one's access to coping
resources, both material and interpersonal. In this sense, what is regulated

is the availability of external support for managing emotional arousal. Adults turn to friends and family for advice when anxious, comfort when bereaved, and a cool head when angry, and young children are aware of the benefits of eliciting nurturance from others when experiencing negative emotion (Masters, Ford, & Arend, 1983; McCoy & Masters, 1985). In these cases, access to coping resources is enhanced by seeking familiar and trusted social partners, and this mode of emotion regulation begins early in life. Indeed, the "secure base behavior" commonly observed in infants who encounter threatening or stressful circumstances with their caregivers reflects the extent to which access to interpersonal coping resources can assist in emotion management from a very early age. The social expectations underlying a secure infant-mother attachment suggest that this perceived access can have broader consequences for socioemotional functioning (see also Cassidy, in this volume). Moreover, parents also enlist the aid of material coping resources (e.g., a favorite toy, blanket, or book) to assist their offspring in coping with emotional demands.

With increasing age, access to coping resources as an aspect of emotion regulation becomes more planned and strategic. Friends are sought out for their emotional support and understanding (Gottman & Mettetal, 1986), and peers may be selected as confidants who have been especially sympathetic on previous occasions. Indeed, when others are expected to be supportive, children may sometimes enhance the intensity of their expressed emotion in order to foster a desired reaction from another that supports one's own emotionally self-regulatory efforts (Dunn & Brown, 1991; Saarni, 1992). For example, a child may exaggerate the hurt that she experiences when tripping and falling to elicit sympathy rather than derision from peers who are looking on as well as to avoid embarrassment, and this helps her feel better. By age 6, children are aware that emotion displays can be altered to mislead onlookers about the quality of one's distress (Harris & Gross, 1989), but we know little about their capacity strategically to manipulate their emotion displays for purposes of emotion regulation, and this constitutes another important research task. As an aspect of emotion regulation, however, enhancing access to coping resources—especially interpersonal resources—can entail the strategic as well as the incidental use of social partners and material resources.

Regulating the Emotional Demands of Familiar Settings

Another answer to the question, What is regulated? is that emotion regulation commonly involves predicting and controlling the emotional requirements of commonly encountered settings. That is, emotion experience is managed as one selects and creates living circumstances that have manageable emotional demands.

Like other modes of emotion management, regulating the emotional demands of familiar settings is one way that parents extrinsically manage the emotion experience of offspring. They often restrict or expand the opportunities for emotional arousal experienced by young offspring by controlling the emotional demands of caregiving routines and other common experiences (e.g., frequency of parent-child separations, promptness of responding to distress cries, etc.). In doing so, parents take into account both their own child's temperamental strengths and vulnerabilities and the socialization demands of the emotion culture. Thus, one parent may use somewhat nondemanding or permissive childrearing practices in light of her child's proneness to distress but will nevertheless increment expectations for emotional tolerance as the child's increasing age permits greater emotional self-control.

With increasing maturity, however, individuals become more capable of selecting or constructing environmental settings in light of their self-perceived needs and characteristics, including consideration of the emotional demands with which they are comfortable (Lerner & Busch-Rossnagel, 1981). Within certain limits, for example, social relationships are chosen, home and workplace settings crafted, and commitments scheduled to create desirable incentives, supports, and expectations, including manageable emotional requirements. For young children, this may involve making choices as simple as playing alone or with congenial peers rather than selecting competitive games; for older people, the range of choices can be much broader. Although this necessarily leads in idiosyncratic directions according to individual constellations of personality and temperament, there are also some developmental trends in the kinds of emotional demands that adults integrate into the environmental and interpersonal settings that they select.

Carstensen (1991; Fredrickson & Carstensen, 1990) has noted, for example, that older adults select settings and relationships that ensure manageable and predictable socioemotional demands, maximize positive affect, and conserve physical energy. Their capacity to regulate the emotional demands that they experience is also reflected in their ability to restructure their lifestyles to accommodate unexpected emotional needs (e.g., clearing the schedule for a mid-afternoon "time-out"), escape from a given situation (e.g., by a spontaneous or planned retreat), or renew or strengthen ties to supportive individuals (e.g., by more frequent visits, calls, or letters to a sibling or an offspring). These ways of structuring and restructuring one's lifestyle can have emotionally managing functions at all ages.

Selecting Adaptive Response Alternatives

A final answer to the question, What is regulated? is that emotion regulation commonly involves expressing emotion in a manner that has satisfactory consequences—in other words, that is concordant with one's personal goals for the situation. For adults, this might entail enlisting anger in a search for solutions or a persuasive argument rather than insults or physical attack. For a preschooler, this might involve insisting that a peer who has destroyed a block tower help reconstruct it rather than angrily attacking the perpetrator or using language to negotiate a parent's demands rather than erupting into angry crying. In each case, it is not just that emotion is regulated in order to achieve personal goals (e.g., reconstructing the tower, finding a solution) but that the expectation of goal achievement also facilitates emotion regulation because of the prospect of beneficial outcomes. In this respect, the availability of satisfactory response alternatives can promote emotion management by offering modes of emotion expression that have predictably satisfactory outcomes for the individual. By implication, emotion regulation is undermined when there is a very limited range of response possibilities or, alternatively, when existing options are perceived to lead consistently to undesirable outcomes.

Students of display rules have noted, of course, that individuals often minimize or intensify the expression of felt emotion and that doing so commonly has emotionally managing consequences (cf. Saarni, 1990). There are, of course, situations in which managing emotional responses has little effect on underlying emotion experience, especially when arousal is strong and salient. Moreover, certain modes of expressing emotion (such as venting anger) can undermine rather than enhance emotion regulation. The strong connections between emotional feeling and emotional responding suggest, however, that emotion regulation is often best accomplished by altering how one expresses emotion—especially when there are available means of conveying emotion that can help accomplish one's goals. In these situations, emotion management occurs because emotion has potentially satisfactory outlets.

This analysis implies that, as young children acquire a broader repertoire of modes for expressing emotion (owing to developmental changes in expressive capabilities as well as a broadened behavioral repertoire), their capacities for emotion regulation are likely to be enhanced as this repertoire is strategically employed. For example, in her longitudinal home-observational study of young children, Kopp (1992) noted that crying peaked in frequency late in the second year, with a progressive decline in crying throughout the third and fourth years. This trend replicates observations by earlier investigators, and Kopp has suggested that crying declines at this time because this is when language emerges as a significant alternative means for expressing emotion and emotion-related experiences (indeed, older children in her study showed many more verbal refusals and "off-task negotiations" in circumstances where younger children simply fussed). In many circumstances, language can express emotion more effectively than crying while at the same time accomplishing situational goals, and this may account for its enhanced utility during the preschool years.

With increasing age, the range of expressive alternatives for emotion broadens, of course, but the expression of emotion also begins to be channeled in directions that the emotion culture finds acceptable. This is because, on the basis of the socialization practices of parents and other authorities, children acquire emotion schemas that, among other things, guide their predictions of the consequences of expressing various emotions in certain situations (cf. Saarni, 1990). For example, on the basis of the verbal (e.g., "Use words rather than hitting") and behavioral guidance of socialization agents, they learn the consequences of responding to an aggressive peer by taking revenge, crying, tattling to adults, or asserting themselves. In doing so, they can more thoughtfully evaluate these alternatives in terms of their relative suitability for accomplishing personal goals in particular circumstances.

The reactions of others are, of course, especially important in evaluating the predictable consequences of different modes of emotional responding for accomplishing one's goals. Because of this, some reactions will be better suited to certain social settings than others and will thus better advance one's regulation of emotion. Recourse to an adult when frustrated by a peer may be praised by a preschool teacher but regarded negatively by a parent. Similarly, crying may be maladaptive for toddlers in some settings (e.g., when used to resist the mother's request to clean up toys) but accomplish valuable strategic ends in others (e.g., when calling attention to sudden danger or an older sibling's aggression). In short, the most adaptive means of expressing an emotion is often situation specific rather than transsituational and is based on the child's expressive repertoire, the demands of the setting, the goals of the child, and the values of social partners. This can be a complex calculus (as most adults know from experience with emotionally charged situations) and suggests not only that selecting an adaptive response alternative can be complicated but also that this facet of emotion regulation is tied to the growth of social cognition and social competency in childhood.

Implications

There are clearly diverse developmental pathways toward emotion regulation, deriving both from the efforts of external agents to manage the emotions of children and from the child's growing capacity to self-regulate (for an insightful analysis, see also Calkins, in this volume). These are built on emerging neurophysiological foundations for arousal regulation and include controlling attention processes, altering construals of emotionally arousing situations, modifying the encoding of internal emotion cues, strengthening access to coping resources, regulating the emotional demands of familiar settings, and selecting adaptive modes for expressing emotion. Each of these pathways provides different answers to the definitional question, What is regulated?

Competent emotion regulation can thus involve any of these processes, taken individually or in combination. Because we know very little about developmental changes in the use of these strategies and their consequences for children's management of emotion, the tasks of constructing a developmental analysis of the growth of emotion regulation skills and identifying the origins of individual differences in capabilities for emotion management are complex indeed. In embarking on these tasks, for example, it is important to understand the diverse constituents of developmental growth in emotion regulation skills. To what extent does growth in emotion management skills derive (a) from children's developing awareness of the *need* for emotion regulation, (b) from a growing repertoire of emotion regulation strategies (if so, which ones emerge at which ages?), (c) from enhanced strategic knowledge of the potential utility of different regulatory approaches in different situations, (d) from growing flexibility in substituting one regulatory approach for another, (e) from an emerging capacity to adapt regulatory strategies to different contexts and situational demands, and (f) from enhanced skills at evaluating (or predicting) the relative success of different regulatory approaches?

New inquiries may also be made concerning the nature and origins of individual differences in emotion regulation among children of a given age. To what extent do these derive (a) from relying on different regulatory strategies, (b) from using strategies that differ in their predictable success, (c) from using strategies that are situation specific rather than transsituational (i.e., that vary in their flexibility), (d) from using an impoverished as opposed to a rich repertoire of alternative regulatory strategies, (e) from a limited understanding of the conditions in which different emotion regulation approaches are useful, suitable, or potentially successful, and (f) from situationally specific success in emotion regulation that is not generalized? These questions and related inquiries constitute an important agenda for future research on emotion regulation and will likely provide considerable insight into processes of emotional development in general as they contribute to an awareness of how emotion changes with increasing age beyond the unfolding of a capacity for discrete emotions.

At the very least, however, the heterogeneity of these emotion regulation processes cautions against regarding the development of emotion regulation as a homogeneous growth process, instead underscoring that *emotion regulation* is a conceptual rubric that encompasses a variety of behavioral strategies, each with likely different developmental timetables and experiential origins.

EMOTION REGULATION AND SOCIAL INTERACTION

The development of emotion regulation has become a central interest of functionalist theorists, who believe that emotion is constituted by the ongoing transactions between individuals and their environments. Within this view, "families" of emotion are crucial to social signaling, communication of needs, enhancement of affiliational ties, self-defense, and other important goals. Strategies of emotion regulation enlist emotion to achieve these goals. The functionalist analysis suggests that social encounters provide the most salient contexts for exercising skills of emotion management and that the efficacy of these skills depends significantly on the responses of social partners and the demands of the social setting as they are pertinent to one's goals. In this view, exploring how the development of strategies of emotion regulation fits into the fabric of social relationships is thus an important task in elucidating the functional significance of processes of emotion management and control.

The social context affects emotion regulation in a variety of ways. One obvious way is that social partners regulate our emotions from early in life. Generalizing from studies of rats, Hofer (in this volume) illustrates the powerful effects that relationships might have on regulating physiological homeostasis and the emotions associated with early attachment and bonding. In humans, a major task of successful parenting is managing and guiding the emotion experience of offspring. This occurs not only through direct intervention to relieve distress, fear, frustration, and other negative emotions (cf. Gekoski, Rovee-Collier, & Carulli-Rabinowitz, 1983; Lamb & Malkin, 1986) but also through modeling and selective reinforcement of positive emotion expression (e.g., Malatesta-Magai, 1991), the direct induction of emotion through such processes as affective contagion, empathy, and social referencing (e.g., Stern, 1985; Thompson, 1987b; Walden, 1991), verbal instruction about emotion and emotion regulation strategies (Dunn & Brown, 1991; Miller & Sperry, 1987), and the control of opportunities for emotional arousal through the organization of caregiving demands and the environment of early development (e.g., early independence training, quality of out-of-home care, etc.). In these and many other ways, caregivers extrinsically manage emotion experience through the emotional demands

41

that they impose on young children and the interpersonal supports that they provide for containing emotional arousal within manageable limits.

With the child's increasing age, the emotional demands of caregivers and the strategies that they use for managing the emotions of offspring evolve in accordance with the child's growing repertoire of emotions and developing skill at emotion management and the changing demands of the emotion culture (e.g., Lewis & Michalson, 1983; Miller & Sperry, 1987; Saarni, 1990). Parents have fairly clearly defined expectations for the emotional behavior of their offspring that change with situational demands and the child's developing capabilities for the self-management of emotion, and they use a broadened range of direct and indirect influence strategies to socialize the child's emotional behavior. But direct efforts to regulate another's emotion are not limited to socialization processes in childhood. As adults, we seek to manage the emotions of others by extending a sympathetic ear or reassurance, emphasizing the consequences of neglected responsibilities, using humor in a distressing situation, and in other ways altering another's experience of emotionally relevant events.

These influences are especially important in the context of meaningful and long-standing social relationships. Such relationships are important not just because partners can have mutual, long-term effects on the arousal and management of emotion but also because of the emotional dimensions of the relationships themselves and the social expectations that they engender. Because attachment figures, friends, parents, spouses, offspring, and significant others constitute valuable interpersonal resources for coping with emotion, expectations concerning their accessibility, helpfulness, and sensitivity can significantly enhance—or undermine—the capacity to manage emotional arousal. A child can more easily cope with a distressing experience because of the anticipated understanding provided by a parent, a friend, or a sibling (as suggested by the research reported by Field, in this volume). Conversely, the anticipation of an uncaring or a denigrating response might cause children to restrict the range or vitality of their expressions of emotion in the presence of such partners or to experience difficulty in coping with strong arousal.

As Cassidy (in this volume) has commented, individual differences in adult attachment representations as well as infant attachments may be associated with distinct styles of emotion regulation that entail minimizing or enhancing different emotions in interaction with attachment figures. In other words, on the basis of expectations concerning the partner's availability and sensitivity, infants as well as adults may learn to disguise or enhance the expression of feelings in a relationship (cf. Thompson & Lamb, 1983). While it is certainly true that there are multiple catalysts underlying these differences in attachment and attachment representations, social expectations may be one important influence on the development of strategies for regulating emotion and emotion displays within these relationships.

In addition to the expectations engendered by close relationships, social partners also influence emotion regulation by affecting the interpretation of emotionally arousing situations and the coping resources that are available. They may reinforce attributional styles that enhance or inhibit certain emotions (e.g., "It's *not* your fault!") and may foster certain coping responses by direct instruction or modeling, by providing instrumental or material assistance, or by offering counseling and emotional sustenance (cf. Miller & Sperry, 1987). For example, offspring who regularly observe parents suppress emotion displays, perhaps in conjunction with verbal comments (e.g., "We don't have to fly off the handle!"), are likely to internalize such strategies as first-resort approaches to managing their own emotion experiences. Furthermore, these relationships may themselves impose emotional demands that can undermine as well as enhance effective regulatory efforts. While offering significant support, close relationships are often simultaneously sources of emotional stress or turmoil that can also affect efforts to manage emotion (Thompson, 1992).

In sum, the development of emotion regulation is well integrated into the fabric of social relationships not only because of the direct and indirect ways that people seek to manage emotion in others but also because of the social expectations generated by close relationships with friends and relatives (especially expectations of support and understanding), their influence on how individuals interpret emotionally arousing situations and the resources that are available to them, and the emotional dimensions of these relationships, including the demands as well as the support that they provide.

Recent research in developmental psychopathology provides informative, albeit distressing, illustrations of the diversity and importance of the influence of relationships (Thompson, Flood, & Lundquist, in press). Young offspring of parents with affective disorders are at heightened risk of emotion regulation problems owing not only to the caregiver's limited availability as a source of emotional support but also to the adult's modeling of negative attributional styles and use of discipline practices that enhance the child's feelings of responsibility and helplessness (Zahn-Waxler & Kochanska, 1990). Parent-child relationships shape not only children's construals of emotionally arousing situations but also their resources for regulating emotion: these offspring (like their parents) have difficulty devising appropriate strategies for modifying emotion and lack confidence in the efficacy of these strategies (Garber et al., 1991). Children from homes characterized by marital conflict show a heightened sensitivity to distress and anger that is manifested in excessive guilt and diminished coping with adult arguments

(Cummings, Zahn-Waxler, & Radke-Yarrow, 1984; Cummings et al., 1989; Katz & Gottman, 1991). The effects on emotion regulation of the emotional demands of distressed caregivers are manifested most clearly in children maltreated by their parents, who sometimes respond with depressed affect, heightened lability, or marked anger (Gaensbauer & Sands, 1979). Thus, diverse facets of significant relationships—expectations of helpfulness or insensitivity, the partner's influence on the interpretation of emotionally arousing situations, instruction in and modeling of strategies for managing emotion, and the emotional requirements of these relationships themselves—can have important effects on the development of emotion regulation strategies.

Thus far, we have been considering how relationships affect the development of emotion regulation. But it is important to note that the reverse is also true: emotion regulation strategies can significantly influence the course of social interaction and the development of social relationships. In a series of well-known investigations, Dodge and his colleagues have found that aggressive children tend to be deficient processors of social cues—especially when they feel threatened—and consequently construe hostile intent in ambiguous or uncertain social encounters with peers (e.g., Dodge, 1991a; Dodge & Somberg, 1987). But it is quite likely that deficiencies in emotion management as well as social information processing contribute to their social dysfunction: under threatening circumstances, the affective salience of social cues, their interpretation, and the thoroughness of one's search for and evaluation of alternative response options are all likely to be affected by skill at self-regulating emotion. Children who can "keep their cool" when threatened may be better able to think carefully about the situation and devise competent and successful response strategies. In a sense, emotion management may be both a contributor to and a result of the quality of social information processing that leads to successful or unsuccessful encounters with peers.

Needless to say, the development of the skills involved in emotion management is affected by a panoply of significant relationships in varied settings: in the context of parent-child relationships, out-of-home care settings, peer interactions, school settings, and, later, workplace associations, strategies for emotion self-regulation are fashioned and refined. A number of important questions arise from such an analysis. Given the challenges to "emotional competence" in troubled parent-offspring relationships noted above, for example, can children acquire more successful strategies of emotion management through extrafamilial support, such as with a teacher or with peers? Are there qualitatively different kinds of emotion regulation strategies—or skills for different emotional demands—acquired in peer as opposed to family contexts? Finally, how do variations in the "emotion culture" (Gordon, 1989) observed cross-nationally affect the interpretation of emotion experience and the requirements for the self-regulation of emotion? These and other questions are fascinating catalysts for the study of the development of emotion regulation, and especially of individual differences in regulatory capacities, in the context of close relationships.

THE CORRELATES OF INDIVIDUAL DIFFERENCES
IN EMOTION REGULATION

Current enthusiasm for the study of emotion regulation doubtlessly also derives from its practical applications. The study of emotion regulation provides an arena within which problems of social competence and incompetence, behavioral self-control, and even intellectual and cognitive functioning can be regarded in a new light. By characterizing these differences as partly a function of individual differences in emotion regulation processes, researchers not only contribute new ideas about the origins of these social and cognitive differences but also begin to identify new intervention and remediation strategies. Implicit in these efforts is the view that differences in emotion regulation skills can be reliably identified and that a coherent formulation of adaptive or "optimal" emotion regulation can be framed as a guide to intervention efforts.

The preceding discussion indicates why this is both a worthwhile goal and a compellingly challenging one. Because emotion regulation encompasses heterogeneous developmental processes, individual differences in emotion regulation are likely to occur along multiple dimensions rather than on a single axis. Individuals likely vary, for example, in their knowledge of the need for emotion regulation in specific situations, their awareness of alternative strategies, their flexibility in applying different regulatory strategies, and other components of emotion control. There is no necessary reason why individuals should exhibit deficiencies in all aspects of emotion regulation or in all situations; individual patterns of skill, difficulty, and compensation may be the rule. This makes the tasks of identifying the nature of these individual differences and of designing effective intervention approaches considerably more complex.

Adding to this complexity is the need to define clearly rather than intuitively what we mean by *optimal* emotion regulation (or, on the other hand, emotion *dysregulation*). As Cole, Michel, and Teti (in this volume) have noted, various clinical approaches emphasize different facets of optimal regulation, and most are difficult to operationalize. In general, *optimal* emotion regulation could be defined for either clinical or research purposes as a process or an outcome. Many formulations of emotion regulation regard optimal regulation in terms of its outcomes: the individual is capable of keeping emotions under sufficient control to allow for interpersonal relatedness and sociability, prosocial initiatives when appropriate, sympathy toward others, personal assertiveness when needed, and/or other indices of successful functioning. Effective emotion regulation is believed to be an ingredient of these behaviors, and signs of "emotion dysregulation" are commonly perceived in the absence of these capacities. But, in other respects, optimal emotion regulation can be regarded as a process: the enlistment of strategies that permit flexibility, quick reappraisals of emotionally provoking situations, access to a broad range of emotions, and efficient goal directedness. In this respect, *emotion regulation* is defined in terms of the quality of emotion that results, regardless of its other behavioral consequences.

The problem with these formulations is that the construct *optimal emotion regulation* is so broadly defined that it becomes confounded with intuitive values of what a well-functioning personality is like. Like the construct of ego control that characterized earlier research on personality development, emotion regulation is often regarded by contemporary researchers as a stable component of personality functioning with broad manifestations in diverse behavioral domains, with those who are "optimally" regulated showing many positive sociopersonality characteristics that avoid the excesses of either under- or overregulation. In these circumstances, it is helpful to remember that *optimal emotion regulation* (or *emotion dysregulation*) is often better defined by the demands of the immediate social situation and the goals of the individual than as a global, personological construct. What is "optimal" may vary for different individuals, in different situations, and with different goals.

Consider, for example, the case of a child who gets angry at a peer who has wronged her. In that situation, does "optimal" emotion regulation involve retaliation, or tattling to an authority, or avoiding the perpetrator, or insisting on the perpetrator's apology, or crying—or some combination of these responses? I suspect that this depends on many factors that are specific to this situation, such as the child's power relative to that of the wrongdoer, the values of the adults to whom the child might turn, the behavior of other children in the setting, and the overarching values of the sociocultural milieu (cf. Miller & Sperry, 1987). I suspect that "optimal" emotion regulation also depends on the child's goals for that situation. In this example, these goals might include reestablishing a sense of personal well-being, ensuring that the wrongdoing does not recur, reestablishing good relations with the perpetrator, restoring a sense of esteem within the peer group—or some combination of these. In other words, emotion management does not necessarily involve diminishing unpleasant affect (although it may); depending on the child's goals, anger might be enhanced (to stand up to the perpetrator), modulated (to enlist the assistance of friends in self-defense), or blended (to provoke an adult's intervention through salient distress). In a sense, the "optimal" choice depends on the child's goals for a given situation.

Similar questions can be raised about other features of individual variations in the self-regulation of emotion. In certain circumstances, for example, well-regulated emotion sensitizes the child to the emotions of others and fosters an appropriate emotional response to them. In these situations, the optimal self-regulation of emotion is likely to be associated with empathy and prosocial initiatives (cf. Eisenberg & Fabes, 1992b). In other circumstances, however, this is a potentially dysfunctional outcome, such as when the child witnesses domestic violence (and is thus at considerable risk by intervening prosocially) or has a parent with an affective disorder (in which case empathy may be disorganizing). Given differing circumstances, optimal emotion regulation processes may yield different behavioral outcomes—indeed, one might regard a child's manifest distress or avoidance as a more "optimal" self-regulatory strategy than one that yields emotional engagement in a parent's personal turmoil.

Children do, of course, acquire characterological styles of emotion management that become increasingly important facets of successful or dysfunctional aspects of personality functioning with increasing age. But a premature research focus on identifying and labeling these styles may cause researchers to miss noticing the social-contextual processes and personal goals that help define what *optimal* regulation is *in that context*. Researchers may also neglect the fact that children can be effective managers of their emotions in some situations (e.g., encounters with peers) and not in others (e.g., sibling interactions) or that they may effectively accomplish some emotional goals and not others. Moreover, in situations involving extreme emotional demands (such as child maltreatment, marital conflict, or a parent's psychopathology), "optimal" emotion regulation may be manifested in behavior that looks very different from what a more typical, well-functioning personality manifests. Finally, a research emphasis on the social-contextual constituents of emotion regulation will also sensitize researchers to the standards by which members of a culture (and subculture) define *optimality*.

In the future, I suspect that individual differences in emotion regulation will be defined much less globally and in a manner that is far more situationally specific than is presently the case, with careful attention to the nature of the child's goals, other developmental capacities, and the contextual demands that the child faces. This will contribute, I hope, to a developmental picture in which individual patterns of compensation and specialization, rather than "optimality" and "dysregulation," characterize our portrayals of developing individuals. And, in this context, I suspect that future research will link the growth of emotion regulation to the growth of self-understanding and of social cognition as these processes are jointly involved in the child's construction of emotion and its functions in social contexts.

NEW APPROACHES TO THE STUDY OF EMOTION REGULATION

Definitions of psychological processes are closely allied with measurement strategies, so it is perhaps appropriate that this essay close with a brief overview of new methodological approaches to the study of emotion regulation that have been explored in my lab with students and colleagues. The purpose in doing so is not to propose that these approaches are necessarily useful for all research purposes but rather to contribute to the variety of research methods that are currently available to researchers in this burgeoning field of study.

Consistent with the definition of *emotion regulation* discussed earlier, our methodological strategy has focused on measuring the dynamic features of emotional responses observed in the infants we have studied. This is because some of the most informative features of emotional arousal entail not variations in discrete emotions (which often covary) but rather changes in the temporal and intensive features of emotion that reflect the appraisal and regulatory processes related to emotion and that, in turn, influence many of the functional properties of expressions of emotion (such as the reactions that they elicit from social partners). We call these response features *emotion dynamics* because, while the discrete emotion may "play the tune" of an individual's response, emotion dynamics (like the dynamic markings on a musical score) significantly influence quality, intensity, timing, and modulation and thus significantly color emotionality. These response parameters have long interested students of infant temperament and child clinical researchers (especially those concerned with emotion regulation), but they have seldom been effectively operationalized in studies of early emotional development. This is the task that we have undertaken, together with studying the meaning and correlates of individual differences and developmental changes in these dynamic features of emotional responding.

We use either continuous time-sampled ratings or on-line temporal assessments of facial and vocal measures of emotion to index response parameters like the *latency* of the response (i.e., time from the onset of the eliciting stimulus until onset or peak of the emotional response), *rise time* (i.e., time from the onset of the emotional response until peak intensity is achieved), *persistence* (i.e., duration) of the emotional reaction, and *recovery* (i.e., time from the terminus of the eliciting stimulus until emotional responses reach a neutral baseline). More broadly, we also examine the *range* and *lability* of emotional responsiveness as well as indexing the *intensity* of emotional reactions over short- and longer-term periods (see Thompson, 1990).

Needless to say, these response dynamics are multidetermined: many factors are influential in shaping the latency, intensity, and other characteristics of an emotional response, some of which involve emotion regulation processes. Consequently, we have examined these response parameters in the context of specific hypothesis-testing studies in which we have sought to predict group differences in these emotion dynamics on the basis of characteristics of the infants themselves or of their experiential history that might contribute to differences in emotion regulation. Such an approach addresses the study of emotion regulation strictly in terms of its influence on emotional response parameters, somewhat independently of the broader consequences for psychosocial functioning.

In one study, for example, the emotion dynamics of a sample of Down syndrome (DS) infants in the Strange Situation procedure were compared with those of a sample of typical infants observed twice in this procedure: once when their ages were equivalent to those of the DS sample and also earlier, when their mental age was more comparable to that of the DS sample. Our purpose was to evaluate whether the emotion dynamics of Down syndrome infants were uniquely different from those of the comparison sample or could instead be interpreted in terms of the DS infants' cognitive lags (Thompson, Cicchetti, Lamb, & Malkin, 1985). Our results indicated that the emotional responses of the DS sample differed significantly from those of the typical sample at *each* age: Down syndrome infants showed diminished emotion intensity, a decreased emotion range, limited lability, a more prolonged latency to distress onset during separation episodes, but a quicker recovery during reunions compared with typical infants regardless of whether they were matched for age or cognitively comparable to the DS sample.

These differences suggest that the organization of emotional behavior for DS infants is unique owing both to their physiological difficulties in modulating arousal and to the cognitive retardation that blunts the speed and efficiency of their appraisals of situations and events. Both physiological and cognitive factors regulate the emotional behavior of DS (and typical) infants via attention, interpretive, as well as physiological processes. This conclusion has had, in turn, important implications not only for our understanding of how DS infants manage to address the socioemotional challenges of early growth but also for intervention and parent education (cf. Cicchetti, 1990).

In other studies, we have examined whether the difficulties in alertness, physiological stability, and arousal modulation commonly observed in premature babies would be manifested in differences (compared to full-term infants) in their regulation of emotional arousal at the end of the first year.

We discovered that the emotion dynamics of relatively healthy preemies (i.e., without compromising medical complications) were no different than those of typical infants at 12 months (Frodi & Thompson, 1985) but that medically compromised premature infants showed significantly different dynamics in their emotional behavior in the second year that reflected their continuing difficulties modulating arousal (Stiefel, Plunkett, & Meisels, 1987). Such findings not only underscore the importance of considering the long-term influences of early biological insult on emotion regulation but have also indicated how the quality of infant-caregiver interactions can support healthy emotional responsiveness in both healthy and medically compromised premature infants.

In these studies as well as others (e.g., Connell & Thompson, 1986; Thompson, Connell, & Bridges, 1988; Thompson & Lamb, 1984), we have examined differences in emotion dynamics in the context of attachment and found that variations in emotionality assume a central role in the nature and stability of the differences between securely and insecurely attached infants. These differences in emotion dynamics have temperamental as well as nontemperamental origins (cf. Belsky & Rovine, 1988) and are likely shaped by the ongoing features of caregiver-infant interaction that affect other components of attachment-system functioning (cf. Thompson & Lamb, 1983). This conclusion is consistent with emerging views of how early caregiving contributes to the development of "emotional biases" in infants (Malatesta, 1990) as well as of the role of temperamental individuality in emotion regulation.

More recently, we have explored developmental changes in the dynamics of emotion in a longitudinal study of infants observed in mother-infant play, an encounter with a stranger, and a separation episode at ages 6, 9, and 12 months (Thompson, 1990). This half year of life is a period of striking changes in emotion regulation owing to rapid cognitive advances that affect emotion appraisals (e.g., the growth of means-ends understanding and of evocative memory skills), neurophysiological maturation in the frontal lobes related to arousal regulation, the consolidation of social expectations for familiar partners, the emergence of social referencing as a means of construing emotionally arousing events, and the growth of self-propelled locomotion, which alters the child's transactions with the social and nonsocial world in that it offers a new potential for goal attainment and feelings of self-efficacy and frustration (Campos, Kermoian, & Zumbahlen, 1992). Consequently, we expected that across this developmental transition infants would show progressively enhanced emotion intensity, growing persistence in their emotional responses, and decreased response latency and rise time in their reactions—indicators, in short, of growing emotional "vitality."

This is precisely what we found across *both* positive and negative emotion elicitors. That is, regardless of whether infants were positively or negatively aroused, they showed greater speed and intensity in their emotional reactions from 6 to 12 months owing, in part, to the regulatory changes in emotionality outlined above. This emotional "vitality" appears to assume an important role in the nature of the infant's transactions with the social world during this period (cf. Tronick, 1989).

However, even though these developmental changes in emotionality were consistent across positive and negative situations, the valence of the reaction *did* make a difference for the organization of these dynamic features. To summarize briefly, negative emotional arousal in infants was characterized by a biologically based "emergency reaction" in which high distress intensity was accompanied by a short latency, long persistence, but prolonged rise time to provide a rapid mobilization of the baby's resources in the face of threat and to evoke a preemptory response from adult listeners. By contrast, high positive emotional arousal involved a longer latency, a shorter escalation to peak intensity, and much less persistence, fostering a more sustained appraisal of situational events and a capacity to respond to changes in those events but also an ability to become quickly engaged in positive stimulation. In sum, these findings indicate significant developmental changes in emotion dynamics from 6 to 12 months against a background of a consistent organizational structure of these dynamic features, as one might predict on the basis of an appreciation of both the biologically adaptive and the psychologically flexible features of the emotion regulation processes discussed in this essay.

These studies underscore what the literature reviewed here also attests: that continued study of the development of emotion regulation processes is compelling because of the potential insights that it can contribute to our understanding of emotional growth. With greater conceptual clarity concerning the meaning of *emotion regulation* and its constituents and consequences, many of these potential contributions are bound to be realized.

SUMMARY

Contemporary interest in emotion regulation promises to advance important new views of emotional development as well as offering applications to developmental psychopathology, but these potential contributions are contingent on developmentalists' attention to some basic definitional issues. This essay offers a perspective on these issues by considering how emotion regulation should be defined, the various components of the management of emotion, how emotion regulation strategies fit into the dynamics of social interaction, and how individual differences in emotion regulation should be conceptualized and measured. In the end, it seems clear that *emotion regulation* is a conceptual rubric for a remarkable range of developmental processes, each of which may have its own catalysts and control processes. Likewise, individual differences in emotion regulation skills likely have multifaceted origins and are also related in complex ways to the person's emotional goals and the immediate demands of the situation. Assessment approaches that focus on the dynamics of emotion are well suited to elucidating these complex developmental and individual differences. In sum, a challenging research agenda awaits those who enter this promising field of study.

ORIGINS AND OUTCOMES OF
INDIVIDUAL DIFFERENCES IN EMOTION REGULATION

Susan D. Calkins

Although the construct *emotion regulation* is subject to a variety of definitions and interpretations, it is often conceived as being the processes or strategies that are used to manage emotional arousal so that successful interpersonal functioning is possible (Cole, Michel, & Teti, in this volume; Garber & Dodge, 1991; Thompson, in this volume). In describing the process of development in this domain, researchers have been investigating the role of both internal and external sources of regulation during infancy and childhood (Dodge, 1989; Kopp, 1982, 1989; Thompson, 1990, in this volume). The progression from relying on parents for regulation of arousal to being able to self-regulate is a process that begins in infancy and continues through early childhood (Cicchetti, Ganiban, & Barnett, 1991; Kopp, 1989; Tronick, 1989). The caregiver's role in this process is extensive; initially, the provision of food, clothing, and physical soothing assists the infant in state regulation; later, more complex communications and interactions with the caregiver teach the child to manage distress, control impulses, and delay gratification.

During this lengthy process, the infant gradually uses developments in the sensorimotor arena to respond differently to different events and people. For instance, the advent of locomotion allows the child to control emotionally comfortable proximity. And the acquisition of social referencing skills gives the child access to new sources of relevant information. The growing ability to modulate attention further contributes to the infant's abilities to exert control in interactions. By the end of the second year of

I wish to thank Nathan A. Fox and Ross A. Thompson for their assistance with earlier drafts of this essay. Direct correspondence to Susan D. Calkins, Institute for Child Study, Benjamin Building, Room 3304, University of Maryland, College Park, MD 20742.

life, owing to major developments in both gross motor and cognitive abilities, infants have become skilled at monitoring their own behaviors, interpreting the behaviors of others, and responding to social demands. Although these developments in self-regulation follow a fairly predictable path in infancy and early childhood (Kopp, 1982, 1989), important individual differences nevertheless exist in both the way that infants learn to regulate their affective states and the strategies that they acquire as a result of this learning process.

Describing the individual differences that exist among young children in emotion regulation is not simply a matter of identifying the different strategies that they use in particular emotionally arousing situations; the developmental process by which these strategies are acquired is itself subject to individual differences. Moreover (and as Thompson, in this volume, points out), given that this process of acquiring emotion regulation skills is a function of the interaction among numerous internal and external factors and takes place over the course of several years, it is not surprising that the study of individual differences in this domain is quite complex.

A multicomponent, longitudinal approach to studying the developmental processes of emotion regulation is quite valuable in such circumstances. Using such an approach permits addressing the issue of the effects that short-term, context-bound strategies may have on the development of more formalized, stylistic emotion regulation strategies that evolve over a number of months or years. Emotional arousal may facilitate, inhibit, or disrupt behavior, and the adoption of particular short-term strategies may therefore engender different experiences for different individuals (Thompson, in this volume). Identifying differences in the developmental process of acquiring the particular adaptive and functional emotion regulation strategies that make up a child's behavioral repertoire may help us isolate the origins of dysregulating behaviors, which can, over time, contribute to the development of a maladaptive behavioral style that places a child at risk for psychopathological disorders such as internalizing and externalizing problems (Cole et al., in this volume). Thus, a process approach to emotion regulation that focuses on individual differences can provide information on the development of both adaptive and maladaptive behaviors.

The aim of this essay is to examine the development of individual differences in regulation and the role that specific styles of emotion regulation and dysregulation play in affecting young children's interactive behavior with peers. Specifically, I propose a general developmental pathway that conceptualizes individual variations in terms of both infant traits and parents' caregiving practices and discuss the role that each set of factors may play in the process of acquiring the emotion regulation skills and strategies used in social interactions. Several specific pathways to particular styles of emotion regulation and dysregulation are delineated, and the manner in which these may influence subsequent peer interaction will be discussed. In the concluding paragraphs, suggestions are made regarding the way that future research aimed at testing these and other models of the emotion regulation process may be conducted.

SOURCES OF INDIVIDUAL DIFFERENCES IN EMOTION REGULATION

A number of steps enter into any conceptualization of how the process of acquiring emotion regulation strategies occurs. First, it is essential to identify the elements, both internal and external to the child, as well as the reciprocal processes that may enter into the interplay between temperament and social interaction. Second, it is necessary to propose a timetable for specifying when and how these elements exert their influence. Finally, the relative strength of association between and among particular elements must be indicated, and the influence of each on the outcome of emotion regulation strategy or style needs to be specified.

The first issue, that of identifying the potentially essential elements of this developmental process, has been addressed by a number of researchers working on diverse aspects of this problem (Cicchetti et al., 1991; Fox & Calkins, 1993; Gable & Isabella, 1992; Rothbart & Derryberry, 1981; Rothbart, Ziaie, & O'Boyle, 1992). Thompson (in this volume) discusses many of the elements that may influence emotion regulation; a number of these are considered to be internal to the child, whereas others are external influences, in particular effects exerted by parents or other significant others. For the purpose of specifying possible pathways to emotion regulation, I have clustered these various components according to the general categories of internal versus external sources of emotion regulation; examples of several types of each of these are listed in Table 1.

At least three potential sources of individual differences that are endogenous to the infant or young child are listed in this table. Differences in the infant's neuroregulatory or biological systems are one such source. Recently, a number of researchers have studied the link between personality characteristics and physiological reactivity during the period of infancy, and Gunnar (1990) has provided an excellent review of work centered on exploring relations between emotional reactivity and such biological phenomena as heart rate, brain electrical activity, and endocrine response. This research demonstrates that there are observable individual differences in infant reactivity to specific emotion-eliciting events and that these differences may also be reflected in the reactivity of particular physiological systems (Fox, 1989; Gunnar, 1986; Kagan, Reznick, & Snidman, 1987; Porges, 1991).

A strong link between two potential sources of individual differences in infancy—biological reactivity and behavioral traits—is thus implied: reac-

TABLE 1

SOURCES OF INDIVIDUAL DIFFERENCES IN EMOTION REGULATION

	Examples		Examples
Internal sources:		External sources:	
Neuroregulatory systems	Endocrine activity Heart rate/vagal tone Brain electrical activity	Interactive caregiving styles	Responsive, contingent vs. insensitive Cooperative vs. intrusive, controlling Reciprocal vs. unilateral Accessible, attentive vs. ignoring Supportive vs. overprotective Accepting vs. neglecting
Behavioral traits	Attentiveness Interest level Adaptability/reactivity in response to novelty Resistance/reactivity in response to frustration Soothability Smiling/sociability	Explicit training	Modeling Reinforcement Discipline
Cognitive components	Social referencing Beliefs/expectations about others and environment (internal working models) Awareness of need for regulation Ability to apply strategies		

tivity to particular kinds of events will vary across infants, and, when displayed behaviorally, this may have important implications for the development of emotion regulation skills for at least two reasons. First, infants who experience extreme distress in response to particular types of events may become too disrupted to permit their acquiring internal mechanisms for the regulation of that distress (Fox & Calkins, 1993). Second, frequent displays of distress in response to particular types of events may affect a caregiver's response in a dyadic interaction (Calkins & Fox, 1992; Crockenberg, 1981; Sagi et al., 1985; van den Boom, 1989). For example, the parent may be unable to respond contingently at all times given the frequency of distress episodes. Over time, then, the behavioral display of particular temperamental dispositions or biological susceptibilities influences both internal and external efforts at emotion regulation.

With development, a third internal factor, cognition, comes into play: as infants mature cognitively, they acquire an understanding that the people around them will respond or behave in a particular manner. Table 1 also lists a number of examples of how the child may use cognitive abilities both to acquire and to utilize emotion regulation skills. For instance, given early experiences of sensitive and responsive caregiving, the infant is likely to come to believe that those around her will support her efforts to learn about her world, protect her in time of trouble, and comfort her in moments of distress (Bretherton, 1985). This internal "working model" of the world shapes the child's interpretations, expectations, and understanding of how others will respond and hence exerts a strong influence on the child's subsequent social interactions.

Developments in cognitive abilities that permit older infants to gather information by visual inspection and assimilation of maternal cues also serve an adaptive value in circumstances where the child confronts novelty and change in the environment (Rothbart, 1988). Later, as the child becomes more sophisticated in social interactions, she will learn when it is necessary and appropriate to regulate displays of affect and will develop the ability to apply any of a variety of strategies to suit the circumstance. At this point, the child will utilize a complex sequence of information-processing skills that enable her to recognize, interpret, and evaluate a given set of circumstances prior to generating a suitable emotion-regulating response (Dodge, 1991a; Garber, Braafladt, & Zeman, 1991).

Although these biological, behavioral, and cognitive factors clearly play a prominent role in the emergence of emotion regulation skills, they are influenced, to varying degrees, by numerous external factors as well (Cicchetti et al., 1991; Thompson 1990, in this volume). As noted in Table 1, primary among these are factors that are a function of both early interactions with caregivers (cf. Cassidy, in this volume; Field, in this volume) and, later, more explicit methods of training children to behave in accordance with given standards, norms, and parents' expectations. As I have argued earlier, the nature of both these sorts of interactions is strongly influenced by an infant's early temperamental dispositions and by her developing capacity to handle affective stimuli on her own; nevertheless, the nature of early interactions with caregivers can act to shape both the infant's cognitive interpretation of given affect-eliciting events and the emotions displayed in response to those events. For example, an infant's capacity to manage distress, coupled with support provided by the mother, can facilitate the development of an ability to self-comfort and rely less on parents as well as a growing sense of security (Fogel, 1982a), whereas an inability to develop this sort of tolerance may lead to both withdrawn behavior and feelings of insecurity on the part of the infant.

In sum, the development of self-regulation seems to hinge on both the infant's own capacity for utilizing necessary regulatory strategies and the parent's sensitivity in meeting the regulatory needs of the infant. Cassidy (in this volume) discusses in great detail the nature of secure versus insecure attachment relationships and the consequences that such relationships have in affecting emotional responsivity and regulation during infancy and early childhood. In describing the interactional nature of secure and insecure relationships, she provides examples of how particular caregivers may shape their child's emotional development. Other examples of styles of caregiving in dyadic interaction that are readily observed during routine parent-child interactions and that may influence the child's acquisition of particular emotion regulation skills are listed in Table 1. As the child becomes older and more adept at managing her own responses, parents will use increasingly more explicit methods of modeling, of reinforcing desirable behaviors, and of disciplining the child for inappropriate behaviors.

Thus, the process of developing emotion regulation skills and strategies is fundamentally an interactive one—it depends on both infant and parent contributions, and, moreover, its success is likely to depend on whether the goals of both participants are in agreement. Determining how this process evolves and the specific manner in which various components exert their influence is clearly crucial to our understanding of the origins of individual differences in emotion regulation; equally clearly, the problems encountered in attempts to study the development of both context-specific regulatory strategies and more general styles of regulation in a systematic, empirical fashion are quite complex. Any attempts to move toward developing models that can eventually be tested require making simplifying assumptions as well as numerous decisions among a host of alternative formulations. The approach that my colleagues and I have adopted in the course our programmatic studies is to focus on the young child's style of interaction with peers as an index of her skills at emotion regulation—a choice that we believe follows logically from the definition of *emotion regulation* given at the outset of this essay (i.e., "the processes or strategies that are used to manage emotional arousal so that successful interpersonal functioning is possible"). Because of our interest in the origins of individual differences in what become the child's characteristic regulatory strategies, our formulations begin with individual difference factors (both internal and external) that can be identified in earliest infancy; given the central role that management of emotional arousal is accorded in our definition of *emotion regulation,* indices of the infant's disposition provide our early internal individual difference factor of choice.

DEVELOPMENTAL PATHWAYS TO EMOTION REGULATION

To enhance clarity of communication, the following descriptions of the various proposed pathways are discussed in the most straightforward terms possible; clarification of various assumptions that are embedded in these formulations as well as other appropriate caveats are deferred to a later section.

The General Case

In specifying a pathway to emotion regulation, the goal is to propose the way that traits or behaviors of particular child and caregiver dyads may affect each other so as to produce an outcome. Focusing on the sources of individual differences in emotion regulation that are discussed by Thompson (in this volume) and outlined in Table 1 above, it is possible to (1) develop a general pathway, or template, that specifies how these sources may work together to produce regulatory skills; (2) create specific models that allow us to speculate on the path to particular outcomes with respect to the way that young children negotiate peer interactions; and (3) describe potentially dysregulating strategies and their origins. Figure 1 displays a simple template that organizes the endogenous and exogenous sources of individual variation discussed in the previous section. The figure depicts three important hypotheses. First, it indicates the relations among the different factors; second, it shows the proposed direction of influence of these factors; and, third, it specifies the relative power of each factor to predict other factors and, eventually, an outcome.

As shown in Figure 1, the proposed pathway is initiated by some biological or neuroregulatory mechanism that predisposes an infant to a particular behavioral trait. On the basis of the recent work from our laboratory as well as that of others who study infant psychophysiology (Calkins, Fox, & Marshall, in press; Gunnar, 1986, 1990; Kagan & Snidman, 1991b; Stifter

INTERNAL COMPONENTS   EXTERNAL COMPONENTS

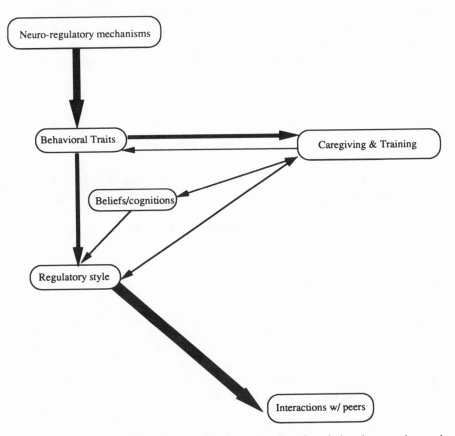

Fig. 1.—This general developmental pathway describes the relations between internal and external sources of emotion regulation to predict the outcome of peer interaction.

& Fox, 1990), it is hypothesized that this link is a fairly strong one, hence the bold arrow in the figure. However, it is the behavioral display of this biological predisposition to which the caregiver reacts. In infancy, this response emerges primarily during typical caregiving routines, simple games, and interventions when the infant is distressed. Later, these responses become more formalized as the caregiver attempts to train or discipline the child to behave in a particular manner. As the figure indicates, this proposed model hypothesizes a strong bidirectional association between infant behavior and the adult's caregiving and training. However, because the focus is on mediation via individual differences in emotion regulation, this association is characterized as being weaker than that between neuroregulatory mechanisms and behavior. In some cases, parents may not adapt their behavior very successfully to the behavioral displays of their infant and thus limit their ability to control or alter the child's early reactivity.

The pathway depicting associations between the internal and the external sources of individual variation in emotion regulation indicates that caregiver behavior affects children reciprocally and in at least three domains. First, it affects the child's immediate emotional reactivity in a given situation. Second, it may affect the child's beliefs and cognitions about the world and the caregiver and, in turn, the way that the child responds to the caregiver's behavior. Third, it may exert a direct effect on the regulatory strategies that the young child uses in particular situations as well as in response to the caregiver's overtures; furthermore, beliefs and cognitions may of themselves influence the way that the child manages affect in given circumstances. These links are shown as the weakest associations within the pathway; within this conceptualization, the child's behavioral traits are viewed as being a stronger direct predictor of her ability to develop strategies for controlling affective reactions.

Our own research (Calkins et al., in press), as well as that of Kagan's group (Kagan & Snidman, 1991b), has indicated that, at the extremes of the distributions of infants, early behavioral profiles are strongly predictive of later social behavior. Thus, for example, among a group of infants selected for extreme displays of negative affect coupled with motor activity, a significant portion displayed inhibited behavior during the second year of life (Calkins et al., in press). This finding suggests that extreme cases of reactivity to given kinds of events may make the process of acquiring more adaptive behavioral repertoires rather difficult. Such extreme types of reactivity may be impervious to caregiver interventions, or, at the very least, make parents' efforts to change early infant behavior somewhat difficult.

The final link in the path model depicted in Figure 1 indicates what we believe is a strong relation between emotion regulation style and interaction in a peer setting. In our operationalization of the construct, *emotion regulation* is the child's ability to control extreme states of negative and positive arousal or reactivity in such a way that mutual, reciprocal interaction becomes possible. Operating in a peer setting places such demands on the child, whose success in negotiating peer interactions in early childhood will depend on the use of a style of regulation that is adaptive and functional. The nature of these early interactions will, in turn, have an important effect on subsequent developments in both social and nonsocial domains (Rubin & Lollis, 1988).

The fundamental proposition embedded in this general path model is that the young child's regulatory style begins to develop quite early in infancy and that it is subject to both infant predispositions and caregiver

61

behaviors. These two facts account for the diversity that we may observe both in the paths to particular styles of emotion regulation and in the way that these skills or styles are displayed in social interactions. This diversity can best be captured by identifying the way that specific infant characteristics and/or specific caregiving styles influence the management of affect in particular contexts. In the next section, I propose several paths that are unique in terms of variations in both these internal and external process components.

PATHWAYS TO PRO-SOCIAL, AGGRESSIVE, AND SOCIALLY WITHDRAWN INTERACTIONS

Figures 2–5 below depict four hypothetical pathways to distinct styles of regulation and subsequent peer interaction; in all four cases, the origin of the various styles of interaction is proposed to lie in a biological predisposition to be reactive to one of two sorts of events. These two types of reactivity are used for illustrative purposes primarily because they have been the focus of our recent research (Calkins & Fox, 1992; Calkins et al., in press; Stifter & Fox, 1990); in a later section, hypotheses regarding other early predispositions and their possible outcomes for peer interaction are advanced.

Reactivity to Frustration

Figure 2 illustrates a developmental pathway by means of which early reactivity to frustration—which may be reflected in particular patterns of heart-rate activity (e.g., Stifter & Fox, 1990)—interacts with a particular caregiving style. In this case, an infant who is resistant to control and easily distressed by events or objects that interfere with exploration is assisted in the process of affect regulation by an unintrusive and supportive style of caregiving. Here, parents respond to the infant's desires for few restrictions on movement and activity by providing an independent environment in which they set few limits on the child's behaviors. The infant's experience leads to perception of the environment as friendly rather than restrictive and is likely to be reflected in a high degree of uninhibited exploratory behavior. Given this view of the environment and the tendency to approach it rather than to withdraw, such a child is also likely to be outgoing and friendly in interactions with others (Fox & Calkins, 1993).

The pathway depicted in Figure 2 describes a course of development that is a function of sensitive caregiving in the service of affective control, and the outcome is positive social interactions for the child. In other instances, however, the outcome may be very different: the pathway depicted in Figure 3 hypothesizes what can happen within the emotion regulation

INTERNAL COMPONENTS

EXTERNAL COMPONENTS

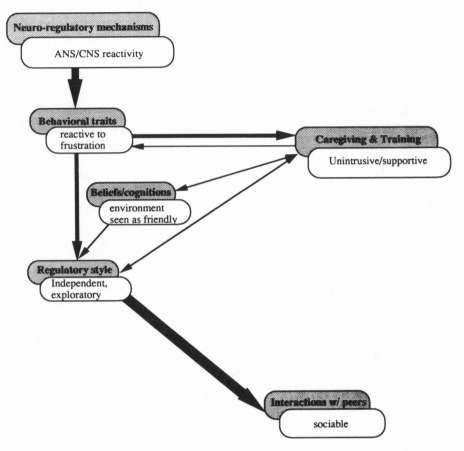

Fig. 2.—This pathway demonstrates how reactivity to frustration leads to sociability with peers when met with supportive parenting.

process when the parent's response to biological and behavioral reactivity is not sensitive.

Here, the infant's tendency to be easily frustrated by barriers and restrictions is met by caregiver attempts to control and coerce the infant. The result is a belief on the part of the infant that the environment is hostile and that external efforts to control behavior should be met by anger (Dodge, 1991b). A coercive style of interaction is likely to develop between parent and child. This, in turn, can lead the child to view interactions with peers as opportunities to exert control or to achieve the upper hand and, in

INTERNAL COMPONENTS   EXTERNAL COMPONENTS

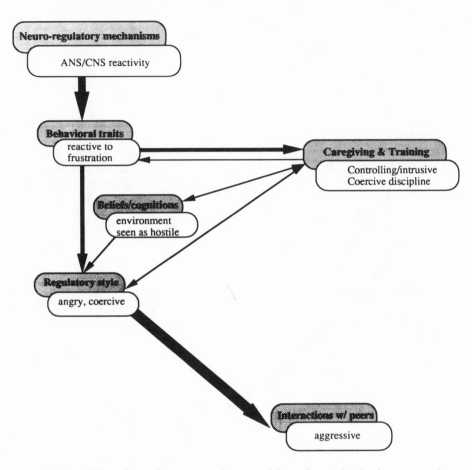

FIG. 3.—This pathway demonstrates how reactivity to frustration leads to aggression with peers when met with controlling parenting.

consequence, lead to a prevalence of aggressive and antagonistic interactions (Bates, Bayles, Bennett, Ridge, & Brown, 1991).

It is clear that, although initial reactivity is proposed to exert a strong effect on the child's failure to develop appropriate regulatory strategies to deal with barriers and issues of control, the particular caregiving style that the child experienced will have contributed to this dysregulation as well. It should also be evident that this outcome may come about through the use of other, equally inadequate caregiving strategies. For example, failure to help a child regulate frustration by ignoring her distress and failure to model appropriate behavioral responses to frustration are two different types of parenting behavior that have also been implicated in the development of aggressive behavior (Bates et al., 1991). Moreover, in cases of extreme early reactivity, the infant's behavior may be difficult to control or shape even under conditions of the most sensitive caregiving; hence, the proposed pathway includes a direct association between early reactivity and subsequent emotion regulation style.

Reactivity to Novelty

To this point, the template depicted in Figure 1 above has been used to specify the way that infant traits and caregiving experiences may influence the role that early reactivity to frustration plays in the emotion regulation process. In the next two figures (Figs. 4 and 5 below), the focus is on another form of initial reactivity—namely, early sensitivity to novelty, which the data suggest is also related to particular biological differences (Calkins et al., in press; Kagan & Snidman, 1991b). As in the previous instances, this early reactivity to new objects, events, and people may be met by a variety of caregiving strategies. Figure 4 depicts circumstances in which caregivers respond sensitively to their infant's behavior by being unintrusive (i.e., not forcing novelty on the child so that they will "get used to it") and providing support in situations that may elicit distress.

Such caregivers may also model approach and interest behaviors, rather than apprehension and anxiety, when they see the child confronted by potentially fear-inducing stimuli. Infants exposed to these sorts of experiences are led to see the environment as inviting and interesting rather than as frightening and hence are able to develop the capacity to cope with the distress and fear aroused by confronting new people and stimuli. Although they may be somewhat cautious and wary, they will nevertheless be ready to control their negative affective response so that interaction with the environment is possible, and the social outcome for these children may well be an ability to interact successfully with their peers.

However, and again as in the previous instances, early reactivity to novelty may be met with caregiving experiences that will not serve to ameliorate the distress. Figure 5 depicts one such possible problem pathway. In this case, frequent displays of distress to new people or places are met by overprotective and controlling caregiving. Although such parenting may protect the child from short-term distress, it can also encourage a withdrawing style of regulation that will fail to assist her in developing appropriate strategies for interacting with the environment. The child is likely to learn to view the environment as frightening and threatening and to display a fearful and inhibited style of interaction (Calkins, Fox, Rubin, Coplan, &

INTERNAL COMPONENTS   EXTERNAL COMPONENTS

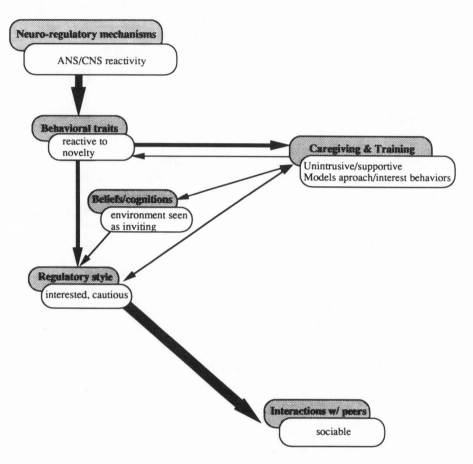

FIG. 4.—This pathway demonstrates how reactivity to novelty leads to sociability with peers when met with supportive parenting.

Stewart, 1994). Such a child will likely be socially withdrawn in interactions with peers (cf. Rubin & Lollis, 1988).

CAVEATS ABOUT AND CLARIFICATIONS OF THE PROPOSED PATHWAYS

The pathways depicted in Figures 2–5 above reflect a number of assumptions that need to be made explicit. First, all these paths hypothesize

INTERNAL COMPONENTS   EXTERNAL COMPONENTS

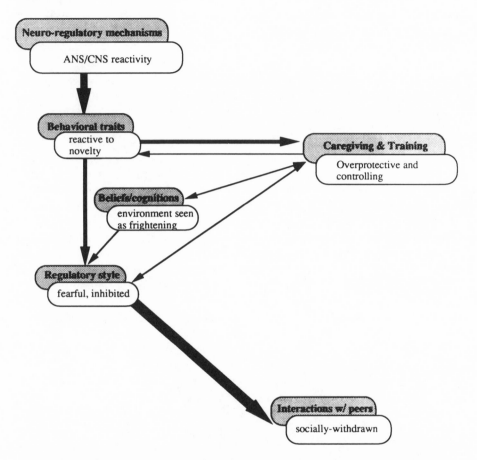

Fig. 5.—This pathway demonstrates how reactivity to novelty leads to social withdrawal with peers when met with controlling parenting.

that the strongest link in the process lies between inborn neuroregulatory mechanisms and behavioral traits. This position represents a theoretical bias and as such underscores the belief that whether caregiver behavior acts to ameliorate, exacerbate, or have no effect on the child's behavior depends on the strength of the infant's reactive tendencies. The relation between infant temperamental reactivity and interactions with the caregiver hypothesized here differs somewhat from that proposed by those who hold that the attachment relationships play a stronger role in affecting infant and child socioemotional development; indeed, Cassidy (in this volume) presents the arguments most commonly used by such theorists in the temperament versus attachment debate. Our own position is that there are enough data to suggest a relation between what is characterized variously as emotionality, reactivity, or temperament and attachment classification and that, for at least some infants, the attachment relationship will reflect early temperamental tendencies (Fox, Kimmerly, & Schafer, 1991; Goldsmith & Alansky, 1987). Early infant reactivity may in fact constrain the development of regulatory skills, limiting the effect of a parent's caregiving style at least in some instances and contributing to a degree of stability of temperament from early infancy through toddlerhood for particular types of infants.

Nevertheless, the interactions hypothesized to exist among the components in these developmental pathways clearly allow for a potent caregiving influence. In using early behavioral/physiological profiles to predict subsequent inhibited behavior, Kagan and Snidman (1991b) report that half the infants they classified as "high motor, high cry" in response to novelty at 4 months (a response that these authors attribute to a low threshold for arousal rooted in the limbic system) showed high fear at 14 months. An important question that they have not addressed, however, is why the other infants who displayed this early pattern of reactivity developed only moderate amounts of fear or were simply not observed to be fearful in later infancy. A similar pattern obtained in our selected longitudinal sample of infants (Calkins et al., in press): some of the infants who displayed the profile of behaviors predictive of inhibition in the second year of life did not in fact become fearful. The proposed pathway suggests that these infants have made accommodations to their initial reactivity, quite likely with the help of their parents, and that the accommodations have allowed them to cope with their low threshold for fear. Thus, while we believe that the nexus of interactions among internal and external sources of effects that we depict in our template in Figure 1 above represents the general case, we recognize that the relative strength assigned to individual links can in fact vary under differing circumstances.

A second point that needs to be stressed is that there are undoubtedly multiple paths (undepicted) to the same outcome. For example, two children may display similar interactive behavior with peers despite the presence of differences in their initial reactive tendencies (or, indeed, despite the fact that one may have been born reactive to particular events and the other not). It is equally possible to see two children who are similar in initial reactivity end up displaying similar styles of dysregulation and poor social skills despite exposure to two very different styles of caregiving. Moreover, the models that we propose are limited to specifying the consequences of early reactivity to novelty and to frustration, yet it is quite probable that a number of other infant behavioral traits are subject to the same developmental processes and affect emotion regulation in a similar manner. Thus, for example, early attention problems may be associated with later behavior problems owing to the role that attention plays in the success of early interactions with caregivers. Behaviors that reflect interest level, soothability, or sociability—all of which are also likely implicated in the process of early dyadic interaction—deserve similar consideration.

A third caveat is that, given their level of simplicity, it is apparent that emotion regulation as examined in these pathways has been reduced to a small set of observable behaviors in particular contexts. However, as Cole et al. (in this volume) make clear, there are many facets of emotion regulation that may or may not include observable behavior. Thus, for example, in considering emotion regulation in the face of novel social stimuli, our pathways take into account only the response of approach versus withdrawal in response to the emotional arousal precipitated by exposure to novelty. In fact (and as Cole et al. point out), emotion regulation also depends on such factors as having access to the full range of context-appropriate emotions, adhering to culturally imposed display rules, and being able to experience mixed emotions. It is clear that these as well as other dimensions of affect management may come into play when an individual is confronted by novel stimuli and that consideration of these additional factors would clearly improve the specificity of the developmental pathway proposed here.

With regard to the development of emotion dysregulation, two distinctions are helpful in differentiating the pathways that I examine here from those that may lead to psychopathology. First, it is important to draw a distinction between specific short-term strategies and long-term stylistic patterns of behavior in thinking about affect management in different contexts. Cole et al. (in this volume) make this distinction in describing ways that dysregulating behaviors may become debilitating psychopathologies. Although it is not the intent of this essay to describe pathways to psychopathology, it is nevertheless important to recognize that, over time, nonadaptive or dysregulating coping strategies may develop into internalizing or externalizing disorders. Thus, what may initially appear to be an effective strategy for coping with novelty (such as withdrawal and retreat to security) may become a more problematic pattern if it is maintained into childhood. The early strategy could establish a pattern of social withdrawal that, while perhaps not a severe behavior problem in itself, may become one if the child's missed opportunities for peer interaction result in depression and low self-esteem. The dysregulation that caused the child to withdraw from social novelty may not of itself have been psychopathological in nature, but its consequences could nevertheless enhance the risk of developing internalizing disorders at a later point in childhood or adolescence (Rubin, Mills, & Rose-Krasnor, 1991).

The second important consideration is that the pathways that are proposed here apply to instances of relatively "normal" caretaking environments, in which the development of extreme forms of dysregulation, and thus psychopathology, is less likely. The distinction here is between aberrant or abusive caregiving situations and those in which the caregiver is simply not as sensitive, contingent, or supportive as would be considered optimal. Aberrant caregiving environments are likely not only to be characterized by caretaker insensitivity but also to consist of additional, more chronic problems that place even the most biologically well-regulated child at risk. Thus, the contribution of the child characteristics—which are viewed as playing such an important role in the proposed developmental pathways—may be overridden in such extreme circumstances.

Finally, the template depicted in Figure 1 above has been used to describe hypothetical pathways to three fairly commonly considered categories of peer interactive behavioral outcomes (pro-social, withdrawn, and aggressive behavior). Clearly, however, this template could be applied to pathways to a multiplicity of other categories of social behavior outcomes. Indeed, different styles of emotion regulation and dysregulation may be central to the emergence of submissive, controlling, hyperactive, impulsive, empathic, altruistic, or anxious patterns of behaviors, each of which is most likely to have implications for a given child's behavior in a peer setting. In each of these possible additional instances, the goal would be to specify what types of caregivers' responses to the infant's biologically driven behavioral systems will allow the child to develop the strategies that are most useful in negotiating the environment and to propose how the use of inappropriate strategies influences the process of emotion dysregulation.

FUTURE DIRECTIONS

In continuing to meet the complex challenge of studying emotion regulation from a process orientation, a number of issues must be addressed. To date, much of the body of research has focused almost exclusively on the influence of either temperament or parenting styles; each approach acknowledges the existence of the other, but neither has made significant progress in examining the relative contributions of each factor. Two problems face researchers who wish to study the question of individual differences without neglecting important issues. First, it is essential that we begin to conceptualize such differences in terms of the effects of transactions between infant reactivity/temperament and parents' responsivity and begin to develop methodologies for examining empirically the developmental nature of this reciprocity. Second, our investigations of the effects of both temperamental reactivity and regulatory strategies must be longitudinal in nature so as to permit complementing our observations of concurrent effects with subsequent behavior changes.

Clearly, current conceptualizations of emotion regulation do acknowledge the reciprocal influences of temperament and parenting; however, there have been few attempts to capture dyadic differences in how this reciprocity evolves. One possible approach to this issue has been suggested by a recent report by Vaughn and his colleagues (Vaughn et al., 1992) on several studies of the relation between infant temperament and attachment. On the basis of their findings, the authors conclude that infant emotionality does indeed exert an effect in shaping the attachment dyad, although the strength of this effect varies. We may speculate that the extent to which infant reactivity influences developing relationships may be a function of the degree to which the nature of this bond is affected by the child's temperamental disposition and the parents' responsivity. Thus, the quality of infant attachment is conceived to be a consequence of some combination of the child's temperament and that child's relationship with the mother. The strength of the influence of each of these two factors may itself reflect a dimension of individual difference: what conditions will affect the relative degree of influence for a given child? In some cases, responsive parenting may override the effects of an irritable temperament; conversely, an easy temperament (or a well-regulated neonate) may be impervious to the effects of unresponsive parenting. Capturing this fundamentally dyadic relation empirically should enhance the predictability of a given child's prospects for the development of particular kinds of emotion regulation skills.

The second issue that needs to be addressed in future research concerned with individual differences is how best to capture the long-term influence of both internally generated and externally derived current regulatory strategies. The focus here might be on some specific types of self-regulatory strategies commonly used by infants since it seems probable that flexibility and adaptability in social interactions would be a function of the child's developing ability to self-regulate, an ability that is aided by parents' support and feedback. Thus, strategies that reflect the child's failure either to self-regulate or to use the mother for the purpose of regulation would be predictive of inhibited behavior, or alternatively, of aggressive and impulsive behaviors. For example, an infant who turns away from a distressing event and distracts herself with a toy may succeed in controlling her immediate negative affect; however, over time, object-oriented regulatory behavior may in fact be a very poor strategy for managing distress. Similarly, if an infant is incapable of self-regulating and looks to an outside source for assistance, failure to choose an appropriate source of feedback (or the caregiver's failure to provide feedback) will prevent the child from learning successful distress-managing strategies.

Studies that assess regulatory strategies used by the infant over a period of time are needed to determine the effect that the deployment of particular strategies may have on subsequent emotional responsivity to social and environmental challenges. Regulatory strategies that are guided by parents need similar investigation—these not only have short-term effects on infant emotional reactivity and regulation but also exert important long-term effects as well. To capture the evolution of an infant's regulatory repertoire, the parent-infant reciprocal relationship needs to be followed over a period of months and in the context of different types of events that elicit emotional reactivity and regulation; only then can the actual process of acquiring regulatory skills be chronicled.

Considerable progress has been made in the last decade in efforts to describe the acquisition of emotion regulation skills in the first few years of life, the underlying physiology of such processes, and the pathologies that may be observed in less than optimal circumstances (cf. Garber & Dodge, 1991). Nevertheless, considerable work remains to be done, particularly with regard to individual differences in the way that this development occurs. This will be a complicated endeavor, primarily because it requires us to examine the complex relations among temperament, emotion, and social relationships, and it is clear that progress will be best achieved in this area by concentrating on capturing the interrelations and reciprocities between temperament and caregiving.

SUMMARY

Recent discussions of emotion regulation in infants and young children have focused on the individual differences that exist in this domain of development. Such differences may be seen at the outcome level, in terms of variations in emotion regulation strategies, or at the process level, in terms of variations in the development of particular strategies as a result of infant or caregiver effects. In this essay, a general hypothetical pathway to emotion regulation and dysregulation comprising interactions among a number of internal and external factors thought to impinge on the emotion regulation process has been proposed. Relations among these factors were hypothesized, and examples of pathways to particular types of social behavior in a peer setting were advanced. It is suggested that empirical confirmation of these pathways would enhance our understanding of adaptive regulatory behavioral patterns as well as patterns that may be dysregulating and potentially place the child at risk for the development of psychopathological disorders. To be successful, such studies must include consideration of the reciprocal interaction between the infant's behavioral and cognitive traits and the caregiving environment over extended periods of early development.

THE DEVELOPMENT OF EMOTION REGULATION AND DYSREGULATION: A CLINICAL PERSPECTIVE

Pamela M. Cole, Margaret K. Michel,
and Laureen O'Donnell Teti

Anger is a short madness.—Horace

The movements of expression in the face . . . are in themselves of much importance for our welfare.—Charles Darwin

The ancient Greek philosophers conceptualized the emotions as irrational, animistic, visceral phenomena that interfered with the higher-order processes of thought and reason. From that early conceptualization, emotion has had a long history of being construed as a psychological underground that disturbs or disrupts rational thought and behavior (Mora, 1980). The emphasis in Freudian theory on unconscious affective processes shaping personality and psychopathology reinforced the image of the disruptive influence of emotion (e.g., Freud, 1915/1957). Impulses were viewed as primitive emotions that dominated early life and were subjugated to reason and internalized social control after age 7.

The Darwinian perspective offered a different vantage point, one that is represented in modern theories of emotion and its development (e.g., Arnold, 1960; Campos, Barrett, Lamb, Goldsmith, & Stenberg, 1983; Frijda, 1986; Izard, 1977; Mandler, 1982; Plutchik, 1980; Tomkins, 1963). These theories argue that emotion organizes human functioning and that each emotion serves specific functions, coordinating organismic needs with

We wish to thank Rheta DeVries, Claire Kopp, Doug Teti, Ross Thompson, and Carolyn Zahn-Waxler for their thought-provoking comments on earlier drafts of this essay. Address correspondence to Pamela M. Cole, Department of Psychology, Pennsylvania State University, University Park PA 16802.

environmental demands. For example, anger serves progress toward goals in the face of obstacles. Sadness serves the relinquishing of desired objects and goals, preventing wasted effort and eliciting nurturance from others. Thus, emotion has a regulatory influence on other processes, such as focusing attention and communicating with others. Emotion is also regulated in that the experience and expression of emotion can be modulated to meet situational demands. For example, one may attenuate intense anger in expression to avoid damaging a relationship.

Views of emotion as poorly controlled or disorganizing are still central in popular conceptualizations of psychological immaturity and deviance and in clinical conceptualizations of maladaptive behavior and psychopathology. Clinical models of psychopathology and therapeutic change focus on the problematic aspects of emotion, implicitly or explicitly, and assume that awareness and flexible control of emotion states are indices of adjustment and treatment success (Bradley, 1990; Greenberg & Safran, 1987; Hart, 1983; Luborsky, 1984; Safran & Greenberg, 1991). That is not to say that emotion is deemed the sole cause or most important variable in clinical conceptualizations but rather that emotion and emotion-related events are critical factors in the etiology of maladjustment and in therapeutic change.

Can these two different emphases be integrated? If emotions are inherently adaptive and organizing, how do we define and understand the poorly modulated and disorganizing emotions observed in clinical work? In this essay, we take the position that emotion is inherently regulatory and regulated, two processes that are subsumed under the term *emotion regulation*. Emotion regulation is an ongoing process of the individual's emotion patterns in relation to moment-by-moment contextual demands. These demands, and the individual's resources for regulating the related emotions, vary. Individual differences in patterns of emotion regulation become characteristics of personality. Under certain conditions, patterns of emotion regulation jeopardize or impair functioning, and such patterns may support or become symptoms of psychopathology. That is, basic emotion patterns can develop into patterns that interfere with functioning. This interference may involve the disruption of other processes, such as attention or social relations, or a failure to regulate emotion experience and expression flexibly. When emotion regulation patterns become linked with such problems, we use the term *emotion dysregulation*.

An important agenda for research on the etiology and prevention of child mental health problems involves understanding individual differences in emotionality that distinguish psychopathology from more adaptive functioning and identifying the processes by which adaptive emotionality becomes associated with risk, maladjustment, and psychopathology. Every emotion researcher knows that individual differences in emotionality are the norm; the issue is how to differentiate normative variability from variations that are indicative or predictive of maladjustment. Also, we need to identify the developmental trajectories that link individual differences in emotion regulation at one point in time with later clinical problems. How does the emotionality that serves the elicitation of caregiving, the communication of needs, the defining of the world of objects and persons, and the selection of behavioral plans relate to the emotionality that disturbs relationships with caregivers, confuses others about the need of the moment, distorts perception and understanding, and interferes with the execution of plans? This essay attempts to integrate modern emotion theory and clinical perspectives on emotion regulation and dysregulation, describe dimensions of emotionality that might serve to differentiate normative and maladaptive patterns, and outline how adaptive emotion patterns might acquire dysregulatory qualities over the course of development.

Developmental psychopathology provides a framework for understanding atypical development in the context of typical development (Cicchetti, 1989b, 1990; Rutter & Garmezy, 1983; Sroufe, 1990). This framework suggests ways to integrate the study of basic developmental processes with the study of individual differences that have implications for the evolution of mental health problems (see also Calkins, in this volume). The development of emotion regulation is an important and central theme of developmental psychopathology. Studies that trace the development of emotion characteristics and their regulatory aspects in samples of typical, at-risk, and atypical populations provide much-needed information on normative aspects of emotional development, conditions that create deviations from these norms, and the nature of the deviations that become symptomatic and develop into disorders. There is an acute need for identifying the development of mental health problems in early childhood, and clinical researchers and epidemiologists look to developmentalists for guidance in conceptualization and assessment (National Institute of Mental Health, 1992).

In discussing the development of emotion dysregulation, we turn to several conceptual frameworks: emotion theory, developmental research on emotion regulation, and clinical research and practice. Contemporary emotion theories and developmental research provide a means of conceptualizing and studying emotion as both regulatory and regulated. Clinical research and practice offer perspective on the range of variation in emotionality that is associated with psychopathology and suggest directions for developmental psychopathology research. We use these literatures to define *emotion regulation* and *emotion dysregulation,* to suggest dimensions of emotion regulation that may distinguish adaptive and maladaptive qualities, and to discuss how adaptive emotion patterns evolve into patterns of dysregulation and become part of a psychopathological condition. Throughout the essay, there is an emphasis on identifying clinically relevant emotion patterns in young children, on the implications of individual differences in emotion regulation patterns for risk for emotion dysfunction in later years, and on the importance of social context in emotion dysregulation and the development of psychopathology.

EMOTION REGULATION

As noted by Thompson (in this volume), the term *emotion regulation* has no single definition; nonetheless, common threads that bind varying definitions can be discerned. These definitions generally emphasize one of two aspects of emotion regulation. Some focus on the regulatory functions of emotions in organizing internal processes (e.g., attention, memory, action readiness) and social communication, which permit the individual to react quickly to situational demands. Others emphasize the ways in which emotion is regulated (e.g., cognitive control, internalization of social expectations) that allow the individual to monitor, delay, and adjust those preparatory reactions and adapt them to the complexities and subtleties of those situational demands (Frijda, 1986; Izard, 1977; Plutchik, 1980). A few authors emphasize both aspects (Barrett & Campos, 1987; Campos, Campos, & Barrett, 1989). In fact, *emotion regulation* might be defined as the ability to respond to the ongoing demands of experience with the range of emotions in a manner that is socially tolerable and sufficiently flexible to permit spontaneous reactions as well as the ability to delay spontaneous reactions as needed.

In the first 7 years of life, the child has many emotion-based developmental tasks to accomplish: frustration tolerance, engaging and enjoying others, recognizing danger and coping with fear and anxiety, defense of self and property within the bounds of acceptable behavior, tolerating being alone for reasonable periods, interest and motivation in learning, and development of friendships. All these developmental tasks involve the regulation of emotion.

Emotion regulation as a developmental process has been discussed and defined articulately in several books and articles (e.g., Barrett & Campos, 1987; Campos & Barrett, 1984; Eisenberg & Fabes, 1992a; Garber & Dodge, 1991; Kopp, 1989; Sroufe, 1979; Thompson, 1990). The regulatory aspects of emotion are especially emphasized in infancy research that demonstrates that emotion organizes the development of social relations (e.g., Sroufe, Schork, Motti, Lawroski, & LaFreniere, 1984) and physical experience (Klinnert, Campos, Sorce, Emde, & Svejda, 1983) and influences such internal processes as attention (Rothbart & Posner, 1985). Beyond infancy, developmental research has emphasized the development of the child's ability to regulate her own emotions. Most developmentalists regard the acquisition of the ability to regulate emotions and related behaviors as a major developmental task (Cicchetti, Ganiban, & Barnett, 1991; Dodge, 1989; Eisenberg & Fabes, 1992a; Kopp, 1989).

Psychopathology is associated with a range of emotion symptoms that interfere with various developmental tasks. This argues for an examination of how children come to feel and express all emotions adaptively and how typical adaptive patterns may evolve into patterns of emotion dysregulation. Unfortunately, individual differences research in child development has not been well integrated with clinical conceptualizations of emotion dysregulation. We now turn to a discussion of emotion dysregulation and the role of emotion from a clinical perspective.

EMOTION DYSREGULATION

Emotion dysregulation is a common dimension of most categories of psychopathology and a defining feature of many. One quick illustration of the prevalence of emotional difficulties in the conceptualization and differentiation of mental health problems is given by a review of diagnostic criteria in the DSM-III-R classification system (American Psychiatric Association, 1987). Table 1 provides a list of emotion-related symptoms of the major diagnostic categories of children and adults. Inappropriateness of affect, chronic worry or tension, blunting or avoidance of emotions, constriction of affect, unpredictable fluctuation between emotionlessness and rage, elation, or dejection, the predominance of one emotion and the relative absence of another, and sustained negative emotions are common examples of emotion characteristics associated with clinical disorders.

In addition, clinical research has been interested in the dysregulatory potential of emotion. For example, clinical studies have provided evidence of the role of emotion in the incidence of relapse of clinical problems (e.g., Koenigsberg & Handley, 1986) and of the negative influences that emotion can have on cognitive processes (Bower, 1981; Isen, 1984). These data provide empirical support for the position that emotion can dysregulate social and cognitive processes and does so in clinical conditions.

Definitions of *emotion dysregulation* tend to be relatively few and rather diverse, despite its importance to clinical conceptualization. Typically, they include reference to interference in the processing of information and events (e.g., Dodge, 1991a; Plutchik, 1980), difficulties with the flexible integration of emotion with other processes (Cicchetti et al., 1991; Katz & Gottman, 1991), and poor control over affective experience and expression (Izard, 1977; Kopp, 1989; Lazarus, 1966; Thoits, 1985). More broadly, emotion dysregulation has been described as failures to meet the developmental tasks of emotional development (Cicchetti et al., 1991; Dodge & Garber, 1991).

TABLE 1

Disorders of childhood and adolescence	
Autistic disorder	Lack of awareness of feelings of others; little or no facial expressivity for communication; distress over trivial changes in environment; abnormal comfort seeking under distress
Disruptive behavior disorder	Lack of concern for feelings of others; lack of guilt or remorse; readily blaming others for own misdeeds; low self-esteem; irritability, resentfulness; temper outbursts; low frustration tolerance; argumentative; deliberately annoying; easily annoyed; spitefulness, vindictiveness; comorbid anxiety and depression
Anxiety-related disorders	Unrealistic, persistent worries and fears; lack of self-confidence, timidity; marked feelings of tension, inability to relax
Adult disorders	
Affective disorders	Elevated, expansive mood; depressed, irritable mood; diminished interest, pleasure; excessive, inappropriate guilt; low self-esteem; comorbid anxiety, worry, panic
Anxiety disorders	Intense, sudden apprehension, fear, or terror; persistent, recurring fears and worries; comorbid depression
Posttraumatic stress disorder and related disorders	Intense distress in response to reminders, recollections, and dreams; detachment from feelings, numbness; restricted affect; irritability, anger outbursts; depression, anxiety, painful guilt
Schizophrenia	Flat or grossly inappropriate expression of affect; lack of subjective emotion intensity; emotional detachment from others
Eating disorders	Intense fear of gaining weight, lack of worry about symptoms; depressed mood, anxiety about adequacy of self
Substance disorders	Mood disturbance, lability; anxiety, irritability; depression, anhedonia; suspiciousness, paranoia
Personality disorders	Irritability, rage, or absence of hostility; easily hurt or highly critical; inappropriate, constricted, or exaggerated affect; chronic emptiness, boredom; preoccupation with envy, suspicion, or fear; lacking in remorse, inappropriate anger; affective instability, rapidly shifting and shallow emotions

Although clinical theory has not defined *emotion dysregulation* explicitly, emotion regulation is an implied goal of most treatment models. Understanding emotion patterns and their historical roots, learning to recognize emotions and to express them appropriately, and experiencing problematic emotion patterns in order to modify them are major goals of many therapies. It has been suggested that all psychotherapies, including pharmacotherapy, are aimed at influencing emotion regulation (Bradley, 1990) and that the emotion patterns must be experienced in treatment in order to be better regulated and to modify their regulatory influences on thought and behavior (Greenberg & Safran, 1987).

For example, traditional psychoanalytic theory outlines a developmental process in which individual differences in emotion regulation shape personality and psychopathology. Early childhood emotions such as anxiety, despair, and disappointment are regulated by the individual; if these regulatory attempts are not flexible or do not change over time, they constrain personality and produce symptoms. Defense mechanisms are postulated to be emotion regulators; they are cognitive and behavioral strategies for avoiding, minimizing, or converting emotions that are too difficult to tolerate because of their powerful latent meanings. The concepts of catharsis and abreaction emerged from Freud's contention that hysterical symptoms resulted from the "strangulation" of strong emotion. The goal of treatment was to gain insight into these emotions and their roots and thereby cope with them in a more mature manner.

In modern variants of psychodynamic therapy, emotion signifies meaning about interpersonal relationships, and emotions as symptoms lead the therapist to an understanding of the patient's impaired adult relationships (Luborsky, 1984; Strupp & Binder, 1984). The therapist first helps clients recognize emotions that they have not been acknowledging and then facilitates the integration of these emotions into conscious experience and expression. This perspective is also articulated in attachment theory (Bowlby, 1973). Emotion organizes the security or insecurity of the mother-infant relationship, which is then internalized as a working model and carried into subsequent relationships (Bretherton, 1985; Sroufe & Fleeson, 1986). This conceptualization is reflected in interventions with mothers meant to help them resolve emotional themes from their families of origin in order to be more interpersonally attuned and responsive to their own children (e.g., Fraiberg, 1980; Lieberman, Weston, & Pawl, 1991).

The cognitive-behavioral clinical perspective emphasizes the role that patterns of action and thought play in regulating emotion. Learned behaviors, attributional styles, belief systems, and self-statements contribute to the development and maintenance of maladaptive emotion symptoms. Treatment emphasizes the reduction of negative emotion states: anger control

(Novaco, 1975; Williams & Williams, 1993), modification of depressive beliefs or self-control patterns that sustain sadness, hopelessness, and despair (Beck, 1976; Rehm, 1977), and anxiety management (Suinn, 1990). An underlying assumption of these cognitive-behavioral perspectives is that the individual has either learned a set of beliefs and coping strategies that sustain a negative emotion or failed to learn the skills necessary to regulate those emotions.

Cognitive-behavioral anxiety-reduction techniques involve exposure, symbolically or actually, to situations that arouse anxiety in order to acquire alternative strategies for regulating the emotion experience. Emotion-focused and expressive therapies are designed to elicit negative emotions (Greenberg & Safran, 1987; Hart, 1983; Luborsky, 1984).

THE RELATION BETWEEN REGULATION AND DYSREGULATION

If emotions are fundamentally adaptive reactions that are regulated and regulating by their very nature, then what is emotion dysregulation? There are assumptions that we believe to be integral to a perspective that respects the fundamental regulatory qualities of emotion as well as the potential for dysregulatory qualities and risk for psychopathology.

Dysregulation versus Absence of Regulation

First, *dysregulated* does not mean *unregulated*. When individuals' emotion-related behavior is extreme and deviant, they may appear to be unregulated, but we would argue that emotion regulation is still present. The term *dysregulated* is preferable to *unregulated* because it connotes that a normal regulatory process is operating in a dysfunctional manner. That is, the pattern of emotion regulation involves a cost reflected in an impairment or restriction of functioning.

There are many facets of dysregulation, and it may be an oversimplification even to attempt to limit dysregulation to two forms—over- and underregulation. For example, an individual may appear underregulated in the intensity or amount of expressed emotion but may also be overregulating a particular emotion state, as in the case of the disruptive child who behaves in a silly, giddy manner but steadfastly avoids allowing himself to experience personal distress. Dysregulation may also take the form of overregulation, as in the case of blunted emotion expression or experience (Thoits, 1985). However, in some cases, the overregulated expression of emotion may be masking high levels of internal distress. Overregulation of distress is inferred in insecurely attached–avoidant infants who fail to show distress on the departure of their primary caregivers (Main, 1981). The interpretation is that an infant can learn to avoid the rebuffing of the parent and develop a pattern of emotion expression that avoids revealing anxiety to others.

Emotion dysregulation serves some regulatory function but in a manner that has serious implications for adjustment. That is, even the most dysregulated emotion serves some adaptive purpose in the present, even as it interferes with optimal adjustment or development. A critical component of effective psychotherapy, in fact, is the clinician's detection of the adaptive function that a symptom serves. We provide two detailed examples from clinical work that illustrate both the immediate functional value of and the immediate or long-term dysfunction of emotion symptoms.

The first example is based on a case of a psychiatrically hospitalized adolescent boy with severe oppositional defiant disorder. On the unit, he frequently provoked other residents through hostile, aggressive behavior. Traditional insight-oriented treatment was not yielding change, so a behavior-modification program was instituted. After many weeks, he earned the privilege of a weekend home visit. He eagerly awaited his mother (who was believed to have borderline personality disorder), but she never came. Eventually he called her, and she lightheartedly said that she was busy and was not coming. He hung up the phone, showing no emotional reaction. A few minutes later he was observed poking another youth with a sharp pencil.

Staff initiated the behavioral program; the boy was reminded that failure to stop would involve a demerit. He rudely claimed indifference, and standard procedures for handling a youth who appears to be losing control were begun. Each time he was reminded what to do to regain control, he escalated. His affect transitioned from arrogant sarcasm to belligerent yelling to shouting a stream of expletives and then screaming and flailing his arms and legs as staff moved to restrain him. As he was carried to a time-out room, he was foaming at the mouth, unable to articulate even curses. In essence, language and action were subjugated to raw rage. Isolated, his rage subsided, and he collapsed, whimpering, on the padded floor. This is about as close to unregulated as dysregulated emotions become. Most dysregulated emotion is under some form of regulation, however, although this is not always obvious.

This event indicates the complex relation between regulation and dysregulation. First, despite his hostile and aggressive problem behavior, this youth never expressed or reflected on his anger directly. He had no history of such emotional outbursts. He did have episodes of violent behavior that were not accompanied by expressed anger. (Once he threw a 20-pound barbell at a staffperson with no accompanying expression of emotion.) His rage reaction communicated the dangerousness of his anger and made us aware of the regulation underlying his albeit inappropriate hostility and acts of aggression. He had been regulating angry impulses that might have led to violence toward his mother.

Borderline personality disorder often elicits intense anger in others. In the safety of the hospital setting with its physical and social protections, the boy finally revealed to himself and to the staff the depth of his pain and frustration. This event permitted the staff and this youth to realize his anger and the reasons for it and to develop alternative ways to express and regulate it. Anger functions adaptively to promote the overcoming of obstacles. One interpretation is that this oppositional youth was still striving to achieve some action that would correct the problems in his life. To have relinquished his protest and efforts to change the relationship with his mother may have led to depression and suicidality. In fact, this event marked a turning point in individual therapy; feelings of grief and despair emerged, and he was helped to cope with the reality of the loss of hope that his mother would be sensitive to his needs.

The regulatory and dysregulatory aspects of emotion are seen in the functioning of many father-daughter incest survivors. As adults, many of these women do not recollect either a part or all of their abusive experiences; they report feeling "numb" or having periods of time lost to them. The origins of this emotional "cutting off" are hypothesized by many clinicians to be protective mechanisms that served to protect the young victimized child from the overwhelming emotional distress typically associated with incest. In fact, denial and dissociation appear to be part of the normative repertoire of early childhood (Cramer, 1991; Dunn, 1988; Gardner & Olness, 1981), and they characterize the predominant coping style of adult survivors (Putnam, 1985). Most young victims are unable to use alternative solutions that might apply to more ordinary social problems. Help-seeking, instrumental, and avoidant behaviors are not as viable when one's father is sexually abusive. To survive the intense emotions and generalized distress that they experience, many children seem to cut off from the sensations, blunt the experience, and absent the sensations and emotions from consciousness (Cole & Putnam, 1992).

At the time of the incest, and later in adulthood, this emotion style protects the individual from the overwhelming, disorganizing emotion associated with the memories. However, it is a profound truncation of emotionality that has serious long-term consequences for adult functioning. This represents dysregulation in that valuable emotions are inaccessible when needed, memory processes are restricted, and relationships are strained.

In sum, we argue that notions of emotion as regulatory and dysregulatory are mutually consistent because emotions serve protective and communicative functions even when they are creating risk to or interfering with adaptive development. Most symptomatic behavior involves regulation of emotion that is over- and/or underregulated in some dimensions and that is difficult for the individual to modify because of the adaptive functions being served.

Regulation versus Control

There is an important distinction between regulation and control. Emotion regulation involves the ability to respond emotionally and to attune one's emotion experience and expression to the ebb and flow of life's moment-to-moment situations. The term *regulation* is preferable to the term *control* because the former implies a dynamic ordering and adjusting of the emotion to the environment whereas the latter connotes restraint.

Emotion regulation is not simply a matter of stopping distress. It involves many kinds of adjustments that organize human functioning and promote the adaptation of the individual to life circumstances, both momentary and ongoing. Emotion regulation is not solely the reduction of the intensity or frequency of states (e.g., frequency of negative thoughts, intensity of anxiety). It includes the capacity to generate and sustain emotions in order to carry out activity and to communicate and influence others, particularly in coordination with the emotion of others.

The well-adjusted individual is usually emotionally well regulated, attentuating and curtailing the intensity and duration of emotions as needed, and amplifying and extending emotion states when necessary. The speed and immediacy of emotional reactions constitute one of their values, permitting an individual to bypass more prolonged, planful processes. A model of emotion regulation that focuses only on restraint overlooks the fact that deficiencies in the capacity for spontaneity and immediacy can be as dysfunctional as deficiencies in the ability to attenuate strong emotion. Imagine an intense negative reaction in which an adult becomes very angry and loud, screaming at a child, perhaps even handling the child roughly. If she is doing this to prevent her child from walking into the street in front of an oncoming car, it is adaptive. She is bypassing internal controls of the display of anger and fear in order to initiate a rapid, critical response and thereby protect her child. A mother who is too inhibited to do so would be responding maladaptively.

Positive versus Negative Emotion

The perspective that all emotions are adaptive offers the opportunity to reexamine the tendency to equate positive affect with adaptation and negative affect with maladaptation. Clearly, an overall affectively positive demeanor is associated with social competence in young children (Denham, McKinley, Couchoud, & Holt, 1990; Shantz & Shantz, 1985; Sroufe et al.,

1984) and adults (Tellegen, 1982; Watson & Clark, 1984). From the perspective of organizational, functional models of emotion, however, negative emotions have their adaptive place and are not inherently dysfunctional. For example, negative emotions are often essential in marking salient issues in communication, as shown in the mother's ability to prevent her child from running out into the street. Toddlers respond to the emotional quality of their mothers' prohibitions more than to the semantic content. Mothers often begin a prohibitive episode in "motherese" prosody but then shift to a more firm, angry tone to convince the child that the prohibition is serious.

Alternatively, positive emotion can be dysregulatory and dysregulated. Such inappropriate responses as smiling when describing problems in one's current or past experience or laughing at another's misfortune represent two different examples of dysregulated positive affect. In the first example, the positive emotion indicates a potential problem with the person's reality testing or insight. In the second, the expression of positive affect is not modulated so as to take account of the other's distress. While most positive emotion in social situations is regulatory in that it engages and sustains interaction, silly, giddy behavior in the classroom or in peer interaction disrupts the achievement of goals. In fact, children with attention deficit disorder often experience peer rejection because of their poorly timed, poorly regulated positive affect (Barkley, 1990; Sroufe et al., 1984).

Emotion Regulation and Dysregulation as Context Bound

Finally, it is important to consider that no single aspect of emotion provides an absolute measure of emotion regulation or dysregulation without a consideration of context (Campos et al., 1989; Izard, 1977). Emotion regulation is embedded in experiences and plans that are further embedded in their relation to contextual demands. Emotions are linked to the promotion of goals (e.g., sustaining a relationship, overcoming an obstacle, relinquishing an unattainable goal, escaping danger). Emotion dysregulation occurs when a pattern of emotion regulation jeopardizes or impairs productive and appropriate functioning (e.g., to preserve relationships, to think clearly, to venture into unfamiliar situations, to solve problems with a spouse or child, to get out of bed, to hold one's job, to inhibit destructive impulses). The key component is the functional relation between the emotion and the immediate events (of the outside world or their internal representations) in light of the larger life context of achieving developmental goals (Cicchetti et al., 1991).

From our view, emotions are regulatory and regulated. Context provides the frame of reference from which dysregulation is determined. Specifically, dysregulation implies that emotion regulation patterns are interfering with current functioning or jeopardizing development. The ability to regulate positive and negative emotions along a number of dimensions and in ways that support cognitive, behavioral, and social functioning is emotion regulation. In the next section, we describe dimensions of emotion regulation and dysregulation that are used in clinical judgments.

DIMENSIONS OF EMOTION REGULATION AND DYSREGULATION

Emotion dysregulation involves difficulty modulating emotion experience and expression in response to contextual demands and controlling the influence of emotional arousal on the organization and quality of thoughts, actions, and interactions. In this section, we present dimensions that underlie clinical judgments of emotion dysregulation. Although emotion dysregulation may occur only as an occasional event in the emotion regulation process of most people, clinicians work with individuals who have developed stable, problematic emotion styles that have become attributes of their psychopathology (Malatesta & Wilson, 1988). Later, we discuss the developmental links between instances of emotion dysregulation and the emotion symptoms of psychopathology. The list of dimensions is offered to suggest ways that patterns of emotionality that are relevant to both typical and atypical development can be assessed. Individual differences in emotion regulation will be more valuable to developmental psychopathology if measurement moves beyond aggregated totals of positive and negative emotion.

Access to the Full Range of Emotions

If emotions are basically adaptive in quality, preparing individuals to engage quickly in actions that support social and individual survival, then it follows that access to the full range of emotions is a characteristic of emotion regulation. Joy, anger, sadness, and social emotions such as guilt and pride are all necessary for optimal functioning. The individual who experiences fear when threatened, sadness when a loved one is lost, and anger when goals are blocked has access to the emotions that appear to be designed for coping in such situations (Barrett & Campos, 1987; Frijda, 1986; Izard, 1977).

When an emotion that is held as typical and appropriate to a particular situation is inaccessible, it is a signal that some basic, adaptive function is blocked. A pattern of inability to access a typical emotion in a pertinent situation is emotion dysregulation. A stable pattern of such blockage interferes with such adaptive functions as affective communication in close relationships and successful problem resolution. Access to the range of emotions is therefore taken to be a goal of psychotherapeutic treatment (for a review, see Greenberg & Safran, 1987).

Access to the range of emotions is an aspect of personality assessment (Greenspan, 1981; for theoretical discussion, see Malatesta & Wilson, 1988). When a person's emotion style is disproportionately dominated by a particular affect (e.g., anger or sadness), it may be that the person has difficulty perceiving, experiencing, and/or expressing other emotions. The inability to access certain emotions may be as critical in defining the dysregulation as the dominant emotion. For example, we often regard depression in terms of excessive sadness, but the inability to generate positive affect is an equally critical component. Anger is seen as dominant in conduct problems, and a bias toward perceiving the world as hostile has been shown in highly aggressive children (Dodge, Murphy, & Buchsbaum, 1984). However, diminished anxiety and guilt, particularly in relation to wrongdoing and harming others, are critical features of antisocial individuals. Their hostile, aggressive presentations are often interpreted as covering over feelings of loss, sadness, and low self-esteem that cannot be tolerated (Winnicott, 1958/1975). Therefore, we think that the emotion dysregulation associated with psychopathology does not necessarily involve a single emotion but that the dominance or absence of a single emotion reflects a state of dysregulation in the overall emotion system.

One implication of this dimension for research is the need for assessment in multiple contexts to assess the range of emotions. Such research would require carefully conceived hypotheses that a particular emotion that would be present in most individuals in a certain context is not evinced by an individual with a particular risk factor or with associated symptoms.

Modulation of Intensity and Duration of Emotion

The classic Yerkes-Dodson principle holds that there is an inverted U function relation between the intensity of felt anxiety and its effect on performance of a task. That is, some increase in anxiety optimizes performance, but, once a certain level of arousal has been reached, any further increase in anxiety interferes with performance. This suggests that the intensity and duration of an emotion are as important as its mere presence in judging the degree to which the emotion supports the individual's reaction to situational demands.

Typically, developmental and clinical research associates emotion regulation with the reduction of intensity and duration of negative emotion. As stated earlier, adaptation requires the flexibility to generate and sustain negative emotion and the ability to modulate positive emotion, as befits the circumstance. At times, the generation of intense, strong emotion is desirable, and even necessary, for a quick and effective response to a situation. In fact, the elicitation of strong emotion is encouraged in many psychotherapies. Assertiveness training, for example, teaches the individual to generate *all* the emotions appropriate to various situations rather than to be paralyzed by anxiety (Wolpe, 1982), and cognitive-behavioral performance-enhancement strategies often include psyching up or anxiety arousal (Suinn, 1990).

In the same way that amplification and sustenance of negative emotions may be a focus of treatment, positive emotions may require some minimization or reduction. In emotionally conflicted situations, disruptive children may deal with conflict by laughing or acting silly or giddy and thus failing to demonstrate the seriousness of another's concern. Their positive affect interferes with adult and peer relationships and the ability to solve problems effectively. Troubled children and adolescents become disorderly and distracted when difficult emotional themes are stirred. The inappropriate laughing and happy interpersonal exchanges allow them to avoid difficult problems. Research is needed to understand how these quantitative aspects of emotion support or interfere with behavior in specific contexts.

Fluid, Smooth Shifts

Fluid, smooth shifts or transitions from one emotion state to another are one more aspect of flexible, coherent functioning. Typically, an individual appears to be in a relatively calm, neutral state, and the onset and offset of emotions are experienced and expressed relatively gradually. Certain circumstances, such as surprise, are associated with a discrete, sudden change in emotion. In general, however, change in emotion is more gradual and bracketed by what the observer perceives as neutral periods. Abrupt, unexpected, frequent, or dramatic changes in emotion and mood suggest emotional difficulty, particularly when those changes are inexplicable to the observer. The term *lability,* borrowed from the biological and physical sciences, is used to convey the instability and potential disorganization that is assumed to underlie a high degree of emotional reactivity or change in emotion. Emotional lability is identified as a symptom of emotional disturbance, particularly of such serious diagnoses as personality disorders.

This aspect of emotion has received some empirical attention in the infancy literature (Hirshberg & Svejda, 1990; Malatesta & Haviland, 1982; Thompson, Cicchetti, Lamb, & Malkin, 1985; Wolff, 1987). Emotional lability appears to diminish with age. Younger infants and children engage in more rapid and more frequent changes of emotion than older children. One common scenario is the adult distracting the distressed baby or toddler with a toy and the child's affect changing from angry tears to delighted surprise. Most parents discover that this technique becomes less effective as children gain more control over the transitions in their own emotional reactions and can sustain the emotion on the basis of internal cues.

Even in infancy, however, there is a pattern to the emotional communication between mother and infant that appears to be smooth and expectable, related predictably to changing physical and social events (Emde, Gaensbauer, & Harmon, 1976; Fogel, 1982b; Tronick, 1989; Wolff, 1987). When clinicians observe labile, unpredictable emotion in adolescents or adults, serious psychopathology such as personality disorder is considered.

Paradigms that are sensitive to the problematic features of rapid changes in emotion (e.g., the interference in communication in a peer interaction) and those that are sensitive to the need to change quickly (e.g., the ability to respond quickly when a threatening situation arises) would be a valuable aspect of developmental research.

Conformity with Cultural Display Rules

The well-regulated person expresses emotions within the boundaries of cultural display rules (Saarni, 1990). This individual can coordinate emotion expression with the social standards of display behavior in the cultural group (Ekman, 1977). Inappropriate affect is associated with either the presence of an emotion (e.g., laughing at another's misfortune) or the absence of an emotion (e.g., being affectively flat while discussing a highly emotional event). Clinical work often focuses on some adjustment of the personal display rules that have been acquired in the socialization process. Some individuals can flexibly coordinate their emotion expression with situational variation, while others appear to be rigid and unable to modulate expression regardless of context (Malatesta & Wilson, 1988).

Over the course of development, for example, people develop rules about the appropriate contexts and forms for the expression of anger, and, in a culture as diverse as that in the United States, there is wide variation in the manner and amount of anger that individuals express in their relationships. We know from adult cases that, owing to internalized family display rules, many people limit their anger displays even though they may be experiencing acute frustration and anger. There are also children who seem to fail to learn subcultural rules for the display of anger and who appear rude and unruly. Research is needed to distinguish children who are more emotionally reactive (e.g., get more angry when frustrated) from children who are simply failing to control their expressions of emotion (e.g., failing to conform to rules about displaying anger to authority figures). Paradigms that show individual differences in one social context but not in another (e.g., peer vs. adult, other vs. alone) will be useful in this regard.

Integration of Mixed Emotions

A basic premise of adult ego development is that the mature individual is capable of integrating emotions—for example, feeling anger and sadness, or even happiness and sadness, simultaneously. This capacity is fundamental to being able to experience self-worth in conjunction with a disappointment or an embarrassment, to realize one's fondness for a person even when angered by that person, or to resolve ambivalence. An inability to integrate multiple emotions is indicative of emotion dysregulation.

For individuals who have very basic difficulties in integrating the mixed emotions that are an inevitable aspect of life, clinicians often use a concept referred to as *splitting* (Blanck & Blanck, 1976). The concept is derived from object relations theory and describes the adult's difficulty perceiving or experiencing the mixed affective valence of many human circumstances, particularly in their most important relationships. For example, some clients will present an overly positive portrayal even while describing serious physical and emotional abuse. In adult clinical work, this phenomenon is associated with personality disorder (Hamilton, 1988; Mendelsohn, 1987). The concept of splitting has been applied in the coding of the Adult Attachment Interview (George, Kaplan, & Main, 1985). Most developmental research, however, has focused on children's knowledge of mixed emotions (e.g., Gnepp & Hess, 1986; Harter, 1990). Observational research that examines expressive aspects of the integration of emotion in naturalistic or quasi-naturalistic situations is also needed.

Verbal Regulation of Emotion Processes

The ability to think and talk about emotion is one important dimension of self-regulation (Bruner, 1983; Luria, 1961; Vygotsky, 1987). This is not to say that, à la 1960s pop psychology, everyone should be urged to express every feeling. Language is a communicative system by means of which experience is internalized. It is adaptive to be able to label, describe, conceptualize, and understand one's feelings. Insight into one's emotional reactions is a goal of many therapies. Many outpatients' work is focused on learning to think and talk about emotional reactions and memories against which they have defended. In a technique called *emotion restructuring,* for example, a problematic emotion is evoked and the client helped to construct a new, more mature cognitive reorganization of the emotion experience (Greenberg & Safran, 1987). The ability to conceptualize emotion experience facilitates the self-reflective process (e.g., Malatesta & Wilson, 1988) and enhances self-regulation (e.g., Cicchetti et al., 1991).

In terms of its communicative aspects, the verbal expression of feelings is assumed to be associated with more control or better regulation of nonverbal expression. Young children are encouraged to "use their words" when distressed rather than to act out aggressively or to collapse in tears. This communicative value must be balanced against the frequent clinical concern for individuals who talk about difficult events without any sign of emotion. Clinicians use discrepancies between the content of the spoken word and its affective quality to identify clinical issues, to assist clients in recognizing their feelings, to recognize that a certain physiological state is anxiety or anger, and to help them use the language of emotion to access and to regulate their emotion states. A well-balanced relation between talking about emotion-related issues and conveying the content of speech with modulated emotionality supports effective communication and enhances opportunities for the social regulation of affective experience.

The Management of Emotions about Emotions

Part of the metacognitive process, known to many clinicians as the *observing ego,* is the ability to monitor and react to one's emotion state. This ability means that one can evaluate one's emotional responses and have emotional reactions to an emotional reaction. If a person becomes very angry at someone, she can witness her own anger and understand why she behaved so. She may also forgive or take pride in herself.

Negative emotions about an emotional reaction are regarded as pathogenic. Defense mechanisms (e.g., isolation and displacement) are regarded as strategies that the individual uses to cope with anxiety generated by feeling sadness or anger (Freud, 1966). Tomkins (1963) describes the "neurotic paradox" in which individuals become distressed by their own emotional responses. Tomkins also describes the "multiple suffering bind" in which negative affect is organized in such an overly generalized manner that stimulation of a particular affect system tends to activate the other negative affect systems.

Empirical support for the interrelationship of emotions remains to be developed. Depression research offers some corroborative support. A characteristic of depression appears to be that a negative emotional reaction to an event is followed by negative emotions about the prior negative reaction. Cognitive behaviorists in particular have documented this depressive cycle in terms of critical self-talk (Beck, 1972; Rehm, 1977). Depressed persons experience distress that is followed by distress about the distress, such as feelings of self-criticism or guilt about being unhappy (for a review, see Alloy & Abramson, 1988).

Each of these dimensions of emotionality has been associated with psychopathological functioning. We hope that such clinically conceptualized emotion dimensions will be reflected in research projects designed to study the emotional concomitants of the presence and risk of psychopathology. Next, we attempt to integrate these dimensions into our understanding of the links between emotion regulation, emotion dysregulation, and the emotion symptoms of clinical disorders.

EMOTION DYSREGULATION AND THE DEVELOPMENT OF PSYCHOPATHOLOGY

Evidence that emotion is regulatory and regulated appears early in life, and both aspects of emotion develop over the life span. Various reviews provide perspectives on the normative aspects of the development of emotion regulation (Kopp, 1989; Sroufe, 1979). In this section, we summarize briefly some findings on typical and atypical emotional development. We use these to suggest how, in the course of the development, adaptive emotion regulation comes to have dysregulating qualities and how such patterns become symptoms of developing disorders.

Cognitive development and social development contribute to the evolution of emotion regulation. Cognitive development influences the manner in which emotional events and emotions themselves can be perceived and understood (Kopp, 1989; Lewis & Michalson, 1983; Malatesta & Wilson, 1988). Self-conscious emotions like guilt or worthlessness require a certain level of self-evaluative thought. Social influences such as modeling, sex-role socialization, and cultural display rules teach children emotion-context relations (Campos et al., 1983) and communicate parameters of emotionally expressive behavior (Saarni & Crowley, 1990).

Relatively little is known about the socialization and acquisition of the self-regulation of emotion. It is generally believed that positive attributes in parents are correlated with positive attributes in children, but the dynamic exchange by which children's emotional lives are co-constructed with those of their parents (and other important people) is not charted. One general underlying assumption of many developmental and clinical models is that children internalize the strategies of their caregivers. Parents under stress and with psychopathology will themselves have dimensions of emotion dysregulation that promote those patterns in their children. Children in treatment for anxiety disorders, for example, have a greater likelihood of having a parent with anxiety disorder than children with other clinical problems (Bradley, 1990; Reeves, Werry, Elkind, & Zametkin, 1987). Many empirical data are needed to examine the interactional influences involved in the regulation of emotion.

Our discussion of emotion dysregulation and the development of psychopathology is organized around three periods of childhood—infancy and toddlerhood, the preschool years, and later childhood. We begin with the premise that the child's capacity to self-regulate emotion starts to develop in infancy but that infancy is a period of relative dependence on adult regulation. Episodes of emotion dysregulation during this period are typically managed by caregivers. When this does not occur, development is severely compromised.

The preschool years are marked by the emergence of periods of sustained self-regulation and periods of child and adult co-regulation. During this time, the scope and nature of emotion regulation increases and diversifies (Kopp, 1989). This period of time may be important in that the child is selecting emotion regulation patterns that may become characteristic. During the preschool years, children try to cope autonomously with the emotional demands of their lives and receive social feedback on their emotional reactivity and expressivity. By middle childhood, emotion regulation processes may be more internalized, less accessible to influence, and may become more stylized and characteristic (Malatesta & Wilson, 1988). While the balance tips toward self-reliance in emotion regulation during middle childhood, social regulation still plays a large and critical role, as it does in adult relationships (e.g., Coyne & Downey, 1991).

Infancy through Toddlerhood

In the first year of life, infants are largely dependent on adults to regulate their environments and their experience, including their emotions, in ways that promote well-being and minimize stress and danger. Infants, however, have some mechanisms for self-regulating their arousal level (Demos, 1986; Rothbart, 1989). They initiate tactile stimulation and gaze aversion to generate a positive state or to minimize negative states. These strategies are of course limited, and the infant relies on adults much of the time. This reliance reveals the regulatory aspects of infant emotion. Infant emotions communicate information about infant states and needs, signaling and directing the caregiver's behavior (Bridges & Connell, 1991; Campos et al., 1983; Trevarthen, 1984; Tronick, 1989). For example, crying signals distress that infants cannot regulate on their own and cooing enjoyment in activities that they wish to sustain.

Although the exact nature of the acquisition of the range of emotions is not known, it does appear that within the first two years most children express the basic emotions of anger, joy, sadness, fear, disgust, and surprise as well as the rudiments of some "social" or "moral" emotions like guilt and pride (Sroufe, 1979; Zahn-Waxler & Kochanska, 1990). Although it is unlikely that infants are cognizant of emotion states and experience them in a self-conscious manner (Lewis & Michalson, 1983), they do appear to experience the range of basic emotions in a sensate way that organizes their experience (e.g., Emde, Biringen, Clyman, & Oppenheim, 1991).

The infant-caregiver relationship provides the context for the socialization of emotion regulation. Very young infants appear to follow the emotional lead of the mother in face-to-face interaction, but by age 6 months they take autonomous turns in the affective exchange (Kaye & Fogel, 1980). Gender-related socialization appears in mothers' face-to-face contingent responses to infant emotion expressions (Malatesta & Haviland, 1982). In addition to face-to-face interaction, parents respond to distress in young children with state-change strategies such as picking up, cuddling, feeding, and distracting (Wolff, 1987), strategies that parallel infant self-regulatory strategies of self-stimulation and gaze aversion. It would be interesting to know how parenting techniques like distraction relate to developmental changes in emotional dimensions such as lability or emotion state changes.

Emotion dysregulation in these first years occurs in the context of a poor fit between the infant's resources for emotion regulation and situational demands. One profound example is autism, in which the infant's ability to coordinate emotional exchanges with the caregiver and to derive meaning via emotion cues is impaired (Rutter, 1983). Emotion dysregulation in infancy and toddlerhood also emerges in the context of dysfunctional parenting. For example, depression interferes with a mother's synchrony with and responsivity to her infant. When the infant's emotion is not successful at eliciting corrective action on the mother's part, the infant's emotion patterns begin to change (Tronick, 1989). The changes reflect increased irritability, listlessness, and disinterest in communicating with adults (Field, 1984a; Tronick, 1989). For some infants, inadequate responsiveness to their emotional communications can have serious mental health consequences, such as functional depression (Cole & Kaslow, 1988; Spitz, 1965), nonorganic failure to thrive, rumination disorder, and reactive attachment disorders of infancy (Mayes, 1992). In such cases, the infant's range of emotion experience becomes restricted and flat in intensity. Thus, a breakdown in the dyadic co-regulation of emotion in early childhood results in emotion dysregulation in the infant, whether the cause is found in the child or in the caregiver (see also Calkins, in this volume).

During the typical first year, there is an increase in the vitality of infant emotion (Thompson, 1990) as well as some learning about control of emotional arousal (Demos, 1986; Rothbart, 1989; Stern, 1985). Between 6 and 12 months, infant emotion episodes increase in intensity and duration and decrease in response latency, yielding a more animated, responsive child (Thompson, 1990, in this volume). Episodes of dysregulation in the form of problematic modulation of emotion intensity and duration and mood changes are seen at this time. For example, temperamentally difficult children appear to have a lower threshold for negative emotional reactions and/or a tendency not to regulate negative affect via gaze aversion and self-soothing (Calkins, in this volume; Fox, in this volume). Such negative emotionality creates stress in the parent-child relationship (Belsky & Vondra, 1989; Mangelsdorf, Gunnar, Kestenbaum, Lang, & Andreas, 1990) and risk for the development of later psychopathology (Bates & Bayles, 1988; Bates, Bayles, Bennett, Ridge, & Brown, 1991; Bates, Maslin, & Frankel, 1985).

Temperament appears to have strong biological underpinnings, but its relation to symptomatology and mental disorders is probably dependent on environmental factors (Egeland, Kalkoske, Gottesman, & Erickson, 1990). We assume that the fit between parent and young child is important. For example, both parent and infant characteristics influence the quality of the attachment relationship, the important affective bond between infant and caregiver that varies in terms of differences in the regulation of affect (Sroufe et al., 1984). The infancy and toddlerhood period is dependent on adequate, responsive social interactions for the promotion of adaptive emotion regulation patterns. Failures in this process can have life-threatening or long-term deleterious effects on the child.

Three to Six Years

After about age 3–4 years, episodes of negative affect, such as tantrums, intense crying, and distress, appear to diminish (e.g., Fabes & Eisenberg, 1991; Goodenough, 1931; Kagan, 1976; Kopp, 1989, 1992). Researchers have tended not to focus on changes in positive affect, but it is possible that these patterns also change. Preschoolers' ability to self-regulate can be seen in their generation of emotion expressions in play and their modulation of expressions in actual circumstances. By age 3 years, young children mimic emotions in play (Dunn, 1988) and mask or minimize expressions of negative feelings under certain conditions (Cole, 1986; Fabes & Eisenberg, 1991).

Individual differences in emotional reactivity and emotion regulation differentiate problem preschoolers from nonproblem children. Behavior-problem preschoolers show intense and prolonged distress and protest during separations, unlike their nonproblem peers (Speltz, Greenberg, & DeKlyen, 1990). It has been suggested that insecurely attached infants regulate emotion differently, in ways that organize the affective behavior of their relationships throughout their lives (Hofer, 1980b; Sroufe & Fleeson, 1986). For example, insecure children age 3–7 appear angry, hostile, sad, fearful, or overly bright in their relationships (Cassidy, 1990; Crittenden, 1992). In situations calling for the masking of disappointment, behavior-problem preschoolers show negative emotions more quickly and for longer periods than nonproblem children (Cole & Smith, 1993).

Not all clinically relevant variations, however, involve the underregulation of emotion expression. Children exposed to concentration camps, one form of sustained trauma, appear to have difficulty sustaining feeling (Wilson, 1985). In fact, a major component of clinical lore is that dysfunctional environments, such as abusive and alcoholic homes, contribute to the child's muting emotionality in some situations (e.g., in the presence of dysfunctional parents) while appearing poorly modulated in others (e.g., at school).

The preschool period marks important social changes as children's networks expand to include new siblings, classroom and neighborhood peers, and teachers. These social influences provide new and different information about emotion, its regulatory influences, and its social acceptability. For example, research has found that displays of anger, disgust, and contempt are associated with achieving one's goals in peer negotiations (Camras, 1982; von Salisch, 1992) and that sad, submissive expressions are associated with capitulation (Zivin, 1982). Frequent and intense displays of dominant emotions like anger, however, are related to lower levels of social competence (Cummings, 1987; Fabes & Eisenberg, 1991). The development of the ability to attune the intensity and duration of the emotion to best support the situational demands of accomplishing goals and preserving relationships is an important accomplishment, probably occurring within the preschool years and continuing through childhood.

These years are also a period of cognitive and linguistic growth, which influences emotion regulation. Recently, interest has been shown in the role of the development of the frontal lobes and executive function with regard to emotion regulation and psychopathology (Bradley, 1990; Fox, in this volume). Individuals who suffer brain damage in the frontal area tend to be emotionally impulsive, labile, and intense (Stuss & Benson, 1986), characteristics that are associated with dysinhibitory psychopathology (Gorenstein & Newman, 1980). Although there is evidence that some children with conduct disorder may show deficits in executive function task performance (Moffitt, 1990), there is a need for work that relates this aspect of development to emotion regulation. The preschool years may mark important transitions in the protracted development of executive functions (Pennington, 1991); during this period, children with difficulties modulating attention and impulses distinguish themselves from their peers in terms of the latency, intensity, duration, and quality of shifts in emotion states, including joy and excitement.

Emotions may also come under greater verbal control during the preschool years, but little is known about the complex relation between emotional and language development in this period (Kopp, 1989, 1992). It is commonly believed that around ages 5 and 6 children more often verbalize their feelings instead of acting on them. By the third year, children have fairly developed language repertoires and are able to think and talk about emotions (for a review, see Bretherton, Fritz, Zahn-Waxler, & Ridgeway,

1986). Their emotion knowledge can be promoted by their caregivers; communication about affective states in the interactions of mothers and their young children enhances the child's developing social understanding (Dunn, 1988; Harris, 1989) and self-regulatory skill (Cicchetti et al., 1991; Hesse & Cicchetti, 1982).

Children who are exposed to atypical levels of distress are at risk for developing difficulties in the regulation of emotion experience and expression. For example, abused children are less likely to verbalize about internal states like emotions, and insecurely attached children are less elaborated and complex in their descriptions of feeling states (Bretherton & Beeghly, 1982; Cicchetti, 1989b; Cicchetti & Beeghly, 1987). An important aspect of the development of dysregulated patterns of emotion may be deviations in the social interactional process by which children acquire and use language to talk about their own and others' emotions.

During the preschool years there is an increase in strategies for self-regulating. Novel emotion experiences typically elicit a search for adult intervention and support. When situations tax the child's developing patterns of coping emotionally, the child is likely to resort to more immature coping, such as denial, dissociation, or misbehavior. The fatigued preschooler may become upset more easily than usual and have a tantrum in which the developing abilities to use anticipation and reasoning, and even adult reasoning, are preempted. This is an instance of emotion dysregulation.

Of clinical concern, however, are circumstances that tax the child's emotion regulation strategies repeatedly or traumatically and that lack adequate adult intervention. One client, aged 9 years, was unable to handle the stress of confrontation by peers. Under provocation, he would turn away and begin to "hallucinate," that is, turn to an imaginary world in which the present stress could be ignored. He was self-regulating fear and perhaps anger but resorting to a strategy that was psychotic-like. The child was taught assertive skills and eventually had the courage to reveal that he was being sexually abused by his father. He had learned to retreat into his imaginary world as a means of coping with overwhelming, emotion-laden circumstances from the age of 4.

In sum, during infancy and early childhood, relationships and life experiences provide opportunities to experience emotions, observe how they function, learn the consequences of emotion states, talk about emotions, and acquire initial strategies for modulating emotion experience and utilizing emotion successfully. Conditions like exposure to interpersonal anger, discord between parents, a parent's psychopathology, and abusive parenting quickly strain and overwhelm the developing emotion regulation patterns of infants. Child characteristics that make it difficult for parents to decipher how to read and soothe infant distress interfere with the infant's ability to experience and learn from parents' emotion regulation strategies. On the other hand, a life in which stress is preempted and opportunities to learn to communicate about and cope with thwarted goals, threatening or novel experiences, and the relinquishing of goals are infrequent fails to afford opportunities for development. Probably the optimal life circumstance for the development of early patterns of emotion regulation is exposure to manageable distress embedded in a responsive, approachable world (see also Demos, 1986).

Childhood

The elementary school years mark new accomplishments in emotion regulation development. Changes in cognitive and social development create the context for greater reliance on the self-regulation of emotion and for patterns of emotion dysregulation to become more stable and less accessible to outside influence. During these years, the manner in which children have internalized their experiences with emotion and its regulation may become more stylized.

Perhaps the most interesting aspect is the development of abilities to reflect on, conceptualize, and verbalize ideas about emotion more abstractly. The development of emotion display rules provides an example. The socialization of emotion displays begins in early infancy (Malatesta & Haviland, 1982); thus, cultural display rules are being acquired at the same time as other rules of conduct. The explicit understanding of display rules, however, emerges during the elementary school years (Gnepp & Hess, 1986; Saarni, 1979, 1984).

Cognitive factors appear to play an important role in the transition toward greater self-regulation. Visuospatial skills support the perception of emotion in others, which in turn influences knowledge about emotion-situation contexts and cultural display rules. Verbal abilities link images to memory and provide alternative ways to communicate inner states. Children with visuospatial and language delays are more likely to have emotional disturbances (Cantwell, Baker, & Mattison, 1979; Rourke, 1989). Children with behavioral problems show difficulties in processing information; peer-rejected and aggressive children appear to misread interpersonal situations, and this leads to frustration and disappointment (Dodge et al., 1984; Putallaz & Sheppard, 1992).

Cognitive development also supports the child's ability to self-reflect on her behavior, thoughts, and emotions. This ability is seen in children's conscious awareness of the possibility of experiencing simultaneous, mixed emotions. A model example of the integration of clinical issues and basic developmental psychopathology research is reflected in an interesting case study reported by Harter (1977) of a 6-year-old client who felt "all bad" some days and could not be reassured and "all good" other days and had no interest in discussing the "bad" days. By offering the child a concrete physical representation of the emotional "parts" of a person, Harter was able to assist the child in integrating her strongly opposed feelings.

Harter's empirical work focused on children's conceptual understanding of mixed emotions, using a Piagetian perspective on social cognition. In this work, it appears that the integration process is a slowly evolving one. Young children seem relatively less able to entertain simultaneous opposite emotions and eventually come to conceptualize them as temporally contiguous ("First I was bad, but now I'm good"). Only in middle childhood do children seem to understand the simultaneity of opposite emotions. Moreover, Harter has shown that the increasingly complex and diversified aspects of self and their integration over time is a continuing process still under way during adolescence (Harter, 1990; Harter & Monsour, 1992).

Early childhood trauma is one condition that is thought to influence the integration of aspects of self, including the integration of multiple emotions (Cole & Putnam, 1992; Kluft, 1985). Symptoms such as splitting, a kind of affective oversimplification of events or self as all good or all bad, are associated with severe psychopathology, notably personality disorders. When early childhood trauma occurs during periods of normative transition in the ability to conceptualize emotion experience as being integrated, it may interfere with this development in such a way as to create dissociations that then continue through later development. In fact, many symptoms associated with personality disorders seem to reflect dysfunctions in the integrated achievement of the tasks of middle childhood.

As children become consciously aware of and able to judge their own inner life, it becomes possible to have emotional reactions about emotional reactions. The development of this emotion cycle capability has not been studied. It is known that, prior to the development of self-reflective skills, young children show emotional reactions to their own violations of behavioral standards (Cole, Barrett, & Zahn-Waxler, 1992; Kagan, 1981) and that preschoolers cope better with a stressful event if they were experiencing positive rather than negative feelings in the preceding moments (Barden, Garber, Duncan, & Masters, 1981; Carlson & Masters, 1986). As children become able to reflect on their own internal states and to think about the implications of those states, the reflections are not "cold" cognitions but rather value judgments that carry emotional valence. Middle childhood may be an important period for examining the emergence of problems in emotions about emotions.

Social influences, such as the reactions of others to one's emotions, also contribute to the internalization of emotions about emotions. One interesting developmental approach might be to study the emotional flow in a conflictual parent-child interaction. For example, it would be interesting to examine how the self-regulation of emotion by the adult relates to emotional communications made to the child about his or her emotionality (for an interesting discussion, see Dix, 1991). If a parent feels guilt, sadness, or anxiety about an angry exchange with the child, the parent may model an emotion/emotion cycle. In addition, such a cycle could also develop if a child is scorned for or chastised about an emotional reaction, such as feeling angry at the parent. One is reminded of Hoffman's (1982) statement that, when trying to promote moral development, parents should focus their reprimands on the inappropriate behavior rather than the felt emotion.

In sum, there are many examples of developmental research that can be integrated into a developmental psychopathology perspective and many aspects of emotionality that are relevant to clinical work and that remain to be studied in both typical and atypical samples. Emotional development is a complex transactional evolution in which child characteristics, caregiver characteristics, and experience converge and transform. Circumstances that stress children beyond their capacity to self-regulate, particularly when there is a lack of adequate alternative sources for regulation in the child's social world, create an opportunity for stable patterns of emotion dysregulation to develop.

Emotion dysregulation begins as emotionally regulatory events that occur in a context. Over the course of development, these events influence the development of stylized patterns of emotion regulation, and dysregulatory qualities can become part of this style. Emotion dysregulation then becomes an attribute of a person. Such dysregulatory patterns may accompany a developing disorder or be causal factors in the etiology of other disorders. They will probably not characterize the individual in all situations but rather be specific to particular types of contexts. A 4-year-old's temper tantrum is an instance of emotion dysregulation but is not necessarily a symptom of or predictive of psychopathology. Yet all forms of psychopathology have concomitant symptoms of emotion dysregulation.

SUMMARY

Clinical conceptualizations of emotion that stress its disruptive influences and functional models of emotion that emphasize its adaptive aspects can be integrated into a developmental psychopathology framework. Under certain conditions, emotion regulation may develop dysregulatory aspects that can become a characteristic of an individual's coping style. This style may then jeopardize or impair functioning and become associated with symptomatic, disordered functioning. Emotional development provides a critical vantage point from which to study the development of symptomatology and psychopathology, particularly given the prevalence of emotional symptoms in various forms of psychopathology. Dimensions of emotionality that can be used to characterize dysregulation include access to the range of emotions, flexible modulation of intensity, duration, and transitions between emotions, acquisition and use of cultural display rules, and the ability to reflect on the complexity and value of one's own emotions in a self-supporting manner. Developmental psychopathology provides a framework within which to examine how emotions are regulatory, how their regulation changes over time, and under what conditions an adaptive emotion process can develop into a pattern of dysregulation that then becomes, or sustains, some symptoms of mental disorders.

Such research requires samples that include children with and without risk or presence of particular mental health problems, paradigms that allow the examination of dimensions of emotionality in context and provide multiple assessments that include observations of children's reactions beyond what they themselves can report, and analyses that extend beyond simple global aggregates such as positive and negative emotion. We believe that it is particularly important to study children and their families in situations that challenge their emotional adaptation.

The developmental tasks of emotional life evolve in exchanges between the child and the world of events and relationships. The emotional conditions of early childhood appear to be very important in optimizing or interfering with how the child's emotionality regulates his or her interpersonal and intrapsychic functioning and how the child learns to regulate emotion. The experiences that accrue around emotional events influence the stable aspects of the developing personality and become trait-like aspects of the person (Malatesta & Wilson, 1988). Dysregulation occurs when an emotional reaction loses breadth and flexibility. If a dysregulatory pattern becomes stabilized and part of the emotional repertoire, it is likely that this pattern is a symptom and supports other symptoms. When development and adaptation are compromised, the dysregulation has evolved into a form of psychopathology.

The line between normative variations and clinical conditions is not clearly drawn. There is as yet no standard by which to state that an emotionally dysregulated style is not of clinical concern. Persons with dysregulated styles may never seek treatment or be diagnosed. They may live relatively ordinary, functional lives, and their friends and family might be startled to learn of their emotional difficulties, as is often the case in marital and family therapy. Individuals may be so accustomed to patterns of emotion regulation that have been part of their repertoire since early childhood that the thought that this style may be problematic may never occur. We contend that an emotion style that has dysregulated features is a vulnerability. The advantage of a developmental psychopathology approach is that it makes it possible to identify variations in emotion regulation and how they correlate with other variables in normative, at-risk, and clinical samples.

INTRODUCTION TO PART 2

Two themes introduced in the first part of this *Monograph* are applicable to the research presented in Part 2. The first theme involves an attempt to apply similar empirical approaches to the study of emotion regulation. The second theme is the focus on the functional role of physiology in understanding emotion regulation. These two themes are intermingled within each of the essays in this part. Scientists interested in the physiological correlates of emotion and emotion regulation have studied a number of different systems in their quest for understanding this complex interplay. Among the systems represented here are the responses of the autonomic nervous system, the hypothalamic-pituitary adrenal (HPA) axis, and electrical activity of the central nervous system.

The research described in this part utilizes a common approach to understanding these systems. First, there is an attempt to describe the position of the physiological system within the nervous system. A good deal of effort is spent understanding the biology of the different parts of the system, how they interact, and how the given system fits in and interfaces with the more general set of physical systems in the body. For example, Kathy Stansbury and Megan R. Gunnar present important detailed information on the biology and physiology of the HPA axis, information that is critical for an understanding of response differences among subjects and response differences as a function of different stimuli.

Second, there is an attempt to understand the range of naturally occurring variability of the system when it is not challenged. All the investigators represented in part 2 make use of notions of tonic or basal level as reflecting important information regarding the individual's potential for response. In addition, this tonic or basal level is seen as reflecting the degree of organization of the system—that is, the threshold from which it may respond—and the integrity of the system as it might interface with other physiological systems. Thus, for example, Stephen W. Porges, Jane A. Doussard-Roosevelt, and Ajit K. Maiti argue that the tonic level of vagal tone reflects the degree of organization of the autonomic system and is a reflection of the underlying integrity or health of the system.

Third, each of the investigators is concerned with the response of the individual system to challenge. Each observes the degree to which there is a change from a tonic or basal level and the direction of that change. These changes are then interpreted within a particular theoretical model and via an understanding of the biology of the physiological system. Nathan A. Fox, for example, interprets decreases in EEG power measured from electrodes placed over different scalp locations as reflecting activation of the cortical regions under these sites.

Fourth, each investigator anchors the physiological response to the behavior of the subject—that is, changes in physiology are interpreted insofar as they accompany the infant or child's response to a defined stimulus event. Although there has been a tradition in psychophysiological research that interprets physiological responses in the absence of any behavioral evidence of a response, the workers represented here have, in general, consistently attempted to link physiological changes to behavior rather than to depend solely on physiology for interpretation. This approach is particularly critical for work with preverbal infants, where self-report of feeling state is unavailable. So, for example, Geraldine Dawson interprets changes in EEG activation that are precisely linked to the affective response of the infant.

Finally, each investigator in part 2 is concerned with the responses of a *developing* physiological system. As such, this presents particular challenges since the development of these systems (EKG and vagal tone, EEG and cortical activity, cortisol and activity of the HPA) is not necessarily complete at birth. Part of the challenge for research in the interface of biology and behavior is an understanding of the role of each physiological system as that role changes with neurophysiological and organismic growth in the early years of life.

Although the essays in Part 2 reflect a common approach to the study of the physiological correlates of emotion regulation, there is also an apparent lack of integration across the three areas under investigation. Thus, although the principles of observation noted above underlie the reported work on the HPA axis and cortisol, on the autonomic nervous system and vagal tone, and on EEG activity and frontal asymmetry, no one approach integrates the three physiological responses at a systems, anatomical, or physiological level. While focusing on different systems, all the investigators are studying the same behavioral phenomena, namely, emotion and emotion regulation. However, there is little synthesis of the findings from these disparate systems into a unified approach to understanding physiological responses underlying emotion and emotion regulation. This situation is somewhat reminiscent of the fable of the four blind men, each touching a different part of the elephant and each providing a very different description of the beast.

There are a number of reasons for this lack of synthesis. First, and perhaps most obvious to those who utilize psychophysiological measures in the study of behavior, is the difficulty of first mastering the complexities of multiple systems and developing models in the context of which research examining their interaction can take place. It is rare to find studies in the psychophysiological literature that combine measurement of central, autonomic, and hormonal responses. Perhaps more to the issue is the notion that each of these systems may underlie different components of the behavioral response to which they are anchored. Each system has its unique time course, differing in the latency of the response of the system, the speed at which the system responds to peak, and the time course it takes for the response to return to a basal, prestimulus level. Brain electrical activity (EEG) may be measured in milliseconds after the onset of a stimulus, heart rate and vagal tone have time courses that occur within 1 to a few minutes after stimulus onset, while cortisol responses may peak only 15–30 min following an eliciting event. Each of these physiological systems may therefore reflect a unique component of the emotional or regulative response. Each system is, as well, functionally interconnected with other behavioral systems, which makes an integrative picture of how they function with respect to emotion difficult.

It is of course ultimately important to provide an integrated model of these various systems and to explain how they influence and are influenced by behavior. There is some suggestion from recent work on yet another physiological system, the immune system, that this synthesis is beginning to occur. Research examining immune responses to certain emotional events has found systematic changes in certain immune parameters associated with unique patterns of central, autonomic, or hormonal activity. It is possible that an integrated physiological approach to understanding how the body regulates and is regulated by emotional stimuli may be moderated through an understanding of the immune system's functioning. This area holds great promise for future research.

The second theme of the essays in this part and of the *Monograph* itself is the agreement among investigators in their focus on the functional significance of the responses being measured. All four essays in this part posit that physiological changes underlie the regulation of emotion and, moreover, that physiology itself may be regulated by emotion and consequently lead to behavioral regulation. This is similar to viewing emotions both as being regulated and as themselves regulating other emotion states. This dual conceptualization has consequences for the study of physiological processes as it has for emotion itself in that it speaks to the functional role that physiological systems may have for emotion regulation. For example, conceived in this way, the basal level of the system may reflect the threshold for the expression of certain emotions or the level of organization of the system. When challenged, the system may respond by changing its physiology and facilitating adaptive regulation or by increasing the level of a disorganized response. This dual role of physiology—as a regulator of behavior and being regulated as a response system—necessitates the measurement during both basal and challenge conditions. This conceptualization is common to all four essays contained in this part.

The questions raised here inevitably lead to the issue of "first causes" of behavior. That is, are the individual patterns of physiological reactivity that we observe an origin or an outcome of other behavioral regulators? At the very least, the essays in this part challenge the common assumption that, in studying the physiological correlates of emotion regulation, we come closer to the "true" origins of these behaviors. Rather, they highlight the complex interplay between behavior and physiology and the feedback systems that seem to be at work in the modulation of affective responses.

Stansbury and Gunnar provide an extensive overview of the adrenocortical system as well as a review of research on its measurement and use as an index for understanding emotional responses to stress. Through detailed description of the feedback system of the adrenocortical system, their essay shows how a physiological system both functions as a regulating system within the body and is regulated in interaction with the environment.

Porges et al. offer a second perspective on the role of a specific physiological system in the control and modulation of emotion. They describe in some detail the role of the parasympathetic nervous system in the organization of behaviors thought to be critical for emotion regulation and make an important link between peripheral and central control of autonomic function as representing relations between these systems and emotion. The remaining two essays, by Dawson and Fox, present evidence for the role that differences in brain activity play in the expression and regulation of emotion. Dawson presents compelling evidence of how two anterior brain systems are involved in the expression and regulation of emotion. One of these is involved in the expressive aspects and the other in the intensive aspects of emotion, and both have unique control systems that are involved in the modulation of affective behavior.

Fox reviews the clinical literature on brain damage and its effect on emotion, concluding that the major behavioral changes seen as a result of brain injury or the WADA test are with respect to the patient's ability to regulate mood state. He discusses the different positions regarding the etiology of these behavioral changes and then goes on to illustrate the issues with data on emotional reactivity and EEG asymmetry obtained in his laboratory. He presents evidence for a relation between changes in central nervous system activity and the infant's ability to react with positive or negative mood state and concludes with a discussion of the implications that these differences in brain asymmetry have for individual differences in infant emotion regulation.

Together, these essays give an insight into the physiological correlates of emotion and emotion regulation. They each provide system models that relate both basal levels of activity and response to challenge to the overt expression of emotion regulation as well as testable hypotheses regarding relations between behavior and physiological change. Future research may lead to achieving a higher-order integration of these models that could result in a synthesis of the roles of various physiological systems in the modulation or regulation of emotions.

N.A.F.

ADRENOCORTICAL ACTIVITY AND EMOTION REGULATION

Kathy Stansbury and Megan R. Gunnar

As repeatedly noted by the contributors to the first part of this volume, emotions consist of. physiological, behavioral, and subjective-experiential components. Accordingly, an understanding of the physiology of emotion is essential to understanding emotion processes, and the concept of emotion *regulation* also requires an understanding of the relations between physiology and behavior. Thus, like Campos, Campos, and Barrett (1989), we view emotion regulation not as a response to emotion but rather as a process- or systems-oriented perspective on the study of emotions. From this perspective, an understanding of emotions requires an understanding of the dynamic, reciprocal relations between the behavioral expression of emotions— including action tendencies and coping processes (see Dawson, in this volume; Lazarus, 1991)—and the physiological processes associated with emotion experience.

Given that physiological processes are integral to emotions and their regulation, investigators working in this domain have become increasingly interested in identifying emotion-relevant physiological systems that can be studied in healthy, normal children (see Dawson, in this volume; Fox, in this volume; and Porges, Doussard-Roosevelt, & Maiti, in this volume). One of these is the hypothalamic-pituitary-adrenocortical (HPA) system. Corti-

Portions of this essay were supported by an Alcohol and Drug Administration Mental Health Association (ADAMHA) Postdoctoral Fellowship in Child Development (5T32-MH15755) to Kathy Stansbury and by a National Institutes of Health research grant (HD-16494) and a National Institute of Mental Health research scientist award (MH-00946) to Megan R. Gunnar. We wish to thank Seymour Levine for reviewing a draft of this essay, Kaye O'Geay for secretarial help, and the many graduate and undergraduate students from our research group whose work we review. Please direct correspondence to Megan Gunnar, Institute of Child Development, 51 East River Road, University of Minnesota, Minneapolis, MN 55455.

sol, the hormonal product of this system, can now be measured easily and noninvasively in small samples of saliva. In addition, the adrenocortical system plays a major role in stress resistance (Selye, 1950), and many believe that emotions mediate the magnitude of the adrenocortical response to environmental challenge (Mason, 1975). The combination of ease of measurement and hypothesized sensitivity to emotion processes makes assessment of adrenocortical activity a highly attractive option in studies of early emotion development. In the following essay, we first provide an overview of the psychobiology of the HPA system and then relate the activity of this system to processes of emotion regulation.

THE PSYCHOBIOLOGY OF THE HPA SYSTEM

Cortisol is the primary hormonal product of the HPA system in humans. The adrenocortical system is a neuroendocrine system, which means that the production of cortisol is regulated, in large part, by centers in the central nervous system (CNS). The hypothalamus is the principle brain region involved in the regulation of cortisol, with centers in the limbic system serving to modulate and coordinate hypothalamic activity with perceptual and cognitive inputs from higher centers in the brain (de Kloet, 1991). Cortisol and its precursor hormones also affect the CNS and influence emotion and cognition.

Control of Cortisol Production

Figure 1 shows a schematic of the HPA system. The production of cortisol is under the control of cortisol-releasing hormone (CRH) and vasopressin, which are produced in the hypothalamus. Vasopressin (whose effects are not schematized in the figure) potentiates and acts synergistically with the action of CRH on the cells in the anterior pituitary that produce adrenocorticotrophic hormone (ACTH) (Palkovits, 1987). ACTH is then released into general circulation and stimulates cells in the cortex of the adrenal glands to produce cortisol and release it into the bloodstream. Once in circulation, most of the cortisol immediately binds to cortisol binding globulin (CBG). It is the unbound fraction of the cortisol in circulation that is biologically active. Activity in the HPA system occurs in pulses; increases in circulating cortisol reflect an increase in the frequency of pulses of CRH.

Basal Activity

A certain amount of cortisol is essential for normal, nonstressed activity. These basal levels of cortisol follow a daily or circadian rhythm in adults

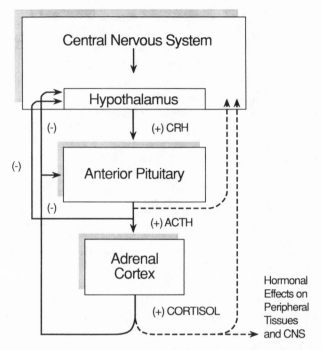

FIG. 1.—Schematic diagram of the hypothalamic-pituitary-adrenocortical axis in normal children and adults. Solid lines represent feedforward and feedback regulation; dotted lines represent physiological effects. The vasopressin influence on ACTH synthesis and secretion is *not* shown in this figure. (Adapted from Gunnar, 1986.)

that is regulated primarily by the suprachiasmatic nuclei in the hypothalamus. Input from the limbic system serves to modulate the rhythm in accordance with the timing of such normal daily activities as napping and meals (de Kloet, 1991). In adults who are on a normal day/night cycle, peak levels of basal cortisol are produced during the last hours of nighttime sleep (Anders, 1982). This results in high early morning levels that help sustain the energy available for action and stimulate the appetite for carbohydrates. Early morning peak levels decline sharply during the first hours after awakening and more gradually thereafter. During the day, however, there is evidence for a temporary postprandial surge in cortisol production. The timing of the circadian rhythm can be altered by gradually shifting sleep/ wake cycles; however, it takes nearly 2 weeks to reorganize the rhythm completely following 12-hour shifts in sleep/wake patterns.

While this circadian pattern is well established by 2 years, it is absent in the newborn, emerging only at about 3 months (Price, Close, & Fielding, 1983). However, during the entire first year, the daily pattern appears notably different from the adult pattern in that it fails to show a consistent

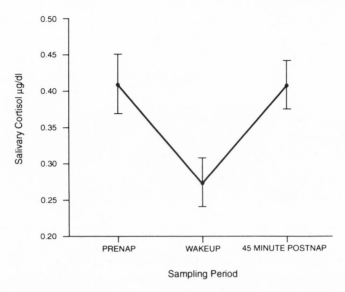

FIG. 2.—Salivary cortisol concentrations in 24 8–11-month-olds obtained immediately before, immediately after, and 45 min after their normal morning nap. (From Larson, Gunnar, & Hertsgaard, 1991.)

decrease over the middle portion of the day (Spangler, Meindl, & Grossman, 1988). This infant pattern may reflect the coordination of basal cortisol activity with napping and feeding schedules. Indeed, morning naps do appear to be associated with a transient decrease in cortisol (see Fig. 2), which rebounds to prenap concentrations 45 min after the nap (Larson, Gunnar, & Hertsgaard, 1991).

Stress Activity

Three major pathways mediate the HPA stress response (de Kloet, 1991). One pathway involves direct stimulation of the pituitary and hypothalamus by biochemicals arriving from general circulation. Another involves direct visceral and sensory stimulation, including pain and blood pressure changes, traveling to the hypothalamus through brain-stem pathways. The third pathway involves the transmission of psychological stimuli reaching the hypothalamus from the cerebral cortex via the limbic circuits. It is believed that the amygdala plays a major role in facilitating the initiation of the stress response while the hippocampus plays a major role in terminating the response and returning the HPA system to basal regulation (de Kloet, 1991; Smuts & Levine, 1977). Following the onset of a stressor, it takes about 10–15 min to produce a rise in circulating cortisol levels and

20–30 min for cortisol to reach peak stress concentrations in plasma. Even if the response is acute, it may take several hours for the "extra" cortisol to be cleared from circulation.

Adequate Measurement of Basal Levels

This brief discussion of the basal and stress-induced activity of the HPA system should serve to alert researchers to the importance of adequately measuring basal levels of cortisol. A determination of whether a change from basal to stress regulation of the system has been produced requires knowledge of what the concentrations of cortisol would have been in the absence of the stressor (Levine & Coe, 1985). When the system is functioning under basal regulation, decreases in cortisol are expected over the day. During the morning hours, when basal levels are declining rapidly, a small cortisol response may not yield increases in cortisol over prestimulation levels. The significance of the response might be apparent only when cortisol levels are compared to levels obtained under similar conditions at the same time of day but in the absence of the stressor. This can be seen in the data on separation from mother shown in Figure 3. The effects of a 30-min separation were evident only when cortisol levels of babies separated from their mothers were compared to levels obtained from the same babies when their mothers stayed with them during the 30-min period (Gunnar, Larson, Hertsgaard, Harris, & Brodersen, 1992).

Cortisol and Stress Resistance

Although stress is often thought of as bad, the ability to mount a stress response is necessary for survival. An individual without a functioning HPA system could not survive even the normal perturbations of daily life and could exist only in physically and emotionally protected environments (Selye, 1950). The adrenocortical system appears to perform three major functions in stress resistance. First, along with other hormones and systems, it participates in the mobilization of energy resources that are needed for action. Second, cortisol serves a homeostatic function in regulating the activity of other stress-sensitive systems including the central and peripheral catecholamine systems, the endogenous opiate system, and the immune system (Munck, Guyre, & Holbrook, 1984). Third, cortisol, ACTH, and CRH act in the brain and can affect memory, learning, and emotions (McEwen, de Kloet, & Rostene, 1986). Clearly, healthy adaptation requires the capacity to produce increased cortisol under conditions of threat and to return its production to basal levels as soon as the threat has passed.

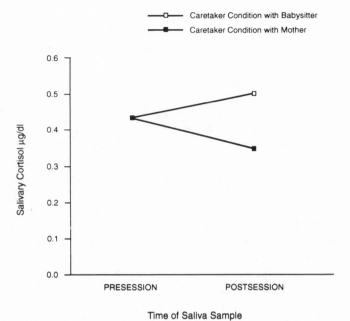

FIG. 3.—Salivary cortisol concentrations in 19 infants, aged 9 months, tested twice: once separated for 30 min from their mothers and once playing in the mother's presence for 30 min (order counterbalanced). Salivary cortisol measures were obtained immediately before and after the 30-min periods. Standard errors were approximately 0.03 μg/dl. (Adapted from Gunnar, Larson, et al., 1992.)

CNS Effects

The CNS effects of glucocorticoids (e.g., cortisol, corticosterone, and related steroid hormones) on behavior are of most relevance to research on emotion regulation. Most of the information that we have about the CNS effects of glucocorticoids has been derived from animal research, a fact that the reader should keep in mind in reading the following section. Because in rodents the steroid produced by the HPA system is corticosterone and not cortisol, the more general term *glucocorticoids* will be used in discussing these data.

It has been hypothesized that the effects of glucocorticoids on behavior are largely mediated by their actions on steroid receptors in the brain-stem reticular formation, the hippocampus, and the frontal cortex (for more extensive reviews, see de Kloet, 1991; McEwen et al., 1986). Glucocorticoids do not have unitary excitatory or inhibitory influences on neural tissue. Instead, the effect of these steroid hormones depends on the type of steroid receptor that is stimulated and on the point in the process at which the response is being measured. Glucocorticoids have both fast membrane and slow gene-mediated effects on neuronal activity (de Kloet, 1991). The fast effects of glucocorticoids take milliseconds to seconds to develop, while the slow effects take minutes to hours to emerge and may last hours after hormone concentrations have returned to basal levels.

Elevations in glucocorticoids in response to stress initially stimulate cortical arousal via excitatory action on brain-stem reticular activity. In emotionally stable adults, these excitatory brain-stem effects are associated with feelings of increased energy and ability to concentrate (Born, Hitzler, Pietrowsky, Pauschinger, & Fehm, 1989). In contrast, the more slowly developing effects of glucocorticoids largely function to lower neuronal excitation, which may produce a reversal of the initial stimulatory influences (de Kloet, 1991). Thus, in normal subjects who are maintained on increased glucocorticoids for several days, there is some evidence for a decrease in energy (hypomania), a loss of ability to concentrate, and an increase in depressive affect (Wolkowitz et al., 1988).

These inhibitory effects develop even when elevations in glucocorticoids are relatively short lived, and they may influence the consolidation and storage of memories for the events transpiring during and after the stressor. They are also involved in the inhibitory effect of glucocorticoids on REM sleep, which persists for hours after stress levels of cortisol have been cleared from circulation (see Fig. 4; and also Gunnar, Malone, Vance, & Fisch, 1985). Thus, in response to a noxious stimulus, glucocorticoids may initially help support the increased cortical arousal needed to sustain heightened behavioral and emotion activity and then facilitate the behavioral withdrawal and quiescence that may be needed to help recover from the physical and emotional effects of the stressor. This dual role of glucocorticoids has clear implications for our understanding of emotion regulation.

Another major effect of glucocorticoids is to raise sensory thresholds via decreasing evoked sensory potentials (Born et al., 1989). At the same time, increased corticoids facilitate the integration and interpretation of incoming sensory information (Henkin, 1970). Thus, once the slow-action effects of glucocorticoids have developed, elevated corticoid levels may be associated with a reduction in an individual's actual sensitivity to auditory, tactile, or visual stimuli, including pain stimuli, along with improved abilities to interpret the meaning of stimulation and to integrate information about the stressor arriving from different sensory modalities.

Elevated glucocorticoid levels also have complex effects on learning and memory. de Kloet (1991) has hypothesized that these effects serve to facilitate the elimination of behavior that is no longer of relevance and to consolidate behavioral strategies that serve to reduce real or perceived threat. Many of the effects on learning and memory may involve corticoid receptors in the hippocampus. Two types of receptors (Type I and Type

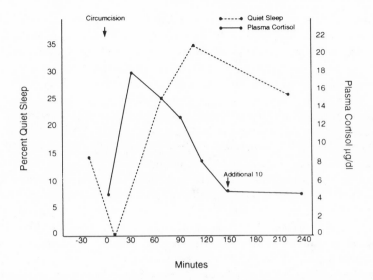

FIG. 4.—Plasma cortisol and behavioral state before, during, and after routine circumcision of normally developing newborn males. Quiet sleep was defined as eyes closed, no or minimal rapid eye movement, and little movement. State was scored every 30 sec. Plasma cortisol was obtained from all subjects immediately before circumcision and from groups of 20 subjects at 30, 90, 120, and 240 min following the beginning of circumcision. An additional group of 10 newborns was added at the 150-min time point. (Adapted from Gunnar, Malone, Vance, & Fisch, 1985.)

II) are responsive to corticoids, and, in the hippocampus, these receptors may work in a coordinated fashion to facilitate three processes: (*a*) modulating basal cortisol levels, (*b*) setting the threshold for the transition from basal to stress activity, and (*c*) influencing the termination of the stress response. These two types of receptors may also form the substrates for quite different cognitive and behavioral strategies in response to stressful stimulation. de Kloet and his colleagues (Bohus, de Kloet, & Veldhuis, 1982) have argued that Type I receptors in the hippocampus are the first to be affected by elevations in cortisol and that stimulation of these receptors facilitates the inhibition of ongoing behavior, facilitates passive avoidance learning, and facilitates attention to changes in the external environment.

Effects of glucocorticoids on the hippocampus that are mediated by Type I receptors are sometimes followed by effects mediated by Type II receptors. Whether the Type II receptors become involved in the response depends on the extent to which cortisol is elevated over basal concentrations. Because corticoids have a higher affinity for Type I receptors, only under conditions in which Type I receptors become occupied are significant numbers of Type II receptors activated (de Kloet, 1991). Thus, Type II receptors in the hippocampus may be activated primarily when a true "stress" response of the HPA system has been elicited. The exact levels of corticoids that denote the "stress" cutoff will vary during the day because the availability of Type I receptors varies with the daily cortisol rhythm (de Kloet, 1991). There are no clear guidelines for determining these levels; however, it is estimated that Type I receptors are 80%–90% occupied under basal conditions. Thus, perhaps a 10%–20% increase in cortisol can be accommodated by Type I receptors, with larger increases affecting Type II receptors and constituting a qualitatively different response.

Once Type II receptors in the hippocampus have been activated, their effects may modulate hippocampal-mediated integration of newly learned behaviors with previously learned material. Thus, activation of Type II receptors in the hippocampus may be associated with changes in response to the stressor over time or with repetitions of the stressful event. These well-modulated effects on brain activity and behavior tend to characterize the effect of low to moderate stress levels of glucocorticoids. When the response to a stressor is intense and corticoids rise rapidly to extreme levels, disruptions in learning and adaptive behavior may be observed. Individual differences related to both genetic and experiential factors also influence the balance between Type I and Type II receptor-mediated behaviors. All these effects are clearly relevant to our understanding of emotion regulation processes.

Negative Feedback and Stress Threshold

Levels of glucocorticoids in circulation are regulated by negative feedback. The hypothalamus appears to be the major site of negative feedback regulation, but other structures, including the pituitary and hippocampus, also play a role. Three types of negative feedback have been distinguished: fast, intermediate, and slow. Fast feedback involves multisynaptic control of ACTH release. It occurs within 10 min of the rise in glucocorticoids (i.e., about 20–25 min after stress activation). Fast feedback appears to be desensitized or "overridden" with chronic stress exposure and may play a role in increasing HPA reactivity in chronically stressed individuals (Young, Akana, & Dallman, 1990). Intermediate feedback may operate at the limbic and forebrain system level to alter reactivity to stimulation, thus dampening continued activation of limbic stress circuits in prolonged stressful encounters. Finally, slow feedback involves the blockade of the CRH-vasopressin system in the hypothalamus and ACTH production in the pituitary. This feedback action takes 30–60 min to begin to develop (i.e., 45 min or more after activation), and its effects may not become pronounced for hours (de Kloet, 1991; Jacobson & Sapolsky, 1991).

de Kloet and his colleagues (de Kloet, 1991; McEwen et al., 1986) have hypothesized that regulation of the HPA stress response is related to Type I and Type II receptor density in the hippocampus. According to these researchers, Type I receptor density may set the threshold for HPA reactivity, with a greater density being associated with lower reactivity (and possibly higher basal cortisol levels). Under this model, Type II receptors modulate negative feedback, with greater density being associated with a greater capacity to terminate the HPA stress response.

There is evidence in the animal literature for individual differences in the number of Type I and Type II receptors in the hippocampus (de Kloet, 1991). In rodents, stressful stimulation experienced during infancy *increases,* while chronic elevation in cortisol experienced after infancy *decreases,* the number of Type II receptors (Meaney, Aitken, Van Berkel, Bhatnager, & Sapolsky, 1988). Several different strains of rats have also been identified that differ in number of Type I and Type II receptors. Strains with more Type I and Type II receptors show a higher threshold for the lifting of tonic inhibition of the hypothalamic CRH neurons and a lower threshold for the termination of the stress response (Walker, Rivest, Meaney, & Aubert, 1989). These strains also show reduced fearfulness or negative emotionality and increased capacity to respond to and learn under stressful environmental circumstances. These behavioral differences have been shown both for receptor differences resulting from prior stress experiences and strain and for genetic differences (Meaney et al., 1988; Walker et al., 1989).

EMOTION REGULATION AND PERIODS OF THE HPA RESPONSE

This overview of the psychobiology of the HPA system clearly points to the relevance of this system for the study of emotion regulation. It also points to the need to consider mutual and reciprocal relations between emotion processes and HPA activity. Furthermore, it is clear that time is an important parameter in relating HPA activity to the behavioral regulation of affect. As an aid to investigators new to the use of cortisol measures in their research, in what follows we briefly consider the major "periods" or "phases" of the HPA response to a stressor as they relate to emotion regulation processes. Our time estimations are only rough approximations. The actual timing of events would depend on numerous factors, including the magnitude and the rate of the HPA response. A consideration of these response periods is relevant to research on both adults and children; however, in what follows, we focus on children.

Initial Reaction

Before a psychological stressor can activate an HPA stress response, the stressor must be perceived and interpreted, at least to some extent (Zajonc, 1984). If after this rudimentary processing the event is perceived as threatening, stress circuits in the limbic system and hypothalamus may be activated. This period of initial reaction probably encompasses only the first moments after the child alerts to the event. One critical issue to consider in relating HPA activity to emotion regulation for this "period" is the delineation of types of emotion reactions that are associated with elevations in cortisol.

Preelevation

If a stress response is activated, the physiological changes set in motion begin to create the substrates necessary to sustain increased physical and psychological activity. For the first 5–10 min following stress activation, cortisol levels will still be at, or close to, basal concentrations, and thus the effects of cortisol on the CNS will not be a major factor influencing behavior. Increases in CRH, vasopressin, and ACTH, however, may begin to influence CNS activity at this time.

While these physiological changes are occurring, we can assume that the child is engaged in a more complete appraisal of the emotional meaning of the event, perhaps incorporating the immediate subjective experience of her altered physiological state (Lazarus & Folkman, 1984). The child may also begin to assess his or her coping and emotion regulation resources. The processes involved in both continued emotion appraisal and emotion regulation may either increase or decrease the activity in the limbic circuits involved in the stress response. As a result of this continued appraisal, the child may decide that the event is not actually threatening, thereby decreasing the stimulation of limbic stress circuits and terminating the stress response. Conversely, the child may experience the event as even more threatening, and stimulation of the limbic stress circuits may increase.

For many of the emotionally distressing situations that we are able to study in the laboratory, psychological and central nervous system processes occurring in these first two periods may not be sufficient to produce a significant, detectable cortisol stress response in enough subjects to permit an adequate examination of hormone-behavior relations. For ethical reasons, the stressors that we use are mild, the situations brief, and the supports provided to the child sufficient to prevent demonstrable elevations in cortisol in most subjects. For example, it is now clear that even such seemingly stressful events as separation from the mother may be insufficient to produce elevated cortisol concentrations when separation occurs in a supportive environment with other caregivers available to respond to the baby's needs (Gunnar, Larson, et al., 1992; Tennes, Downey, & Vernadakis, 1977). Furthermore, it has been shown that, for monkeys, the presence and availability of the mother buffers the HPA stress response to many potentially stressful events (Levine, 1970), and in the laboratory the human mother is typically present unless separation is the stressor being examined. The problem of identifying sufficiently salient stressors in research on children has led many researchers to seek naturally occurring or real-life stressful contexts in which to examine the relations between HPA activity and emotion regulation.

Period of CNS Effects: Fast-developing Influences

Once cortisol levels have risen sufficiently above basal values—about 10–15 min after stress activation—cortisol can begin to have effects on CNS activity. The initial effects will involve those that can occur quickly, and, as discussed earlier, should include changes leading to a sense of increased energy and concentration, facilitation of passive avoidance, and attention to changes in the environment. These effects may facilitate emotion regulation through facilitating avoidance of noxious or threatening elements of the situation. Avoiding behaviors that lead to increased distress may, in turn, increase the likelihood that the child will try other behaviors that may be more adaptive. Fast negative feedback effects may also begin to exert influence on continued CRH-vasopressin and ACTH production at this time.

Period of CNS Effects: More Slowly Developing Influences

The neuronal effects that develop more slowly take at least 15 min after cortisol has risen above basal levels (i.e., after the onset of period 3). Thus, the earliest "slow gene-mediated effects" may not occur until about 20–30 min after stress activation of the HPA system. Furthermore, most of these influences will take much longer, including the slow negative feedback effects described earlier. The point is that these more slowly developing effects are probably taking place after the child has left the laboratory and/ or an acute stress experience is over. Nonetheless, because many of the gene-mediated effects influence memory processes and the integration of new information, they will be important to the study of emotion regulation and may help explain how emotion regulation experiences alter the child's responses to arousing events on subsequent exposures.

TABLE 1

PLASMA CORTISOL AND PERCENTAGE OF CRYING IN RESPONSE TO CIRCUMCISION AND
HEEL-STICK BLOOD SAMPLING IN NEONATES

Stimulus	N	Time Point (min)[a]	r	p[b]
Circumcision	9	30	+.71	< .05
Circumcision (with soothing)[c]	20	30	+.44	< .05
Circumcision (with soothing)	20	90	+.50	< .05
Circumcision (no soothing)	13	20	+.35	N.S.
Heel stick (no soothing)	18	20	+.54	< .05
Heel stick (with soothing)	13	20	+.50	N.S.
Heel stick (no soothing)	12	20	+.55	< .05

SOURCE.—Adapted from Gunnar, Marvinney, Isensee, & Fisch (1989).
NOTE.—N.S. = not significant.
[a] Time point indicates minutes between onset of stimulation and poststimulation blood sampling. Behavior was always obtained during stimulation.
[b] $Z = 7.47$ for the combined significance of the seven correlation coefficients presented in this table.
[c] Soothing indicates that all subjects were given pacifiers.

ILLUSTRATIONS FROM RESEARCH ON CHILDREN

Most of the work on normally developing human children examines acute, brief stressors and changes in cortisol at approximately 20–30 min after stressor onset. Because of this, our data on children deal primarily with questions relating behavior to HPA activity during the first two to three periods outlined above. These questions include asking which emotions are related to activation of the HPA stress response, which emotion regulation processes are involved in mediating the stress response, and how individual differences might be understood in the context of these first two questions.

Emotions Associated with Activation

It has long been believed that negative emotions play a primary role in activating the HPA stress response (Mason, 1971). This view finds support in data showing that crying during infancy is at times correlated with post-stressor cortisol concentrations (see Table 1). These data on newborns in Table 1 conform well with data on adults showing that conditions of work stress and military training lead to correlated increases in cortisol and self-reports of boredom, impatience, irritation, fear, and anxiety (Franken-haeuser, 1980; Ursin, Baade, & Levine, 1978).

While states of negative affect do appear to be associated with elevations in cortisol, it is not clear that they are sufficient to cause activation of the HPA stress circuits. The literature on HPA activity and emotion behavior is replete with instances of statistical dissociations (Levine, Wiener, Coe,

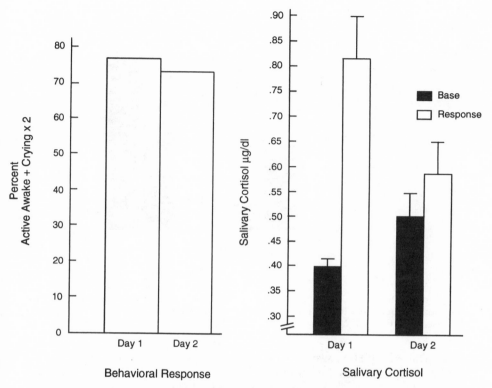

FIG. 5.—Behavioral distress and HPA activity in response to two physical exams separated by 24 hours in normally developing human newborns. Behavioral distress is defined as the weighted average of the percentage of 30-sec coding intervals in the states of active awake or crying. Salivary cortisol in µg/dl obtained before and 30 min after the beginning of a 6-min physical exam. (Adapted from Gunnar, Connors, & Isensee, 1989.)

Bayart, & Hayashi, 1987). For example, on repeated exposure to a psychological stressor, we found that the newborn HPA stress response habituated (Gunnar, Connors, & Isensee, 1989; Gunnar, Hertsgaard, Larson, & Rigatuso, 1992) but that crying did not (see Fig. 5). Similarly, during a prolonged separation, cortisol levels in rhesus monkey infants returned to basal concentrations within 24 hours, while behavioral distress continued for days (Gunnar, Gonzales, Goodlin, & Levine, 1981). A decade ago, in a review of the adult research, Rose (1980) pointed out that rapid adaptation was also highly characteristic of the human adult HPA stress response.

Dissociations between HPA activity and a negative emotion response have led many to question how closely negative emotions are linked to stress

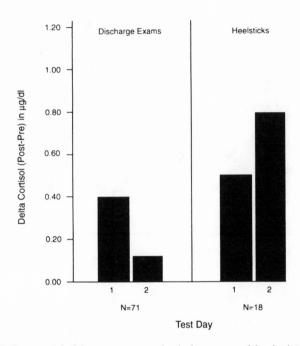

Fɪɢ. 6.—Salivary cortisol in response to physical exams and heel sticks in normally developing human newborns. Trials were separated by 24 hours. (Adapted from Gunnar, Hertsgaard, et al., 1992.)

activation of the HPA system. Levine (Hennessy & Levine, 1979), for example, has suggested that cortisol is not the "emotion juice." Instead, novelty, uncertainty, discrepancy, and/or incongruity serve as the primary psychological factors that activate the HPA response. This, of course, might explain why, with repetitions of a stressor, one can see adaptation of the HPA response.

To add to the complexity, data also exist that appear to contradict the novelty/uncertainty hypothesis. First, when stressors are repeated and thus become more familiar, stress elevations in cortisol sometimes increase rather than decrease. Sensitization of the cortisol stress response occurs with more noxious or intense stressors (Groves & Thompson, 1970; Natelson et al., 1988). This is demonstrated in Figure 6 using data from a study comparing the neonatal HPA response to repeated heel sticks (more noxious) with the response to repeated physical exams (less noxious). Second, novel experiences occurring in pleasant emotion contexts do not elevate cortisol. At times, in fact, pleasurable situations have been associated with a lowering of cortisol below basal concentrations (Wadeson, Mason, Hamburg, & Handlon, 1963). In a study that we conducted with 6–13-month-olds, we contrasted the novelty of a first-time swimming experience with the positive emotion typically engendered in mother-baby swim classes (Hertsgaard, Gunnar, Larson, Brodersen, & Lehman, 1992). Rather than elevating cortisol levels, as the uncertainty hypothesis would predict, swimming lowered cortisol below baseline, as the emotion hypothesis would predict.

To summarize, neither the emotion nor the uncertainty hypothesis appears sufficient to explain the various types of results that have been reported. Perhaps one reason the relative contributions of emotions and uncertainty are still unclear is that these factors need to be considered within an emotion regulation framework. As we have suggested previously, uncertainty may play a role in mediating the effect of emotion on the HPA system. However, the critical aspect of uncertainty may not be novelty or unfamiliarity but rather uncertainty about how to control or influence the stressful event and one's behavioral and emotion reactions to it (Gunnar, Marvinney, Isensee, & Fisch, 1989). Thus, uncertainty about the effectiveness of emotion regulation processes may be the critical mediating factor. This idea is not new. It permeates the literature on coping and HPA regulation (Rose, 1980) and to some extent the literature on "ego defenses" and HPA activity (Wolff, Friedman, Hofer, et al., 1964).

Emotion Regulation Processes Mediating the HPA Response

We are viewing emotion regulation behaviors as those actions initiated by the child that function to reduce negative emotions or sustain positive emotions and their associated physiological processes (see also Masters, 1991). Many of the regulatory behaviors described below correspond to those discussed by Thompson (in this volume). They are also, of course, similar to those discussed by Lazarus and Folkman (1984) and others studying stress and coping in adults.

Control

The controllability of stimulation is among the most important factors determining the effect of noxious stimulation on HPA activity. There is now good evidence that the HPA stress response is affected more by the perception or expectation of control than by the actual "fact" of control (Weiss, 1971). Thus, when individuals believe that they can effectively control potentially threatening events, even noxious stimuli such as electric shocks (Weiss, 1971) and loud noises (Hanson, Larson, & Snowden, 1976) produce only a small HPA response compared to the responses observed in yoked subjects, who experience the same stimulation but believe that they are unable to control it.

Not only does perceived control reduce elevations in cortisol in the

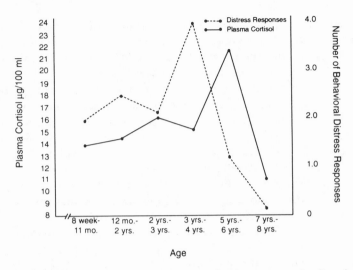

Fig. 7.—Observer-rated distress and plasma cortisol in a cross-sectional study of children with PKU (phenylketonuria) during anticipation of and reaction to venipuncture (Gunnar, Marvinney, et al., 1988).

context of noxious stimulation, but it also appears to lower cortisol below basal levels in the context of pleasant and interesting stimulation. Frankenhaeuser, Lundberg, and Forsman (1978) allowed adults to work at a complex task at their own, preferred work pace and found that, compared to adults who performed the task at the experimenter's set pace, those who had control actually showed a lowering of cortisol below their normal basal levels. In addition, these subjects reported feelings of increased interest and effort combined with reduced boredom and impatience.

In human children, control also plays an important role in emotion regulation (e.g., Gunnar, 1980). Although no studies have directly examined the effect of control on children's HPA activity, the results of one study do suggest that developmental changes in children's knowledge of emotion control may influence the HPA stress response. These results come from a cross-sectional examination of plasma cortisol and behavioral distress in children with PKU (phenylketonuria), from whom blood samples were repeatedly taken as part of the treatment for this disorder (Gunnar, Marvinney, et al., 1989). These children were developing normally and had good dietary control of phenylalanine concentrations.

As shown in Figure 7, age changes in distressed behavior were dissociated from age changes in cortisol concentrations. When crying was low, cortisol was high. In interviews with these children, we found that elevations in cortisol and reductions in crying were noted for those who verbalized the display rule that children should "act tough" or "not cry" when they come to the clinic (Saarni, 1979) but who could not generate strategies that allowed them to maintain such self-control (Harris, Olthof, & Meerum Terwogt, 1981; McCoy & Masters, 1985). The older children who exhibited low levels of crying and of cortisol, on the other hand, both verbalized the display rule and generated a number of strategies for controlling their overt displays of distress. One interpretation is that these older children were more certain about their ability to maintain self-control whereas the younger ones were uncertain about their emotion control.

Distraction and Attention Regulation

Distraction and/or attention regulation is another emotion regulation strategy that may influence HPA activity (see Thompson, in this volume). Rothbart (e.g., Rothbart & Derryberry, 1981) has suggested that the development of attention regulation underlies the changes in emotion behavior and self-regulation abilities that are noted between infancy and childhood. There is currently no evidence that distraction buffers or lowers the cortisol stress response in young children. However, there is evidence that attention to pleasant, relaxing stimulation under nonstressful conditions lowers cortisol below basal levels. Activities like watching nature films, meditation, and hypnosis lower cortisol in human adults (Handlon et al., 1962; Sachar, Fishman, & Mason, 1965; Wadeson et al., 1963). In infants, we have found that riding in the car lowers cortisol below home basal levels. Furthermore, babies who stayed awake during the whole car trip showed decreases in cortisol similar to the decreases observed for babies who got drowsy and fell asleep (Larson et al., 1991). Thus, the effect appeared to be related to the car trip itself, not to sleeping or napping. The lowering of cortisol during parent-infant swim classes may be another instance in which attending to pleasant, interesting stimulation operated to reduce HPA activity (Hertsgaard et al., 1992).

Self-Soothing and Adjunctive Behavior

Self-grooming, nonnutritive sucking, rocking, and rhythmic stroking are all behaviors that increase under noxious conditions and that have been hypothesized to play a role in emotion regulation (Kopp, 1989). The opportunity to perform these behaviors reduces the HPA stress response to some noxious stimuli in rodents (Brett & Levine, 1979). Furthermore, Levine (e.g., Brett & Levine, 1979) has shown that how often the animal performs these behaviors is not related to how effective the behavior is in buffering the adrenal response. Instead, what appears to matter is that the environment supports the opportunity to engage in the behavior. Thus, the data on these behaviors are similar to the data on control; it is the opportunity to use the behavior, not the performance of the behavior, that appears to modify the stress reaction. The effects of these types of behaviors on HPA activity have not been studied in children.

Social Companionship

Social support plays a major role in modulating the effect of noxious life events (Lazarus & Folkman, 1984). In infant monkeys, familiar conspecifics lower the HPA response to separation from the mother (Levine, Johnson, & Gonzales, 1985). We also found that a playful baby-sitter buffered the HPA response of 9-month-olds to 30-min separations from their mothers (Gunnar, Larson, et al., 1992). And, of course, one reason that swimming did not elevate cortisol among our 6–13-month-old infants may have been because the babies were with their mothers.

The proximal mechanisms for the effects of social companions may include all the emotion regulation strategies described above as well as others. Certainly, the presence of a responsive adult increases infants' personal control over the environment and over their own internal state. A playful baby-sitter also supports distraction and attention regulation. Additionally, interactions with caregivers provide a rich context for learning regulation strategies, including cognitive restructuring and other complex cognitive strategies.

In summary, the behaviors and/or psychological processes that are known to modify HPA activity are the same processes and behaviors that are studied by emotion regulation researchers. Positive social relationships, pleasant, challenging tasks, and self-stimulatory actions are known to be part of the strategies that children use to regulate emotion states (Kopp, 1989; McCoy & Masters, 1985; Stansbury, 1991; Thompson, in this volume). Although the effects of emotion regulation behaviors on HPA activity have not been studied extensively in human children, this will be an important avenue of inquiry.

Individual Differences

There are large individual differences in neuroendocrine responsivity. While some stressors are intense enough to activate the HPA and other stress systems in the majority of individuals, most stimulate increases in HPA activity in only some. Many factors may contribute to these differences in response, including such factors as experiential history, developmental level, current resources and strategies, and physiological differences in the HPA system. Models relating these various factors to differences in HPA reactivity in children (and adults) have not been worked out. However, temperamental variations among children may reflect the combined influence of many of these factors and thus may serve as a useful heuristic in approaching the study of individual differences in HPA reactivity and emotion regulation.

To organize our discussion of individual variation, we use two major temperament factors that have also been considered as bases for childhood emotion problems. These dimensions are a fear of novelty and distress in response to limitations (Rothbart & Derryberry, 1981). In considering fear of novelty, we also include other temperamental and emotion dispositions that seem to involve inhibition in the face of arousing stimulation and that have been viewed by others as composing negative orientations associated with anxiety, depression, and emotion and behavioral withdrawal (Davidson, 1984b; Dawson, in this volume; Roth & Cohen, 1986). These are emotions associated with internalizing behavior disorders (Kagan, Reznick, & Snidman, 1988; Rosenbaum et al., 1988). Distress in response to limitations, in contrast, has been viewed as a disposition toward externalizing behavior problems (Bates, 1989; Magnusson, 1988). This affective orientation includes anger, aggressiveness, and a low tolerance of frustration. While these are also negative emotions, they can be contrasted with the negative affects listed earlier because they involve an outward orientation and approach (Davidson, 1984b). In discussing these individual differences, we consider variations in both the normal and the pathological range because such a joint consideration can be informative for both normally developing and at-risk populations (Cicchetti, 1989a). Having said this, however, we recognize that, although in some instances pathology may reflect extremes in normal functioning, in others it may indicate a reorganization of the relations between physiological and behavioral processes.

Behavioral Inhibition and Withdrawal

There is a strong theoretical basis for expecting HPA reactivity to be associated with behavioral inhibition, anxiety, fearfulness, internalizing behavior disorders, and depression (e.g., Henry & Stephens, 1977). Indeed, much of the current research on the HPA system in humans is motivated by an interest in identifying the physiological substrate of negative emotions associated with withdrawal (e.g., Young, Haskett, Murphy-Weinberg, Watson, & Akil, 1991). This orientation is reflected in Kagan's theory of behavioral inhibition (Kagan et al., 1988), according to which extreme behavioral inhibition in the face of the unfamiliar is the result of a constitutionally lower threshold for activation of the stress circuits in the limbic lobes. This lower threshold for reactivity should be reflected in greater HPA and sympathetic reactivity. Kagan and his colleagues have repeatedly demonstrated that extremely inhibited children show higher and less variable heart-rate responses to mildly novel stimulation than do extremely bold children (see, e.g., Kagan, Reznick, & Snidman, 1987).

HPA activity has been less clearly linked to behavioral inhibition. Kagan did report higher home and laboratory salivary cortisol concentrations among extremely inhibited children when compared to bold children (Kagan et al., 1987). Suomi (Scanlan, Suomi, Higley, & Kraemer, 1982) also noted that monkeys bred for inhibition showed greater HPA reactivity than did those bred for boldness. On the other hand, research by Tennes and Kreye (1985) showed that second graders with higher basal cortisol levels were more socially outgoing rather than inhibited.

The relations between behavioral inhibition and HPA reactivity are likely to be complex. We expect that they may depend on the amount of social support provided to the child. Indeed, we recently found that fearful toddlers showed elevations in cortisol during testing with arousing, novel stimuli only if they were insecurely attached to the parent who accompanied them for testing. If the relationship was secure, then the fearful children did not show any increase in cortisol (see Nachmias, Gunnar, Mangelsdorf, Parritz, & Buss, 1993).

In addition to social support, a child's willingness to take risks may also play a role. In a study of nursery school children, we found that cortisol reactivity during the first weeks of school was greater for children whose parents described them as highly active and attracted to highly stimulating activities. Shy children did not show high reactivity during this time. The more inhibited children, however, avoided the kinds of social and physical activities that would elicit elevations in cortisol. Thus, social support and the inhibited child's options to choose safe, less risky activities and events may be important moderators of the relations between inhibition and HPA activity (see Gunnar, 1992).

Anxiety and Ego Defenses

There are relatively few studies of the relations between generalized trait anxiety and HPA reactivity in children. The few studies that do exist suggest that, for children as well as for adults, measures of anxiety are relatively poor predictors of children's HPA activity even when they are more specific to the stressor (i.e., test anxiety) (see McBurnett et al., 1991; Tennes & Kreye, 1985). Dissociations between anxiety measures and HPA activity typically have been explained in the clinical literature by reference to the mediating effects of ego defenses (Wolff et al., 1964). Strong or effective ego defenses are expected to prevent the experience of anxiety, maintain the individual's ability to engage in normal cognitive and interpersonal functioning, and buffer stress-reactive physiological systems. The adult research on ego defense effectiveness has largely supported these predictions (Mason, Sachar, Fishman, et al., 1965; Wolff et al., 1964). Similarly, both of the two studies conducted with school-age children have also shown that strong ego defenses, as measured by Rorschach tests and clinical interviews, were associated with lower cortisol during hospitalization for minor surgery (Knight et al., 1979) and, in hemophiliacs, during hospitalizations for observation and following a major bleed (Mattsson, Gross, & Hall, 1971).

Given these data, it would seem that ego defense effectiveness may be an important construct to measure in studies relating anxiety-eliciting events to emotion regulation and HPA activity in children. However, there are at least two reasons for caution at this point. First, in correlating the components of ego defenses with cortisol, Knight et al. (1979) found that only the *affective distress* component predicted HPA activity. Children who scored higher on affective distress had higher cortisol levels. This association could have been predicted independently of the ego defense construct. Second, strong ego defenses are, at times, associated with immature or maladaptive emotion regulation behaviors. Thus, the children with hemophilia who were judged to be coping effectively with the trauma of the condition and the hospitalization were more poorly defended according to the ego defense measures and also showed *higher* cortisol levels (Mattsson et al., 1971). Thus, at least with regard to normal children, once coping or emotion regulation processes are taken into consideration, strength of ego defenses may not add significantly to our understanding of the relations between anxiety-eliciting events and HPA activity. It is possible that measures of intrapsychic defense processes may become important in understanding emotion processes and neuroendocrine activity in clinically disturbed children.

Depression

Some of the earliest interest in cortisol and psychological functioning focused on clinical depression; many depressed patients have elevated basal cortisol levels and fail to suppress HPA activity in response to dexamethasone, a synthetic corticosteroid (Carroll et al., 1981). Researchers now suspect that disturbed regulation of the HPA system in clinical depression and other, possibly related, clinical syndromes (e.g., anorexia nervosa) may be the result of feedback mechanism dysregulation. Young and her colleagues (Young et al., 1991) demonstrated weakened fast feedback in depressed adults; depressed subjects did not show the expected suppression of precursor hormones in response to exogenous increases in cortisol. As noted, the animal literature is fairly clear in showing that chronic or repeated stress-elevated concentrations of glucocorticoids in the brain down-regulate the receptors involved in the fast negative feedback studied by Young and her colleagues (Jacobson & Salposky, 1991; Young et al., 1990).

The links between weakened fast feedback and depression in childhood and adolescence are not clear at this point. Cortisol hypersecretion has sometimes been shown among clinically depressed children and adolescents (Puig-Antich, 1982), but at least one methodologically sound study of depressed adolescents has shown that these subjects have normal levels of cortisol over nearly all the daily cycle (Dahl et al., 1991). Furthermore, although failure to suppress cortisol with dexamethasone is noted in a large percentage of adult patients with major depression, it is less characteristic in childhood and adolescent depression (Goodyer, Herbert, Moor, & Altham, 1991). Indeed, in one recent study, adolescents with more severe depression actually showed greater suppression of cortisol in response to dexamethasone (Birmaher et al., 1992). There is now evidence that ACTH may be down-regulated in response to CRH challenge in a subset of clinically depressed children by the age of 8–12 years (Ryan & Dahl, 1993). Down-regulation of ACTH may explain the apparently normal concentrations of cortisol observed in these studies of depressed children and adolescents.

Internalizing Behavior Problems

Several research groups have reported that depressed adults frequently exhibited internalizing behavior problems as children, and this pathway has also now been demonstrated in several prospective studies as well (Robins, 1966, 1986; Rutter, 1970). Thus, it may be useful to seek antecedents of adult depression in the relations between internalizing behavior problems and HPA reactivity in children. These relations have been examined in two studies. Granger and Stansbury examined preschool children who scored in the clinical range for internalizing and externalizing behavior problems. In response to novel social settings, which should theoretically elicit distress in internalizing children, greater increases in cortisol were associated with higher scores on measures of social withdrawal, unhappiness, and anxiety (see Granger, Stansbury, & Henker, 1994).

In contrast, McBurnett et al. (1991) did not find that 8–16-year-old boys with anxiety disorders alone (i.e., in the absence of conduct disorder) exhibited higher cortisol levels. However, boys with both anxiety and conduct disorders had elevated cortisol levels relative to the other clinically diagnosed subjects in the study. This finding suggests that a focus on emotion behavior associated with affective withdrawal, fear, and anxiety may be too exclusive. HPA reactivity during childhood may also be related to negative affects associated with approach, anger in response to loss of control, externalizing behavior, and conduct disorder.

Distress in Response to Limitations and Approach Emotions

Behavioral tendencies toward distress in response to limitations, a low tolerance of frustration, anger, and aggression are considered to be orthogonal to those behavioral tendencies discussed in relation to emotion withdrawal. Rothbart (1981) has shown that there is only a low correlation in infancy between temperaments characterized by a fear of novelty and those characterized by distress in response to limitations; however, in older children, internalizing and externalizing behavior problems are often exhibited by the same child (Puig-Antich, 1982; Wolff, 1971). Therefore, although we have just discussed evidence indicating a relation between adrenocortical reactivity and behavioral inhibition, it is also possible that similar reactivity forms part of the physiological substrate for anger, aggression, and other negative dispositions associated with approach in response to psychological stress.

The evidence that HPA reactivity is associated with a temperament prone to greater distress in response to limitations comes from research on the effects on infants of separation from the mother. In several studies of 9-month-old infants, Rothbart's (1981) Infant Behavior Questionnaire was used to predict behavioral and salivary cortisol responses to a 30-min separation from the mother. A temperament prone to distress in response to limitations predicted distress and cortisol responses on separation, while one characterized by a fear of novelty did not (Gunnar, Larson, et al., 1992). Thus, babies who showed greater HPA responses on losing control over access to their mothers were also the ones who cried and fussed more when forbidden objects were taken away, when they had to wait for food, when they were told no, and so on. A tendency to resist or react against threats to personal control may be the common factor in these results (Frankenhaeuser, 1980).

Angry reactions to loss of control are also a core component of the Type A, coronary-disease-prone behavior pattern (Glass, 1977). Impatience, time urgency, high standards, aggressivity, and hostility are characteristic of Type A individuals (Rosenman & Chesney, 1980). Although most often studied in relation to the activity of the sympathetic nervous system, HPA activity and Type A behavior have been directly examined in several studies (Frankenhaeuser & Lundberg, 1985). As long as Type A individuals experience personal control, they do not have higher cortisol levels or greater cortisol reactivity than Type B individuals, even though they frequently choose to work harder, faster, and to higher standards. Type As do show greater HPA reactivity than Type Bs, however, when they must perform tedious, boring tasks and have little control over the work environment.

It is not clear that Type A behavior patterns can be identified in children under the age of 5 years (Matthews & Angulo, 1980). In preschool children, behavior labeled as Type A primarily reflects aggression and a low tolerance of frustration, and it is not clear that these behaviors are the antecedents of later Type A coronary-prone patterns. Furthermore, Lundberg (1986) has found few relations in preschoolers between these behaviors and either sympathetic or adrenocortical measures.

Externalizing Behaviors and Conduct Disorder

Aggression and a low tolerance of frustration during the preschool years have more often been examined as antecedents of later externalizing behavior disorders than as antecedents of Type A behavior patterns (see Hinshaw, 1987). In the studies described earlier, the children identified as displaying clinically significant externalizing behavior patterns (Granger et al., 1994) or conduct disorders (McBurnett et al., 1991) were not found to show elevated levels of cortisol in response to novel social settings. If anything, children scoring in the clinical range for the use of anger, aggression, hostility, and destructiveness in their social interactions (unless coupled with an anxiety disorder) exhibited significantly lower cortisol concentrations than did the other children. These data suggest that, rather than being associated with elevations in cortisol, externalizing behavior disorders may be linked to a buffering of the HPA system in social situations.

If children with externalizing behavior disorders are buffered from experiencing HPA activation in many social settings, how might this be integrated with an understanding of HPA activity and emotion regulation? In animal research, there is some evidence that a reflexive kind of fighting that is elicited under stressful conditions in rats can lower or buffer the HPA response to foot shock (Connor, Vernikos-Danellis, & Levine, 1971). Thus, some kinds of aggressive behavior may be akin to adjunctive activities known to lower the HPA response to otherwise stressful stimulation. Alternatively, Sroufe (1983) has reported that, for some children (those classified insecure/avoidant), hurting other children appears to be pleasurable. For such children, bullying others may be a form of diversion that they can use to make themselves feel good and to "tune out" other emotionally distressing stimuli. Finally, children who use aggression frequently and who are "good" at it may also believe that aggressive, externalizing behaviors give them control over events. If extremely aggressive, externalizing behaviorally disordered children are shown to be buffered from HPA reactions to stress when they have the opportunity to engage in externalizing behaviors, any or all of these explanations might account for the pattern of HPA activity observed.

Although children exhibiting externalizing behaviors in the clinical range appear to be somewhat buffered from HPA responding in their peer relations, the opposite may be true of children exhibiting normal or nonclinical levels of these behaviors. In several pilot studies, we have examined HPA activity in a laboratory preschool by sampling children's saliva for cortisol determination repeatedly just prior to snack time. Most children exhibited a narrow range of values over days, with variation within the error of measurement of the cortisol assay. Some, however, showed greater variation and more days when cortisol was elevated. These "high reactor" children did not score higher on scales of internalizing or externalizing behavior problems. Indeed, all the children scored well within the nonclinical range on these scales. However, for boys especially, scoring higher on items specifically related to peer conflict and aggression was associated with HPA reactivity. These data suggest that, for normally developing children, conflict and aggression may activate the HPA system. Why these associations reverse for children with clinically relevant externalizing behavior is not clear but may be an important avenue of inquiry.

SUMMARY AND CONCLUSIONS

Activity of the HPA system does appear to be related to emotion regulation processes in children. The conditions known to modulate HPA activity in animals, adults, and children correspond well to the behavioral strategies often discussed in the domain of emotion regulation. Individual differences in emotion processes related to negative emotion temperaments appear to be associated with individual differences in HPA reactivity among normally developing children, with both fearful, inhibited temperaments and distressed, angry temperaments being associated with greater HPA reactivity. Among children exhibiting behavior problems in the clinical range, however, it may be the "internalizing" patterns that are associated with greater HPA reactivity.

The body of research concerning the psychobiology of the HPA system strongly suggests that associations between emotion regulation styles and HPA activity are not merely correlations, that they do indeed reflect potential causal connections. HPA activation and regulation has been shown in animals both to influence and to be influenced by emotions and their corresponding behavioral and psychological processes. Despite a reasonable body of research that now exists on children, many questions regarding the relations between HPA activity and emotion processes remain to be examined. In addressing these questions, it may be useful to consider several periods of the HPA response. Most of the work on children involves the interrelations between emotion and adrenocortical systems during the first 10–15 min of the stress response. This would include the initial activation of the system and the subsequent emotion and physiological processes involved in continuing or terminating the response. Little attention has been paid to more slowly developing effects of HPA activity on the central nervous system in children, particularly with regard to its influence on children's memories for stressful events and the emotion regulation strategies that they employed during the event. Studies of change or continuity of these interconnections over several exposures to a stressor, as well as between earlier and later points in the activation and regulation process, will be especially important to our understanding of the regulation of affective behavior.

FRONTAL ELECTROENCEPHALOGRAPHIC CORRELATES OF INDIVIDUAL DIFFERENCES IN EMOTION EXPRESSION IN INFANTS: A BRAIN SYSTEMS PERSPECTIVE ON EMOTION

Geraldine Dawson

An emotion can be characterized by both the type of emotion expressed (e.g., sadness vs. happiness) and the intensity with which it is expressed. This distinction is believed to be important because it is likely that individual differences in these two aspects of emotion vary independently and account for different dimensions of temperament, personality, and vulnerability to psychopathology. In this essay, I review empirical evidence that suggests that these two aspects of emotion expression are associated with distinct and independent patterns of frontal electroencephalographic (EEG) activity in infants. The essay concludes by considering the role of the frontal lobe and related brain systems in emotion expression and regulation from a developmental perspective. This discussion highlights the importance of frontal lobe development in developmental changes in emotion regulation during the first years of life.

The financial support of the National Institute of Mental Health (grant MH47117) and the John D. and Catherine T. MacArthur Foundation is gratefully acknowledged. Appreciation also is expressed to the mothers and infants who participated in the studies reported and to several people whose contributions were essential to this work: Heracles Panagiotides, Laura Grofer Klinger, Susan Spieker, Don Allen, Kari Blanchard, Julie Johnson, Esther Kim, Justine Loebel, Diana Patterson, Al Ross, and Susan Tapert. Direct correspondence to Geraldine Dawson, Psychology Department, NI-25, University of Washington, Seattle, WA 98195.

FRONTAL LOBE ACTIVATION AND EMOTION

As evinced in the early writings of Darwin (1872/1965), James (1884), and Cannon (1927), those who study emotion have a long tradition of using psychophysiological measures and constructs. The most frequently used among them have focused on the autonomic nervous system. Measures of heart rate, blood pressure, finger pulse volume, and skin conductance have been thought to index a variety of psychological processes, including generalized emotional arousal (Duffy, 1962; Schachter, 1964), receptivity to sensory intake (Lacey, 1967), specific type of emotion expression (Ekman, Levenson, & Friesen, 1983), covert emotion state (Schwartz, Brown, & Ahern, 1980), and valence of emotional response (Petty & Cacioppo, 1983), among others. Autonomic indices have also been used in studies of infant emotion. For example, measures of heart rate and vagal tone have been found to be associated with individual differences in infant emotional reactivity and emotion regulation (Fox, 1989; Kagan, Reznik, & Snidman, 1987; Porges, 1991; see also Porges, Doussard-Roosevelt, & Maiti, in this volume).

These studies have provided unequivocal evidence that the expression of an emotion is associated with reliable changes in autonomic activity. Current research efforts are aimed at establishing the directional causality and specificity of autonomic correlates of emotions and at determining the degree to which certain autonomic measures are indicative of individual differences in emotion expression and regulation.

Relatively less attention has been paid to the relation between emotion and electrocortical activity. For example, in a recent book in which research on psychophysiological correlates of emotion was reviewed (Wagner, 1988), there were 18 references to measures of heart rate and emotion and only three to EEG activity. The measures of EEG used in these studies were generally global in nature, involving generalized suppression of alpha frequency.

One exception to this tendency to ignore electrocortical activity in studies of emotion is the series of studies of asymmetrical frontal EEG activity and emotion conducted by Fox and Davidson and their respective colleagues. The results of these studies, which involved both adults and young infants, indicate that asymmetries in frontal lobe activation and function are related to the expression of different emotions (Davidson, 1984a, 1984b; Davidson & Fox, 1982, 1988, 1989; Dawson, Panagiotides, Grofer Klinger, & Hill, 1992; Fox & Davidson, 1986, 1987, 1988; Tucker, 1981). Specifically, relatively stronger right frontal activation has been found during crying and sadness and relatively stronger left frontal activation during happiness and anger.

Originally, it was speculated that frontal activation asymmetries were dependent on the valence of an emotion. More recently, however, both

Davidson and Fox (Davidson, Ekman, Saron, Senulis, & Friesen, 1990; Fox, 1991) have argued that frontal lobe asymmetries are linked to innate action tendencies, namely, the tendency to approach and explore (left) or to withdraw and flee from (right) the external environment. Thus, frontal asymmetries are believed to be linked to the directional component of emotions. Moreover, evidence suggests that frontal activation asymmetries can serve as indices of individual differences in infants' responses to emotionally stressful situations. Davidson and Fox (1989) found that infants with greater right than left frontal activation during a baseline condition were more likely to cry when later separated from their mothers.

My colleagues and I (Dawson, Grofer Klinger, Panagiotides, Hill, & Spieker, 1992; Dawson, Grofer Klinger, Panagiotides, Spieker, & Frey, 1992) found that, compared with infants of nondepressed mothers, infants raised by mothers experiencing depression exhibited reduced left frontal activity during a baseline and a playful condition. Davidson and Fox (1988) have hypothesized that baseline frontal activation asymmetries represent biological differences corresponding to a "vulnerability" to experience negative affect in stressful situations. According to this view, individuals exhibiting asymmetries favoring right frontal activation have a lower threshold for the experience of such right-hemisphere-mediated emotions as distress and irritability. Furthermore, Dawson (Dawson, Grofer Klinger, Panagiotides, Hill, & Spieker, 1992; Dawson, Grofer Klinger, Panagiotides, Spieker, & Frey, 1992) has argued that socialization, particularly parents' responses to the infant's emotional behavior (Malatesta & Haviland, 1982), can influence tonic frontal activation asymmetries.

TYPE AND INTENSITY OF EMOTION EXPRESSION IN INFANTS ARE INDEXED BY DISTINCT AND INDEPENDENT PATTERNS OF FRONTAL EEG ACTIVITY

In this essay, I explore further the relation between emotion expression and frontal EEG activity in infants. It is proposed that measures of frontal EEG activity can serve to index not only the type of emotion expression (e.g., happiness vs. sadness), as demonstrated by Fox and Davidson, but also the intensity with which emotions are expressed. The notion that emotions can be characterized by both their direction (approach-withdrawal or valence) and their intensity has long been held by emotion theorists (e.g., Duffy, 1962; Schachter, 1964; Tomkins, 1984). Like Duffy and others, I believe that this distinction is important because it is likely that individual differences in these two dimensions of emotion expression vary independently and account for different aspects of temperament, personality, and psychopathology. For example, in his study of infant reactivity, Fox (1989) found that 5-month-old infants with high vagal tone were more emotionally reactive to both positive and mildly stressful stimuli. These same infants were more positively reactive to novel events at 14 months and also more reactive to separation from the mother (i.e., they cried more quickly after their mother's departure).

Hence, the vagal tone measure indexed not the type of emotion displayed but rather the degree of reactivity to both positive and negative events. In contrast, frontal EEG asymmetries typically have been found to be associated with the expression of different types of emotions or the vulnerability to display different types of emotions (Davidson, 1984a, 1984b; Davidson & Fox, 1982, 1988, 1989; Dawson, Panagiotides, Grofer Klinger, & Hill, 1992; Fox & Davidson, 1986, 1987, 1988; Tucker, 1981). In subsequent sections, I provide evidence that these two different components of emotion are associated with distinct and independent patterns of frontal EEG activity.

Specifically, our studies support the following hypothesis: Whereas the *type* of emotion expression is associated with asymmetries in frontal EEG activity, the *intensity* of emotion expression is associated with generalized activation of both the right and the frontal regions, regardless of type of emotion. Measures of intensity consist of both the time it takes to respond to an emotion stimulus and the level of emotional response (mild to strong). These two measures have been found to be highly correlated in our studies. A corollary of this hypothesis is the following: Measures of *asymmetrical frontal activity* will be better predictors of individual differences in the tendency to express certain emotions, such as distress and sadness, whereas measures of *generalized frontal activity* will be better predictors of individual differences in emotional reactivity and emotion intensity. Three sets of data, derived from studies of infant emotion and EEG activity, will be described that support these hypotheses.

INTENSE EMOTIONS ARE ACCOMPANIED BY GENERALIZED INCREASES IN FRONTAL LOBE ACTIVATION IN INFANTS

I turn now to the evidence collected in two independent studies that supports the proposal that the type and intensity of emotion expressed by infants are associated with distinct patterns of frontal EEG activity (Dawson, Panagiotides, Grofer, & Hill, 1991; Dawson, Panagiotides, Grofer Klinger, & Hill, 1992). In both studies, my colleagues and I examined the relation between measures of frontal and parietal lobe activation (as revealed by EEG recordings) and individual differences in emotion expression in young infants.

Study 1 involved 21 infants, aged 21 months, and Study 2 14 infants between 12 and 15 months of age; male and female infants were equally represented in both cases. Indices of frontal lobe activation consisted of measures of right and left frontal EEG power in the 6–9 Hz frequency range, a dominant high-frequency band in infants. On the basis of the traditional notion that increased brain activation is characterized by desynchronized alpha EEG activity (Berger, 1930), reductions in EEG power in infant "alpha" (indexed by decreased EEG amplitude in the 6–9 Hz frequency range) were interpreted as evidence of increased brain activation. Frontal lobe activation was examined in terms of (a) asymmetries and (b) levels of generalized activation of both right and left frontal regions. It was predicted that frontal activation asymmetries would be associated with displays of specific emotions whereas generalized frontal activation would be associated with the intensity with which emotions were displayed, regardless of the type of emotion.

The experimental paradigm was the same for both studies. During EEG recording, infants sat in a high chair while being exposed to several conditions designed to elicit different emotions. We were especially interested in the conditions that were designed to elicit the lowest and highest levels of emotion intensity, namely, the baseline and separation-from-mother conditions. In the baseline condition, infants observed bubbles cascading from behind a black curtain situated across from them. In the separation-from-mother condition, mothers were asked to wave goodbye, walk slowly toward the door, and then leave the room. Infants were videotaped from a camera hidden behind a curtain situated directly in front of them. A videotimer recorded continuous time on the videotapes and was synchronized with EEG recording.

As illustrated in Figures 1 and 2, in both studies we found that *both* the left and the right frontal regions became highly activated in the separation-from-mother condition, during which the infants expressed intense emotions (all infants cried). This pattern was reflected in our statistical analyses by a strong condition × region (frontal vs. parietal) interaction effect obtained in both studies.

Note that the direction of EEG asymmetry in the frontal region recorded while the infants were separated from their mothers differs for the 21-month-old (Fig. 1) and the 12–15-month-old (Fig. 2) samples. Although these asymmetries were not found to be statistically significant, it is interesting to note that coding of the infants' facial expressions—using Ekman's Facial Action Coding System (EM-FACS; Ekman & Friesen, 1984)—revealed that the 12–15-month-old infants tended to express anger during separation whereas the 21-month-old infants more often expressed sadness. Thus, the asymmetries are consistent with previous research indicating that anger is mediated by the left frontal region and sadness by the right. I wish to underscore, however, that these rather subtle asymmetries were

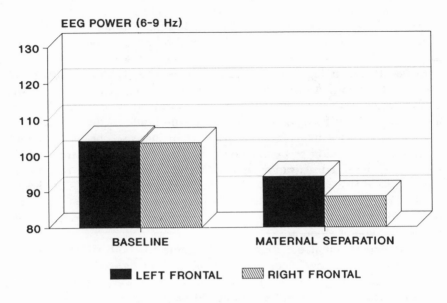

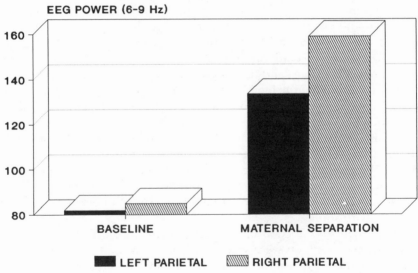

FIG. 1.—Frontal and parietal EEG power (6–9 Hz) recorded from 21-month-old infants ($N = 21$) during conditions of low (baseline) vs. high (separation from mother) emotion intensity. Lower power indicates increased brain activation. (Reproduced with permission from Dawson, Panagiotides, Grofer Klinger, & Hill, 1992.)

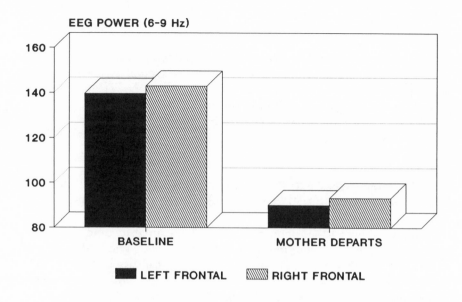

EEG POWER (6-9 Hz)

■ LEFT FRONTAL　▨ RIGHT FRONTAL

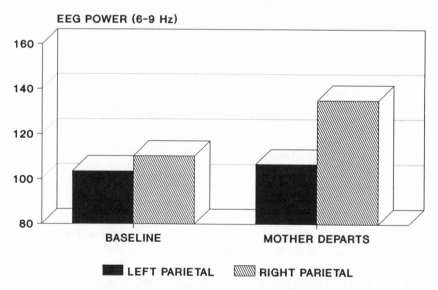

EEG POWER (6-9 Hz)

■ LEFT PARIETAL　▨ RIGHT PARIETAL

FIG. 2.—Frontal and parietal EEG power (6–9 Hz) recorded from 12–15-month-old infants (N = 14) during conditions of low (baseline) vs. high (separation from mother) emotion intensity. Lower power indicates increased brain activation. (From Dawson, Panagiotides, Grofer, & Hill, 1991.)

superimposed on a more robust pattern of activation of both the left and the right frontal regions.

Importantly, separate measures of right and left frontal activation (EEG power) bore no statistical relation to measures of frontal asymmetries. Correlations between measures of right and left frontal power and measures of frontal asymmetries (right minus left frontal power) ranged from −.08 to .08. Thus, these measures appear to be tapping independent aspects of brain activity.

INDIVIDUAL DIFFERENCES IN GENERALIZED FRONTAL ACTIVATION ARE PREDICTIVE OF THE INTENSITY OF INFANTS' EMOTIONAL RESPONSE

In the study of 12–15-month-old infants, the intensity of infant distress during the separation-from-mother condition was coded on a 13-point scale developed by Thompson and Lamb (1984). The scale assesses variations in infant vocal activity, ranging from positive vocalization to fussing to hyperventilated crying, with an emphasis on distress vocalizations. Measures of latency to the onset of distress were also taken. We predicted that there would be significant correlations between level of *both* right and left frontal activation and the intensity of infants' behavioral distress.

As predicted, increases in both right and left frontal activation (lower EEG power) when the infants were separated from their mothers were strongly and equally associated with higher intensity of behavioral distress (r's = −.72 and −.69, right and left frontal, respectively, p's < .005) and shorter latencies to the onset of distress (r's = .62 and .61, p's < .01). Peak intensity ratings and latency to the onset of distress were highly correlated (r = −.88, p < .000). Importantly, baseline measures of right and left frontal activation were also predictive of the intensity of distress (r's = −.48 and −.49, right and left frontal, respectively, p's < .05). In contrast, no significant correlations were obtained between measures of frontal and parietal asymmetries and either intensity of distress or latencies to the onset of distress. Thus, the measures of generalized frontal activation were found to be better predictors of the intensity of emotional distress than were measures of frontal asymmetry.

Another aim of the study was to determine whether measures of frontal lobe activation were predictive of an infant's emotional behavior in situations outside the psychophysiology laboratory. These measures were taken on a different day than that of psychophysiological testing and consisted of the infants' attachment classifications and ratings of disorganization (Main & Solomon, 1990). Thompson and his colleagues (Frodi & Thompson, 1985; Thompson & Lamb, 1984) found that infants who differed in their attachment classifications also differed in the peak intensity of their negative affective expression during separation episodes with their mothers. Avoidant (A) infants showed the lowest level of distress, longest latency to the onset of distress, and quickest recovery time; in contrast, resistant (C) infants exhibited the highest level of distress, shortest latency to the onset of distress, and longest recovery time. Securely attached (B) infants showed patterns that fell in between these two extremes.

Using Main and Solomon's system, five of the 14 infants in the 12–15-month-old sample were classified as insecure; one of these had a primary classification of A, and four had a primary classification of disorganized (D). The remaining nine were classified as B. Attachment classification was unrelated to any of the EEG measures. However, an infant's level of disorganization (as measured by Main and Solomon's nine-point rating scale) was significantly correlated with measures of both right and left frontal brain activation obtained during the separation-from-mother condition in the psychophysiology assessment (r's $= -.59$ and $-.64$, right and left frontal, respectively, p's $< .01$). Infants who exhibited greater frontal activation were rated as more disorganized. Frontal EEG asymmetries and parietal EEG measures were not correlated with either ratings of disorganization or secure/insecure classifications.

FACIAL EXPRESSIONS OF NEGATIVE EMOTIONS ARE ACCOMPANIED BY BOTH ASYMMETRICAL AND GENERALIZED ACTIVATION OF THE FRONTAL LOBE

The final piece of evidence supporting the hypothesis that generalized frontal activation indexes intensity and asymmetrical activation type of emotion expression is based on measures of EEG taken while infants were displaying either neutral facial expressions or facial expressions indicative of intense negative emotions (anger and sadness). In the study of 21-month-old infants described above, videotapes of infant behavior recorded during all emotion-eliciting conditions were coded using EM-FACS (Ekman & Friesen, 1984), which yielded measures of specific instances of facial expressions of sadness and anger as well as neutral expressions. Figure 3 displays frontal and parietal EEG power obtained from the right and left hemispheres during neutral, sad, and angry emotion expressions.

Consistent with previous research, asymmetrical activation of the right and left frontal brain regions was found during specific facial expressions of emotion (sad vs. angry). Relatively greater left frontal activation occurred during angry expressions and relatively greater right frontal activation during sad expressions. Moreover, these small asymmetries in frontal lobe activation found to exist during specific facial expressions of emotion were superimposed on more pronounced, significant increases in activation of

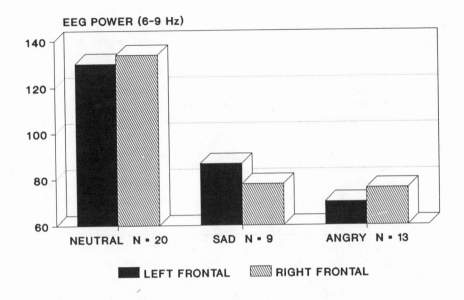

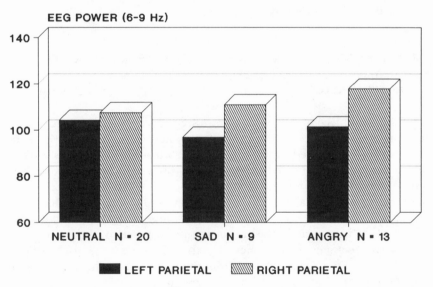

FIG. 3.—Frontal and parietal EEG power (6–9 Hz) recorded from 21-month-old infants during facial expressions of low (neutral) vs. high (sadness and anger) emotion intensity. Lower power indicates increased brain activation. (Reproduced with permission from Dawson, Panagiotides, Grofer Klinger, & Hill, 1992.)

both the right and the left frontal regions. Notably, these generalized increases in frontal lobe activation were obtained during facial expressions of both happiness (approach) and sadness (withdrawal), indicating that the generalized frontal activation was not linked to the specific type of facial expression.

SUMMARY OF EMPIRICAL FINDINGS

I have presented evidence that infants exhibit increased activation of both the right and the left frontal regions during intense emotion states (induced by separation from the mother) and during intense negative emotions (anger and sadness). Increases in parietal activation were not found to occur during intense emotion, a finding that underscores the role of the frontal lobe in emotion. As hypothesized, infants who became distressed more quickly and more intensely when separated from their mothers exhibited higher levels of generalized frontal activation.

Specifically, measures of both right and left frontal lobe activation taken during a baseline condition and during separation from the mother predicted the level of intensity of the infants' distress; in contrast, measures of frontal asymmetry were not found to be related to the intensity of distress. Furthermore, measures of generalized frontal activation, but not of frontal asymmetry, taken in the psychophysiology laboratory during the separation-from-mother condition were found to be related to the infants' degree of behavioral disorganization in the Strange Situation when observed on a separate day. Infants who displayed higher levels of generalized frontal brain activation when separated from their mothers were rated as more disorganized during the Strange Situation. Measures of parietal activation were unrelated to the infants' emotional behavior either in the psychophysiology laboratory or in the Strange Situation.

Asymmetrical frontal activation, on the other hand, was found to be associated with the type of emotion displayed. Replicating previous studies conducted by Fox and Davidson, my colleagues and I found that infants' angry facial expressions were associated with relative left frontal activation and sad facial expressions with relative right frontal activation.

These results extend the work of Davidson and Fox (e.g., Davidson et al., 1990; Fox, 1991; see also Fox, in this volume) on the relation between frontal lobe activation and infant emotion. We have demonstrated that it is important to distinguish between the type and the intensity of emotion expression and that distinct patterns of frontal lobe activation accompany these two dimensions of emotion expression. Specifically, we have discovered that generalized frontal activation is an important correlate of emotion, indexing the intensity, but not the type, of emotion expression. Furthermore, we found that measures of generalized frontal activation provided a better predictor of the intensity of infant emotion expression than did measures of asymmetrical activation of the frontal lobes. The theoretical implications of these findings are discussed in the next section.

WHAT DO MEASURES OF FRONTAL EEG ACTIVITY REFLECT?

What processes are indexed by measures of frontal EEG activity? In considering the role of the frontal lobe in emotion expression and regulation, it is useful to view this region in the context of a group of interrelated cortical and subcortical brain structures known to be involved in emotion. Papez (1937) was one of the first to attempt to build a model of emotion firmly anchored in neuroanatomy. Elaborating on earlier notions introduced by Cannon (1927), Papez proposed that the hypothalamus (interacting in conjunction with the thalamus, cingulate gyrus, and hippocampus) mediates emotion expression and the neocortex emotion experience. Eventually, the concept of a *limbic system* evolved, designating an emotion system of the brain consisting of cortical (orbital frontal, anterior temporal, cingulate gyrus, and hippocampus) and subcortical (amygdala, hypothalamus, brain-stem reticular formation) regions (MacLean, 1952). On the basis of studies of animals who had undergone selective brain lesions or electrical stimulation, hypotheses eventually evolved regarding the unique contribution of each brain region of the limbic system to emotion.

Recently, LeDoux (1987) has proposed a neuroanatomical model of emotion in which the amygdala is centrally involved in coding the biological significance of stimuli (see Fig. 4). Like previous theorists, LeDoux suggested that neocortical regions, especially those involved in language and other higher cognitive functions, mediate emotion experience (conscious awareness of emotion). According to LeDoux, primitive emotional responses can be processed rapidly at the subcortical level (amygdala). This type of emotion processing requires only crude stimulus representations that activate hard-wired, species-typical behaviors related to survival. Complex emotion stimuli, such as the facial expressions of others, are believed to require the perceptual capabilities of the neocortex. In this case, reciprocal cortical-subcortical interactions are involved in the mediation of emotional behavior, as illustrated in Figure 4.

Generalized frontal lobe activation during emotion may reflect, in part, the relatively diffuse influence of subcortical structures on the cortex. In particular, the ascending influences of the brain-stem reticular activating system serve to increase the infant's "readiness" to receive and respond to external stimuli (Steriade, 1981), as would be adaptive when the infant is separated from the mother. Recent physiological evidence suggests that

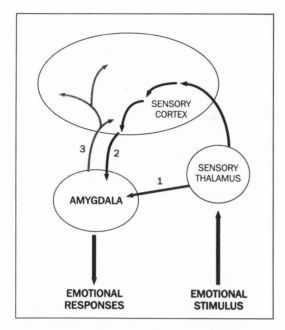

Fig. 4.—Thalamo-amygdala and thalamo-cortico-amygdala emotion-processing pathways. According to LeDoux, the emotional significance of sensory stimuli is processed by multiple input systems to the amygdala. In some situations, emotional reactions may be based entirely on primitive stimulus representations received from the thalamus (1). In other situations, the amygdala may start emotional reactions on the basis of primitive sensory representations derived from the thalamus (1) but may then utilize higher-order information derived from the cortex (2) to fine-tune the reaction. In still other situations, the emotional reaction may be based entirely on cortical inputs to the amygdala (2). The amygdala also projects to widespread areas of the cortex (3), possibly allowing emotion processing to influence cognitive processing. (Reproduced with permission from LeDoux, 1991.)

the brain mechanism of electrocortical desynchronization involves reticular activation of thalamocortical neurons, which in turn have inhibitory influences on cortical interneurons (Gonzalez-Lima, 1989; Gonzalez-Lima & Scheich, 1985; Steriade, 1980).

Physiological and behavioral studies indicate that reciprocal relations exist between the reticular formation and the frontal cortex (Heilman, Watson, Valenstein, & Goldberg, 1987). It has been hypothesized (Heilman et al., 1987; Skinner & Yingling, 1977) that, whereas arousal and alerting responses are mediated by the ascending influences on the cortex of the reticular formation, the reciprocal frontocortical-thalamic-reticular system prepares the aroused organism to respond to a meaningful stimulus.

What do frontal asymmetries reflect? As indicated earlier, Davidson and Fox (Davidson et al., 1990; Fox, 1991) have argued that frontal lobe asymmetries are linked to innate action tendencies, namely, the tendency to approach and explore (left) versus withdraw and flee from (right) the external environment. Although the notion of frontal lobe mediation of innate action tendencies, such as approach and withdrawal, is intuitively appealing, there is some evidence to suggest that such action tendencies can be mediated by lower centers in the brain. As early as the first part of the nineteenth century, it was established that many forms of fully integrated emotional responses, including rage, escape, and attack responses as well as fear and pleasure, do not depend on the cerebral cortex. LeDoux (1987) has provided a thorough review of the evidence suggesting that primitive emotional responses related to survival can be mediated at the subcortical level. Indeed, rage, escape, attack, fear, and exploratory behaviors can be observed in decorticate animals. Interestingly, however, the emotional responses of decorticate animals are often extreme and unusually easily elicited, suggesting that the cortical regions are important for the regulation of emotional behavior.

It is known that the frontal lobe is involved in higher-level processing of the meaning of environmental stimuli and in the regulation of voluntary motor behavior. As LeDoux (1987) has argued, the subcortical regions are capable of forming only primitive sensory representations of the stimulus, which allow for the hard-wired, rapid responses necessary for survival. The frontal lobe, on the other hand, is involved in forming internal representations of reward and punishment that are based on experience and that can be generalized from one stimulus to another (Goldman-Rakic, 1987; Jones & Mishkin, 1972), in inhibiting prepotent responses (Diamond, 1990), and in monitoring temporal sequences and contingencies (Fuster, 1989). Dawson has described how the emergence of emotion regulation behaviors during infancy is linked to the early development of frontal lobe functions (see Dawson, Panagiotides, Grofer Klinger, & Hill, 1992). As noted by Diamond and Goldman-Rakic (Diamond, 1990; Diamond & Goldman-Rakic, 1989), periods of rapid frontal lobe development in humans and monkeys (Chugani, 1994; Huttenlocher, 1979, 1994) coincide with the acquisition of specific inhibitory behaviors, such as those involved in the delayed-response test used with nonhuman primates and object-permanence tasks used with human infants.

I propose that, rather than reflecting innate approach/withdrawal responses, frontal activation asymmetries that accompany specific facial expressions of emotion may reflect regulation/coping strategies. As pointed out by Dodge and Garber (1991), the regulatory significance of facial expressions was recognized by early theorists (Darwin, 1872/1965). For example, the facial expression of disgust reduces contact with distasteful food by expelling the unpleasant stimulus.

During development, as facial expressions of emotion come under voluntary control and acquire social communicative value, they increasingly function as regulators of emotion. Crying, for example, can be used to signal to the parent the need for regulatory assistance. As the young child develops, the ability to override and inhibit action tendencies by mobilizing intentional regulation strategies during states of high emotional arousal is an important achievement in the development of emotion regulation. After reviewing the experimental evidence mapping the prefrontal-premotor-motor pathways, Goldman-Rakic (1987) concluded that the frontal lobe could regulate the voluntary motor responses of any part of the upper body, including the head, mouth, and eyes, to react or not react to the environment. As the infant's motor responses come to be increasingly under voluntary control, they are likely to involve the frontal lobe. Examples of this kind of motor behavior include facial expressions that have intentional communicative value and directed gaze such as is observed in social referencing.

Considering the frontal lobe's involvement in inhibition and in planned, voluntary behavior, Dawson suggested that the right and left frontal regions are specialized for different kinds of emotion regulation/coping strategies (see Dawson, Panagiotides, Grofer Klinger, & Hill, 1992; for a similar view regarding hemispheric differences in self-regulation strategies, see also Tucker & Williamson, 1984). As Lazarus (1991) has suggested, these coping processes can be either consistent or in conflict with action tendencies and can override or inhibit them. We hypothesize that the left frontal region is specialized for regulation/coping strategies that involve sequentially organized action schemes, such as language. Left hemisphere regulation strategies, moreover, serve to maintain continuity and stability of the organism-environment relation and of ongoing motor schemes (Tucker & Williamson, 1984). The right frontal and parietal regions, on the other hand, appear to be specialized for processing novel stimuli that tend to disrupt ongoing activity. On the basis of several studies of normal and brain-damaged adults (e.g., Heilman, Schwartz, & Watson, 1978; Heilman & Van Den Abell, 1980), Heilman and his colleagues have demonstrated right hemisphere dominance for attention and response to novel information. Regulation strategies mediated by the right hemisphere, then, call for selection of novel actions rather than for continuity and elaboration of current actions.

We also propose that individual differences in frontal activation asymmetries may reflect experiential rather than innate factors. Given the paramount importance of the parents' participation in the infant's developing capacity for emotion regulation by explicitly teaching, directing, and scaffolding infant-initiated self-regulation behaviors (Garber & Dodge, 1991; Kopp, 1982, 1989; Stern, 1985; Tronick, 1989), it is very likely that socialization influences account, at least in part, for individual differences in frontal brain activity. Parents, for example, selectively reinforce positive facial expressions of emotion (Malatesta & Haviland, 1982), and the failure to provide such reinforcement can lead to diminished positive expression by an infant (Tronick, 1989). This is especially apparent in infants of depressed mothers, who have been found to be more irritable and less contingently responsive toward their infants (Cohn, Matias, Tronick, Connell, & Lyons-Ruth, 1986; Field, Healy, Goldstein, & Guthertz, 1990).

To explore therefore whether mothers' responsiveness affects infants' frontal brain activity, we recently examined the brain activity and emotional behavior of infants of depressed mothers (see Dawson, Grofer Klinger, Panagiotides, Hill, & Spieker, 1992; Dawson, Grofer Klinger, Panagiotides, Spieker, & Frey, 1992). We found that, compared with infants of nondepressed mothers, infants of depressed mothers showed less left frontal activation during baseline and during a playful condition designed to elicit positive affect. The two groups of infants did not differ significantly in their patterns of generalized frontal activation, however, suggesting that this aspect of frontal activity may be less susceptible to environmental influences than are patterns of frontal asymmetries. While the possibility of genetic influences cannot be ruled out, our data suggest that frontal asymmetries can be influenced by socialization. Longitudinal studies will be essential in gaining a richer understanding of environmental influences on frontal lobe activity in infants and children and in determining whether measures of frontal lobe activity can enable us to better predict who will be vulnerable to developing emotional disorders in later life.

The task of psychophysiologists is to understand the biological underpinnings and correlates of emotion appraisal, expression, and experience as well as of action tendencies and regulatory processes. Physiological measures hold the promise of providing information that supplements rather than duplicating measures of overt emotional behavior and subjective accounts of emotion experience. The advantage of using physiological measures is that they may offer unique insights into such phenomena as unconscious appraisals (LeDoux, 1987), predispositions to emotion tendencies and temperament (Finman, Davidson, Colton, Straus, & Kagan, 1989; Fox, 1991), and vulnerabilities to such emotional disorders as depression (Davidson, Schaffer, & Saron, 1985; Dawson, Grofer Klinger, Panagiotides, Hill, & Spieker, 1992; Dawson, Grofer Klinger, Panagiotides, Spieker, & Frey, 1992; Henriques & Davidson, 1990).

SUMMARY

Emotion expressions can be characterized by both the type of emotion displayed and the intensity with which the emotion is expressed. Individual differences in these two aspects of emotion appear to vary independently and may perhaps account for distinct dimensions of temperament, personality, and vulnerability to psychopathology. We reviewed several sets of data gathered in our laboratory that indicate that these two dimensions of emotion expression are associated with distinct and independent patterns of frontal EEG activity in infants. Specifically, whereas the type of emotion expression was found to be associated with asymmetries in frontal EEG activity, the intensity of emotion expression was found to be associated with generalized activation of both the right and the left frontal regions. Moreover, we reviewed and provided evidence that measures of asymmetrical frontal activity are better predictors of individual differences in the tendency to express certain emotions, such as distress and sadness, whereas measures of generalized frontal activity are better predictors of individual differences in emotional reactivity and emotion intensity.

The neuroanatomical bases of emotion were discussed with special reference to the role of the frontal lobe in emotion regulation. It was hypothesized that the frontal activation asymmetries that have been found to accompany emotion expressions reflect specific regulation strategies. The left frontal region is specialized for regulation strategies involving action schemes that serve to maintain continuity and stability of the organism-environment relation and of ongoing motor schemes, such as those involved in language and the expression of happiness and interest. In contrast, the right frontal region appears to be specialized for regulation strategies that involve processing novel stimuli that disrupt ongoing activity, such as might occur during the expression of fear, disgust, and distress. Furthermore, it was proposed that individual differences in patterns of frontal EEG asymmetries during emotion may be related to socialization influences rather than solely innate factors. It was speculated that the pattern of generalized frontal lobe activation that accompanies the experience of intense emotions may reflect, in part, the relatively diffuse influence of subcortical structures on the cortex and may serve to increase the infant's general readiness to receive and respond to significant external stimuli.

DYNAMIC CEREBRAL PROCESSES UNDERLYING EMOTION REGULATION

Nathan A. Fox

There is a large, although diverse, neuropsychological literature linking both subcortical and neocortical structures to the expression and perception of emotion (Borod, 1992; Stuss, Gow, & Hetherington, 1992). This literature has focused on studies of adults with various types of cerebral damage, injury, or psychopathology and has reported relations between the locus of damage or activity and emotion perception and expression. In the main, this literature suggests that the side of the brain that is damaged or hyperactive is of some significance to emotional behavior. Adults with damage to the right side are more likely to express positive types of emotions, while damage to the left side is associated with negative emotions. This is known as the *valence* model of brain-emotion relations (cf. Borod, 1992). The pattern of findings from this literature was one factor motivating researchers to study cerebral lateralization in normal human adults and infants and its effect on emotion behaviors (Davidson, 1984a; Fox & Davidson, 1984). If damage to one side of the brain affected the expression or perception of certain emotions, then perhaps the source for these competencies in the intact brain could be identified and insights into normal emotional behavior gained.

An important distinction that has been drawn by these studies is that brain injury or surgical intervention has differential effects on the perception versus the expression of affect (Silberman & Weingartner, 1986). These differential effects depend on whether damage was anterior or posterior in the hemisphere. In general, damage, injury, or activation of posterior re-

Support for writing this essay and for the research presented in it was provided by a grant to Nathan A. Fox from the National Institutes of Health (HD 17899) and to the Graduate School at the University of Maryland for a Semester Award.

gions of the right hemisphere affected the perception of affect. Damage, injury, or activation of anterior foci of either the right or the left hemisphere was associated with changes in expression of emotion. There has been widespread agreement that changes in the perception of the affective quality of a stimulus (in the visual or auditory domains) are associated with insult to the right hemisphere (Ahern et al., 1991; Bryden & Ley, 1983). There has been less agreement with regard to the lateralization of function in the expression of affect. Recent reviews contain evidence both for a valence interpretation (e.g., left hemisphere control of positive emotion, right hemisphere control of negative emotions; Silberman & Weingartner, 1986) and for right hemisphere dominance of all types of emotion expression (Borod, 1992).

THREE MECHANISMS UNDERLYING THE REGULATION OF EMOTION

A reanalysis of the data from the clinical areas of this research literature suggests that three different neural processes or brain mechanisms may underlie the regulation of emotional behavior: (a) contralateral disinhibition of cortical centers; (b) ipsilateral (top-down) disinhibition of subcortical centers; and (c) excitation of specific subcortical or neocortical centers. These mechanisms may be inferred from two literatures, one on the effects on emotional mood after the administration of sodium amytal prior to neurosurgery for epilepsy, the second on the effects of mood change due to insult such as cerebral stroke.

The Evidence from Studies of Sodium Amytal

Sodium amytal is often injected into the carotid artery during a surgical procedure conducted on patients who have intractable epilepsy. The procedure is designed to enable the physician to identify the area of language facility in the brain, prior to an attempt to eliminate the focus of the epileptic seizure in brain tissue. The procedure is known as the WADA test and has been used for a number of years by neurosurgeons. The early studies of unilateral injection of sodium amytal into the left carotid artery reported production of severe emotional reactions (Perria, Rosadini, & Rossi, 1961; Serafetinides, Hoare, & Driver, 1965; Terrazian, 1964). Descriptions of individual patients' behaviors including crying, pessimistic statements, feelings of nothingness, indignity or despair, and an inability to hold back fears or negative thoughts even though, in some instances, the patient simultaneously reported no apparent reason for such feelings. Unilateral injection into the right carotid artery elicited an opposite response that has been characterized as a euphoric reaction, including smiling, optimism, and an overall sense of well-being. A recent review of data from a number of studies points to a relation between side of injection and affective response (Lee, Loring, Meader, & Brooks, 1990).

In general, the results of the WADA test studies have been interpreted to mean that mood changes are the result of the release of one hemisphere from the contralateral inhibitory influences of the other. Thus, when not counterbalanced, the right hemisphere would produce dysphoria and the left hemisphere euphoria. The point arising from these studies is that the change in behavior was one in mood control, which is viewed as being a function of the dynamics of balance or imbalance between the left and the right hemispheres.

The Evidence from Studies of Brain Injury Due to Stroke

The pattern of findings from the WADA test studies have been paralleled by investigations of the effects of unilateral brain injury on affect. Here too the findings have been contradictory, in part owing to problems associated with identification of the extent of damage from stroke or other injury to brain tissue. Research conducted by Robinson has shown the closest parallel to the WADA test results (see Robinson, Kubos, Starr, Rao, & Price, 1984; Robinson & Szetela, 1981). Robinson studied patients suffering from unilateral stroke and found that those with left-sided lesions were more likely to suffer from depressive symptomatology. In an important qualification, Robinson also found that location of the lesion within the hemisphere may be as important as side of damage in determining the emotional consequences.

Further, Robinson demonstrated that mood was independent of overall level of cognitive impairment. For example, Robinson et al. (1984) found that patients with unilateral stroke in the left hemisphere were more likely to show signs of depression if the stroke was localized to the anterior portion of the hemisphere, even when controlling for degree of language impairment. Robinson has argued that these unilateral effects are the result of asymmetries in neurotransmitter pathways. In a number of animal studies, he has demonstrated greater depletion of central catecholamines (e.g., norepinephrine) with left as opposed to right ischemic lesion (Robinson, 1985; Robinson & Coyle, 1980).

Robinson et al. (1984) are among those who argue that insult to one hemisphere releases activity within the contralateral hemisphere. Their model refers to this process as *contralateral inhibition* or, in the case of damage, *disinhibition*. Damage to centers in the left hemisphere disinhibits right hemisphere arousal; excitation of centers in the right hemisphere changes

THE DEVELOPMENT OF EMOTION REGULATION

or distorts the balance between the two sides. Both instances produce a shift from left hemisphere control over right hemisphere negative affect to either a loss of control or an increase in the probability of negative expression.

An important paper published by Sackeim et al. (1982) some years ago addressed this issue. The authors collected a large number of cases from the clinical literature on pathological laughter and crying. These are instances of uncontrollable bouts in which the individual sometimes reports a dissociation between the loss of control and the feeling state; however, more often there is a concordance between loss of control and feeling state. The authors reviewed 122 cases of this phenomenon in the literature and then, using a set of independent judges, determined the lateralization of brain damage in each case. They found a greater probability of left-sided damage being associated with pathological crying and right-sided damage with pathological laughter. Sackeim et al. (1982) linked unilateral cortical damage to release from inhibition (contralateral disinhibition); however, the mechanisms of disinhibition remained unknown.

In a second study reported in the same paper, Sackeim et al. (1982) reviewed the data on patients with hemispherectomy. Here, obviously, mood changes could not be attributed to release of ipsilateral cortical centers. Nineteen patients were identified, 14 with removal of the right and five of the left hemisphere. Of the 14 patients with right removal, 12 were judged to be euphoric in mood postsurgery; of the five patients with left removal, three were judged as depressed. The results of right hemispherectomy argued that the left hemisphere may be a site for the generation of positive mood states. After all, the experience of increased positive affect following removal of the right hemisphere could not be due to release (disinhibition) of right-sided cortical centers. Nevertheless, it was possible that mood changes seen in the 12 patients were due to release of ipsilateral subcortical centers within the left hemisphere.

In an attempt to answer this question, Sackeim et al. (1982) performed a third study in which cases of alteration in mood as a function of ictal manifestations of epilepsy were examined. The authors argued that associations between lateralization of foci and type of ictal emotional outburst should most likely reflect the excitation of brain centers ipsilateral to the focus. In contrast to the finding that pathological laughter was associated with right-sided destructive lesions, foci of pathological laughter associated with epileptic seizure (gelastic epilepsy) were more frequently left sided. Similarly, in contrast to cases of pathological crying being associated with left-sided damage, cases of pathological crying related to seizure (dycrystic epilepsy) were more frequently associated with right-sided foci. Sackeim et al. (1982) argued that, taken together, these data suggest that uncontrollable outbursts could result either from disinhibition or from excitation within the left or right sides of the brain. In the case of brain damage, the consequent

NATHAN A. FOX, ED.

behaviors are the result of disinhibition, while, in the case of ictal seizures, it is excitation within the hemisphere that produces the mood change.

A PROPOSED MODEL OF DYNAMIC BRAIN ACTIVITY AND EMOTION REGULATION

The Sackeim et al. (1982) findings are presented in some detail because they underscore four issues in the study of lateralized hemispheric activation and affect. First, it appears that changes in dysphoric affect can be the result of either right-sided excitation or the lack of left-sided inhibition (disinhibition). Indeed, the manifestations of negative affect may be critically different in these two cases—crying as a result of right hemisphere excitation, negative thoughts and mood state as a result of left-sided disinhibition. Second, it may be the case that the right hemisphere inhibits certain left hemisphere affect-related behaviors. Cases of pathological laughter and indifference reactions were found in instances of destructive right hemisphere lesions as well as ictal left hemisphere excitation. Third, there were numerous exceptions to the prevailing pattern across these case reports. It is likely that, as in the case of lateralization of cognitive functions, there are individual differences in the degree and direction of affective lateralization. Finally, very few cases in either the brain injury, WADA test, or seizure literature describe patients who are unable to perform certain expressions. Thus, it is not the existence or patterning of discrete affects that is impaired but the individual's ability to regulate these emotions.

These studies also highlight two additional aspects of brain-behavior relations, particularly with regard to emotional behaviors. It is clear that static notions regarding activity in one hemisphere versus another are inadequate to describe the dynamic changes that occur within the brain. Except for cases of commissurotomy (cutting of the connections between the two hemispheres), there is ongoing active communication between left and right sides. Notions of cerebral lateralization must take into account this dynamic interaction in attempting to explain the role that hemispheric specialization plays in emotion and emotion regulation (cf. Fox et al., in press).

It is also clear that the frontal region of the neocortex plays a unique and significant role in the regulation of emotional behaviors (Dawson, Panagiotides, Grofer Klinger, & Hill, 1992). The frontal region is uniquely qualified for this role. It receives input from every sensory cortical area as well as from the motor areas of the neocortex (Nauta, 1971). It also has important and well-mapped-out reciprocal connections with the limbic system, particularly the amygdala (Kelly & Stinus, 1984). With its various nuclei, this structure in the limbic system is thought to play a definitive role in the basic behavioral-emotional responses of the animal to fear stimuli

Crying/Distress	Negative Thoughts and Mood
Right hemisphere activation	Left-sided disinhibition
Laughter/Positive Affect	Indifference Reactions/Impulsivity (Euphoria)
Left hemisphere activation	Right-sided disinhibition

FIG. 1.—After Sackheim et al. (1982)

(LeDoux, 1987). The frontal region has also been identified across the many studies of brain damage as the site that, when affected, produces the greatest as well as the most complex effects on affective behavior (Stuss et al., 1992).

It is possible, therefore, to propose a model of brain activity and its relation to emotion regulation based on the issues raised above. The neural regulation of emotion is a function of the dynamic interplay of anterior regions of the left and right hemispheres. The functional consequence of the inhibition or activation of certain centers in the frontal cortex is a change in the ability to modulate the expression of certain emotions and/or other affect-related behaviors. As can be seen in Figure 1, activation of the right frontal region is associated with control over the expression of negative affect; activation of the homologous left frontal region is associated with control over the expression of positive affect. Inhibition of activity (due either to contralateral activity or to ipsilateral subcortical activity) results in a distinctly different set of affect/regulation responses.

In the discussion presented above, emotion is a response that both is to be regulated and has a regulatory capacity. This dual function is a consequence of the role that emotions play in psychological life. Emotions are elicited as a consequence of and in response to environmental events. Fear, for example, may be evoked in response to a threatening stimulus, yet the fear response (including active withdrawal or flight) regulates the individual's interaction with the fear-provoking stimulus. However, this fear response need not persevere once the threat has subsided. Thus, the fear response must be modulated as the emotional behaviors involved in fear act as a regulatory force for the individual. The complex interplay that allows emotion to act as a regulator of behavior is subserved and guided by activation of the frontal cortex.

THE FUNCTIONAL MEANING OF BRAIN ASYMMETRY

An important issue in the area of lateralization and emotion involves the search for a functional (behavioral) interpretation of the underlying patterns of brain asymmetry. Why should the two hemispheres be differentially specialized for the expression or regulation of certain emotions? A number of researchers have argued that this asymmetry reflects a fundamental dichotomy between the two hemispheres in the control of behaviors underlying either approach or withdrawal (see Davidson, 1984a; Fox, 1991; Fox & Davidson, 1984; Kinsbourne, 1978). Kinsbourne (1978), for example, has argued that the different motor components involved in approach or withdrawal behaviors (whole body and gross motor for withdrawal, fine motor for approach) and the differing temporal aspects of the control of these motor components (immediate for withdrawal, sequential for approach) resulted in asymmetrical specialization for approach and withdrawal rather than bisymmetry.

My colleagues and I have discussed the development of different discrete emotions as a function of their association with either approach or withdrawal behaviors and have speculated that the infant's initial responses to the environment are based along this motivational dimension rather than reflecting discrete emotional responses (see Fox, 1991; Fox & Davidson, 1984). Indeed, Fox and Davidson (1987, 1988) found differences in EEG activation based on the approach/withdrawal dichotomy and not on any other categorical parsing of discrete affects. We have also speculated that, with development, social behavior may be viewed as maintaining a balance between approach and withdrawal tendencies (Fox, 1991).

One may extend the utility of the approach and withdrawal system beyond its role in the expression of certain emotions to the regulation of emotion states. That is, activation or inhibition of approach or withdrawal behaviors may be involved in the regulation of a person's response to emotionally arousing stimuli. Active engagement or a heightened withdrawal from a stimulus can maintain or reduce arousal level. Activation of the approach system increases exploratory behavior, maximizes chances for social interaction, and, in the infant's case, may be involved in the promotion of a secure bond with the caregiver. Activation of the withdrawal system decreases contact with noxious or novel stimuli and can serve to reduce arousal.

Inhibition of the approach system is to be distinguished from active withdrawal. In the former, there is an absence of active approach or social engagement of the environment; in the latter, there is the presence of negative affect and avoidant behavior. Inhibition of withdrawal also presents a unique state in which the balance between approach and withdrawal tendencies maintained by the vigilant organism is upset. Inhibition of withdrawal results in the lack of modulation of approach tendencies and may be reflected in impulsivity and high levels of activity. Each of these conditions describes a particular pattern of dynamic balance between the left and the right hemispheres in activation. Emotional responses that are a function

Left Frontal Activation	Right Frontal Activation
Active approach	Active withdrawal
Positive affect	Negative affect
Exploration	Fear/anxiety
Sociability	

Left Frontal Hypoactivation	Right Frontal Hypoactivation
Absence of positive affect	Disinhibition of approach
Depression	Impulsivity
	Hyperactivity

FIG. 2.—Four possibilities that are a consequence of left or right hemisphere activation or inhibition.

of differential hemispheric activation are thus regulating or modulating a person's interaction in the environment.

Four possibilities (listed in Fig. 2) that are a consequence of left or right hemisphere activation or inhibition can be proposed: active approach (left hemisphere activation); active withdrawal (right hemisphere activation); a deficit in approach (left hemisphere inhibition); and a deficit in withdrawal (right hemisphere inhibition). Each of these four might be associated with a different dynamic pattern of hemispheric arousal, and each pattern may have specific consequences with regard to the regulation of emotion and social behavior.

Thus, individuals with a pattern of left frontal activation would be more likely to express patterns of approach behavior. This would be evinced by more positive affect, increased sociability, and, importantly, the ability to utilize left frontal analytic strategies to regulate both positive and negative mood states. Individuals with a pattern of right frontal activation would be likely to evince withdrawal behavior in response to environmental challenge. Increases in negative affect and anxiety behaviors would be the hallmark here, and these behaviors would also be the typical manner in which these individuals regulate their responses to stress and novelty.

Deficits in approach behavior would be associated with lack of activation of the left frontal region (i.e., left frontal hypoactivation) and might be characterized by the absence of positive affect rather than by the exhibition of negative emotions. Henriques and Davidson (1990), for example, found that depressed adults exhibit left frontal hypoactivation, and they discuss depressive symptomatology as the absence of positive affect rather than the presence of negative emotions. In a similar vein, Dawson, Grofer Klinger, Panagiotides, Spieker, and Frey (1992) found patterns of reduced left frontal activation in the infants of depressed mothers. Indeed, Dawson (in this volume) has suggested that general frontal activation may reflect the recruit-ment of frontally mediated behaviors in the service of emotion regulation.

Finally, deficits in withdrawal behavior would be associated with right frontal hypoactivation and might involve the inability to inhibit positive approach activities. Children exhibiting high levels of activity may be unable to modulate initial approach tendencies and motor actions. If unchecked, these behaviors may progress into antisocial conduct problems in which the child's unrestrained behavior is viewed as aggressive or impulsive.

INDIVIDUAL DIFFERENCES IN FRONTAL ASYMMETRY: WHAT DO THEY MEAN?

Obviously, one cannot assume that the two hemispheres or regions within each of the two hemispheres operate independently of each other. It is therefore necessary to understand these different behavioral outcomes as the outcome of the dynamic balance between the two hemispheres (Fox et al., in press).

Individual differences in the activation or inhibition of the approach or withdrawal systems have been investigated on both a behavioral and an electrophysiological level. For example, Larsen and Ketelaar (1991) investi-gated differences in susceptibility of individuals to positive and negative emotions. They found that extroverts expressed more positive affect than introverts in response to a positive mood induction but did not differ in response to a negative mood induction. On the other hand, neurotics ex-pressed more negative affect than stable individuals in response to a nega-tive mood induction but did not differ in response to a positive mood induc-tion. Larsen and Ketelaar speculate that individual differences in the activation of either a behavioral approach system or a behavioral inhibition system (cf. Gray, 1981) might account for these individual differences in affect susceptibility; in other words, there may be individual differences in the threshold at which individuals experience different emotions.

This argument is similar to one put forth by Davidson with regard to individual differences in frontal brain electrical activity. Davidson proposed that differences in frontal activation reflect the threshold at which individu-als express negative affect (see Henriques & Davidson, 1990). Davidson and his colleagues found that individual differences in frontal brain activation were associated with an individual's predisposition to express positive or negative affect (Tomarken, Davidson, & Henriques, 1990; Tomarken, Da-vidson, Wheeler, & Doss, 1992). For example, subjects with resting right frontal asymmetry were more likely to rate film clips in a negative manner (Tomarken et al., 1990), and clinically depressed subjects exhibited right frontal asymmetry that was a function of less left frontal activity (Henriques

& Davidson, 1990). Davidson argues that differences in frontal activation reflect a stress-diathesis, that is, a disposition to experience situations in a negative manner, with individuals who exhibit right frontal activation displaying a lower threshold for stress.

The model presented in this essay differs in two crucial respects. First, rather than viewing individual differences in frontal asymmetry patterns as reflecting the tendency to express positive or negative affect or as marking the threshold at which an individual responds, I view these hemispheric differences as reflecting differing regulatory abilities of the individual. In some instances, positive or negative emotions may be utilized in the service of regulation; in others, cognitive processes specific to the frontal region (executive functions, planning, sustained attention, motor planning) may be the behaviors evoked to enable behavior regulation. From the perspective of the individual, the critical element is the degree to which she is able to regulate her emotion state. Second, EEG activation is viewed as a dynamic process. While traditional measures of asymmetry are useful as a first level of analysis, they must be supplanted by more precise measures of the dynamic interplay of left and right hemisphere activity so that the pattern of balance or imbalance between the two hemispheres can be accurately described.

In part, the assumptions underlying our model are based on an argument presented by Levy (1983). Levy suggested that there were important individual differences in the level of hemispheric arousal that affected performance on certain tasks designed to tap lateralized/specialized skills, noting that not all right-handed individuals performed equally well on tasks designed to tap left hemisphere function. She proposed that these differences in performance were, in part, due to differences in hemispheric arousal. When she assessed right-handed subjects for the degree of their left or right bias, she found that some had right and others left hemisphere arousal (see Levy, Heller, Banich, & Burton, 1983). These differing levels of arousal interacted with specialization either to enhance or to diminish an individual's utilization of certain hemispheric competencies and hence performance. So, for example, all other things being equal, individuals with greater right hemisphere arousal might perform better than those with greater left hemisphere arousal on tasks that involve the right hemisphere.

This argument has been extended to the area of emotion (Davidson & Fox, 1988) and emotion regulation (Fox, 1991). For example, individual differences in hemispheric arousal could interact with specialization for either approach or withdrawal tendencies either to exacerbate or to diminish an individual's disposition to respond in a particular way to affect-eliciting stimuli. Or individual differences in hemispheric arousal could interact with regional specialization for certain executive functions that are critical for behavior regulation, increasing the likelihood that these functions will be executed. In either case, the degree of hemispheric arousal may be a marker of important individual differences in either one's threshold for either positive or negative affect or one's ability to call on approach or withdrawal tendencies or other regulation strategies to control behavior.

EMPIRICAL SUPPORT FOR THE ROLE OF INDIVIDUAL DIFFERENCES IN FRONTAL ACTIVATION IN EMOTION REGULATION BEHAVIORS

For the past few years we (Calkins, Fox, & Marshall, in press) have investigated the possibility that individual differences in hemispheric activation as reflected in the pattern of the resting EEG may be utilized as a marker of the disposition to display approach or withdrawal behaviors in response to stress or novel situations. In a series of studies, we examined the relations between EEG activity and infant responses to a brief separation from their mothers.

In two studies, we found that baseline patterns of EEG recorded from anterior frontal scalp locations (F3 and F4) were associated with the infant's response to separation (see Davidson & Fox, 1989; Fox et al., 1992). Infants who subsequently cried when separated from their mothers displayed right frontal asymmetry, while infants who did not cry exhibited left frontal asymmetry. The effects appeared to be a function of power in the right frontal lead. That is, infants who had a tendency to cry in response to separation exhibited greater activation in the right frontal region.

The data indicated that there are individual differences in infant response to separation that are associated with a specific pattern of frontal activation. The data also suggested that these differences are stable across the second half of the first year of life. However, the implications of these brain-behavior relations for child personality (e.g., temperament) were unclear. In order to study the possibility that frontal EEG differences were a marker for certain temperamental traits, we performed a separate study with a selected group of subjects.

Data from our own laboratory and from others (Kagan & Snidman, 1991a) had indicated that infants who display a high degree of irritability and negative affect during the early part of infancy may be more likely to exhibit inhibited social behavior as toddlers. For example, Calkins and Fox (1992) found that, in an unselected sample, infants displaying negative reactivity during the first 6 months of life were more likely to be classified as insecurely attached and display distress at separation at 14 months of age and that they were also more likely to display signs of behavioral inhibition at age 2 years. Kagan and Snidman (1991a) reported that 4-month-old infants selected for similar characteristics (i.e., high motor activity and high frequency of crying) were likely to exhibit behavioral inhibition as toddlers. If frontal EEG asymmetry indexed a temperamental disposition, it was possible that the irritable active infants who displayed behavioral inhibition as toddlers would display a unique EEG activation pattern.

In order to investigate this issue, we screened over 300 infants at 4 months of age and selected three distinct groups: those infants who exhibited high motor behavior and high frequencies of crying and negative affect; those infants who exhibited high motor behavior and high frequencies of smiling and positive vocalizations; and those infants who exhibited low motor behavior and low frequencies of either positive or negative affect. These infants were seen in the laboratory twice—first at 9 months of age, at which time EEG was recorded while the infants attended to an attractive visual stimulus, and again at 14 months of age, at which time they were presented with a series of novel stimuli designed to elicit approach or withdrawal behaviors. The findings from this study confirmed our hypotheses regarding the relations between approach and withdrawal behaviors, infant temperament, and the patterning of frontal EEG activity (see Fox et al., in press). Infants selected at 4 months for the temperamental characteristics of high motor behavior and high frequencies of crying exhibited right frontal asymmetry, while infants selected for the temperamental characteristics of high motor behavior and high positive affect exhibited left frontal asymmetry. In addition, the high motor/high cry infants who exhibited right frontal EEG pattern were more likely to exhibit inhibited behaviors at 14 months.

Two results from this study are of note. First, by selecting infants at 4 months of age, we were able to predict which infants would display withdrawal and inhibited behavior 10 months later. Second, the combination—or interaction—of temperament indexing behavior and EEG pattern was the best predictor of withdrawal behavior at 14 months. Infants who were classified as high motor/high cry but did not show right frontal activation were less likely to exhibit inhibition; it was the combination of both factors that significantly predicted inhibited response. Of importance here is the fact that the significant differences in EEG obtained between the high motor/high cry and the high motor/high positive children were in right frontal power; there were no differences between groups in the magnitude of left frontal power. The groups also did not differ in parietal or occipital asymmetry, indicating that the group differences were not a function of generalized arousal. As predicted by our model, the increase in right frontal activation in the high motor/high cry group was accompanied by increased signs of negative affect and withdrawal in response to novelty and stress.

A third study was recently completed in our laboratory on a group of 4-year-olds (Fox et al., in press). Again, we found relations among frontal EEG and the disposition to display negative or positive affect in a social situation. We were interested in the possibility that resting frontal asymmetry may be associated with the pattern of social behavior in preschool children. Reports from Kagan's lab had indicated that there was a small group of children who exhibit vigilant and anxious behavior when confronted with mild stress and novelty, particularly in social situations. Kagan and his colleagues have argued that these children reflect a unique temperamental type who are sympathetically aroused and may exhibit other specific physiological characteristics. For example, Finman, Davidson, Colton, Straus, and Kagan (1989) reported that children selected for characteristics of behavioral inhibition (a high degree of proximity to their mothers during a laboratory play session) were more likely to exhibit right frontal asymmetry when assessed in a subsequent laboratory session.

Fox et al. (in press) observed a sample of 4-year-olds in laboratory play sessions involving four children of the same sex. The children came into the laboratory as a group and were videotaped in two free-play sessions that were separated by a cleanup session, a cooperation task, and a self-presentation task (describing their recent fourth-year birthday party). These sessions were coded using Rubin's Play Observation System (Rubin, 1989), and measures of inhibition and social competence were computed (Coplan, Rubin, Fox, Calkins, & Stewart, 1994). Each child returned to the laboratory some 2 weeks later, at which time EEG from left and right frontal, parietal, and occipital scalp locations was recorded during a visual attention task.

Our analyses of relations among behavior observed during the quartet session and measures of EEG activation at the lab visit indicated that children who exhibited inhibited behavior were more likely to present with right frontal asymmetry that was a function of greater left frontal power (left frontal hypoactivation). Children who exhibited a high degree of sociability in the group session, on the other hand, exhibited left frontal asymmetry that was a function of less left frontal power (increased left frontal activation).

It is interesting to note that the differences in frontal asymmetry between the two groups (inhibited vs. uninhibited children) were a function of power in the left and not the right frontal region. This pattern differs from that found for the inhibited toddlers and is similar to those reported by Davidson and his colleagues for adults exhibiting depression. This is not to argue that the 4-year-olds we studied were depressed or at risk for depression but rather that similar patterns of emotion regulation and cerebral dynamics (an absence of positive affect and approach behavior in the inhibited children) may characterize both types of social interactions. The reticent child fails to respond with positive affect in the quartet session. The depressed adult is also unable to generate appropriate positive affect.

CONCLUSION

Emotion regulation may operate on at least two levels with respect to frontal activation. The first level is the one that I have been discussing, and it involves the activation of motivational tendencies and their associated affective behaviors in response to environmental challenge. The 4-year-old's response to being confronted with three unfamiliar peers in an unfamiliar setting may be to withdraw and avoid interaction: the underlying affective quality may be fear and anxiety, or it may be an inability to activate approach behaviors (social interactive skills) that would facilitate social interaction. These two responses to challenge may at first look identical; in fact, they reflect different ways in which children reach a position of social isolation and solitude (Coplan et al., 1994), and each may involve a different dynamic pattern of balance/imbalance between the left and the right hemispheres.

A second level on which emotion regulation may operate is in the area of cognitive strategies or resources that the child has for successful coping with stress. A number of investigators have outlined the different skills that mature and develop over the preschool and school years and that turn the 2-year-old child who has a tantrum when overexcited or distressed into a child who can verbalize her anger or anxiety or plan strategies for successful coping with stress (Kopp, 1992; Thompson, 1990). These skills, particularly those that we put under the rubric *executive function and planning*, are uniquely frontal lobe tasks and may interact with the affective disposition to promote successful emotion regulation. That is, the child who becomes overaroused and excited when confronted with novelty or an anxiety-producing situation may be able to utilize these frontal skills to inhibit or modulate approach or withdrawal tendencies. This second level of frontal involvement in emotion regulation has been investigated indirectly in the literatures on hyperactivity, conduct disorder, and aggression in children and in the perseverative behavior and lack of executive-function skills in delinquent children (Moffitt & Henry, 1989). It has been less directly implicated in the cases of internalizing disorders, although recent work by Kagan and his colleagues on anxiety disorders in inhibited children suggests a possible link between frontally mediated functions and such disorders (Hirshfeld et al., 1992).

Although it is possible that different frontally mediated competencies are lateralized to the two frontal regions, little is known about these relations. It may be, however, that differences among individuals in the use of frontal strategies for emotion regulation may be reflected not in the asymmetry or balance between the left and right sides but in the overall activation of the region (see Dawson, in this volume). That is, individuals engaged in emotion regulation may be more likely to display activated frontal EEG patterns compared to those less involved in regulation behavior. There is indirect and speculative evidence for this relation. Dawson (in this volume) reports differences in EEG power between infants who are more and those who are less likely to be engaged in affect regulation. She attributes these overall power differences to intensity level; thus, in her model, increased generalized frontal activation reflects the degree of affect intensity. It may be that these overall frontal differences reflect the degree to which individuals engage this region in the service of emotion regulation. Individuals displaying greater overall frontal activation may do so as a result of the engagement of both left and right frontal regions in the service of modulation of affect.

Finally, an important factor in the pathways toward developmental outcome that should not be ignored is the effects of different environmental events on emotion regulation (see Thompson, in this volume). It is most likely that at least two factors interact in this process. The first of these is the parents' response to infants with certain extreme patterns of temperament. Caregivers may reinforce, ignore, or intervene in responding to a child who has a low threshold for distress in response to novelty, and each rearing pattern may produce a different pathway and end point in social development (cf. Calkins, in this volume). The second factor is the frequency of novel or stressful events to which the infant is exposed since repeated exposure to such experiences may exacerbate an infant's negative reactivity. Thus, differences in frontal asymmetry are not predictive of subsequent social development in and of themselves. Rather, the interaction of individual patterns of frontal activity and specific environments will be most telling of the pathways to adaptation or maladaptation in social development.

VAGAL TONE AND THE PHYSIOLOGICAL REGULATION OF EMOTION

Stephen W. Porges, Jane A. Doussard-Roosevelt,
and Ajit K. Maiti

Because emotions are psychological processes, the experience and regulation of emotion should be functionally dependent on the state of the nervous system. If a major source of emotion variation is dependent on the nervous system, how would this be evaluated? The goal of this essay is to address this problem by introducing vagal tone as a measurable organismic variable that contributes to individual and developmental differences in the expression and regulation of emotion.

We propose that understanding the mechanisms determining individual and developmental differences in emotion expression and regulation might provide a rationale for identifying subjects who differentially express the ability to regulate emotion. Thus, there is the possibility that individual differences in the nervous system might mediate the expression and regulation of emotion. Most research on the autonomic correlates of emotion has focused on *sympathetic* activation (e.g., GSR); here, we attempt to demonstrate that individual differences in *parasympathetic* tone are related to the regulation of emotion by focusing on a construct called *vagal tone,* which reflects the vagal control of the heart.

PHYSIOLOGY AND EMOTION: THE AUTONOMIC NERVOUS SYSTEM

The autonomic nervous system (ANS) regulates homeostatic function and is composed of two subsystems, the parasympathetic (PNS) and the sympathetic (SNS) nervous systems. The PNS and SNS represent neural systems that originate in the brain stem and contribute to the regulation of a variety of target organs, including the eyes, lacrimal, salivary, and sweat glands, blood vessels, heart, larynx, trachea, bronchi, lungs, stomach, adrenal glands, kidneys, pancreas, intestines, bladder, and external genitalia. In general, the PNS promotes functions associated with growth and restorative processes. In contrast, the SNS promotes increased metabolic output to deal with challenges from outside the body. However, there are states that require dual excitation (e.g., sexual arousal). Recent conceptualizations of the ANS by Berntson, Cacioppo, and Quigley (1991) provide insight into the complex dynamic relation between SNS and PNS processes.

In general, when a visceral organ is innervated by both the SNS and the PNS, the effects are antagonistic. For example, SNS neurons dilate the pupils, accelerate the heart, inhibit intestinal movements, and contract the vesical and rectal sphincters. The PNS neurons constrict the pupils, slow the heart, potentiate peristaltic movement, and relax vesical and rectal sphincters. The PNS deals primarily with anabolic activities concerned with the restoration and conservation of bodily energy and the resting of vital organs. In contrast, stimulation of the SNS prepares the individual for the intense muscular action required to protect and defend in response to external challenges. The SNS quickly mobilizes the existing reserves of the body.

Darwin provides insight into the potential importance of PNS processes in the regulation of emotions. Although Darwin defined emotions as facial expressions, he acknowledged the dynamic relation between parasympathetic structures and central nervous system activity that accompanied the spontaneous expression of emotions. Darwin speculated that there were specific neural pathways that provided the necessary communication between the brain states and the specific pattern of autonomic activity associated with emotions. For example, he stated, "When the mind is strongly excited, we might expect that it would instantly affect in a direct manner the heart; and this is universally acknowledged. . . . When the heart is affected it reacts on the brain; and the state of the brain again reacts through the pneumo-gastric [vagus] nerve on the heart; so that under any excitement there will be much mutual action and reaction between these, the two most important organs of the body" (1872/1965, p. 69).

Darwin attributed these ideas to Claude Bernard. Bernard developed the construct of *le milieu interieur,* which included physiological mechanisms responsible for maintaining the constancy of the internal environment. This construct evolved into our present-day concept of *homeostasis.*

In Darwin's formulation, when emotion states occur, the beating of the heart changes instantly, the change in cardiac activity influences brain activity, and the brain-stem structures stimulate the heart via the cranial nerves (i.e., vagus). Although Darwin did not elucidate the neurophysiological mechanisms that translate the initial emotion expression to the heart, this formulation provides us with three important points. First, by emphasizing the afferent feedback from the heart to the brain, Darwin anticipated the views of William James linking autonomic feedback to the experience of emotion. Second, he acknowledged the afferent capacity of the vagus to transmit sensory information from visceral organs independent of the spinal cord and the sympathetics. Third, Darwin's insight regarding the regulatory role of the pneumogastric nerve (renamed the *vagus* at the end of the nineteenth century) in the expression of emotions anticipates the major theme of this essay.

Contemporary models of emotion and emotion regulation (e.g., Ekman, Levenson, & Friesen, 1983; Kagan, in this volume; Schachter & Singer, 1962), as did their historical antecedents, have focused on the sympathetic nervous system and ignored the vagal system, the primary component of the parasympathetic nervous system. Thus, although Darwin speculated about the bidirectional communication between the brain and the heart more than 100 years ago, the importance of vagal afferents and efferents in the expression, experience, and regulation of emotion has not been addressed.

VAGAL TONE: BACKGROUND AND DEFINITION

The vagus is the tenth cranial nerve. It originates in the brain stem and projects, independently of the spinal cord, to many organs in the body cavity, including the heart and the digestive system. The vagus is not a single neural pathway but rather a complex bidirectional system with myelinated branches linking the brain stem and various target organs. These neural pathways allow direct and rapid communication between brain structures and specific organs. Because the vagus contains both efferent (i.e., motor) and afferent (i.e., sensory) fibers, it promotes dynamic feedback between brain control centers and the target organs to regulate homeostasis.

The peripheral autonomic nervous system is asymmetrical. The peripheral target organs of the autonomic nervous system are clearly lateralized; for example, the heart is oriented to the left, the stomach is tilted, one lung is larger, and one kidney is higher. The neural wiring of the autonomic nervous system requires asymmetry, and the central regulation via the vagus is lateralized. Although asymmetry of cortical function is well known and has been theorized to contribute to emotion regulation (see Fox, in this volume), asymmetrical regulation of autonomic function has been ignored.

The vagus is bilateral, with a left and a right branch. Each branch has two source nuclei, with fibers originating either in the dorsal motor nucleus or in the nucleus ambiguus. Traditional texts in neuroanatomy and neurophysiology (e.g., Truex & Carpenter, 1969; Williams, 1989) have focused on the dorsal motor nucleus of the vagus and neglected both the asymmetry in the vagal pathways and the important functions of the pathways originating from source nuclei in the nucleus ambiguus.

The dorsal motor nucleus is lateralized. Pathways from the left and right dorsal motor nucleus to the stomach have different regulatory functions. The left dorsal motor nucleus innervates the cardiac and body portions of the stomach that promote primarily secretion of gastric fluids (Kalia, 1981; Loewy & Spyer, 1990). The right dorsal motor nucleus innervates the lower portion of the stomach that controls the pyloric sphincter regulating the emptying into the duodenum (Fox & Powley, 1985; Pagani, Norman, & Gillis, 1988).

The nucleus ambiguus is also lateralized. While the right nucleus ambiguus provides the primary vagal input to the sino-atrial (S-A) node to regulate atrial rate (Hopkins, 1987) and determine heart rate, the left nucleus ambiguus provides the primary vagal input to the atrio-ventricular (A-V) node to regulate ventricular rate (Thompson, Felsten, Yavorsky, & Natelson, 1987). Given the ipsilateral control of efferent pathways regulating the nucleus ambiguus, characteristics of right-side brain damage are associated with defective right nucleus ambiguus regulation. In this manner, the observed deficits in prosody (e.g., Ross, 1981) and in heart-rate changes during attention-demanding tasks (Yokoyama, Jennings, Ackles, Hood, & Boller, 1987) associated with right-side brain damage implicate the right nucleus ambiguus in the regulation of vocal intonation and attention. Asymmetrical nucleus ambiguus regulation is less clear in other organs, such as the soft palate, the pharynx, and the esophagus.

Functionally, the dorsal motor nucleus is involved with the vegetative functions of digestion and respiration. In contrast, the nucleus ambiguus is more involved with processes associated with motion, emotion, and communication. For example, rapid mobilization of the body may be achieved by regulating heart rate via removal of vagal input to the S-A node. Vocal intonation, mediated by vagal connections to the larynx, is intimately related to the processes of emotion and communication. Facial expressions, critical to the expression of emotion and the signaling of information, are related to vagal function. In cats, vagal afferent fibers have direct influences on facial motoneurons (Tanaka & Asahara, 1981). Thus, the vagus originating from the dorsal motor nucleus might be labeled the *vegetative vagus*, in contrast to the emotive or *smart vagus* originating from the nucleus ambiguus. Table 1 provides a list of target organs associated with each branch of the vagus.

Sympathetic innervation of the heart is also asymmetrical (Randall & Rohse, 1956). Moreover, lateralized sympathetic input to the heart has been hypothesized to relate to emotion state (Lane & Schwartz, 1987). As with vagal control of the heart and larynx, research has demonstrated that damage to the right hemisphere has greater sympathetic consequences than does

TABLE 1

TARGET ORGANS ASSOCIATED WITH THE DORSAL
MOTOR NUCLEUS AND THE NUCLEUS AMBIGUUS

Dorsal Motor Nucleus	Nucleus Ambiguus
Trachea	Heart
Lungs	Soft palate
Stomach	Pharynx
Intestines	Larynx
Pancreas	Esophagus
Colon	Bronchi

left hemisphere damage (Hachinski, Oppenheimer, Wilson, Guiraudon, & Cechetto, 1992).

The central control of the vagus is ipsilateral. Thus, the right vagus originates in either the right dorsal motor nucleus or the right nucleus ambiguus. As noted above, the right nucleus ambiguus contains the primary source for the branch of the right vagus that provides input to the S-A node. Thus, output from the nucleus ambiguus can be monitored by measuring changes in vagal control of the S-A node. The S-A node is the primary pacemaker of the heart. Vagal stimulation of the S-A node delays the onset of the heart beat (i.e., slows heart rate), and vagal withdrawal (i.e., a delay or blocking of the neural transmission) shortens the time between heart beats (i.e., speeds heart rate). Most rapid heart-rate changes (i.e., chrono-tropic mechanisms) are mediated by the vagus. When metabolic demands increase, such as during exercise or fight-flight demands, the sympathetic nervous system influences heart rate. Thus, the study of vagal control of the heart might provide an important window on the rapid autonomic changes associated with gradations of emotion state.

Vagal Tone: Measurement Strategies

An easily accessible method for evaluating the vagal control of the S-A node (i.e., cardiac vagal tone) is to quantify respiratory sinus arrhythmia (RSA). RSA is characterized by a rhythmic increase and decrease in heart rate. The heart-rate increase is associated with phases of inspiration, when respiratory mechanisms in the brain stem attenuate the vagal efferent action on the heart. The heart-rate decrease is associated with phases of expiration, when the vagal efferent influence to the heart is reinstated.

Measurement of RSA requires detection of the heart beat from the electrocardiogram (i.e., R-wave) and timing between heart beats (i.e., heart periods). To quantify the cardiac vagal tone index ($\hat{V}$) from RSA, it is neces-sary to detect and time with millisecond accuracy. The cardiac vagal tone index is extracted via time-series procedures. These procedures require heart-period rather than heart-rate data. On a beat-to-beat level, heart periods are the sequential time intervals between heart beats. Heart-rate data require a transformation of the heart period by determining how many of each of the heart periods scored in milliseconds could occur in a minute (i.e., 60,000 msec per minute/heart period in milliseconds). The data are processed by a method developed and patented by Porges (1985). This technique includes the application of time-domain filters designed to extract only RSA, the heart-period pattern in the spontaneous breathing frequencies. The resulting heart-period pattern is sinusoidal with an amplitude and time period. The amplitude represents the changing vagal influences to the S-A node, and the period represents the medullary inspiratory drive frequency. By calculating the amplitude or variance of the extracted pattern, RSA amplitude provides an excellent measure of cardiac vagal tone.

VAGAL TONE: POTENTIAL LINK WITH EMOTION

Changes in RSA amplitude in response to sensory, cognitive, and visceral challenges represent a "central command" to regulate vagal efferents originating in the right nucleus ambiguus and terminating in the heart, soft palate, pharynx, larynx, bronchi, and esophagus. These changes in nucleus ambiguus regulation of peripheral autonomic activity support the expression of motion, emotion, and communication by regulating metabolic output (i.e., shifts in heart rate) and organs involved in the production of vocalizations (Porges & Maiti, 1992).

When there are no challenging environmental demands, the autonomic nervous system, through the vagus, services the needs of the internal viscera to enhance growth and restoration. However, in response to environmental demands, homeostatic processes are compromised, and the autonomic nervous system supports increased metabolic output to deal with these external challenges by vagal withdrawal and sympathetic excitation. By mediating the distribution of resources, the central nervous system regulates the strength and latency of autonomic responses to deal with internal and external demands. Perceptions and assumed threats to survival, independent of the actual physical characteristics of the stimulation, may promote a massive withdrawal of parasympathetic tone and a reciprocal excitation of sympathetic tone. These changes promote fight-flight behaviors. Less intense environmental demands, often associated with emotion expressions, might be characterized by less withdrawal of parasympathetic tone independent of, or in concert with, slight increases in sympathetic tone. This trade-off between internal and external needs is monitored and regulated by the central nervous system.

Vagal tone measured via RSA has been documented to be related to affect, attention, and metabolic demands (see below). Although the vagus is bilateral, the right branch originating in the nucleus ambiguus is the primary determinant of RSA. This laterality in the vagus is not a developmental or an individual difference. Rather, the laterality is dependent on the neurophysiology and the neuroanatomy of the mammalian nervous system. In the mammalian nervous system, the right side of the brain stem provides the primary central regulation of homeostasis and physiological reactivity. Thus, right-brain-stem structures initiate peripheral physiological states via shifts in vagal tone to facilitate the processes of attention, the expression of emotion, and the initiation of shifts in metabolic output.

THE RIGHT HEMISPHERE: THE REGULATION OF EMOTION

Right hemisphere function, evaluated via EEG or disrupted by localized damage, is related to the same cluster of behaviors that has been linked to the vagal tone measure. Research demonstrates that the right hemisphere is implicated in both the expression and the interpretation of emotions (e.g., Bear, 1983; Heilman, Bowers, & Valenstein, 1985; Pimental & Kingsbury, 1989; Tucker, 1981) and in the regulation of attention (e.g., Heilman & Van Den Abell, 1980; Mesulam, 1981; Pimental & Kingsbury, 1989; Voeller, 1986). Research has also linked right hemisphere deficits with aprosody or lack of emotion expression in speech (e.g., Ross, 1981; Ross & Mesulam, 1979; Zurif, 1974) and attenuated autonomic reactivity (e.g., Heilman, Schwartz, & Watson, 1978). Several investigators have argued that the right hemisphere provides the primary control of emotion (for detailed reviews, see Molfese & Segalowitz, 1988; Pimental & Kingsbury, 1989; Silberman & Weingartner, 1986).

EEG research has been used to provide support for laterality theories of emotion. Fox and his colleagues (e.g., Dawson, in this volume; Fox, in this volume; Fox & Davidson, 1984) present a model of emotion expression in which positive (e.g., interest) emotions are associated with the left hemisphere and negative emotions (e.g., disgust or distress) with the right. Asymmetry of hemispheric control of negative and positive affect has also been posited by Tucker (1981). Other laterality theories focus primarily on the role of the right hemisphere in the regulation of negative emotions and fight-flight behaviors (for a review, see Silberman & Weingartner, 1986). The data strongly support the relation between right hemisphere EEG activity and the expression of negative emotions in infants, children, and adults; however, research demonstrating the relation between left hemisphere EEG activity and the expression of positive emotions is less conclusive.

In children, right hemisphere dysfunction has been associated with attentional, social, and emotional problems. Voeller (1986) reported data on 16 children with unilateral right hemisphere lesion or dysfunction as assessed by neuropsychological exam and/or CAT scan. Fifteen of these children were extremely distractible and inattentive, meeting the DSM-III criteria for attention deficit disorder; moreover, eight were also hyperactive. Eight children were shy and withdrawn, sharing some of the behavioral characteristics of the inhibited child described by Kagan (in this volume), and nine expressed atypical emotion expression (i.e., prosody, facial expression, and gesture). Most of these children made little eye contact with others, and virtually all had poor relationships with peers.

In their survey of studies with both normal and lesioned subjects, Silberman and Weingartner (1986) suggested that the right hemisphere is superior for recognizing emotional aspects of stimuli. They propose that right hemisphere dominance for emotion regulation reflects a nervous system organization that gives priority to avoidance or defensive mechanisms that have a high survival value. By inference, these avoidance and defensive mechanisms require massive and immediate shifts in autonomic function.

THE RIGHT HEMISPHERE: AUTONOMIC REGULATION AND REACTIVITY

The right side of the brain also plays a special role in the regulation of emotion. Data supporting laterality theories of emotion have been based on studies of electrophysiological recordings from the scalp (e.g., Fox, in this volume) and neuropsychological studies of dysfunction in individuals with brain damage (e.g., Silberman & Weingartner, 1986). We propose a convergent approach by emphasizing the right brain's regulation of peripheral autonomic activity.

Asymmetry in the control of the autonomic nervous system has been documented in the previous sections. Because peripheral organs are not symmetrical in shape or placement, it is not surprising that the neural control of the autonomic nervous system is lateralized. For example, the heart is displaced to the left, with the right vagus going to the S-A node and the left vagus going to the A-V node. Other organs with dual vagal innervation are often tilted (e.g., the stomach and intestines), or are located higher on one side (e.g., the kidneys), or are larger on one side (e.g., the lungs).

Emphasis on the asymmetry of autonomic organs has implications for the evolution of central regulatory systems and cortical development. In mammals, the peripheral autonomic organs and brain-stem structures are similar across species. Asymmetrical neural control of autonomic processes is characteristic of mammals. However, the process of encephalization differs among mammalian species, with man possessing a uniquely large cerebral cortex. Because the neural control of the vagus is ipsilateral (e.g., the left vagus originates in the left side of the brain stem), the right hemisphere—including the right cortical and subcortical structures—would promote the efficient regulation of autonomic function via the source nuclei in the brain stem. For example, neuroanatomical and electrophysiological studies demonstrate the important regulatory function of the right central nucleus of the amygdala in regulating the right nucleus ambiguus.

We propose that the functional dominance of the right side of the brain in regulating autonomic function has implications for specialization of motor and language dominance on the left side of the brain. The right-sided responsibilities of regulating homeostasis and modulating physiological state in response to both internal (i.e., visceral) and external (i.e., environmental) feedback potentially enabled the control of other functions to evolve on the left side of the brain. With greater encephalization, which is characteristic of more cognitive mammalian species such as man, lateralized specialization is more observable.

A sharing of central control of voluntary and emotion-homeostatic processes would enable the individual to express complex voluntary levels of communication and movement via the left side of the brain and more intense emotion-homeostatic processes via the right side of the brain. If these processes are lateralized, they might have a degree of autonomous regulation. Of course, the central nervous system is complex and has, in many instances, both ipsilateral and contralateral communication. This provides a small percentage of individuals with central control of both language and dominant hand motor movement on the right instead of the left side of the brain. However, owing to the asymmetry of the peripheral autonomic organs and the medullary control of the autonomic nervous system, the right side of the brain is always dominant in the regulation of autonomic function and, thus, emotion.

Data from stimulation studies using left and right visual fields (e.g., Hugdahl, Franzon, Andersson, & Walldebo, 1983; Weisz, Szilagyi, Lang, & Adam, 1992) indicate that activation of the right cortex results in larger and more reliable autonomic responses. Additionally, studies of brain-damaged individuals have shown that right hemisphere damage or dysfunction is associated with a severe deficit in the facial, vocal, and autonomic components of the expression of emotions (Pimental & Kingsbury, 1989; Silberman & Weingartner, 1986). Similar asymmetry of the sympathetic nervous system has been reported, with the right stellate ganglion having greater cardiovascular control than the left stellate ganglion (Yanowitz, Preston, & Abildskov, 1966). However, no research has focused on assessment of the cardiac vagal tone measure in subjects with right hemisphere disorders. Since the cardiac vagal tone measure is physiologically linked to the right

175

hemisphere regulation of autonomic activity, it might index the individual's functional capacity to regulate autonomic function and to express emotion.

THE VAGAL CIRCUIT OF EMOTION REGULATION: A MODEL

The right vagus and, thus, cardiac vagal tone are associated with processes involving the expression and regulation of motion, emotion, and communication. These processes enable individuals to approach and/or withdraw from objects and events in their environment. The regulation of attention, a major substrate for appropriate social behaviors, is included among these processes. Thus, the approach/withdrawal dimension includes movement in psychological as well as physical space. Vagal regulation of the heart modulates metabolic output to physically approach or withdraw; vagal modulation of vocal intonations provides clues for an individual to approach or withdraw; feedback from our own facial muscles to the vagus and the ability to pay attention to social cues, including another person's facial muscles and verbal commands, allow us to negotiate appropriate approach or withdrawal behaviors.

Just as Schneirla (1959) proposed that all behaviors could be described in terms of approach and withdrawal actions, we too place the dimensions of approach and withdrawal in a central role in our model of the vagal regulation of emotion. Schneirla assumed that stimulus intensities modulated autonomic function to produce sympathetic dominance during high intensities and parasympathetic dominance during low intensities. However, according to our model of emotion regulation, sympathetic modulation is not always necessary, and the vagal system can promote approach or withdrawal behaviors via the right nucleus ambiguus control of heart rate and the intonation of vocalizations.

The vagal circuit of emotion regulation is schematized in Figure 1. The circuit focuses on right hemisphere regulation of emotion states via vagal projections from the nucleus ambiguus to the larynx and the S-A node of the heart. The vagal control of the right side of the larynx produces changes in vocal intonation associated with the expression of emotions. The vagal control of the S-A node produces a cardiovascular state associated with specific emotions and facilitating attention or fight-flight behaviors.

Emotion process may originate on a cortical level or may be initiated and/or regulated by afferent feedback from visceral organs. For example, if the emotion were triggered by a psychological process (e.g., perception of a specific stimulus), the following stages may occur: (1) cortical areas stimulate the amygdala; (2) the central nucleus of the amygdala stimulates the nucleus ambiguus; and (3) the right vagus regulates heart rate and vocal intonation by communicating with the S-A node and the right side of the

THE VAGAL CIRCUIT OF EMOTION REGULATION
Right Side of the Brain

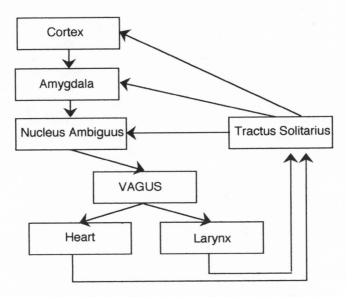

FIG. 1.—Schematization of the vagal circuit of emotion regulation

larynx. Regulation of the emotion response also may follow a specific path:
(1) sensory information regarding the status of visceral organs stimulates
vagal afferents, lateralized vagal afferents stimulate the nucleus tractus solitarius in the brain stem, and projections from the nucleus tractus solitarius
stimulate the cortex, amygdala, and/or nucleus ambiguus to regulate the
emotion expression; or (2) the emotion state could be initiated by the visceral afferent (e.g., stomach pains) and trigger the cortical, subcortical,
brain-stem, and autonomic responses associated with emotion.

Interference with transmission on any level of the circuit may result in
affective disorders, including emotion regulation problems or severe mood
states. Dysfunction in the circuit could be caused by brain damage, neural
transmission problems due to drugs, or learned dysfunction. The learning
model is based on the demonstrations that classical conditioning and other
associative learning paradigms that modify autonomic function are dependent on cortical-autonomic and amygdaloid-autonomic pathways. Thus, autonomic afferents to or from the nucleus ambiguus may be amplified, attenuated, or blocked via neuropathy, drugs, or associative learning to produce
different affective states.

The vagal circuit of emotion regulation that we propose makes several important advances in the conceptualization of the physiology of emotion and emotion regulation. It introduces the importance of the vagal system in the physiology of emotion and emphasizes the bidirectional (i.e., afferent feedback) physiological characteristics of the vagus. Furthermore, the vagal circuit is neuroanatomically dependent on right medullary control of autonomic function via the nucleus ambiguus, has a noninvasive window of measurement via the quantification of respiratory sinus arrhythmia with the vagal tone index ($\hat{V}$), explains individual differences due both to defects in neurophysiology and to associative learning, and is consistent with brain-damage research. Finally, by emphasizing afferent feedback and communications among various levels of the nervous system, the vagal circuit of emotion regulation provides an explanation for the effectiveness of specific interventions (e.g., nonnutritive sucking, massage, eating, exercise, yoga, and cognitive strategies) in the regulation of emotions.

VAGAL REGULATION AND EMOTION

Interest in vagal tone as a regulatory mechanism in the expression of individual differences in autonomic function is not new. Eppinger and Hess introduced the concept of vagal tone as an individual difference construct in their monograph *Die Vagotonie* (1910). They described a form of autonomic dysfunction for which there was no known anatomical basis: "It is often unsatisfactory for the physician . . . to find that he must be content to make a diagnosis of 'Neurosis'. The symptomatology and the impossibility of establishing any anatomical basis for the disease always remain the most conspicuous points in formulating the diagnosis of a neurosis of an internal organ" (p. 1). The objective of their monograph was to identify a physiological substrate that could explain this anomaly and thus provide the mechanisms for a variety of clinically observed neuroses.

Although Eppinger and Hess were interested in clinical medicine, their case studies described a problem in the regulation of autonomic function that might be intimately related to the regulation of emotion. Their observations are relevant to our interest in the regulation and expression of emotion for four important reasons: first, they alerted us to the importance of the vagal system in mediating physiological and psychological responses; second, they related individual differences in physiology (i.e., vagal tone) to individual differences in behavior (i.e., neuroses); third, they recognized the pharmacological sensitivity of the vagal system to cholinergic agents; and, fourth, they brought to the attention of the medical community the commonality of the vagal innervation of various peripheral organs.

In our model of vagal regulation, we adopt a stimulus-organism-response (SOR) approach. The expression and regulation of emotions are the responses, which are dually determined by the stimulus and the organism. It is not just the stimuli that elicit a response; rather, the response is determined by a complex system of behavioral-physiological responses that involve perception of the stimulus, afferent feedback, and the regulation of approach-withdrawal behaviors via the vagal system. Because of the link between the right vagus and the processes of motion, emotion, and communication, individuals with low vagal tone and/or poor vagal regulation would be expected to exhibit difficulties in regulating emotion state, in appropriately attending to social cues and gestures, and in expressing contingent and appropriate emotions. Thus, the possibility exists that the vagal system may provide a physiological metaphor for the regulation of emotion states. Individual differences in vagal tone may index organismic factors related to the competency of the individual to react physiologically and to self-regulate.

VAGAL TONE RESEARCH

In testing our model of vagal regulation, we have been assessing empirically whether individuals with low vagal tone and/or difficulties in regulating vagal tone have problems with the expression and/or regulation of motion, emotion, and communication. The potential to move, express emotion, and communicate enables an individual to maneuver along a continuum of approach-withdrawal with the environment. Several behaviors are critical to this function, including behavioral reactivity, facial expressivity, and emotion regulation.

If vagal tone mediates the expression and regulation of emotion, developmental shifts in vagal tone might contribute to the observed developmental shifts in affective expression. Research has demonstrated that vagal control of the autonomic nervous system increases developmentally as the nervous system matures. We have reported a relation between gestational age and vagal tone in premature neonates (Porges, 1983) and a monotonic increase in vagal tone from birth through the first 18 days postpartum in rats (Larson & Porges, 1982). In the rat pups, these changes were paralleled by increased organization of behavior, including enhanced state regulation, exploration, and attention. Current longitudinal research with human infants has demonstrated that vagal tone increases monotonically from 3 to 13 months (Izard et al., 1991).

To evaluate whether vagal tone as a construct has properties that may be useful in explaining the expression of emotion and the regulation of affective state, the following sections review research on the relation between vagal tone and variables in the domains of reactivity, the expression of emotion, and self-regulation.

Reactivity

Here we provide theoretical justification and empirical support for the hypothesis that individual differences in vagal tone are related to heart rate and behavioral reactivity in young infants. The core proposition is that vagal tone indexes a dimension of central nervous system organization that disposes an individual to be hypo- or hyperreactive. Thus, subjects with higher levels of vagal tone should have more organized (i.e., consistent) autonomic responses with shorter latency and greater magnitude autonomic responses.

Before 1970, heart-rate responses were defined as rapid increases and decreases to discrete stimuli. These response patterns were interpreted as an autonomic correlate of an orienting response (see Graham & Clifton, 1966). Research was not directed at the physiological mechanisms that may mediate individual differences in autonomic reactivity. Observed variations in heart-rate response characteristics were assumed to be dependent on both the physical parameters of the stimulus and the subject's previous history with the stimulus. Individual differences that could not be attributed to these two sources were treated as experimental (i.e., measurement) error.

In the early 1970s, our research demonstrated that individual differences in spontaneous base-level heart-rate variability were related to heart-rate reactivity. These studies stimulated our interest in the vagal mechanisms mediating heart-rate variability and in the development of methods to quantify vagal influences on the heart. The first studies (Porges, 1972, 1973) demonstrated, in a sample of college students, that individual differences in heart-rate variability assessed during baseline conditions were related to heart-rate responses and reaction-time performance. These studies were followed by experiments with newborn infants that demonstrated a relation between baseline heart-rate variability and the magnitude of heart-rate responses to simple visual and auditory stimuli. Newborn infants with higher baseline heart-rate variability reacted with larger heart-rate responses to the onset and offset of auditory stimuli (Porges, Arnold, & Forbes, 1973) and with shorter latency responses to the onset of an increase in illumination (Porges, Stamps, & Walter, 1974). When the illumination was decreased, only the high heart-rate variability subjects responded. Consistent with these findings, only the neonates with higher heart-rate variability exhibited a conditioned heart-rate response (Stamps & Porges, 1975).

Recent studies using the vagal tone index have been consistent with the theme that vagal tone is an index of reactivity. Porter, Porges, and Marshall

(1988) demonstrated in a sample of normal newborns that individual differences in vagal tone were correlated with heart-rate reactivity to circumcision. Neonates with higher vagal tone exhibited not only larger heart-rate accelerations but also lower fundamental cry frequencies in response to the surgical procedures, the latter having been hypothesized to be associated with greater vagal influences (see Lester & Zeskind, 1982). Consistent with these findings, Porter and Porges (1988) have also demonstrated in premature infants that individual differences in vagal tone are related to the heart-rate response during lumbar punctures.

Behavioral reactivity and irritability in response to environmental stimuli assessed with the Neonatal Behavioral Assessment Scale (Brazelton, 1984) are also associated with vagal tone. In a sample of full-term healthy neonates, DiPietro, Larson, and Porges (1987) found that neonates who were breast-fed had higher vagal tone, were more reactive, and required more effort to test. DiPietro and Porges (1991) evaluated the relation between vagal tone and behavioral reactivity to gavage with a sample of preterm neonates. (Gavage is a commonly used method to feed premature infants by passing food through a tube inserted into the stomach via the nasal or oral passages.) Individual differences in vagal tone were significantly correlated with behavioral reactivity to the gavage method of feeding.

Similar relations between spontaneous vagal tone and reactivity have been reported for older infants. Linnemeyer and Porges (1986) found that 6-month-old infants with higher vagal tone were more likely to look longer at novel stimuli, and only those with high vagal tone exhibited significant heart-rate reactivity to the visual stimuli. Richards (1985, 1987) reported convergent findings that infants with higher levels of respiratory sinus arrhythmia (a measure of vagal tone) were less distractible and had larger decelerative heart-rate responses to visual stimuli. Huffman, Bryan, Pedersen, and Porges (1988) observed that high vagal tone infants at 3 months of age habituated to novel visual stimuli more rapidly than those with low vagal tone; the former were more likely to suppress vagal tone during attention-demanding tasks and received a better attention score than the latter.

In summary, vagal tone mediates the behavioral and emotional response of the organism, and the vagal tone index provides a measure of behavioral and emotional reactivity. Neonates, infants, children, and adults with higher vagal tone exhibit appropriate autonomic reactivity and, in turn, appropriate behavioral and emotional responses (e.g., crying, irritability) to stimulation.

Expression of Emotion

Few studies have investigated individual differences in vagal tone as a mediating variable indexing individual differences in facial expressivity.

There are two important reasons for posing this research question. First, both autonomic and facial responses have been theoretically associated with the expression of emotions. Second, measurement of vagal tone may provide an index of the neural organization necessary for facial expressions—a hypothesis suggested by the nature of the neurophysiological mechanisms that mediate facial expressions and autonomic reactions. Facial expressions and autonomic reactions associated with emotion states are controlled by brain-stem structures that are in close proximity (i.e., the source nuclei of the facial nerve and the vagus). Quite often the facial nerve is included as part of the "vagus complex." Therefore, if expressivity is assumed to be an individual difference determined by the neural tone of the facial nerve, measurement of the neural tone of the vagus might be related to the expressivity of the infant. Thus, vagal tone, monitored during a nonstressed period, might index a neural propensity to produce facial expressions.

Support for this hypothesis comes from studies that have related resting levels of heart-rate variability to expressivity. Field, Woodson, Greenberg, and Cohen (1982) reported that newborn infants exhibiting greater resting heart-rate variability were more expressive, and Fox and Gelles (1984) found that 3-month-old infants with higher resting heart-rate variability displayed a longer duration of interest expressions. More recently, Stifter, Fox, and Porges (1989) evaluated the relation between the vagal tone index and expressivity in 5-month-old infants and found that infants with higher vagal tone displayed more interest, more joy, and more look-away behaviors toward the stranger.

Self-Regulation

Self-regulation is a difficult process to operationalize. Behaviors as diverse as sustained attention, facial expressions, and latency to soothe can be interpreted as regulatory. Many studies have demonstrated the relation between vagal tone and attention (for a review, see Porges, 1992). In general, higher vagal tone and proper suppression of vagal tone during an attention-demanding task are related to better performance. More important for the discussion of vagal tone and emotion self-regulation, vagal tone has also been shown to be related to the ability to self-soothe.

In both full-term and premature newborns, the ability to self-soothe is inversely related to vagal tone. The higher vagal tone neonates are more irritable and exhibit greater difficulty in self-soothing. However, a subsequent increasing capacity to self-soothe is clearly seen in the high vagal tone neonates. One might speculate that the high vagal tone neonate's reactivity elicits more caregiving from the mother and that, once such an infant becomes physiologically stable, the capacity for self-soothing is consequently enhanced. Thus, the self-regulatory demands might be different for the neonate and for the older infant, and vagal tone might index this propensity to self-regulate under changing developmental demands. Support for this hypothesis comes from a study of 3-month-old infants that found significant relations between vagal tone and soothability (Huffman, Bryan, del Carmen, Pedersen, & Porges, 1992); high base-level vagal tone was correlated with a low soothing score (i.e., little soothing was required) and a high Rothbart soothability score (i.e., distress was easily reduced).

The studies summarized above support the hypothesis that base-level vagal tone is an important determinant of self-regulatory autonomic and behavioral responses. Unfortunately, the relation is more complex, and there are infants with high vagal tone who do not suppress vagal tone under regulatory demands and who show poor emotion regulation (DeGangi, DiPietro, Greenspan, & Porges, 1991; Doussard-Roosevelt, Walker, Portales, Greenspan, & Porges, 1990). According to Greenspan (1991), infants older than 6 months of age who exhibit fussiness, irritability, poor self-calming, intolerance to change, and/or a hyperalert state of arousal are best described as being regulatory disordered.

Preliminary data suggest two important points. First, these infants tend to have high vagal tone. Second, these infants tend to exhibit a deficit in the ability to suppress vagal tone during attention-demanding situations. Assessed at 9 months of age, this inability to suppress vagal tone predicts behavior problems at 3 years (Portales, Doussard-Roosevelt, Lee, & Porges, 1992). It appears that these "fussy babies" are hyperreactive not only to environmental stimuli but also to visceral feedback. The relation between higher vagal tone and greater reactivity is supported, but the relation between vagal tone and the ability to self-regulate, assessed via behavior and the suppression of vagal tone during tasks, is not consistent with that observed with normal infants.

CONCLUSIONS

What does vagal tone convey about an individual's ability to regulate and express emotion? To answer this question, we have proposed a model that integrates information regarding lateral brain function with the regulation of the peripheral autonomic nervous system. The model is based on the following observations:

1. The peripheral autonomic nervous system is asymmetrical.
2. The medullary regulation of the autonomic nervous system is also asymmetrical, with structures on the right side exhibiting greater control of physiological responses associated with emotion.

3. The right nucleus ambiguus is a source nucleus of the right vagus, which provides control of the larynx and S-A node of the heart and controls vocal intonation and cardiac vagal tone.

4. The right central nucleus of the amygdala has direct influences on the right nucleus ambiguus to promote the laryngeal and cardiovascular responses associated with emotion (e.g., increased pitch of vocalization and increased heart rate).

5. Stimuli that are processed primarily by the right hemisphere produce greater cardiovascular responses than stimuli processed by the left hemisphere.

6. Damage to the right hemisphere blunts facial expression, vocal intonation, and autonomic reactivity.

Although each of these points has been documented, no study has as yet adequately tested the model linking vagal tone to right hemispheric regulation of emotion. Since the cardiac vagal tone index is an accurate measure of the input to the S-A node from the right nucleus ambiguus, it provides a noninvasive measure of right hemisphere capacity to process emotion stimuli and to regulate emotional responses. To test this model adequately, it will be necessary to conduct experiments to evaluate vagal tone and vagal reactivity of individuals with known right hemisphere disorders and evaluate covariations between individual differences in vagal tone and vagal reactivity and the expression and interpretation of emotions in non-brain-damaged subjects.

Providing evidence in support of this model, previous studies have addressed the relation between vagal tone and three dimensions related to the expression and regulation of emotion: reactivity; expressivity; and self-regulation. The literature and our ongoing research permit the following generalizations.

First, independent of developmental stage, vagal tone is highly correlated with autonomic reactivity; individuals with higher vagal tone consistently exhibit larger and more reliable autonomic responses. Second, the relation between vagal tone and emotion expressivity appears to be dependent on development. A preliminary study has demonstrated that higher vagal tone was associated with greater facial expressivity in 5-month-old infants but failed to establish any such relation in 10-month-old infants. These data suggest that there is a developmental shift in the neurophysiological control of facial expressivity: as infants become older, facial expressivity may become more dependent on higher brain control and less related to individual differences in brain-stem function, manifest in the tonic outflow of the cranial nerves.

Third, independent of developmental stage, vagal tone is correlated with self-regulation. Individuals with high vagal tone consistently suppress vagal tone or heart-rate variability to enhance the intake of information from the environment. Fourth, there is a subset of individuals who have high vagal tone and who do not suppress vagal tone or heart-rate variability during information processing. These individuals appear to have a *regulatory* disorder that is displayed on both behavioral and physiological levels; regulatory disordered infants are often labeled as *fussy* because of their continuous crying and disorganized behaviors, and they have difficulty self-soothing and maintaining a calm state.

Finally, as the infant matures, the range of expressivity increases, the self-regulation of emotion is enhanced, and vagal tone increases; in the course of normal development, the increased myelination and regulation of autonomic function associated with enhanced vagal tone parallels the range and control of emotion states. Thus, on both developmental and individual difference levels, vagal tone is clearly related to the processes of reactivity, expressivity, and self-regulation.

We introduce vagal tone as a physiological construct that is useful in explaining individual and developmental differences in the expression and regulation of emotion. As an organizing construct, vagal tone is useful in integrating central, autonomic, and psychological components of emotion. Vagal tone may index individual differences in the homeostatic capacity of the autonomic nervous system to foster rapid expression and attenuation of sympathetic reactions. This function is dependent on neural regulation of the reciprocal relation between the antagonistic branches of the autonomic nervous system.

During emotion states, normal homeostatic function is perturbed to express emotions. Initially, sympathetic activity is expressed owing primarily to the withdrawal of the antagonistic vagal tone. Even without discrete sympathetic excitation, the vagal withdrawal will enhance the expression of sympathetic activity when the two systems have antagonistic influences on specific organs. The vagal withdrawal triggers the autonomic correlates of emotions.

If the emotion state is prolonged, the physiological state will be maintained by activation of sympathetic and endocrine systems. Excessive sympathetic activity reflects a deviation from normal homeostatic autonomic function, which then elicits vagal activity to self-regulate and return the autonomic state to homeostasis. In individuals with high vagal tone and appropriate vagal regulation capacities, the autonomic nervous system has the capacity to react (i.e., appropriate reactivity and expressivity) and to return rapidly to homeostasis (i.e., self-regulation and self-soothing).

The relation among the right hemisphere, the right vagus, and the processes involved in the expression and regulation of motion, emotion, and communication makes apparent the relevance of examining individual differences in vagal tone in studies of emotion regulation. Vagal tone and vagal regulation in the context of the vagal circuit of emotion regulation that we proposed may provide the physiological measures of the individual's ability to regulate motion, emotion, and communication.

SUMMARY

On the basis of current knowledge of neuroanatomy and our previous research with cardiac vagal tone, we have proposed the vagal circuit of emotion regulation. The vagal circuit of emotion regulation incorporates lateral brain function with the regulation of the peripheral autonomic nervous system in the expression of emotion. The vagus and the vagal circuit do not function independently of other neurophysiological and neuroendocrine systems. Research on brain activity (see Dawson, in this volume; Fox, in this volume) and research on adrenocortical activity (see Stansbury & Gunnar, in this volume) demonstrate that EEG and cortisol are related to emotion states and to individual differences similar to those that we have investigated.

The vagal circuit emphasizes not only the vagus but also the lateralization of specific brain structures in emotion regulation. The emphasis of the vagal circuit on right-brain-stem structures stimulates several testable hypotheses regarding the function of specific structures in the right brain in emotion regulation. These speculations are consistent with other reports (see Dawson, in this volume; Fox, in this volume) describing asymmetrical EEG activity during expressed emotions. Moreover, the vagal circuit does not exist independently of the brain structures and peptide systems regulating cortisol (see Stansbury & Gunnar, in this volume). Areas in the brain stem regulating vagal activity are also sensitive to the peptides that regulate cortisol (e.g., vasopressin and corticotropin-releasing hormone).

In this essay, we have provided information regarding the relation between vagal tone and emotion regulation. A review of research indicates that baseline levels of cardiac vagal tone and vagal tone reactivity abilities are associated with behavioral measures of reactivity, the expression of emotion, and self-regulation skills. Thus, we propose that cardiac vagal tone can serve as an index of emotion regulation.

Historically, the vagus and other components of the parasympathetic nervous system have not been incorporated in theories of emotion. Recent developments in methodology have enabled us to define and accurately quantify cardiac vagal tone. Theories relating the parasympathetic nervous system to the expression and regulation of emotion are now being tested in several laboratories.

INTRODUCTION TO PART 3

In a paper published some 10 years ago and based on his presidential address to the Society for Psychosomatic Medicine, Myron Hofer raised the issue of how relationships could act as regulators of behavior (Hofer, 1984). This theme continues to be a central one in Hofer's current research and is, indeed, the central theme of the three essays in the third part of this *Monograph*. The question may be posed in two ways: How do relationships mediate the individual's ability to regulate emotional arousal both within the relationship and on an individual basis? and, What are the factors that influence the pathways of developing relationships, which in turn facilitate successful or dysfunctional emotion regulation?

Developmental theory has been ambivalent regarding the role of relationships in the child's social and cognitive development. On the one hand, there have been many studies of the importance of mother-infant interaction and of the types of behaviors that facilitate positive interaction. On the other hand, only a few researchers have addressed these issues from the perspective of the development of relationships. Most often the concern has been to identify the effects of specific patterns of the mother's behavior: which of these most facilitated cognitive development, which promoted secure attachment. Less often has it been the case that mothers' and infants' behaviors were seen as having important reciprocal regulatory functions for general emotional development and for the development of emotion regulation (for an exception, see, e.g., Stern, 1977).

To some extent this has been the case even for work on the development of attachment. Mother's behavior was seen as important in facilitating feelings of security in the infant, but, while notions of reciprocal regulatory control, first mentioned in Bowlby (1969), were acknowledged, they were not central to research in this area.

There has been, of course, a change in emphasis over the past 10 years. Current theory of emotion development, and attachment theory in particular, now places great importance on the ontogeny of the relationship itself, on the child's internalization of that relationship, and even on the parents' perception of their own original attachment relationships.

Two motivating forces, both reflected in the essays in this part, have contributed to this change. The first, represented in the work of Myron A. Hofer and Tiffany Field, is an increasing acknowledgment of the importance of data from psychobiological research. This research, exemplified by Hofer's work, traces the biological mechanisms underlying mothers' and infants' attachment behaviors. Its findings suggest functional explanations for these behaviors, explanations that have important implications for the growth and development of the neonate and for the formation of the mother-infant relationship. The relationship itself is a regulator of biological change and development. As such, the formation of that relationship becomes crucial to understanding the regulation of essential physiological processes. The role of these relationships as regulators at the biological level was anticipated by Bowlby but heretofore has not been well investigated by developmental psychologists.

This perspective has now been extended by Field and her colleagues to work on the formation of the mother-infant bond and the formation of relationships across childhood. Field has utilized the psychobiological model to suggest that relationships and the interactions that occur within them are critical to social development in early childhood. She has provided data to demonstrate the importance of early social relationships in the child's psychosocial health.

The second motivating force for a renewed emphasis on the development of relationships and their role in regulating behavior has come from within attachment theory itself. There has been an acknowledgment that internal working models of the initial attachment mature and are possibly transformed with the development of more complex symbolic and cognitive representations. Indeed, the attempt to examine security of attachment across the preschool and school years was undertaken in response to an awareness that the function and meaning of internal representations of relationships change over the course of development.

This new work on assessment of security during early and middle childhood deals explicitly with notions of the child's developing complex relationship with her parents. In her essay in this *Monograph,* Jude Cassidy presents an overview of these important new conceptualizations within attachment theory, focusing on proposed linkages between attachment relationship patterns and patterns of emotion regulation. As such, her essay puts attachment theory and research squarely into the mainstream discussion of the manner in which relationships regulate emotions and emotions come to assist in the regulation of relationships.

The three essays in this final part converge to advance our understanding of the role of relationships as regulators. They move us one step closer to understanding the wide range of behaviors that we are coming to view as reflecting emotion regulation.

N.A.F.

HIDDEN REGULATORS IN ATTACHMENT, SEPARATION, AND LOSS

Myron A. Hofer

Love and grief, two of the most intense and complex human emotions, have their origins in the infant's attachment to her parents and in her responses to separation from them. In early development, when these responses are first evident, we have no descriptions of the inner experience of these emotions and no verbal assessment measures to guide us in our research. In this regard, studies of human infants are no different from research with young animals; we must use observations of behavior and of physiological responses to make inferences about the nature of the processes responsible for the elicitation, the control of intensity, and the termination of these early emotion states.

Research on young mammals of widely divergent species has revealed a remarkable similarity between infant animal and human behavior, particularly with respect to behaviors used to maintain proximity and those elicited by separation. In addition, a number of physiological responses to separation have been described that generalize widely across species from laboratory rats to rhesus and pigtail macaque monkeys. These cross-species similarities encourage us to believe that we can learn something about the basic processes underlying attachment, separation, and loss in human infants from experimental studies on the young of other species.

Contemporary concepts of attachment grew out of attempts to understand responses to separation and loss (Bowlby 1969/1982, 1980) but are currently much more focused on individual differences in the development of patterns of attachment behaviors and of the mental representations that

This research was supported by Research Scientist and MERIT Awards from the National Institute of Mental Health. My thanks to Susan Brunelli for helpful suggestions in revising this essay.

are inferred to emerge from these behaviors. The original interest in the emotional responses to separation and loss has subsided, as if this question has been settled. But attachment theory is far from satisfactory as an explanation for responses to separation in very young infants or in animals with underdeveloped cognitive systems, and it cannot adequately explain the profound changes in biological systems that accompany loss and contribute to the nature of the emotions experienced. In the last few years, a new perspective has emerged as a result of experimental work directed at the early behavioral systems on which attachment is grounded. This essay describes this work and the new understanding it has provided.

In the first 6 months after birth, the foundations for psychological attachment are laid down through the web of sensory and behavioral interactions that characterize the parent-infant relationship and by the early emotion and physiological states that are induced by these events. Early behaviors of proximity maintenance as well as reactions to separation and responses to reunion take place, and it is from these experiences and from the interactions involved in feeding, play, and caretaking in the first months of life that the construction of internal working models of highly specified attachment figures gradually evolves.

This early "motivational-behavioral control system" (Bretherton, 1985) thus occupies a key position in the formation of the later attachment patterns that are currently such a focus of study. Yet we know relatively little about the properties of this very early attachment system. Since experimental separations are the best and possibly the only way to explore the first stages of the development of this system fully, such work will probably never be done with humans. Hence, the necessity for research on animal model systems.

What has emerged from our research on early mother-infant interaction and separation in an animal model is the discovery of widespread regulation of early behavioral and biological systems in the infant that is exerted by the mother-infant interaction. These regulatory processes are hidden within the observable transactions between mother and infant during the nursing period in young rats. We found regulators that allow the mother to control the level, intensity, and pattern of the infant rat's response systems in a graded fashion. Thus, the provision of warmth, the tactile and olfactory stimulation of the mother's physical interactions, and the oral sensory and absorptive consequences of nursing were found to provide specific and independent sources of regulation for one or another of the infants' emerging behaviors and neuroregulatory systems.

The discovery of these unexpected regulatory processes provides a new explanation for responses to separation and loss in these animals, one that allows us to understand their form and pattern in detail and to relate it to the nature of the relationship that was lost, for separation of the infant from its mother involves the withdrawal of all these regulatory processes at once. The result is a pattern of changes in different systems as each responds to release from its regulator within the previous mother-infant interaction. What appears to be a centrally integrated pattern is in fact an assemblage of individual processes.

These "hidden regulators" control the behavioral, autonomic, endocrine, and sleep-wake states of the infant rat and thus control the constituent parts of the early emotion states associated with attachment, separation, and loss. The existence of these regulators suggests that emotions may be eventually understood in terms of their subcomponents and that the regulation of emotions may be profitably viewed from a "bottom-up" perspective as well as by the more usual "top-down" approach. The discovery of these hidden regulators gives us a new level of understanding of the processes underlying attachment, separation, and loss and forms a conceptual bridge between the simple sensorimotor processes of very early development and the formation of the mental representations that organize the inner experience of emotional relationships with important figures in the lives of older children and adults—the internal working models of current attachment research.

RESPONSES TO SEPARATION AND LOSS
IN INFANT RATS AND PRIMATES

When I began to study early development in laboratory rats in the late 1960s, I assumed that choosing this convenient species would preclude my studying such complex cognitive-emotion events as attachment and responses to separation. I was prepared to begin with the long-term effects of simpler, physical stressors. It was thus a great surprise to me when I came to the lab one morning to find 2-week-old infant rats with dramatically low heart rates and in an apathetic and unresponsive behavioral state after the mother had escaped from their cage during the night and was unable to reenter the wire mesh top. Charles Kaufman and Leonard Rosenblum (1969) had just discovered a profound behavioral depression in pigtail macaques that had been separated from their mothers, and they had proposed that this demonstrated a "conservation-withdrawal" response analogous to W. B. Cannon's fight-flight response, but one having adaptive value in situations of prolonged danger in which active responses are useless. Suddenly, the responses so eloquently described by Heinicke and Westheimer (1965) in briefly separated human infants seemed to have broad representation across species, suggesting deep biological roots and a long evolutionary history.

Now, 20 years after this first discovery, we have learned quite a few things about attachment, separation, and loss from these relatively simple animal models. There are clearly important differences between species, but the behavioral and physiological responses of the infant rat to separation are remarkably complex and strikingly similar to what we know of the responses in humans and "lower" primates.

Because of their advantages as experimental subjects, we now know much more about these responses in rats than in any other species. Two-week-old rat pups show an immediate response to separation consisting of repeated, high-intensity vocalizations (in the ultrasonic range) accompanied by agitated "searching" behavior and high levels of self-grooming, even though they have reached an age at which they are capable of surviving without their mothers (Hofer & Shair, 1978). All evidence of distress is immediately alleviated by the return of a familiar littermate or dam, even when the infant is in unfamiliar surroundings. If the mother does not return, these behaviors wane over a period of hours, and a number of more slowly developing responses become evident. The pup becomes progressively less responsive, reaching a state of severely slowed movements and diminished alertness after 10–12 hours. Food is ignored, new stimuli are not investigated, and body temperatures and heart rates are reduced (Hofer 1970, 1973a).

This sequential response pattern closely parallels the protest and despair phases described by Bowlby (1969/1982) in humans and by Kaufman and Rosenblum (1969) in monkeys. Reite, Kaufman, Pauley, and Stynes (1974) subsequently found decreases in heart rate and body temperature in their separated monkeys that closely resembled the changes that we had found in rat pups.

Following 12 hours of separation, rat pups also show a central neural inhibition of metabolic mechanisms for generating heat from brown fat (and thereby increasing oxygen consumption) in response to cold (Bignall, Heggeness, & Palmer, 1977). This inhibitory mechanism accounts for the fall in core temperature of separated animals and seems to supply the "conservation" element of the "conservation-withdrawal" response by turning off mechanisms for energy expenditure.

The sleep of human infants separated from their mothers has been described as fitful and restless with frequent awakenings (Heinicke & Westheimer, 1965). When we recorded the sleep-wake states of rat pups separated for 24 hours, we found a fragmentation of states, with more frequent arousals, a greater number of state changes, an overall reduction in REM sleep, and a shortened duration of slow wave sleep periods even when nest temperatures were maintained (Hofer, 1976). Studies by Reite and Short (1978) showed a similar pattern of change in separated macaque infants.

Although the literature since Harlow has generally downplayed the role of feeding and nursing in attachment, separated human infants have been reported to develop increased oral activity and to suck more on their thumbs or on inanimate objects (Heinicke & Westheimer, 1965). Stephen Brake and I developed methods for recording sucking in rats and found three different patterns: one nutritive mode and two nonnutritive patterns. We also found a way to measure the intensity of the pup's seal on the nipple (reviewed in Brake, Shair, & Hofer, 1988). After 24 hours of separation, pups showed high levels of the nutritive sucking pattern even on a dry nipple, and one of the two nonnutritive patterns was greatly increased in frequency, as was the intensity of the nipple seal. These measures represent the most concrete way in which the pup "attaches" itself to the mother, and they were clearly activated by separation.

Finally, it is worth considering a long-term and severe effect of maternal deprivation in humans, growth retardation. It is known that growth hormone levels can be reduced and even the response to treatment with administered growth hormone blunted in the condition known as "psychosocial dwarfism" (Powell, Brasel, & Blizzard, 1967). In a striking cross-species parallel, infant rats have been found to show both these responses, and both can be reversed by reunion with the dam, even if her lactation is blocked (for a review, see Kuhn & Schanberg, 1991).

Thus, we have found some remarkable similarities in the responses of infant rats, monkeys, and humans to short-term separations from, and to longer-term losses of interaction with, their mothers.

A SIMPLE ATTACHMENT SYSTEM IN RATS

The most basic property of attachment is the presence of a number of behaviors by which the infant maintains close proximity to the mother (Bowlby, 1969/1982). From the moment of birth, rat pups show clear behavioral dispositions to follow certain tactile gradients on the dam's body and to search for and locate nipples. Within hours, they can use olfactory and tactile cues that have been associated with contact with the mother or the nipple and will remember such specific odor cues days later without further reminding. Contact with the dam can be shown to be rewarding as soon as pups can show the effects of runway or Y-maze training at 8–10 days of age (for a review, see Rosenblatt, 1983). Their vocalization response to isolation from the nest is quieted by a familiar social companion as well as by warmth alone within 3 days of birth (Carden & Hofer, 1992) and at 7–10 days of age by a variety of additional nest cues (Oswalt & Meier, 1975). By 15 days of age, they can use a long-distance pheromonal cue to find their way to their mother or to the home cage nest (Leon, 1974).

Attachment is also inferred from the responses of an individual to separation from a social companion or a familiar environment. Given this criterion, the results described in the previous section allow us to infer that some sort of attachment must exist between the infant rat and its mother and littermates. But one of the hallmarks of many definitions of *attachment* is its specificity, the presence of a "highly discriminated attachment object" (Bowlby, 1969/1982). This was an important part of Bowlby's original formulation that has since come under considerable criticism because human infants with experience in day care or with multiple caretakers do not show the single-minded responses originally described by Robertson and Bowlby in infants for whom their mother had been the only caretaker. It is clear that rat pups have a full complement of proximity-maintenance behaviors as Bowlby described them, but until quite recently it was thought that they could not discriminate between members of a relatively large social group. Moreover, rat pups will approach, huddle, and cease vocalizing in response to any object that provides the right olfactory, tactile, and thermal characteristics (Hofer & Shair, 1980).

However, in the past 5 years, rat pups have been shown to be capable of remarkable discrimination between individuals. Peter Hepper, an ethologist in England, developed a tunnel system with a choice point and a means of providing currents of air emanating from one or another individual rat, housed at a distance in the system (Hepper, 1986b). Hepper was able to show that rats younger than 1 week old turn toward their own littermate rather than toward a pup from another litter and choose their own dam (whether a foster dam or their biological mother) in preference to another lactating female. But his results went further than this. Pups are also able to tell their biological father from an unrelated male rat and to detect degrees of relatedness among a number of unfamiliar rats (Hepper, 1986a). This capacity stems from the use of a sense—olfaction—that is capable of molecular discrimination far more sensitive than the visual processing used by human infants. Chemical signal detection allows responses to scent cues reflecting genetic similarities as well as to scents associated with prior experience.

These remarkable findings provide a basis for concluding that, given the proper circumstances, highly discriminated attachment objects are not beyond the capabilities of infant rats, although comfort can be derived from a far broader class of individuals. Highly specific comfort responses in some species of birds, humans, and other primates may have more to do with the early maturation of "stranger avoidance" behavior in these species than with the specificity of kin recognition. The implication for human attachment theory is that what appears to be specificity of attachment (the refusal to be comforted by anyone except the familiar caretaker) after 7 months of age may be the product of maturation of another system involving fear of strangers. The capacity for individual discrimination may develop separately from the comfort response, and its integration with attachment and avoidance systems may be subject to considerable variability during subsequent development.

THE DISCOVERY OF REGULATORS
WITHIN THE MOTHER-INFANT INTERACTION

The first clue that regulators might be hidden within the interactions of infants and their mothers came from the effects of warmth supplied to separated pups. The 2-week-old pups described above (those whose mother had escaped from the cage and could not get back in) had very low heart rates (about a 40% reduction) and body temperatures about 2°C–3°C below normal (Hofer, 1973a). They showed the retarded movements and diminished responsiveness described in human infants and in the monkeys of Kaufman and Rosenblum (1969). I wondered whether the low heart rates could be due to cooling of the cardiac pacemaker cells, and to test this idea I supplied thermoregulated heat through the cage floor, maintaining the separated pups' core temperature throughout the 24-hour separation period. To my surprise, cardiac rates were just as low as before, but the pups' behavior was changed by the provision of warmth: instead of being slowed down behaviorally, separated pups with normal body temperatures were hyperactive. Thus, a 24-hour period of separation could produce either an overreactive or a depressed behavioral state, depending on whether one aspect of a mother's care—warmth—was supplied to the pups. Even more surprising, warmth did not appear to have a general effect on separation responses since it did not affect the cardiac response at all.

It occurred to me that different aspects of a mother's care appeared to have relatively specific effects on separated pups, and I wondered what aspect might affect their cardiac rates. This cardiac response interested me because it was so large and because I had found that it reflected a major change in sympathetic-parasympathetic balance within the pups' autonomic nervous system (Hofer & Weiner, 1971). A series of experiments showed that the cardiac response could be prevented by supplying milk but also—to my surprise—that the milk had no effect on the behavioral hyperactivity (Hofer, 1973c). Soon we found that this behavioral response was prevented by a nonlactating foster mother (Hofer, 1973b) without affecting the autonomic cardiac response.

These results drove home to me the fact that different features of the pup's response to separation were affected by different aspects of the experience of separation. The pups' behavioral reactivity could be either reduced or enhanced according to how much warmth was supplied. The pups' cardiac rate could be set at any level between normal and 40% below normal by the rate at which milk was infused to the separated pup through a gastric cannula. Finally, the behavioral interaction between mother and pup appeared to control the level of the pups' behavioral reactivity when their body temperatures were maintained.

Clearly, hidden within the interactions between mother and pup must be processes that regularly influence the pups' behavioral and physiological systems in a graded fashion. These processes appear to control infant systems, and it seems reasonable to think of them as "hidden regulators" of infant physiology and behavior.

Since these initial studies, a number of other regulatory processes have been discovered by us and by other groups. These act on behavioral, metabolic, endocrine, neurochemical, and autonomic systems (see below). We have found that regulators can be classified into three major categories: behavioral-sensorimotor, thermal-metabolic, and nutrient-interoceptive. The first of these categories may well be the largest, involving stimulation over all five senses and including complex elements of the interaction between mother and infant such as rhythm, synchrony, reciprocity, and other aspects of attunement (see Field, in this volume). The other two categories may prove to be complex as well. For example, in attempting to prevent sleep disturbance in separated pups, warmth, exteroceptive stimulation, and nutrient each seemed to be partially effective, but the element most necessary was the temporal aspect of the intervention supplied: milk and stimulation had to be given on phasic or periodic schedules. Apparently, the timing of the interaction was essential for maintenance of the temporal organization of sleep-wake states (Hofer, 1992; Hofer & Shair, 1982).

A NEW MECHANISM FOR RESPONSES TO SEPARATION

The discovery of these multiple regulators of infant physiology and behavior led me to ask if they could provide a new way of understanding the responses to separation, one that might apply to all young mammals. I realized that responses to separation may occur because regulators of behavior and physiology, inherent in the relationship, are withdrawn. Functions that had been maintained at relatively high levels then decline, and others that had been maintained at low levels rise. Patterns established by the timing of certain events within the interaction are lost.

Because the mother-infant interaction embodies multiple regulators of diverse infant systems, the loss of all the regulators at once produces a complex web of responses in different systems, their direction, timing, and intensity varying with the characteristics of individual systems. The response to separation is thus an assemblage of different processes, all of which reflect a single mechanism, release from regulation.

The later course of separation responses has always been somewhat mysterious: the remarkable recovery that children can make even after very intense initial reactions and the long-term effects that brief separations can have on later behavior despite this apparent recovery. The concept of relationships as regulators suggests that other relationships can eventually replace the regulatory processes that were originally lost. Furthermore, self-regulatory processes also exist and increase in effectiveness as animals mature. The recovery of infant humans, primates, and rats after separation is quite remarkable and may be understood as an adaptation involving both self-regulatory systems and the establishment of new regulatory interactions between infants and their new social and inanimate environments.

Below, I consider first the immediate responses to separation— vocalization and agitated behavior, Bowlby's "protest" responses—and then the more slowly developing "despair" responses such as sleep disturbance, changes in behavioral reactivity, and endocrine responses.

Protest and Comfort Responses as Outcomes of Affect Regulation

Attachment theory infers a motivational system in which clinging, following, searching, and crying behaviors are activated by events that disturb proximity to the attachment object (Bowlby, 1969/1982). These behaviors serve to restore proximity and then cease to be activated through feedback within this "goal-corrected system." This is Bowlby's innate homeostatic system, which he believed evolved through its survival value to the young as protection against predators and environmental hazards. Thus, in this conceptual scheme, the protest response to separation is nothing more than highly activated attachment behavior. The comfort response is the termination of this activation.

There are important affective components of these behaviors. As Bowlby puts it, "Intense affects arise during the formation, maintenance, disruption and renewal of attachment relationships. The formation of the bond is described as falling in love, maintaining a bond as loving someone, and losing a partner as grieving. . . . Threat of loss arouses anxiety and actual loss gives rise to sorrow; while each of these [latter] situations is likely to arouse anger" (Bowlby, 1980, p. 40).

However, it is possible to view the comfort response as the result of regulation of the infant's level of affective arousal through defined sensory interactions occurring during contact and close proximity. Tactile, textural, thermal, olfactory, vestibular, auditory, and visual stimuli experienced in predictable patterns may be considered to act in a graded fashion to modulate arousal within a range from quiet alert to sleep, consistent with the experienced affects of comfort and security. The protest response then would occur when these sensory interactions are withdrawn as a result of separation and the source of affect regulation is lost. Released from the down-regulatory effect of close proximity, the infant's affective arousal state rises rapidly to levels of high distress, a possible precursor of anxiety as we know it in adults.

What evidence is there in support of such an idea? Several years ago, Harry Shair and I explored the sensory qualities necessary for an object to attenuate the separation-distress vocalization response elicited by placing a rat pup alone in unfamiliar surroundings (Hofer & Shair, 1980). By using artificial fur, contoured surfaces, warmth, and scents taken from the home cage nest, we found that the rate of ultrasonic calling was reduced in a graded fashion that depended on the number of familiar sensory modalities and on how they were arranged in model surrogates that resembled the pup's littermate to various degrees. For example, a rubber model that was warm but had no soft textural or familiar olfactory cues was ineffective, a piece of soft fur laid flat on the floor was somewhat effective, while a flashlight battery warmed to 36°C, wrapped in fur, and scented with home cage shavings was almost as effective as an anesthetized littermate, reducing vocalization rate by 70%. Other combinations of modalities fell in between. We also observed the amount of time that pups maintained contact with the various test stimuli and found a very close correlation between degree of reduction in vocalization and the amount of contact elicited ($r = .94$).

These results appeared to support the idea that we had identified tactile, thermal, and olfactory cues that reduced affective arousal levels of pups and controlled the proximity that pups maintained with the test object in a graded fashion typical of regulatory control. The distress of separation would then be the result of a release from those sources of regulation that maintain affective arousal at low levels during close proximity. Ordinarily, we think of distress as being stimulated by events, rather than as being held in check by them. But physiological research has shown that the long-term effect of intermittent stimulation is often to *reduce* the level of functions. For example, the repeated action of the cardiac pressure pulses on arterial baroreceptors (pressure-sensitive neural feedback systems) has the cumulative long-term effect of reducing central sympathetic activity, an effect that is revealed by the dramatic surge in blood pressure and heart rate that occurs in the days following section of the arterial baroreceptor nerves that had conveyed this phasic stimulation to the brain stem (Alexander, Velasquez, Decuir, & Maronde, 1980). Similarly, the intense physiological and psychomotor activation of heroin withdrawal appears to be due to the now unopposed action of the excitatory mechanisms that had previously counteracted the chronic down-regulatory action of the drug. These "escape phenomena" are well established in other systems and may apply as well to the release of affect in infants as a response to separation.

More Slowly Developing Responses as Loss of Hidden Regulators

Following the immediate responses to separation come the more slowly developing changes in behavioral reactivity level, body temperature, cardiac rate, sleep-wake states, sucking patterns, growth hormone, and corticosterone levels. Some of these changes were discussed above in the section on the discovery of regulators, where I described how the loss of the mother's thermal input resulted in slowed movements and diminished behavioral reactivity. The mechanism for this effect was explored further, and it was found that brain catecholamines (norepinephrine and dopamine) accumulate at a slower rate in pups separated without a heat source (Stone, Bonnet, & Hofer, 1976). However, if nest temperature was maintained, catecholamine levels of separated pups rose above normally mothered controls, and the pups became hyperactive. If this accumulation was prevented pharmacologically, hyperactivity did not occur (Hofer, 1980a). Thermal input thus appears to be a regulator of central neurotransmitter systems and behavior, within a broad range.

The increased behavioral responsiveness developed only after 4 hours of separation, reaching a maximum at 12–18 hours. It was essentially an intensification of the "searching" behavior (rises, ambulation, etc.) previously described as a part of the immediate "protest" response to isolation in an unfamiliar test area. It could not be related to loss of the mother's thermal input since it occurred in separated pups maintained at nest temperature. We also found that it was not prevented by nutrient infusions at rates resulting in normal or increased weight gain. We were able to attenuate or prevent this response to separation by providing intermittent tactile stimulation or mother-specific olfactory stimulation, but not by vestibular stimulation, novelty, or the presence of familiar littermates (Hofer, 1975). Thus, the development of hyperresponsiveness in pups separated in a nest temperature environment was due to loss of sensorimotor regulators in the mother-infant interaction that normally inhibited or "down-regulated" this behavioral system.

The autonomic changes underlying the fall in heart rate were found to be the result of loss of the nutrient normally delivered by the mother to the infant's stomach during the nursing interaction (Hofer & Weiner, 1975). Observations by Reite suggest that a nutrient mechanism may also underlie the fall in heart rate in separated infant monkeys (Reite & Capitanio, 1985). For rat pups, the gastric route was essential—intravenous nutrient was ineffective, as was mere gastric distention—but not because of some specific milk factor since glucose, protein, and corn oil were equally effective. Apparently, gastric interoceptors provided the afferent route for the regulatory effect that was withdrawn by separation and resulted in the 30% fall in the level of this function.

The central inhibition of the metabolic response to cold in separated pups has also been traced to loss of contact of nutrient with interoceptors in the stomach and/or intestines (Bignall et al., 1977). This effect of separation was reversed with intragastric but not subcutaneous glucose injections. The inhibition of thermogenesis was found to arise centrally, above the pons, on the basis of its immediate reversal by mid-pontine transections but not by hypothalamic lesions.

The fragmentation of sleep-wake states, increased arousals, and decreased REM sleep time of separated infants was found to be due to loss of periodically delivered nutrient and tactile stimulation (Hofer & Shair, 1982). This disturbance occurred even in pups maintained at nest temperature, but it was exaggerated in pups separated also from a source of warmth. Intermittent but not constant infusions of milk were effective in alleviating the sleep-wake disorder of separated pups. It appears that sleep-wake state changes after separation are due to loss of the timed events of the interaction as well as to loss of the more steadily applied warmth. A complex pattern of changes appears to follow these losses.

The increase in rhythmic pattern of nutritive sucking following separation was traced to the loss of the gastric distention provided by the milk previously consumed. However, the increase in the arrhythmic patterns of nonnutritive sucking was due to loss of the orosensory stimulation provided by the nursing interaction (for a review, see Brake, Shair, & Hofer, 1988). Here, increases in two different patterns of the same behavior are consequences of the loss of different regulators acting at two different locations.

The pronounced fall in growth hormone level that follows separation was discovered by Kuhn and Schanberg to be due at least in part to loss of the sensorimotor aspects of the mother-infant interaction (for a review, see Kuhn & Schanberg, 1991). The hormonal change could be reversed by interaction with a nonlactating foster dam and prevented by vigorous tactile stimulation of the separated pup, but the levels of stimulation required to prevent the separation-induced decline in growth hormone had to be greater than the levels present in the interaction. Recently, a more detailed search for regulators of growth hormone in 2–8-day-old rat pups has shown that provision of high levels of ambient temperature (37°C) and some factor carried in the water-soluble solids of rat milk (other than nutrients such as glucose or protein) can reverse the separated pups' growth hormone decline (Kacsoh, Meyers, Crowley, & Grosvenor, 1990). Thus, levels of this hormone appear to fall as a result of the loss of three different forms of regulatory interaction.

The most recent system found to show significant alterations following the separation of young rats from their mother is the hypothalamic-pituitary-adrenal. A fivefold increase in the corticosterone response to novelty or saline injection (Stanton, Gutierrez, & Levine, 1988) and a remarkable fifteenfold increase in basal levels of corticosterone (Kuhn, Pauk, & Schanberg, 1990) have been described in 10–15-day-old pups after a 24-hour separation. Some of the altered function appears to occur in the adrenal response to adrenocorticotrophic hormone (ACTH), but corticosterone responses to saline solution and to novelty also appear to be independently enhanced through a central neural mechanism. The latter change appears to be the result of loss of some regulators present in passive contact with the mother (Rosenfeld et al., 1991).

The factor responsible for heightened adrenal responsivity has not yet been identified, but preliminary data suggest that it will prove to be nutrient based. Thus, this stress-responsive endocrine system appears to be powerfully up-regulated following separation owing to removal of at least two inhibitory regulators formerly present in the mother-infant interaction, one involving tactile and/or olfactory aspects of contact and one involving loss of some aspect of milk delivery (for a detailed description of this system, see Stansbury & Gunnar, in this volume). Thermal metabolic effects have yet to be systematically evaluated.

In summary, there appear to be numerous regulators that arise out of different aspects of the mother-infant interaction and that impinge on the pup in different ways. Furthermore, the physiological transduction mechanisms within the pup are quite intricate and vary widely between regulatory systems. Loss of these regulatory interactions results in changed levels of function through absence of activation of the transduction mechanisms. Levels of function in various systems may increase (e.g., sucking, arousals from sleep, corticosterone output) or decrease (e.g., cardiac rate, REM sleep, growth hormone) during separation according to whether the previous regulatory effect had been to inhibit or to enhance levels of activity within a given system.

FROM HIDDEN REGULATORS TO MENTAL REPRESENTATIONS

The regulatory interactions that we can study experimentally constitute the stuff out of which mental representations and their associated emotions arise. So far as we understand the process, experiences made up of individual acts, parents' responses, sensory impressions, and associated affects are laid down in the child's memory during and after early parent-infant interactions. These individual units of experience are integrated into something like a network of attributes invested with associated affect, and they result in the formation of an internal working model of the relationship. Expectations, longings, and fantasies based on these representations then become the basis for motivational systems, for comparison with ongoing events, and for attitudes and actions toward others. In this way, regulatory interactions in infancy become the building blocks out of which the mental representations and related inner affective experiences of children and adults are built.

As soon as associative memories begin, infants begin to function at a symbolic level as well as at the sensorimotor level of the regulatory processes described above. In infants of species with the necessary cognitive capacities, mental representations of caretakers are formed out of the individual units of their experience with the regulatory interactions that I have described above. It seems likely that, once formed, these organized mental structures come to act as superordinate regulators of biological systems underlying motivation and affect, gradually supplanting the sensorimotor, thermal, and nutrient regulatory systems found in younger infants. This would link biological systems with internal object representations in humans and would account for the remarkable upheavals of biological as well as psychological systems that take place in response to separation signaled only by warning cues or by losses established simply on hearing of a death, for example, by telephone. Thus, in older children and adults, the regulation inherent in an important social relationship may be transduced not only by the sensorimotor and temporal patterning of the actual interactions but also by the internal experience of the relationship in the form of an internal working model or mental representation (Hofer, 1984). And mother-infant relationships that differ in quality, and that consequently involve different levels of regulation in a variety of systems, will be reflected in the nature of the mental representations constructed by different children as they grow up.

The emotions aroused during the early crying response to separation, during the profound state changes associated with the loss of hidden regulators, and during the reunion of a separated infant with her mother are clearly intense. They command our attention and correspond to our inner experiences of attachment and loss as adults. But they occur at a different level of psychobiological organization than the changes in autonomic, endocrine, and neurophysiological systems that we have been able to study in rats and monkeys or in younger human infants. The discovery of regulatory interactions and the effects of their withdrawal allows us to understand not only the responses to separation in young organisms of limited cognitive-emotional capacity but also those in which the familiar emotions and mental representations can be described to us by the child or inferred from higher-order behavioral capabilities. It is not that rat pups respond to loss of regulatory processes while human infants respond to emotions of love, sadness, anger, and grief. As they mature, human infants can respond at the symbolic level *as well as* at the level of the behavioral and physiological processes of the regulatory interactions. Even adult humans continue to respond at the sensorimotor-physiological level in their social interactions, separations, and losses, continuing a process begun in infancy (Hofer, 1984).

SUMMARY AND PERSPECTIVES

Bowlby's concept of an attachment system described its role as one of regulating the closeness of mother and infant. Bowlby saw the system as having the qualities of a physiological homeostatic system, such as that regulating blood pressure, and as being of almost equal importance to infants, although acting at a different level of organization. In this essay, I have looked within the workings of the relationship and described a number of interactions between mother and infant that regulate the infant's behavior and physiology. This form of regulation acts at the level of physiological homeostasis and on the neural systems underlying behavior. Our discovery of these regulators hidden within the observable events of the relationship shows us that the infant's homeostatic systems are more "open" than we had expected and that the infant delegates a portion of the control of her *milieu interieur* to processes within her relationship with her mother. Likewise, the mother's lactational physiology and probably other aspects of her internal states are open to regulation by these same interactions. This linkage of two individuals' homeostatic systems into a superordinate organization we can call *symbiosis* after the first use of this term by the botanist Anton DeBary in 1879 to describe the mutual benefits accruing to plants that grow in close physical proximity to each other.

The discovery of regulators within social interactions has important implications for understanding responses to separation and loss. For the first time, we have a mechanism to explain how these experiences are translated into behavioral and physiological changes, such as those referred to as *protest* and *despair*. This mechanism can act at any stage in development from the fetus to old age and is primarily responsible for these responses before the development of psychological attachment takes place. The relative roles of higher-order mental processes and of interactional regulators in the grief of children and adults is an interesting topic for future research. There are a number of known regulators of adult human function that suggest that human relationships have similar hidden regulators resembling in principle those found in infant rats (Hofer, 1984). Once identified, these regulators can become the basis for clinical interventions, such as in the care of premature babies. Based on the rat studies, Field and Schanberg have carried out controlled studies in which tactile and kinesthetic stimulation was administered to premature babies carefully matched with controls (see Field, in this volume).

Regulation of behavior and biology is not exerted only over the relatively short time periods considered in this essay. The close mother-infant relationship, lasting throughout the early development of most mammals, provides an opportunity for differential regulation of development of the infant by the qualitative and quantitative differences between relationships (Myers, Brunelli, Shair, Squire, & Hofer, 1989; Myers, Brunelli, Squire, Shindledecker, & Hofer, 1989). The mother is thus capable of inducing modifications in her offspring, through the regulators within her relationship with them, that could preadapt them to changing conditions. Vertical transmission of the effects of experience to subsequent generations has been described for both biological (Skolnick, Ackerman, Hofer, & Weiner, 1980) and behavioral (Denenberg & Whimbey, 1963) traits as a result of the mother's prior experience. This constitutes a biological analogue of cultural evolution and could have conveyed a selective advantage to mothers and infants who had strong proximity-maintenance (behavioral attachment) systems.

This form of mutual regulation between infants and mothers originates before psychological attachment develops, with its mental representations and highly differentiated affective states. Indeed, regulatory processes are the precursors of psychological attachment and its associated emotions. Thus, the neural substrates for emotion are regulated by specific aspects of the mother-infant interaction even before emotion expression becomes clearly differentiated and readily recognizable. It is no small wonder then that many emotions are so strongly affected by social interactions, that certain emotions may be considered to be regulated by relationships, even later in life, and that the self-regulation of emotion appears to be intimately tied to the concept of self, a form of internal symbolic relationship constructed out of these early interactional experiences.

THE EFFECTS OF MOTHER'S PHYSICAL AND EMOTIONAL UNAVAILABILITY ON EMOTION REGULATION

Tiffany Field

Infant emotion regulation develops in the context of early mother-infant interactions (for animal models, see also Hofer, in this volume). The mother assumes various roles in these interactions, as does the infant, and together they develop attunement. Emotion dysregulation can occur when the mother is either physically unavailable, as during early separations, or, even worse, emotionally unavailable, as, for example, if she is depressed. Physical or emotional unavailability of the mother contributes to dysregulation because the mother can no longer act as optimal stimulator and an arousal regulator for the infant.

This essay first reviews data on the mothers' and infants' roles during early interactions and how these serve to foster the development of infant emotion regulation. Data and methodologies are then reviewed for the measurement of synchrony, or attunement, during early interactions. Next, illustrations are provided of the ways in which physical unavailability—specifically, early separations due to the mother's hospitalization or her conference trips—contributes to emotion dysregulation. This is followed by illustrations of how the mother's emotional unavailability (due to her depression) contributes to emotion dysregulation. Finally, future research directions are suggested for the assessment of individual differences in the development of emotion regulation and dysregulation.

This research was supported by a National Institute of Mental Health (NIMH) Research Scientist Award (MH00331) and an NIMH research grant (MH40779) to Tiffany Field. I would like to thank all the mothers and infants who participated in these studies. Direct correspondence to Tiffany Field, Department of Pediatrics, University of Miami School of Medicine, P.O. Box 016820, Miami, FL 33101.

EMOTION REGULATION DURING EARLY INTERACTIONS

In a number of earlier papers, my colleagues and I advanced the notion that infants develop emotion regulation, or become behaviorally and physiologically organized, in the context of early mother-infant interactions (e.g., Field, 1978, 1985, 1991a). Because the infant spends most of the time with the primary caregiver, who is typically the mother, this can be considered the primary learning environment for the development of emotion regulation. Mothers' and infants' roles in accomplishing the regulation of infant behavior and physiology are discussed in Field (1978).

Mothers' and Infants' Roles in the Development of Infant Emotion Regulation

As noted in Field (1978), the mother's roles in helping the infant establish behavioral and physiological organization consist of reading the infant's signals and, accordingly, providing optimal stimulation (with respect to stimulation modality, form, intensity, variability, and contingency), which in turn provides arousal modulation that permits the infant to remain behaviorally and physiologically organized. They also include the modeling of behaviors to be imitated by the infant and contingent responsivity of the behavior (meaning that the mother typically simplifies and imitates the infant's behavior), which in turn leads to reinforcement of the infant's behaviors.

Similarly, the infant remains physiologically and behaviorally organized, alert, attentive, and receptive to stimulation; reads the mother's signals during social interactions; seeks out and approaches optimal stimulation (which depends on the infant's stimulus threshold, sleep-wake state, and ability to self-regulate independent of the parent's modulation, all of which depends on the infant's maturity and previous experience); withdraws and averts from nonoptimal stimulation; and contingently responds to the mother's behaviors (mostly via imitation). That contingent response in turn reinforces the mother's behaviors. When the mother and infant are able to assume these roles effectively during their early interactions, behavioral and physiological attunement is achieved, and the interactions appear harmonious and synchronous.

Behavioral and Physiological Attunement

Attunement is a term used to describe the phenomenon that occurs when mothers and infants appear to be coordinated behaviorally and/or are concordant physiologically during early interactions (Field, 1985). It has also been called *behavior meshing, affect matching, synchrony, concordance,* and *en-*

trainment, to name only a few alternate terms. Stern (1974) was one of the first to describe this phenomenon in infants, demonstrating dramatic differences in the mother-child interactions of two twins: the mother and one twin were synchronous during their interactions, whereas the other twin and the mother were unable to arrive at a mutually optimal level of stimulation. Stern suggested that mothers "infantize" their behavior so that the infant can closely match it and they can achieve synchrony together.

More recently, Stern (1983) has labeled that phenomenon *affect attunement,* noting that 48% of the mother's behaviors consist of mirroring/ echoing the infant's visual/vocal behavior in either the same or a different modality. The criterion he used for coding attunement was whether the mother's behavior matched the infant's behavior on shape, intensity, contour, or temporal features (duration, beat, or rhythm). In psychoanalytic terms, Stern suggested that this phenomenon was a matching of inner states of the infant and mother.

Brazelton and his colleagues took a similar approach, plotting rhythmic cycles of the infant's attention and the mother's activity during mother-infant interactions (Brazelton, Koslowski, & Main, 1974). Mothers were seen to meet their infants' needs in one of three ways: by adjusting their rhythm to the infant's, following the baby's gazing-away cues with increases and decreases in stimulation; by not responding to the child's rhythm but rather continuing their own stimulation, thus reinforcing the time the infant spends looking away; or by attempting to impose their own rhythm to regulate the child's. The sensitive timing of these behaviors was illustrated by a series of photographs taken from a similar study by our group (see Fig. 1). As in a dance, the mother and infant can be seen to be sensitively attuned to each other.

Since the publication of these early studies, a number of systems have been developed for the coding of these behaviors and of the affective quality of interactions (see Beebe, Jaffe, Feldstein, Mays, & Alson, 1985; Tronick, Als, & Brazelton, 1977). In these systems, behavioral states are scaled along an attentional/affective dimension (from negative to neutral to positive states or from disengagement to engagement) for each member of the dyad, and the data are then examined for the amount of time the mother and infant share the same behavior state. In harmonious interactions, infants and mothers appear to share and experience the same behavior states (Beebe et al., 1985); furthermore, infants and mothers seem to cycle together across these behavioral states, as if sharing interaction rhythms. Some authors have suggested that interaction rhythms are biologically based, resembling the temporal rhythms of sucking, cardiac, and respiratory rhythms (Stratton, 1982; Wolff, 1967). Others have suggested that the interactions themselves entrain the rhythms of the infant (Beebe et al., 1985; Sander, 1969).

Measurement of Attunement

The measurement of attunement has come to depend on the coding of videotapes, using laptop-computer technology for continuous coding (Guthertz & Field, 1989). This method, combined with the increasing sophistication of time-series data analysis (Gottman, 1989; Warner, 1989), has greatly facilitated the development of this research area. The assumption underlying these methods of data analysis is that synchrony occurs when a behavior cycles with another behavior in rhythm. Any behavior/physiology that occurs rhythmically can be described in terms of cycles, periods, frequencies, and amplitudes; cycles typically occur in ranges of seconds. Once each of the individual cycles has been determined, these are then examined for coherence or concordance. Synchrony is then defined as the degree of coherence or concordance between the behavioral/physiological cycles of the two individuals.

One of the simplest approaches to studying synchrony is to code the behavior streams of each individual for various behaviors or affective states; the proportion of time that both individuals are displaying the same behavior or state is then determined by the computer. Typically, the behavior states are scaled along the attentional/affective dimension of disengagement to engagement, and greater behavior state matching or sharing by the members of the dyad is considered greater synchrony.

Currently, the most popular method for assessing shared rhythmicity in interactions is cross-spectral analysis. Two time series are created by coding the behavior states of each of the two partners second by second. Spectral analysis is first performed to determine whether both individuals' behaviors are significantly cyclic, whether they fall within one basic frequency band, and whether their cyclicities overlap. Then, to demonstrate synchrony, two other functions need to be examined: first the coherence spectrum, which assesses the linear associations of the cycles; then the phase spectrum, which measures the lead-lag relation of the cycles (Gottman, Rose, & Mettetal, 1982) (according to Gottman, 1981, analysis of the coherence spectrum is required to determine whether the time series are related). Cross-spectral analysis is then applied to determine the coherence or shared variance of the two time series at different frequencies. This model is further described in the examples of dysregulation given below.

EMOTION DYSREGULATION IN EARLY INFANCY

Emotion dysregulation occurs when the mother's physical or emotional unavailability deprives the infant of her *zeitgeber,* or regulator. As I have argued earlier (Field, 1987), the mother is a modulator of the infant's opti-

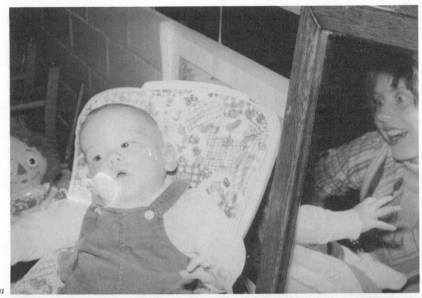

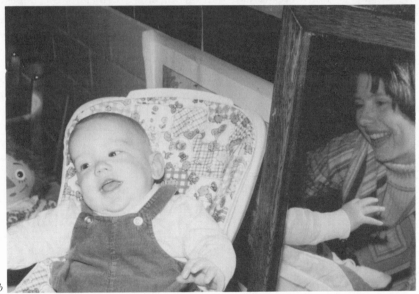

c

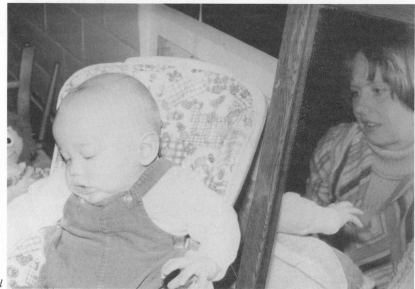

d

Fig. 1.—A typical sequence observed during "attuned" interactions of normal infants and their mothers. *a,* The infant looks at the mother, and the mother shows an exaggerated facial expression (mock surprise). *b,* The infant and the mother smile. *c,* The infant laughs. *d,* The infant looks away. The mother ceases smiling and watches her infant. (From Field & Fogel, 1982.)

mal stimulation and arousal level, and, in optimal interactions, the mother's and the infant's attentive/affective behaviors and physiological rhythms become synchronized. If, however, the mother is physically unavailable (during early separations) or emotionally unavailable (i.e., affectively unresponsive, as, e.g., during a period of depression), the infant experiences behavioral and physiological disorganization, and the mother's and the infant's behavioral and physiological rhythms become asynchronous. This is manifested in affective disturbance and changes in the infant's motor, physiological, or biochemical activity levels, which follow from either temporary or chronic loss of an important external regulator of stimulation that the infant needs for arousal modulation.

A similar model, the mutual regulation model, has been proposed by Tronick and Giannino (1987). According to these authors, "Because of her own emotional state, [the depressed mother] fails to respond to her infant's other-directed regulatory signals, and thus fails to provide the infant with appropriate regulatory help" (p. 9). Tronick and Giannino argue that maintenance of synchrony is not important. Rather, they suggest that such circumstances lead the infant to develop skills to restore or "repair" harmony that are significant for successful early socioemotional functioning. By their reasoning, one might expect infants of depressed mothers to develop even greater skills because of their greater experience with asynchronous interactions.

Physical Unavailability:
Examples Taken from Early Separations

At around 9 months, dysregulation can be seen during separations from the mother. In our model, the dysregulating effect of the mother's physical unavailability is thought to occur because substitute caregivers are less familiar with the infant's signals, thresholds, personal preferences for stimulation, etc. They are less able to provide optimal stimulation than the mother, and, as a result, the mother's absence leads to loss of the external regulator of the infant's arousal level. Because of their lesser familiarity with the infant's stimulation preferences, substitute caregivers tend to be more arousing and have more difficulty regulating the infant's arousal level. The combined effects of missing a source of optimal stimulation and arousal regulation can lead to disorganization of physiology (as indexed by heart rate), play behavior, affect, activity level, sleep, and other vegetative functions during the separations, which sometimes extends even into the postreunion periods.

By the end of the first year, the infant has probably mastered a number of self-regulatory behaviors that should attenuate the stress associated with separation from the mother; examples of such skills are gaze aversion and such self-comforting behaviors as thumb sucking. In addition, the infant will have begun to develop strategies for emotion regulation that are well tailored to particular partners and/or circumstances. Arousal reducing behaviors that are effective with mothers may differ from those that are effective with fathers, nursery caregivers, or peers. Emotion regulation is fostered in different ways by different partners. Emotion dysregulation is probably most apparent in the absence of the infant's primary, most familiar caregiver.

Separations Due to Mother's Hospitalization

We have investigated mother-infant separations using the paradigm developed by Martin Reite and his colleagues to study infant pigtail and bonnet monkeys (Reite & Capitanio, 1985). These investigators surgically implanted telemetry in their infant monkeys and monitored both their behavior and their physiology during a period prior to mother-infant separations, during the separations themselves, and following the pairs' reunions. Generally, they found a period of behavioral agitation followed by a period of depression that often persisted after the mother-infant reunion. The infants moved more slowly than normal, and their play behavior was diminished; they showed sleep disturbances accompanied by increases in both heart rate and body temperature that were followed by decreases to below baseline. For several monkeys, the behaviors did not return to normal following reunion; the authors suggest that the mother continued to be unavailable to the infant in these cases, either because she was coming into estrus during the period of separation or because she needed to reestablish herself in the dominance hierarchy after her return.

In our study, the mother was separated from her infant (0–12 months), toddler (12–24 months), or preschooler (2–5 years) owing to the birth of another child (Field, 1985; Field & Reite, 1984). Similar to the data on the infant monkeys, the data on human infants showed agitated behavior and physiology during the period of the mother's hospitalization and depressed behavior and activity following the mother's return from the hospital. The latter suggests that the mother remained unavailable to the infant despite her physical presence; typically, the mothers were tired, and some experienced postpartum depression. Inevitably, the mother-infant relationship was altered by the arrival of the new sibling. Similar to the monkeys, the infants were agitated during their mothers' hospitalization, showing increases in negative affect, activity level, heart rate, night wakings, and crying. Longer than usual periods of deep sleep at this stage were interpreted as conservation withdrawal. After the mother returned, decreases were noted in positive affect, activity level, heart rate, and active sleep, effects that are suggestive of depression. The parents also noted illnesses, clinging and aggressive behaviors, and changes in eating, toileting, and sleep patterns. The infants were clearly agitated by being separated from the mother even though they were cared for by their fathers.

The fathers may not have been as effective in modulating these infants' arousal because of their lesser experience with the child's arousal modulation needs. Heightened arousal can stimulate the sympathetic adrenergic system, resulting in agitated behavior typically associated with active coping—in this case, active attempts to recall the mother. The emergence of depression as the separation continued may relate to a number of factors. Given our assumptions about the nonoptimal quality of the father's care, the child's depression could have been a homeostatic mechanism acting to offset the sympathetic arousal or agitation arising in the absence of effective arousal modulation, or it might have resulted from inadequate amounts of stimulation. Moreover, the children may have experienced helplessness during the separation because of their failure to recall the mother and during the reunion because the arrival of the new sibling had altered the relationship.

This, of course, is the major confound of this paradigm—it does not permit assessing how much the changes in behavior are related to the separation per se and how much to the altered mother-infant relationship. Thus, in a subsequent study, we examined the effects of a separation that was not confounded by a change in relationship, namely, separation due to the mother's attending a conference (Field, 1991b).

Separations Due to Mother's Conference Trip

In this paradigm, we simply observed infants, toddlers, and preschoolers before, during, and after their mothers' conference trips (Field, 1991b). The observations for this study were conducted in a nursery school. Because the children in this study attended nursery school while those in our study on hospital separations did not, direct comparisons could not be made between the two sets of data. In particular, during our pilot testing we noted that children who remained at home during the mother's trip were more stressed during that period than those who remained in school; hence, it appears that the child's familiar peers and teachers may have served to buffer the usual separation stress. Of course, others (e.g., Cassidy, in this volume) might interpret this behavior instead as a "dampening" of negative emotion expression as in a "stiff upper lip" kind of behavior.

As can be seen in Table 1, changes in the children's behaviors indicate that they experienced stress during the mother's absence. However, as can

TABLE 1

MEANS FOR FREE-PLAY AND SLEEP MEASURES AT BASELINE AND DURING SEPARATIONS
FOR SINGLE AND MULTIPLE SEPARATIONS

	SINGLE SEPARATION (N = 40)		MULTIPLE SEPARATIONS (N = 40)	
	Baseline	During	Baseline	During
Activity level	14.1[a]	19.1[b]	14.7[a]	16.1[b]
Wandering aimlessly	6.1[a]	10.5[b]	6.4[a]	5.8[b]
Watching children	14.3[a]	26.4[b]	15.8[a]	17.7[b]
Cooperative play	24.8[a]	15.5[b]	26.8[a]	32.4[b]
Fantasy play	46.7[a]	30.3[b]	44.7[a]	49.1[b]
Fussiness	5.3[a]	12.1[b]	6.3[a]	5.5[b]

SOURCE.—Adapted from Field (1991b).
NOTE.—Lowercase letters across rows represent post hoc comparisons that are significantly different at $p < .05$ or less.

also be seen in Table 1, comparison of those who had experienced repeated separations with those who had experienced only a single separation suggests adjustment to repeated separation. Also, when later and earlier separations were compared, later separations were found to be less stressful. Thus, it appears that children learn to adapt to separations from their mothers when these are not accompanied by changes in relationships. It should also be noted that, in this sample of dual-career medical faculty and staff families, no differences were seen between the children's responses to separation from mother and from father.

Hospital versus Conference Trip Separations

To permit comparisons that could not be performed with the data sets just described, we undertook another study: using the same nursery school population as before, we compared the child's response to separation due to mother's hospitalization for the birth of another child and to mother's conference trips. As can be seen in Table 2, a number of significant differences emerged. *During the actual separation,* parents reported more sleep and behavior problems when the separation was due to hospitalization than when it was due to a conference trip. In addition, less smiling was noted during the play observations, and the children spent a greater proportion of their nap time in active sleep. This latter difference was interpreted as indicating conservation withdrawal; the children's more agitated behavior during hospital as opposed to conference separations exhausted them more, and they required more sleep. *Following the return of the mother,* parents continued to report more sleep and general behavior problems following hospital as opposed to conference trip separations. During play, the post-

TABLE 2

Means for Children's Behaviors Observed during Separation and after the
Mother's Return from a Conference Trip versus a Hospitalization
for the Birth of a Sibling ($p < .05$, $N = 20$)

OBSERVATION PERIOD	TYPE OF SEPARATION	
	Conference Trip	Hospitalization
Separation:		
Sleep problems (rating)	1.0	2.4
Behavior problems (rating)	.7	1.6
Smiling (% time)	7.4	2.7
Active sleep (% time)	4.3	10.8
After mother's return:		
Sleep problems (rating)	.6	2.4
Behavior problems (rating)	.8	1.6
Smiling (% time)	8.9	5.4
Positive verbal interaction (% time)	13.1	4.9
Fantasy play (% time)	38.7	23.2

hospital separation group also showed less smiling, less fantasy play, and fewer positive verbal interactions. Thus, in general, the hospital separations were significantly more stressful for the children than separations due to conference trips, probably because of the anticipated and actual disruptions and changes in the mother-child relationship.

In sum, both human and primate separation studies have demonstrated that separation from mother is associated with changes in infant affect, play behavior, activity level, heart rate, sleep and eating patterns, general health status, and functional responses of the immune system (Field, 1984b; Field & Reite, 1984; Field, Vega-Lahr, & Jagadish, 1984; Laudenslager, Reite, & Harbeck, 1982; Reite, Short, Seiler, & Pauley, 1981). In studies of monkey mother-infant separations, changes also have been noted in cortisol levels (Coe, Mendoza, Smotherman, & Levine, 1978). This particular constellation of changes is not surprising inasmuch as these functions are thought to be mediated by the hypothalamus and its extensive connections to other areas of the limbic system as well as the pituitary adrenal cortical system (Levine, 1983; McCabe & Schneiderman, 1985; Stansbury & Gunnar, in this volume). A biphasic response to separation, with an agitated period typically followed by a period of depression, has also been established in humans and other primates.

Depressed activity may be adaptive following a period of agitated behavior, particularly in the absence of the infant's primary source of arousal modulation. Furthermore, data from neuroanatomical and pharmacological studies reviewed by Kraemer (1984) suggest that the abnormal behavior of separated subjects might in part reflect the effect of social stimulation that, following deprivation, activates inputs to neural systems whose receptors

TABLE 3

Means Proportion of Time That Mother's and Infant's Interaction Behaviors Occurred during the Separation and Still-Face Perturbations ($N = 40$)

	PERTURBATION			
	Separation		Still Face	
	Baseline	During	Baseline	During
Smiling	8[b]	1[a]	10[a]	3[b]
Vocalizing	5[a]	6[a]	5[a]	9[b]
Motor activity	9[a]	15[b]	8[a]	21[b]
Gaze aversion	35[a]	0[b]	36[a]	50[b]
Distress brow	2[a]	4[b]	1[a]	9[b]
Crying	1[a]	4[b]	2[a]	8[b]

Note.—Lowercase letters across rows represent post hoc comparisons that are significantly different at $p < .05$ or less.

have become supersensitive. As implied by the term *conservation-withdrawal*, depressed activity may serve as a rest from agitation, and, thus, it may serve an adaptive function until physiological equilibrium is restored or until the mother and child become attuned to their new relationship and the latter's arousal modulation needs can again be met.

Physical versus Emotional Unavailability during Brief Perturbation Interactions

The studies that I have described indicate that infants continue to experience stress even after the mother is again physically available if she remains emotionally unavailable. Several experimental perturbations of mother-infant interactions have been tried to mimic the emotional unavailability of a mother who is involved with a new baby or, in the case of monkeys, with reestablishing herself in the dominance hierarchy. In these paradigms, the mother is asked to look depressed or to remain still faced (Stoller & Field, 1982; Tronick, Als, Adamson, Wise, & Brazelton, 1978); in both cases, the mother is affectively unresponsive, and, after attempting to reinstate a normal interaction, the infant becomes significantly distressed. Thus, we know that both physical and emotional unavailability of the mother distresses the young infant; however, no direct comparisons have been made between the infant's different responses to these two conditions. To make that comparison, we subjected 3-month-old infants to the mother's "still face" condition as well as to a brief separation.

As can be seen in Table 3, the infants became more negative and agitated during both these conditions. However, the situation in which the mother was emotionally unavailable (still face) appeared to be the more stressful. During the perturbations, infant motor activity, gaze aversion, distressed brow, and crying occurred more often during still face than separation, perhaps because still face situations are a violation of the infant's expectations. The mother becomes suddenly unresponsive in a typically interactive situation. Emotional unavailability is more distressing to the infant than simply being left alone to rely on her own resources.

Analogous situations in the literature are the anesthetized mother rat who is unresponsive to her pup (Schanberg & Field, 1987) and depressed mothers who tend to leave their infants alone in playpens (Lyons-Ruth, Zoll, Connell, & Grunebaum, 1986). Being left alone by a depressed mother, however, may be less stressful for the infant than experiencing her as emotionally unavailable. In a comparison of home-care versus day-care infants observed in this same still face versus separation paradigm, home-care infants displayed more motor activity and distress brow behavior than day-care infants, again suggesting the buffering effects of day care on the disturbances associated with the physical and emotional unavailability of the mother (Field, Stoller, Vega-Lahr, Scafidi, & Goldstein, 1986).

Chronic Emotional Unavailability Exemplified by Mother's Depression

The data on brief periods of mother's emotional and physical unavailability suggest that the effects of the former may be far more distressing than those of the latter. Although less direct, comparisons of findings obtained in our studies of mother's physical unavailability (the hospital and conference separations) and emotional unavailability (exposure to a depressed mother) also suggest that the latter is more harmful to the infant's development. Whereas the effects of physical separations (both conference and hospital) appear to be short lived, mother's depression is correlated with infant depression as early as 3 months of age (Field, 1984a), and, if the mother remains depressed at 6 months, it is related to growth and developmental delays shown at age 1 year (Field, 1985).

The basic factors involved in emotional unavailability are much the same as those involved in physical unavailability; however, there are some differences. First, although the emotionally unavailable mother's stimulation is not missing (as it is in instances of physical unavailability), this stimulation is disruptive and noncontingent. The mother's sad affect and withdrawn behavior, or angry affect and intrusive behavior, are noncontingent and hence disruptive to the flow of interaction. Dyadic sharing of behavior states is less frequent because of the mother's limited contingent responsivity and the dyads' limited mutual attentiveness. Studies reported by Cohn, Matias, Tronick, Connell, and Lyons-Ruth (1986) show that withdrawn mothers spent approximately 80% of their time disengaged from their infants and were responsive only to infant distress; intrusive mothers, on the other hand, expressed anger and irritation or handled their infants roughly more than 40% of the time. Infants of the disengaged (i.e., withdrawn) mothers protested nearly 30% of the time and watched their mothers less than 5% of the time, whereas infants exposed to the intrusive mothering style protested less than 5% of the time but spent more than 55% of their time avoiding their mothers.

Second, both physical unavailability and emotional unavailability on the part of the mother result in lack of arousal regulation for the infant. Emotional unavailability results when the mother is insensitive and unresponsive to the infant's signals rather than when she is absent. Finally, in the short run, the net effect is very much the same. The child's behavior and physiology are disorganized, but, in the case of emotional unavailability due to mother's depression, the disorganization is more prolonged. Changes in physiology (heart rate, vagal tone, and cortisol levels), in play behavior, affect, activity level, and sleep organization as well as other vegetative functions such as eating and toileting, and even immune system changes persist for the duration of the mother's depression. I have suggested that these changes occur because the infant is being deprived (in this case chronically) of an important external regulator of stimulation (the mother) and thus fails to develop or sustain arousal modulation and organized behavioral and physiological rhythms. Over brief periods, this has been demonstrated in observations of interaction rhythms.

In one study, my colleagues and I investigated shared states and rhythms during interactions between nondepressed and depressed mothers and their infants (Field, Healy, Goldstein, & Guthertz, 1990). Mother-infant interaction synchrony was assessed in 48 depressed and nondepressed pairs at the time the infants were 3 months old. The attentive/affective behavior states of both the mothers and the infants were coded on a negative to positive continuum that included anger and disengagement at one pole and attentiveness and playfulness at the other. The depressed mothers and their infants showed negative behavior states more often and positive behavior states less often than the nondepressed dyads (see Fig. 2). The depressed dyads also spent less time (40% vs. 54%) in shared behavior states.

In a second study, both the behavior states and the physiological rhythms (heart rate) of depressed and nondepressed mothers and their infants were subjected to cross-spectral analyses (Field, Healy, & LeBlanc, 1989). The data were analyzed to determine the coherence of mother-infant behavior states, the coherence of mother-infant heart rate, the within-partner (mother or infant) coherence of behavior and heart rate, and the

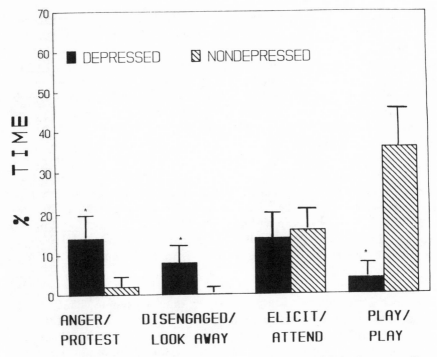

F<small>IG</small>. 2.—Percentage of time that mothers and infants shared behavior states. (From Field, Healy, Goldstein, & Guthertz, 1990.)

coherence of mother's behavior and infant's heart rate and of infant's behavior and mother's heart rate. These coherence values were then compared across depressed versus nondepressed mother-infant dyads to determine whether greater coherence characterized harmonious (nondepressed) than disturbed (depressed) interactions. The sharing of negative behavior states by the depressed dyads and of positive states by the nondepressed dyads was consistent with our previous findings: the coherence functions indicated that the nondepressed dyads had higher mean coherence than the depressed dyads ($M = .46$ vs. $.29$).

Models of the wave forms of these mother/infant behavior states (for the nondepressed and the depressed dyads) are displayed in Figure 3. The model wave forms illustrate the rhythmic structure of the interaction across the 3-min period as a function of the level of affective involvement. Examples of synchrony can be seen at the points where the wave forms of the mothers' and the infants' behavior-state ratings overlap.

Additional analyses also indicated greater coherence between infant's behavior and mother's heart rate for the nondepressed as opposed to the

CONTROL MOTHER/INFANT BEHAVIOR

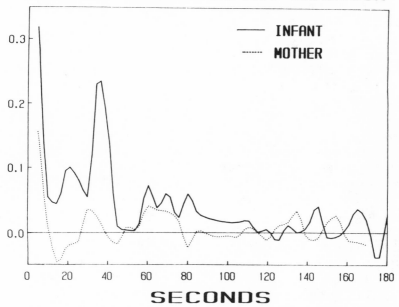

DEPRESSED MOTHER/INFANT BEHAVIOR

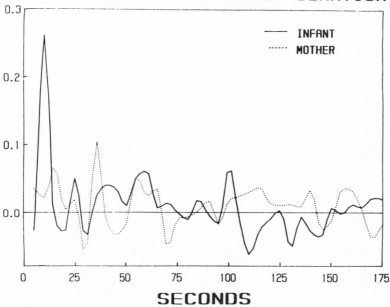

FIG. 3.—Wave forms for the nondepressed control mothers and their infants and for depressed mothers and their infants derived from averaging the sine transformed values of the frequencies in the band .03–.12 Hz ($N = 16$). (From Field, Healy, & LeBlanc, 1989.)

depressed dyads; no group differences for mother's behavior/infant's heart rate, for mother's behavior/heart rate, for infant's behavior/heart rate, or for mother's/infant's heart rate; and greater coherence across partner behavior (i.e., mother/infant) than within partner behavior and physiology (mother's behavior/heart rate or infant's behavior/heart rate).

In sum, these data converge to suggest a greater coherence between mothers' and infants' behavior in the nondepressed than in the depressed dyads. This is perhaps not surprising given that the former shared behavior states more frequently. That the nondepressed dyads also showed greater coherence between infant's behavior and mother's heart rate is also not surprising inasmuch as nondepressed mothers are noted to be more sensitive/responsive to their infants' behaviors. The heart-rate coherence values for both groups of mother/infant dyads were moderately high ($M = .46$ for the nondepressed group and .28 for the depressed group), suggesting that there was a mutual entrainment of physiological rhythms, not unlike that documented for therapist/patient dyads by Ax (1964) and Kaplan and Bloom (1960). As these authors suggested, correlated changes in autonomic arousal may be interpreted as evidence of empathy.

The implication here is that the depressed mothers and their infants were as empathetic as the nondepressed dyads inasmuch as their heart-rate coherence values were equivalent. However, it is possible that the high heart-rate coherence of the depressed dyads was due to their frequent sharing of negative states, which in turn attenuated the expected difference between these groups. Spending a significant portion of time in a shared angry/protesting state would be highly arousing for the depressed mother-infant dyads, just as spending time sharing a positive playful state might be highly arousing for the nondepressed dyads. If so, heart rate would be simultaneously elevated in both states, in both partners, and hence in both groups. These results suggest that both Gottman's (1989) notion that greater physiological coherence would occur in stressed dyads and Chapple's (1970) prediction that greater coherence would occur in nonstressed dyads are correct.

These, then, are some examples of the ways in which infants can become behaviorally and physiologically disorganized and interactions can become asynchronous when mothers are emotionally unavailable. As noted earlier, such early dysregulation of the infant appears to have later consequences, including growth and developmental delays at age 1 year. Seen again at preschool age, these infants are showing high internalizing and externalizing behavior scores, suggesting a predisposition to depression, conduct disorder, or co-morbidity, that is, both depression and conduct disorder (Field, Lang, Pickens, & Yando, 1994). The offspring of depressed mothers are noted to have a predisposition to later psychiatric disorders, and the emotion dysregulation that occurs during early mother-infant interactions may be the pathway for the later disorders.

INDIVIDUAL DIFFERENCES

As in any study of any process, individual differences should be investigated once a phenomenon is established. In the case of dysregulation, individual differences might emerge as a function of several factors in addition to that of the mother being physically or emotionally unavailable. Variations in central nervous system maturity/integrity related to perinatal complications may be one such factor. Limited synchrony has been demonstrated in samples of preterm infants by Lester, Hoffman, and Brazelton (1985). These authors reported greater synchrony (coherence) in term versus preterm infant-mother dyads and in more developmentally mature dyads (5- vs. 3-month-old), suggesting that less mature, preterm infants—who are typically less responsive—achieve limited synchrony with their mothers and that mother-infant interactions become more synchronous as infants become more mature and farther removed from their perinatal complications.

Another factor may lie in differences in behavior repertoires that reflect individual differences in interaction skills, creativity, and probably intelligence. Temperament/personality differences can also play a role; these can be described in a number of different ways, including the distinction uninhibited/inhibited, as in the work of Fox and Kagan and their colleagues (see, e.g., Fox, in this volume; Kagan, in this volume), or in terms of the externalizing/internalizing typology described by Field (1987). Field reported higher thresholds in response to stimulation, slower habituation, greater behavioral reactivity, and lesser physiological reactivity for externalizing than for internalizing neonates. These characteristics would be expected to contribute to less emotion dysregulation and smoother mother-infant interactions in the case of externalizing infants.

Interactive/coping style—as in being a risk taker versus a non–risk taker (Field, 1989) or more ready to approach versus more ready to withdraw from stimulation (Fox & Davidson, 1984)—may also play a role. Differences in attitude toward stimulation are likely to lead to more or less exploratory behavior and more or less interactive behavior and hence dispose the infant to cope more actively (or less passively) with stimulation. Finally, the relative degree of mother-infant match-mismatch, synchrony, and/or empathy could also presumably lead to individual differences in the development of regulation. An example of a potentially consequential mismatch is dissimilarity in temperament between the infant and the mother, the infant being more vocal and gregarious and the mother more withdrawn and inactive. These are only some examples of factors that can be expected to contribute to individual differences in the development of emotion dysregulation, and even these few have rarely been investigated.

SUMMARY

In summary, emotion dysregulation can develop from brief or more prolonged separations from the mother as well as from the more disturbing effects of her emotional unavailability, such as occurs when she is depressed. Harmonious interaction with the mother or the primary caregiver (attunement) is critical for the development of emotion regulation. The effects of the mother's physical unavailability were seen in studies of separations from the mother due to her hospitalization or to her conference trips. These separations affected the infants' play behaviors and sleep patterns. Comparisons between hospitalizations and conference trips, however, suggested that the infants' behaviors were more negatively affected by the hospitalizations than the conference trips. This probably related to these being hospitalizations for the birth of another baby—the infants no longer had the special, exclusive relationship with their mothers after the arrival of the new sibling. This finding highlights the critical importance of emotional availability. The mother had returned from the hospital, but, while she was no longer physically unavailable, she was now emotionally unavailable.

Emotional unavailability was investigated in an acute form by comparing two laboratory situations, the still face paradigm and the momentary leave taking. The still face had more negative effects on the infants' interaction behaviors than the physical separation.

The most extreme form of emotional unavailability, mother's depression, had the most negative effects. The disorganization or emotion dysregulation in this case is more prolonged. Changes in physiology (heart rate, vagal tone, and cortisol levels), in play behavior, affect, activity level, and sleep organization as well as other regulating functions such as eating and toileting, and even in the immune system persist for the duration of the mother's depression. My colleagues and I have suggested that these changes occur because the infant is being chronically deprived of an important external regulator of stimulation (the mother) and thus fails to develop emotion regulation or organized behavioral and physiological rhythms. Finally, individual differences were discussed, including those related to maturity (e.g., prematurity) and temperament/personality (e.g., uninhibited/inhibited or externalizing/internalizing) and those deriving from degree of mother-infant mismatch, such as dissimilar temperaments.

Further investigations are needed to determine how long the effects of such early dysregulation endure, how they affect the infant's long-term development, how their effect differs across individuals and across development, and whether they can be modified by early intervention. Eventually, with increasing age, developing skills, and diversity of experience, infants develop individualized regulatory styles. That process, and how it is affected by the mother's physical and emotional unavailability, also requires further investigation.

EMOTION REGULATION:
INFLUENCES OF ATTACHMENT RELATIONSHIPS

Jude Cassidy

In his essay in this volume, Thompson discusses several defining features and important components of emotion regulation. One of these addresses the adaptive nature of emotion regulation: the notion that emotions can be regulated as an adaptive means, a strategy, to achieve one's goals within a given context. Given that, according to attachment theory (Bowlby, 1969/1982, 1973, 1980), a centrally important, biologically based goal of the child is maintaining proximity to the attachment figure, then, following Thompson's position, children would be expected to regulate their emotions in order to achieve this goal.

My aim here is to examine ways in which individual differences in emotion regulation may be influenced by children's attachment experiences. Throughout, three themes central to Thompson's definition of *emotion regulation* will be considered: (*a*) that emotion regulation involves both the suppression and the heightening of emotions; (*b*) that emotion regulation involves the regulation of attention; and (*c*) that emotion regulation involves factors both intrinsic (e.g., temperament) and extrinsic to the child (particularly the child's relationships with parents). I begin with a brief theoretical discussion of the ways in which attachment theory converges with Thomp-

Preparation of this essay was supported by a Research Initiation Grant from the Pennsylvania State University. Discussions within the Attachment Working Group of the John D. and Catherine T. MacArthur Network on the Transition from Infancy to Early Childhood (principal investigator, Kathryn Barnard) contributed to the formulation of ideas presented here. I am also grateful to Inge Bretherton, Tiffany Field, Nathan Fox, Mark Greenberg, Roger Kobak, Karlen Lyons-Ruth, and Arietta Slade for thoughtful comments on earlier drafts of this essay. Address correspondence to Jude Cassidy, Department of Psychology, 514 Moore Building, Pennsylvania State University, University Park, PA 16802.

son's view of the adaptive nature of emotion regulation. Ways in which individual differences in emotion regulation may be partly accounted for by attachment relationships are then discussed. Finally, interconnections among attachment, temperament, and emotion regulation are considered.

THEORETICAL PERSPECTIVES

Thompson (in this volume) points out that children are continually faced with many options when choosing how to regulate their emotions. He cites an example of a child who, in the face of peer-instigated conflict, can choose among a variety of emotion regulation responses, including, among others, angry revenge, crying, tattling (with sadness, anger, or whining), and direct assertion. The child is thought to select among these responses in a way that will help her achieve her goals. Her choice is viewed as being a situation-specific strategy, with the effectiveness of any particular strategy varying according to such factors as setting (e.g., home vs. day care) and social partner (e.g., mother vs. father).

Thompson emphasizes the important role of parents and suggests that it is largely within the parent-child relationship that children learn about emotion regulation in the service of attaining their goals. Thus, parents help children learn which of several emotion response options will be effective in attaining both their immediate goal and the more general goal of conforming to social demands: "On the basis of the socialization practices of parents and other authorities, children acquire emotion schemas that, among other things, guide their predictions of the consequences of expressing various emotions in certain situations. . . . For example, on the basis of the verbal . . . and behavioral guidance of socialization agents, they learn the consequences of responding to an aggressive peer by taking revenge, crying, tattling to adults, or asserting themselves. In doing so, they can more thoughtfully evaluate these alternatives in terms of their relative suitability for accomplishing personal goals in particular circumstances" (Thompson, in this volume, p. 39).

Thompson's propositions about the adaptive nature of emotion regulation converge with the thinking of Bowlby (1969/1982, 1973) and of Main (Main, 1990; Main, Kaplan, & Cassidy, 1985; Main & Solomon, 1986) about adaptation in relation to attachment. According to Main, just as many biological systems have evolved to permit adaptation and a flexible response to a range of environmental circumstances, so have infants evolved with the capacity to respond to variations in caregiving environment. Thus, when an infant is faced with a particular type of caregiving and learns from these experiences, she is able to tailor her own behavior accordingly. The manner in which the infant tailors her behavior is referred to as a *strategy*, and the infant is thought to have the capacity to use one of several strategies; central to Main's thinking is the notion that strategies are used automatically and need not be conscious (Main, 1990).

This notion of strategies is entirely consistent with Bowlby's proposal that individuals can take into account environmental feedback in modifying their biologically driven behavior toward a goal. Main's (1990) framework of "conditional behavioral strategies" emphasizes the adaptive nature of these infant strategies; in accordance with Bowlby's (1969/1982) notion that the infant is biologically predisposed to maintain proximity to the caregiver so as to increase the likelihood of protection, Main proposes that the child's strategy is adaptive in that it helps ensure this proximity in light of a particular caregiving history.

Within Main's scheme, children are thought to develop strategies as a means of responding to the caregiving that they receive: in the service of implementing a strategy, the infant may regulate behavior, feelings, cognition, perception, memory, and attention (Main et al., 1985). In what follows, I focus on the ways in which emotion regulation can be viewed as one means used by the child in implementing a strategy. I suggest that infant emotion regulation can be regarded as part of an adaptive strategy that, in concert with other strategic means and in response to a particular caregiving history, serves the function of maintaining the relationship with the attachment figure. In an attempt to better understand infant emotion regulation, parent emotion regulation is also examined briefly.

The view of emotion regulation presented here draws not only from the theoretical writings of Bowlby and Main but also from Bretherton's (1990) writings about attachment and communication patterns, from Tomkins's (1962, 1963) affect theory, from the functionalist approach to emotions (Barrett & Campos, 1987; Bretherton, Fritz, Zahn-Waxler, & Ridgeway, 1986), and from family systems theory (Minuchin, 1985). In addition, a foundation for this view is Sroufe and Waters's (1977) conceptualization of individual differences in attachment quality as individual differences in emotion regulation.

INDIVIDUAL DIFFERENCES IN EMOTION REGULATION AS A FUNCTION OF ATTACHMENT HISTORY

Emotion regulation is thought to be influenced by the attachment relationship through the child's expectations ("working models") of the parent's behavior. According to Bowlby, such working models develop during the infant's first year and are based on repeated daily experiences with the parent (Bowlby, 1969/1982, 1973). The secure child is thought to develop an expectation that her emotion signals will be responded to. The insecure child, on the other hand, is thought to develop expectations that her emotion signals will be attended to only selectively. (On the basis of recent animal research, Hofer, in this volume, extends attachment theory by specifying physiological processes that may be additional mechanisms through which emotion regulation is influenced by attachment relationships.)

In this section, individual differences in emotion regulation are first discussed by examining a flexible style of emotion regulation in which a range of emotions is possible. Next (following Thompson's scheme), two further styles of emotion regulation involving a restricted range of emotions are considered: one in which emotions are systematically suppressed and one in which they are systematically heightened. According to Thompson, "Emotion regulation is undermined when there is a very limited range of response possibilities or, alternatively, when existing options are perceived to lead consistently to undesirable outcomes" (in this volume, p. 38). Thus, these styles are viewed as less satisfactory for the child.

Two assessments of attachment are considered in the following discussion. For infants, individual differences in quality of attachment have been identified and examined using Ainsworth's Strange Situation procedure (Ainsworth, Blehar, Waters, & Wall, 1978). During this widely used 20-min assessment, the parent and a stranger alternately leave and return to the infant, who remains in a toy-filled laboratory playroom. There are two parent-child separations and two parent-child reunions. On the basis primarily of the infant's behavior during these reunions, she is classified into one of three attachment groups: secure, insecure/avoidant, and insecure/ambivalent.[1] The reliability and validity of this procedure have been extensively demonstrated (Ainsworth et al., 1978; Belsky & Cassidy, in press; Bretherton, 1985; Waters, 1983; for a divergent view, see Lamb, Thompson, Gardner, & Charnov, 1985).

A second assessment—the Adult Attachment Interview—taps the adult "state of mind in relation to attachment" (George, Kaplan, & Main, 1985). This semistructured interview probes memories of attachment-related experiences during childhood, such as memories of feeling loved or unloved, memories of being upset or ill, and memories of separations and losses.

---

[1] More recently, Main and Solomon (1986) have identified the existence of a fourth attachment group: insecure/disorganized. Approximately 12% of infants in white, middle-class American samples are classified in this group (Main & Weston, 1981). Substantially more infants fall into this group in high-risk samples (Carlson, Cicchetti, Barnett, & Braunwald, 1989; Lyons-Ruth, Connell, & Grunebaum, 1990; Speltz, Greenberg, & De-Klyen, 1990; Spieker & Booth, 1988). Relatively little research has yet been conducted using this classification, and it is not considered in this essay. Note, however, that Main and Hesse (1990) have provided a theoretical discussion of the disorganized group as a variant of the basic secure, avoidant, and ambivalent groups, and as such it is possible that no particular pattern of emotion regulation is associated with this attachment pattern.

Subjects are asked to provide general descriptions of their relationships with each parent and to integrate specific memories with these more general descriptions. Discrepancies, contradictions, and the individual's overall coherence of thought are considered when classifying interviews into three attachment patterns that parallel the three infancy patterns: secure/autonomous, dismissing, and preoccupied.

For each style of emotion regulation, several questions will be considered. First, are there children who show a given emotion regulation style within the Strange Situation? Second, what attachment-related experiences might lead to a strategy that would incorporate this style of emotion regulation, and is there evidence that these children have experienced the hypothesized attachment history? Finally, is there evidence of a more pervasive link between this style of emotion regulation and the proposed attachment pattern?

For parents, the state of mind in relation to attachment that is thought to characterize the parents of infants who most typically use a given emotion regulation style is first examined, and the Adult Attachment Interviews of these parents are described. In relation to styles of emotion suppression and heightening, parents' behaviors that might contribute to infant emotion regulation are then further examined. Finally, the signal function to the parent of the infant's emotion regulation is described.

Open, Flexible Emotion Expression

Children and Parents

The notion of open, flexible emotion expression suggests that the child expresses a range of emotions and that none are systematically distorted. This flexibility is thought to arise in part from experiences with a caregiver who responds sensitively much of the time to a range of infant affective signals, without any selective ignoring (Bretherton, 1990; Kobak, 1985, 1987).

Several studies converge to suggest that infants whose mothers respond sensitively to their signals are more likely to be securely attached (Ainsworth et al., 1978; Belsky, Rovine, & Taylor, 1984; Egeland & Farber, 1984). The secure infant's strategy in response to these mothering experiences is to use the mother as a secure base from which to explore when there is no threat from the environment and as a haven when danger arises (Ainsworth et al., 1978; Main & Solomon, 1986). This strategy allows the infant maximum freedom to explore and to respond to the exciting possibilities of the environment, without jeopardizing access to the attachment figure when needed.

Why might flexible emotion expression be part of a strategy aimed at allowing the infant freedom to explore while assuring her safety? If the infant believes that her emotion signals will be responded to sensitively, she is most likely to signal her wishes directly and freely and to share her emotions with the parent. In most instances, relatively little negative affect is expected from infants who have experienced sensitive caregiving. However, when the secure infant does experience negative affect (as some babies do in the Strange Situation), her strategy involves open, direct, and active expression to the parent; rather than hiding the distress, the child seeks the parent for help in dealing with it. On the other hand, when experiences with a sensitive caregiver give rise to pleasurable feelings, open expressions of joy serve the function of showing an interest in maintaining the relationship. In relation to fear, the secure infant's strategy involves flexible emotion regulation in response to changes in the environment. When an alarming event occurs, the infant moves to the parent; when the parent is present and the situation is not alarming, the infant explores.

The affective communication between child and parent provides the context in which the child comes to understand and organize affective experience. For the secure child, this affective communication is thought to have a positive influence on personality development. Because the parent is sensitive to the child's signals, affects will be experienced as useful in alerting the parent during times of distress. A parent's sensitive response will in turn enhance the child's sense of efficacy in modulating her feeling states (Bell & Ainsworth, 1972). In this type of dyad, the child's experience of negative affects, such as fear and anger, comes to be associated with expectations of the parent's ameliorative response. As a result, the experience of negative affect may be less threatening to the child. The experience of security is based not on the denial of negative affect but on the ability to tolerate negative affects temporarily in order to achieve mastery over threatening or frustrating situations (Kobak, 1985).

The pattern of openness to a range of emotions seen in secure infants is also evident in the Adult Attachment Interviews of most of their parents (who are typically classified as secure/autonomous). If such a parent reports that her own childhood was *secure,* she supports this claim with convincing and coherent memories and can also acknowledge humanly expectable limitations or disappointments within her childhood relationships. If she reports an *insecure* childhood, she has nonetheless come to understand or forgive her parent(s) and acknowledges the importance of attachment relationships.

The notion that an open acceptance of many emotions is associated with secure attachment converges with several theoretical perspectives. One of these is Tomkins's (1962, 1963) affect theory. According to Tomkins, the "most developmentally favorable outcome" is what he calls an "affectively balanced personality," in which no single emotion either dominates or is suppressed and there is room for balance and a range of emotions. Tomkins proposes that such a positive outcome is associated, not with attempts to suppress the child's negative affect, but rather with the parent's acceptance of negative emotions, with continued engagement with the child during times of anger or sadness, with provision of assistance in dealing construc- tively with negative emotions, and with the parent's own comfort with nega- tive emotions.

These ideas are also similar to Bretherton's (1990) proposals concern- ing "open communication." Bretherton makes a convincing case that the flow of communication between partners has important consequences for the security/insecurity of the relationship. She described "open, fluent, and coherent" dyadic communication, in which neither partner is selective about either sending or receiving signals, as characteristic of secure dyads. Her focus is on the importance of communication signals, and these are in large part emotion signals.

Stern's (1985) discussions of "affect attunement" as characteristic of sensitive parenting also converge with the ideas presented here. Stern de- scribes the sensitive mother as one who recognizes her infant's affective signals, accepts these signals, and shares in these with her infant. Through these experiences, the infant learns that a variety of emotions are accept- able and that they can be experiences shared within social relationships. According to Stern, difficulties arise when, because of her own needs and perceptual biases, the mother either undermatches or overmatches her in- fant's emotion signals. These mismatches, in which the mother excessively tries either to dampen or to heighten her infant's affect, are thought to convey to the infant that only some emotions are appropriate.

Empirical evidence of a link between open, flexible emotion expression and secure attachment is contained in later sections where I examine re- stricted emotion expression.

Minimizing Emotion Expression

Children

There is one group of infants who appear to minimize emotion expres- sion within the Strange Situation: those classified as insecure/avoidant. On reunion with the parent, these infants show little interest in proximity or contact and, in fact, actively avoid the parent. In most American samples, about 20% of babies fall into this group (Ainsworth et al., 1978; Campos, Barrett, Lamb, Goldsmith, & Stenberg, 1983). Such children seem in large part affectively neutral, showing neither overt distress on separation nor pleasure on reunion.

What attachment-related experiences might contribute to a strategy within which a child minimizes her emotions? Main and Solomon (1986) propose that, when activation of their attachment system has consistently resulted in rejection, infants develop a reasonable strategy of minimizing attention to the attachment relationship, minimizing the importance of the caregiver as a source of comfort and hence their apparent need for her. Results of several studies converge to suggest that insecure/avoidant infants have experienced consistent rejection by their parents, particularly so in times of distress when they had especially wanted comfort—times when their attachment systems had been highly activated (Ainsworth et al., 1978; Grossmann, Grossmann, Spangler, Suess, & Unzner, 1985).

If a strategy of minimizing the attachment relationship serves the avoidant infant well, how could regulation of emotions best be used to this end? Minimizing negative emotions such as anger, sadness, or distress is thought to be a useful component of a strategy to minimize the relationship. Important to this argument is Main's proposition that this minimizing actually permits the infant to maintain sufficient proximity to the caregiver to ensure protection (Main, 1981). Given that the ultimate goal of the insecure/avoidant infant is to maintain proximity to an attachment figure who is known to reject attachment behaviors, the expression of emotions that can be construed as an attempt to elicit care may have dangerous consequences for the child. If she overtly expresses the anger associated with having had her attachment behaviors rejected, she risks alienating the attachment figure; if she increases her demands and becomes more clingy, she risks being rebuffed further. Avoidance and the masking of negative emotion reduce the infant's arousal level (Bowlby, 1980) and thereby prevent the direct, possibly dangerous expression of anger toward the attachment figure.

Owing to the parent's chronic rejection of her attachment needs, the avoidant infant's anger is so intense that it needs to be muted in order not to disrupt the attachment bond. Masking of negative affect simultaneously protects the infant from the rejection that often results from her attempts to seek contact as well as from the painful fear of alienating the attachment figure on whom she depends for survival (Bowlby, 1980; Main, 1981). Minimizing anger also serves the strategy of minimizing the relationship with the attachment figure in another way. Anger can be engaging. To be angry is, in some way, to be invested in the relationship. Within a strategy of minimizing the relationship, such investment is not acceptable.

Minimization of other emotions in the service of minimizing the relationship with the attachment figure is also expected to characterize insecure/avoidant children. For example, joy might be minimized because it signals an openness and a readiness for interaction. As Malatesta wrote, joy "promotes social bonding through contagion of good feeling" (Malatesta & Wilson, 1988, p. 107). Thus, joy can be viewed as reflecting investment in the relationship. Again, such investment is not acceptable within a strategy of minimizing the relationship. Fear is also minimized with this strategy. According to Main and Hesse (1994), "The infant is thought to respond to mildly alarming events by shifting attention from fear-eliciting cues and from attachment, thereby avoiding or minimizing the disorganization which might well follow an experience of fear in which a caregiver was rejecting."

Does empirical evidence support the expectation that infants who minimize emotion expression are likely to be characterized by an insecure/avoidant attachment pattern? Four studies have shown that a tendency to mask negative affect while interacting with the parent characterizes insecure/avoidant infants. In one of these, observations of the communication patterns of mother-infant dyads during the Strange Situation revealed that avoidant infants communicated directly with their mothers only when the infants were feeling at ease (Grossmann, Grossmann, & Schwan, 1986). Unlike secure infants, when judged to be distressed, these infants tended not to signal the mother directly and did not seek bodily contact. In another, similar study, avoidant infants were found to differ from secure infants in their emotion regulation behaviors on reunion: rather than being mother oriented, the regulatory behaviors of avoidant babies were self-oriented (Braungart & Stifter, 1991). Given that the avoidant infants in this sample showed greater distress during separation than some secure infants (the B1 and B2 infants), this study again provides evidence that, when distressed, avoidant babies do not share their distress with the parent.

A similar connection between infant avoidance and suppression of negative affect emerged from a study by Malatesta and her colleagues in which infants and mothers were observed in face-to-face interactions during the first year and attachment was assessed at age 22 months (see Malatesta, Culver, Tesman, & Shepard, 1989). The authors interpreted their findings as follows: "During stressful situations—when it is more adaptive to communicate one's distress—insecurely attached [avoidant] children, paradoxically, displayed more positive affect (mainly interest) and showed the compressed lips expression more frequently; we interpret these findings as revealing a pattern of emotion suppression and vigilance" (p. 72).

Finally, a recent study that included both behavioral and psychophysiological measures provided data that again suggest a masking of negative affect by avoidant infants (Spangler & Grossmann, 1993). Although heart-rate measures revealed that avoidant infants were as physiologically distressed on separation as the secure babies, and although the post–Strange Situation cortisol levels indicated that the procedure was *more* stressful for avoidant than secure babies, the avoidant babies masked their negative affect: that is, they showed significantly less negative vocalization during the separations than did secure babies. Furthermore, like in the Grossmann et al. (1986) study described earlier, the findings revealed that, unlike secure babies, avoidant babies turned to their mothers, not when they were highly aroused (as assessed by heart rate), but rather only during times of low arousal.

Although a strategy of minimizing negative affect may be adaptive for avoidant infants in the context of the relationship with the attachment figure, it may be maladaptive in other contexts. In particular, the avoidant individual's lack of expectable affective displays in social and problem-solving contexts may appear inappropriate and be maladaptive. Two studies provide examples of the use of restricted affect in situations not involving the attachment figure by older children classified as avoidant; this restricted affect can be viewed as part of an individual's defensive communication that she is unaffected by others.

In an experimental study, Lutkenhaus and his colleagues analyzed the affect and behavior of 3-year-olds who had been assessed in the Strange Situation with the mother at 12 months (Lutkenhaus, Grossmann, & Grossmann, 1985). An unfamiliar adult visitor played a competitive tower-building game with the children, and the children's affective reactions to winning and losing were analyzed. The avoidant children manifested sadness about losing while they were still engaged in the game, but this affective display ceased when the game was over and the experimenter was available for social communication. In fact, during this phase of "social communicative exchange," there was a tendency for the avoidant children to replace sadness with smiling. In contrast, securely attached children showed their sadness after the game, when the adult was more available. It is not the case that avoidant children simply did not feel (or display) sadness because sad expressions were evident before the game was finished and there was no eye contact between child and experimenter, leading the authors to suggest that greater hesitancy to display sad feelings in social situations characterizes avoidant children. It is striking that such masking of true feelings of sadness is evident as early as 3 years of age, and it is also striking that this pattern of masking emotions is used so readily with a new social partner, someone with whom the child has had no history of social interaction.

Restriction in affective expression among avoidant children also emerged in another study. Six-year-olds participating in the Berkeley Social Development Project were asked to "draw a picture of your family" as part of a longitudinal study of infant attachment (Kaplan & Main, 1985). Children who had been classified as avoidant in infancy tended to draw figures that were carbon copies of each other, with little or no individuality. The bodies were tense and rigid. Family members often had no arms: individuals were independent and were literally unable to reach out to each other. This signaling of "emotional unavailability" (Emde, 1980) is congruent with a style of affective communication organized around the attempt to withhold affect. Another characteristic of this group of drawings was that facial expressions often involved stereotyped, overemphasized smiles. This exaggeration of positive affect in the drawings, with the accompanying masking of negative affect, parallels the behavior of the avoidant children in the Lutkenhaus study described above.

No research has examined the suppression of positive emotions in relation to attachment patterns. Generally, little positive emotion is thought to be associated with avoidant attachment. There is some empirical evidence that, compared to secure infants, avoidant infants are less likely to express positive emotions (Matas, Arend, & Sroufe, 1978; Pastor, 1981; Waters, Wippman, & Sroufe, 1979) and are more likely to decrease smiling in interaction with the mother over the first year (Malatesta et al., 1989), but in none of these studies is there evidence that suppression is involved.

Parents

A pattern of emotion regulation in which negative emotions are restricted emerges from the Adult Attachment Interviews of the parents of many of the avoidant infants (adults who are classified as dismissing) (Main & Goldwyn, 1984, 1994). Some of these parents use idealization: they deny that their parents or childhoods had any negative characteristics. Others admit negative characteristics but minimize their own negative responses to them.

What factors support the proposition that masking of negative affect is reflected in these adult narratives? First, because no one is perfect (particularly one's parents), no recognition of any flaws at all is likely to involve perceptual and affective distortion. In addition, descriptions of specific experiences of rejection emerge in the narratives of these idealizing adults that are not incorporated into the global portrayals of their perfect childhoods. For example, in Main and Goldwyn's (1984) sample, the mother of an avoidant infant described her relationship with her mother as "fine," yet later told of hiding from her mother when she was injured out of fear of angering her. Given the absence of the negative affect that would be expected to occur in response to such treatment, masking of negative affect is a likely interpretation. This disconnection of the cognitive representation of an event from the normally accompanying emotion is similar to what Anna Freud (1966) called "isolation of affect."

Additional evidence that a minimizing of negative affect occurs in these adult narratives comes from a study of 50 adolescents that included physiological measures (Dozier & Kobak, 1992). The skin conductance scores of individuals who scored high on a repression scale—as is characteristic of individuals classified as dismissing (Kobak, Cole, Ferenz-Gillies, & Fleming, 1994)—were no different from those of others when subjects were responding to low-stress background questions about their parents and child-hoods. However, when asked more stressful questions about their feelings during times of separation, rejection, or threat, these individuals experi-enced significantly greater conflict than other individuals as evinced by their higher skin conductance scores, even though they claimed to have had no difficulties in their early attachment relationships. Individuals guided by a strategy of shifting attention away from attachment information should experience conflict or inhibition during the interview (as indexed by an increase from baseline skin conductance) because the interview *focuses* atten-tion on this information.

Findings from another study of adolescents also suggest that a minimiz-ing of negative affect characterizes adults with a dismissing attachment pat-tern (Kobak & Sceery, 1988). Kobak interviewed 53 first-year college stu-dents in the fall, collected self-report measures of perceptions of self and others over the course of the first year, and obtained peer ratings of adjust-ment in the spring. Peer ratings of those in the dismissing group indicated that they were viewed by their peers as less ego resilient, more anxious, and more hostile than secure individuals. However, on self-report measures, the dismissing individuals reported no more self-related distress than did secure individuals. The authors interpreted this combination of findings as indicat-ing a cognitive bias among dismissing individuals toward minimizing ac-knowledgment of distress or difficulty in adjustment.

In order to maintain their own state of mind in relation to attachment, parents behave in particular ways toward their infants (Main & Goldwyn, 1994). As argued earlier, a parent's rejection contributes to an infant's sup-pression of negative emotions in a number of ways. But what about any additional ways in which a parent's behavior may contribute to an infant's restriction of negative emotions?

Additional processes through which avoidant infants may learn to mask negative emotions have been identified empirically through observations of mothers' and infants' behavior. Three studies of mother-infant interaction indicated that mothers of insecure/avoidant infants showed a more re-stricted range of emotion expressiveness than mothers of secure infants (Ainsworth et al., 1978; Main, Tomasini, & Tolan, 1979; Malatesta et al., 1989), suggesting that avoidant infants may learn a style of restricted affect through direct modeling. In addition, a study using a mother-infant free-play situation found that mothers of avoidant infants joined in play when the infant was content but withdrew when the infant expressed negative affect (Escher-Graeub & Grossmann, 1983); such withdrawal during times of negative affect may teach the avoidant infant that such affect is inappro-priate (see also Stern, 1985). The pattern was reversed among mothers of securely attached infants, who were more likely to join in play (in a facilita-tive way) when the infant expressed negative affect.

Furthermore, although it must be viewed as preliminary, a small pilot study (Haft & Slade, 1989) provided convergent data. Mothers with dismissing patterns of attachment were described as follows: "Overall, the dismissing group distorted their babies' affect by misreading it primarily when it was negative. . . . Dismissing mothers were most comfortable attuning to their babies' expression of exuberance, especially in the context of mastery in play . . . [and to their infants'] expressions of autonomy and separateness. . . . On the other hand, they tended to be rejecting of their babies' bids for comfort and reassurance" (p. 168).

Finally, overinvolvement, which was found to characterize mothers of avoidant babies in several studies (Belsky et al., 1984; Isabella & Belsky, 1991; Isabella, Belsky, & von Eye, 1989; Lewis & Feiring, 1989; Malatesta et al., 1989; Smith & Pederson, 1988), may also contribute to infants' reduced negative expressivity. Just as the avoidant infant's own increased activity on reunion in the Strange Situation is thought to decrease activation of the infant's attachment system (Ainsworth et al., 1978) and thereby decrease negative expressivity, so might the mother's relatively high activity during daily mother-infant interactions shift attention away from the infant attachment system and any accompanying negative affect. In an attempt to regulate distance, the infant of an overinvolved mother may respond by withdrawing and minimizing interaction in a variety of ways, one of which involves expressivity.

Just as consideration of the mother's behavior is useful in understanding how minimization of emotion expressiveness may be adaptive for avoidant infants, so is consideration of the parent's state of mind in relation to attachment. Given a mother who dismisses the importance of attachment relationships, the restricted negative emotionality of the avoidant infant can be viewed as signaling to the parent that the infant is cooperating in order to help maintain the parent's state of mind. The avoidant infant's limited negative emotionality may be part of a communicative package that signals that the infant will not make demands for comfort or seek care. (For additional discussion of ways in which the masking of negative emotions in both children and adults may characterize avoidant individuals, see Bretherton, 1990; Cassidy, 1988; Cassidy & Kobak, 1988; and Main et al., 1985.)

Heightening Emotion Expression

Children

In the Strange Situation, extreme distress on separation and difficulty in calming on reunion characterize the group of infants classified as insecure/ambivalent. These infants display angry, resistant behavior toward the parent.

What sorts of attachment-related experiences might contribute to a strategy in which a child heightens her emotions? An infant who has experienced a minimally or inconsistently available parent is thought to develop an understandable strategy of increasing her bids for attention. She develops a strategy of *heightening* the importance of the relationship and exhibits extreme dependence on the attachment figure. Main and Solomon (1986) note that, by increasing "dependence upon the attachment figure, this infant successfully draws the attention of the parent" (p. 112). In fact, results from several studies have shown that insecure/ambivalent babies had experienced their mothers as relatively unavailable in the home (Ainsworth et al., 1978; Belsky et al., 1984; Grossmann et al., 1985; for a review, see Cassidy & Berlin, in press). The pathologically extreme form of mother's unavailability—neglect—has also been found to be associated with the insecure/ambivalent attachment pattern (Youngblade & Belsky, 1990).

If an infant wants to heighten the importance of the relationship and show an interest in remaining close to the attachment figure, how might she regulate her emotions to this end? Heightened negative emotionality can be viewed as a component of the child's strategy to gain the mother's attention. The negative emotionality of the insecure/ambivalent child may be exaggerated and chronic because the child recognizes that to relax and allow herself to be soothed by the presence of the attachment figure is to run the risk of then losing contact with the inconsistently available parent. One reasonable strategy involves fearfulness in response to relatively benign stimuli. Through exaggerated fearfulness, the infant increases the likelihood of gaining the attention of a frequently unavailable caregiver should true danger arise (Main & Hesse, 1990). This heightening strategy can be viewed as adaptive if it serves to gain the attention of an unavailable caregiver. However, according to Bowlby (1973), such a strategy can be dysfunctional if the negative emotionality is so pervasive that it threatens the existence of the relationship. It can also be dysfunctional to the extent that it interferes with other developmental tasks such as exploration.[2]

How does attention regulation contribute to the heightened emotionality of these children? One process may involve shifting attention toward attachment-eliciting situations; thus, such children may selectively attend to the frightening aspects of the environment, interpreting "an environment

[2] This strategy of exaggerating negative affect in order to increase care is not restricted to the context of routine parent-child interaction. For instance, it is a strategy commonly used by young children following the birth of a sibling in order to regain the degree of caregiving received before the parent's attention was diverted by the new infant, a tendency long described as *regression* (Dunn, Kendrick, & MacNamee, 1981; Field & Reite, 1984; Trivers, 1974). This strategy is also used by the young of other species; e.g., when their mothers become less available to them during weaning, free-ranging infant baboons dramatically increase their crying (DeVore, 1963).

known at some level to be quiescent as threatening" (Main, 1990, p. 61). Heightened recall of memories that activate attachment-related behaviors and emotions may also occur. Thus, according to Main's speculations, the infant's perception (based on previous interactions) of the parent's probable unresponsiveness is at some level accurate. This *accurate* perception of the parent's behavior is thought to necessitate a *distorted* perception of the environment, which, by serving to heighten attachment behavior, (usefully) increases the likelihood that the child's attachment needs will be met.

Because there are so few infants classified in this group (in American samples, roughly 10%), there are few empirical data to permit assessment of the extent to which heightening of negative emotions characterizes insecure/ambivalent infants. Heightened negative emotionality is indeed a marker of this pattern in the Strange Situation (Ainsworth et al., 1978; Braungart & Stifter, 1991; Shiller, Izard, & Hembree, 1986). In addition, there is some evidence that these infants are more fearful than others. Ainsworth (1992) conducted post hoc analyses of her original Baltimore data and reported that insecure/ambivalent infants were overrepresented among those who showed clear-cut fear in the episode of the Strange Situation before the entrance of the stranger (see also Bretherton & Ainsworth, 1974). These infants have also been found to be more fearful than secure infants in laboratory procedures at age 7 months (Miyake, Chen, & Campos, 1985) and at 2 years (Calkins & Fox, 1992). In addition, these infants have been found to be fearful about exploring a new environment (Hazen & Durrett, 1982; Jacobson & Wille, 1986) and to be fearful and withdrawn in interaction with peers (Pastor, 1981; Renken, Egeland, Marvinney, Mangelsdorf, & Sroufe, 1989).

However, the critical research needed to demonstrate a heightening of negative affect by insecure/ambivalent infants does not exist. With the insecure/avoidant pattern, evidence of minimization of negative affect does exist; infants and adults characterized by this pattern *do* feel negatively aroused, but they suppress expression of such feelings (Dozier & Kobak, 1992; Grossmann et al., 1986; Lutkenhaus et al., 1985; Malatesta et al., 1989). Comparable evidence in relation to the insecure/ambivalent pattern would consist in demonstrating that the insecure/ambivalent individuals show *greater* negative reactivity than they actually feel. The operationalization of "heightening" has not yet been attempted.

Parents

Just as heightened negative emotionality characterizes insecure/ambivalent infants, so does it also characterize their parents. Parents of insecure/ambivalent infants are thought to have a "preoccupied" state of mind in which the importance of attachment relationships is emphasized to such an extent that autonomy is undermined (Ainsworth & Eichberg, 1991; Benoit, Vidovic, & Roman, 1991; Main & Goldwyn, in press; Ward, Botyanski, Plunket, & Carlson, 1991). This state of mind involves a heightened and often incoherent focusing on relationships. The Adult Attachment Interviews of these parents indicate that they are embroiled in current anger with their own parents that they are unable to resolve or even convincingly analyze. They continue to fight their parents; they may rail angrily at their parents' shortcomings, describing recent arguments in great detail. Their attachment-related narratives have been described as "fearful and over-whelmed; or angry, conflicted, and unconvincingly analytical" (Main & Goldwyn, in press).

What aspects of the parent's behavior other than low or inconsistent availability might contribute to the heightened negative emotionality of these children? One factor may be a parent's failure to help the child regulate emotion. The parent may realize, at an unconscious level, that prolonged negative emotionality keeps the child embroiled with her and prevents the child from moving away to explore the environment. Thus, in order to emphasize the attachment relationship, the parent may use a strategy of failing to help the child effectively regulate negative emotions.

Extensive examination of the parent's role in helping children with such regulation is needed. There is, however, already some indication that mothers of insecure/ambivalent infants may not do what is necessary to resolve negative affect. Even during the first few months of their infants' lives, these mothers are less likely than mothers of secure infants to attempt to soothe their distressed babies (Ainsworth et al., 1978). At the end of the first year, during the Strange Situation, these mothers do not provide physical contact to their distressed infants but rather attempt to reinterest them in play (Ainsworth et al., 1978). This choice of comforting style may contribute to the relatively greater and longer-lasting distress of these babies. Congruent with this picture is the finding that mothers of 6-year-olds classified as insecure/ambivalent have difficulty setting limits on their children's behavior (Solomon, George, & Ivins, 1987), which is in turn a parenting style commonly found in coercive, highly negative families (Baumrind, 1973; Patterson, 1982).

It is important to acknowledge that, as with all attachment groups, both the parent's and the child's behavior can be viewed in ways other than as a strategy. Parents of insecure/ambivalent infants may be relatively unresponsive to their infants' signals not only because of an unconscious strategy aimed at eliciting infant attachment behavior but also because they lack the competence to respond differently. Their own backgrounds may not have provided them with opportunities for learning competent parenting skills. When parents do not help their children regulate emotions, it may be that they did not learn how to regulate emotions in their own relationships. Such a possibility is underscored by the responses given by these parents during the Adult Attachment Interview that indicate their continuing consuming anger toward their own parents (Main & Goldwyn, in press).

Given a parent who is preoccupied with attachment, the infant's heightened negative emotionality may serve a signal function to the mother, indicating that the child wants to stay close and emphasize the relationship, thus cooperating with the mother's wish to maintain an attachment-preoccupied state of mind. Heightened anger and fearfulness show the mother that the child is involved with her. They reassure the parent that she will continue to be needed and that the child will remain close to her; in other words, they reassure the parent that the child "will not become an adult and leave" (Bacciagaluppi, 1985, p. 371).

EMOTIONS, ATTACHMENT, AND TEMPERAMENT

The proposition that emotion regulation may be influenced by and, indeed, be part of the infant's strategic response to interaction with the caregiver reflects a relationship-based approach that focuses on an environmental explanation of the connection between emotion regulation and attachment pattern. It is important to note, however, that the perspective offered here is fully compatible with Calkins's (in this volume) comprehensive model of the biological, behavioral, cognitive, and caregiving precursors of emotion regulation. My focus has been on the caregiving (specifically attachment) component, which, as Calkins points out, operates in conjunction with other components and is in fact itself influenced by the infant's emotion regulation. In this section, I address the role played by infant temperament in the connection between emotion regulation and attachment pattern.

The notion of infants' attachment-related strategies that I have described incorporates recognition of contributions made by infant temperament. Biological factors are recognized as being the basic structure that social factors influence and as being important contributors to individual functioning. Converging studies suggest the existence of temperamentally based tendencies toward particular patterns of emotion regulation that are both early to appear and stable over time (Bates, 1987; Garcia-Coll, Kagan, & Resnick, 1984; Izard, Hembree, Dougherty, & Spizzirri, 1983). Thus, when an infant's strategic response to a mother's caregiving is considered, two contributions of temperament are acknowledged: (a) the response is likely to fall within a range that is constrained by the infant's temperament; and (b) infants are not only responsive to their mother's caregiving behavior but also contribute to shaping its nature.

The nature of the effect of infant temperament on emotion regulation within particular attachment patterns is particularly complex. It is unlikely that simple, direct connections exist among temperament, attachment, and emotion regulation. Empirical investigations that have examined infant characteristics in conjunction with attachment classification indicate, for the most part, that the two are not directly associated (e.g., Bates, Maslin, & Frankel, 1985; Belsky & Isabella, 1988; Belsky et al., 1984; Crockenberg, 1981; Egeland & Farber, 1984; Gunnar, Mangelsdorf, Larson, & Hertsgaard, 1989; Mangelsdorf, Gunnar, Kestenbaum, Lang, & Andreas, 1990; Vaughn, Lefever, Seifer, & Barglow, 1989; Weber, Levitt, & Clark, 1986) but that they may relate indirectly via moderating factors such as the mother's social support (e.g., Crockenberg, 1981) and her personality (e.g., Mangelsdorf et al., 1990).

Some investigators of links between temperament and attachment have suggested that the patterns of emotion regulation associated with the two insecure attachment patterns have little to do with attachment history but rather reflect temperament-related assessment artifacts of the Strange Situation (Goldsmith & Alansky, 1987; Kagan, 1984). According to this reasoning, it is temperament that accounts for particular forms of emotion regulation, and it is the emotion regulation that leads to the attachment classification.

From this perspective, the classification of children as insecure/avoidant relates to their being low on the temperamental dimension of fearfulness (what Kagan, 1984, calls *inhibition*, the "vulnerability to becoming anxious in an unfamiliar situation" [p. 58]). In this scheme, it is because such children are not distressed on separation that they find nothing noteworthy in the parent's return and so attend little to her, a type of reunion behavior that contributes to classification as insecure/avoidant. This reasoning is based on the assumption that insecure/avoidant infants are less distressed during separations than secure infants.

Research has contradicted this assumption: in three of the four studies that provide relevant data, insecure/avoidant infants have been found to be as distressed as (or even significantly more distressed than) some secure (B1 and B2) infants during separation (Ainsworth et al., 1978; Braungart & Stifter, 1991; Frodi & Thompson, 1985). In the fourth study, compared to secure infants, avoidant infants were less behaviorally distressed on separation; physiological measures, however, revealed them to be equally (assessment of heart rate) or more (assessment of cortisol level) distressed. Thus, extent of separation distress alone cannot account for classification as insecure/avoidant (see also Thompson & Lamb, 1984). Examination of both behavioral and physiological measures will be particularly important in this regard for future research.

Classification of a child as insecure/ambivalent is thought to relate to temperamental characteristics such as fearfulness or irritability (Goldsmith & Alansky, 1987; Kagan, 1984). Both these characteristics are viewed as making it particularly difficult for the infant to stop crying and be soothed on reunion, a pattern of behaviors that contributes to classification as insecure/ambivalent. Fearfulness is thought to make the separation so traumatic for the child that recovery is naturally more difficult, and, by definition, *irritability* means that the infant is difficult to soothe.

These speculations rest on propositions that can be examined. First, the proposition that fearfulness leads to insecure/ambivalent attachment rests on the assumption that ambivalent infants are more fearful and distressed on separation than secure infants. Two studies provide relevant data. In one, distress on separation was assessed within each 10-sec epoch with a five-point rating scale of negative affect (Braungart & Stifter, 1991). In the other, it was assessed within each 15-sec epoch with a five-point rating scale that included both positive and negative affect and that was used to create a number of composite variables: peak affect expressed, general affect tone, latency to onset of distress, and rise time to peak distress (Frodi & Thompson, 1985). Data from both studies indicated that insecure/ambivalent infants are in fact no more distressed on separation than some secure (B3 and B4) infants. Thus, as was the case with regard to the insecure/avoidant group, fearfulness and separation distress alone cannot account for the classification of infants as insecure/ambivalent.

Certainly, considerably more research examining this issue is needed. Both these studies rely on negative findings, and ambivalent infants may in fact be more distressed than secure infants in ways that were not captured by these assessments. In addition, there may be both temperament- and relationship-based influences on an infant's ability to be soothed following distress.

Second, the proposition that infant irritability leads to classification as insecure/ambivalent rests on the assumption that irritable babies are more likely to be classified in the insecure/ambivalent group than in any other. However, although there is some indication that insecure/ambivalent infants are prone to irritability (Miyake et al., 1985), there is no evidence that most irritable babies become insecure/ambivalent. In fact, two studies have found that large proportions of irritable newborns were not classified as insecure/ambivalent. This was true for 84% of irritable newborns in a study conducted in the Netherlands (van den Boom, 1989) and for 75% of irritable newborns in an American sample (Crockenberg, 1981, personal communication, December 9, 1981). Additional research with samples of irritable newborns is necessary in order to investigate this issue further.

Before closing this discussion of temperamental influences, it may be useful to consider briefly the difference between what infants feel (reactivity) and what they show (expressiveness). Infant reactivity is likely to have both temperamental and caregiving origins. But what about infant expressivity? There may be some direct temperamental influence on the tendency to express that which is felt, and it is certainly likely that what is expressed is linked to what is felt. Nevertheless, expressivity may be more directly linked to environment than reactivity since it seems likely that the children's expressiveness will be influenced by the responses that significant people have made to their expressiveness. Parents engage in a number of behaviors that serve to regulate their children's emotions, both consciously (via emotion socialization practices; Cole, 1985; Lewis & Saarni, 1985; Miller & Sperry, 1987; Thompson, 1990) and unconsciously (e.g., affect attunement; Stern, 1985). Within the range of the infant's reactivity, these processes of socialization and attunement may provide a means for the parent to influence the child's expressivity.

It is intriguing to note that, during the Strange Situation, it is within the secure group that the widest range of emotion expression is evident: some children are quite distressed during separation; others are not. It is worth considering whether parents of secure infants are more willing to accept the temperamental proclivities of the infant whereas parents of insecure infants more strongly attempt to influence their children's expressiveness to suit their own preferences.

In sum, although it is likely that infant temperament plays a role in regulating attachment behavior and may influence the connection between emotion regulation and attachment pattern, it does not appear that the nature of the relevant mechanisms is yet fully understood.

SUMMARY

Emotion regulation and quality of attachment are closely linked. It has been proposed here that one influence on individual differences in emotion regulation may be a child's attachment history. Individuals characterized by the flexible ability to accept and integrate both positive and negative emotions are generally securely attached; on the other hand, individuals characterized by either limited or heightened negative affect are more likely to be insecurely attached. While acknowledging the role of infant temperament, I have focused on the role of social factors in examining the link between emotion regulation and attachment.

The approach to emotion regulation taken here—that emotion regulation is adaptive in helping a child attain her goals—is essentially a functionalist approach (Bretherton et al., 1986; Campos et al., 1983), consistent with earlier views of emotions as important regulators of interpersonal relationships (Charlesworth, 1982; Izard, 1977). It has been proposed that patterns of emotion regulation serve an important function for the infant: the function of maintaining the relationship with the attachment figure. Emotion regulation has been described as serving this function in two ways.

First, the function of maintaining the relationship is thought to be served when infant emotion regulation contributes to the infant's more generalized regulation of the attachment system in response to experiences with the caregiver. Infants who have experienced rejection (insecure/avoidant infants) are thought to minimize negative affect in order to avoid the risk of further rejection. Infants whose mothers have been relatively unavailable or inconsistently available (insecure/ambivalent infants) are thought to maximize negative affect in order to increase the likelihood of gaining the attention of a frequently unavailable caregiver. Both these patterns of emotion regulation help ensure that the child will remain close to the parent and thereby be protected.

Second, the function of maintaining the attachment relationship is thought to be served when the infant signals to the parent that she will cooperate in helping maintain the parent's own state of mind in relation to attachment. The minimizing of negative affect of the avoidant infant signals that the infant will not seek caregiving that would interfere with the parent's dismissal of attachment. The heightened negative emotionality of the ambivalent infant signals to the parent that the infant needs her and thus helps maintain a state of mind in which attachment is emphasized.

The approach to emotion regulation presented here is congruent with much work examining the socialization of emotions (Lewis & Saarni, 1985; Thompson, 1990). Thompson (1990, in this volume) provides a thorough discussion of the ways in which social experiences with parents can influence children's emotion regulation and also describes the diverse reasons that adults attempt to regulate children's emotions: "to promote positive social interactions with the child, to make the child's emotion expressions conform to cultural and familial display rules, to support the child's own coping efforts, or to broaden the child's own emotional repertoire" (1990, p. 416). Here, it has been proposed that an additional reason for such attempts at regulation is to help the parent maintain her own state of mind in relation to attachment. Thompson's further observation that parents' regulation "sometimes requires [of the child] a dissociation of the components of emotion experience (e.g., expressing an emotion that is inconsistent with one's internal experiences in order to conform to parental demands)" (1990, p. 417) is consistent with the view presented here that infant emotion regulation may involve emotion displays that are either heightened or minimized versions of actual feelings.

The ideas that I have presented are preliminary, and much additional research is needed to clarify and extend these theoretical notions. It is hoped that this discussion will be useful in the design of future research. In particular, research is needed on the occurrence of minimizing and maximizing of true feelings, on parents' responses to a wide range of children's emotions in a variety of contexts, on individual differences in the ways in which parents regulate their own emotions, on the nature of emotion regulation during different developmental periods, and on the extent to which children's emotion regulation is relationship specific as opposed to being generalized across relationships. Future research examining the interplay of both temperament and attachment quality as predictive of emotion regulation will be particularly important.

REFERENCES

Adamec, R. E. (1991). Individual differences in temporal lobe sensory processing of threatening stimuli in the cat. *Physiology and Behavior,* **49,** 445–464.

Adamec, R. E., & Stark-Adamec, C. (1986). Limbic hyperfunction, limbic epilepsy and interictal behavior. In B. K. Doane & K. E. Livingston (Eds.), *The limbic system.* New York: Raven.

Ahern, G. L., Schomer, D. L., Leefield, J., Blume, H., Cosgrove, G. R., Weintraub, S., & Mesulam, M. M. (1991). Right hemisphere advantage for evaluating emotional facial expressions. *Cortex,* **27,** 193–202.

Ainsworth, M. D. (1992). A consideration of social referencing in the context of attachment theory and research. In S. Feinman (Ed.), *Social referencing and the social construction of reality.* New York: Plenum.

Ainsworth, M. D., Blehar, M., Waters, E., & Wall, S. (1978). *Patterns of attachment: A psychological study of the Strange Situation.* Hillsdale, NJ: Erlbaum.

Ainsworth, M. D., & Eichberg, C. (1991). Effects on infant-mother attachment of mother's unresolved loss of an attachment figure or other traumatic experience. In P. Marris, J. Stevenson-Hinde, & C. Parkes (Eds.), *Attachment across the life cycle.* New York: Routledge.

Alexander, N., Velasquez, M. T., Decuir, M., & Maronde, R. H. (1980). Indices of sympathetic activity in the sinoaortic denervated hypertensive rat. *American Journal of Physiology,* **238,** H521–H526.

Alloy, L. B., & Abramson, L. Y. (1988). The hopelessness theory of depression: Attributional aspects. *British Journal of Clinical Psychology,* **27,** 5–21.

Altschuler, J. L., & Ruble, D. N. (1989). Developmental changes in children's awareness of strategies for coping with uncontrollable stress. *Child Development,* **60,** 1337–1349.

American Psychiatric Association. (1987). *Diagnostic and statistical manual of mental disorders* (3d ed., rev.). Washington, DC: American Psychiatric Press.

Anders, T. F. (1982). Biological rhythms in development. *Psychosomatic Medicine,* **44,** 61–72.

Arnold, M. B. (1960). *Emotion and personality* (Vol. 1). New York: Columbia University Press.

Ax, A. A. (1964). Goals and methods of psychophysiology. *Psychophysiology,* **1,** 8–25.

Bacciagaluppi, M. (1985). Inversion of parent-child relationships: A contribution to attachment theory. *British Journal of Medical Psychology,* **58,** 369–373.

Band, E., & Weisz, J. R. (1988). How to feel better when it feels bad: Children's perspectives on coping with everyday stress. *Developmental Psychology,* **24**(2), 247–253.

Barden, R. C., Garber, J., Duncan, S. W., & Masters, J. C. (1981). Cumulative effects of induced affective states in children: Accentuation, inoculation, and remediation. *Journal of Personality and Social Psychology,* **40,** 750–760.

Barkley, R. A. (1990). *Attention deficit hyperactivity disorder: A handbook for diagnosis and treatment.* New York: Guilford.

Barrett, K. C., & Campos, J. J. (1987). Perspectives on emotional development: 2. A functionalist approach to emotions. In J. D. Osofsky (Ed.), *Handbook of infant development* (2d ed.). New York: Wiley.

Bates, J. (1987). Temperament in infancy. In J. Osofsky (Ed.), *Handbook of infant development* (2d ed.). New York: Wiley.

Bates, J. E. (1989). Applications of temperament concepts. In G. A. Kohnstamm, J. E. Bates, & M. K. Rothbart (Eds.), *Temperament in childhood.* New York: Wiley.

Bates, J. E., & Bayles, K. (1988). Attachment and the development of behavior problems. In J. Belsky & T. Nezworski (Eds.), *Clinical implications of attachment.* Hillsdale, NJ: Erlbaum.

Bates, J. E., Bayles, K., Bennett, D. S., Ridge, B., & Brown, M. M. (1991). Origins of externalizing behavior problems at eight years of age. In D. Pepler & K. H. Rubin (Eds.), *The development and treatment of childhood aggression.* Hillsdale, NJ: Erlbaum.

Bates, J. E., Maslin, C. A., & Frankel, K. A. (1985). Attachment security, mother-child interaction, and temperament as predictors of behavior-problem ratings at age three years. In I. Bretherton & E. Waters (Eds.), *Growing points of attachment theory and research. Monographs of the Society for Research in Child Development,* **50**(1–2, Serial No. 209).

Baumrind, D. (1973). The development of instrumental competence through socialization. In A. D. Pick (Ed.), *Minnesota Symposium on Child Psychology* (Vol. **7**). Minneapolis: University of Minnesota Press.

Bear, D. M. (1983). Hemispheric specialization and the neurology of emotion. *Archives of Neurology,* **40,** 195–202.

Beck, A. T. (1972). *Depression: Causes and treatment.* Philadelphia: University of Pennsylvania Press.

Beck, A. T. (1976). *Cognitive therapy and the emotional disorders.* New York: International Universities Press.

Beebe, B., Jaffe, J., Feldstein, S., Mays, K., & Alson, D. (1985). Interpersonal timing: The application of an adult dialogue model to mother-infant vocal kinesic interaction. In T. Field & N. A. Fox (Eds.), *Social perception in infants.* Norwood, NJ: Ablex.

Bell, S., & Ainsworth, M. D. (1972). Infant crying and maternal responsiveness. *Child Development,* **43,** 1171–1190.

Belsky, J., & Cassidy, J. (in press). Attachment: Theory and evidence. In M. L. Rutter, D. F. Hay, & S. Baron-Cohen (Eds.), *Development through life: A handbook for clinicians.* Oxford: Blackwell.

Belsky, J., & Isabella, R. (1988). Maternal, infant, and social-contextual determinants of attachment security. In J. Belsky & T. Nezworski (Eds.), *Clinical implications of attachment.* Hillsdale, NJ: Erlbaum.

Belsky, J., & Rovine, M. J. (1988). Nonmaternal care in the first year of life and the security of infant-parent attachment. *Child Development,* **59,** 156–167.

Belsky, J., Rovine, M., & Taylor, D. G. (1984). The Pennsylvania Infant and Family Development Project: 2. The origins of individual differences in infant-mother attachment: Maternal and infant contributions. *Child Development,* **55,** 718–728.

Belsky, J., & Vondra, J. (1989). Lessons from child abuse: The determinants of parenting. In D. Cicchetti & V. Carlson (Eds.), *Child maltreatment: Theory and research on the causes and consequences of child abuse and neglect.* New York: Cambridge University Press.

Benoit, D., Vidovic, D., & Roman, J. (1991, April). *Transmission of attachment across three generations.* Paper presented at the meeting of the Society for Research in Child Development, Seattle.

Berger, H. (1930). Uber das Elecktrenkephalogramm des Menschen. *Journal of Psychology and Neurology,* **40,** 160–179.

Berntson, G. G., Cacioppo, J. T., & Quigley, K. S. (1991). Autonomic determinism: The modes of autonomic control, the doctrine of autonomic space, and the laws of autonomic constraint. *Psychological Review,* **98,** 459–487.

Bignall, K. E., Heggeness, F. W., & Palmer, J. E. (1977). Sympathetic inhibition of thermogenesis in the infant rat: Possible glucostatic control. *American Journal of Physiology,* **233,** R23–R29.

Birmaher, B., Dahl, R. E., Ryan, N. D., Robinovich, H., Ambrosini, P., Al-Shabbout, M., Novacenko, H., Nelson, B., & Puig-Antich, J. (1992). The dexamethasone suppression test in adolescent outpatients with major depressive disorder. *American Journal of Psychiatry,* **149,** 1040–1045.

Blanck, G., & Blanck, R. (1976). *Ego psychology: Theory and practice.* New York: Columbia University Press.

Bohus, B., de Kloet, E. R., & Veldhuis, H. D. (1982). Adrenal steroids and behavioural adaptation: Relationship to brain corticoid receptors. In D. Ganten & D. W. Pfaff (Eds.), *Current topics in neuroendocrinology.* Berlin: Springer.

Born, J., Hitzler, V., Pietrowsky, R., Pauschinger, P., & Fehm, H. L. (1989). Influences of cortisol on auditory evoked potentials and mood in humans. *Neuropsychobiology,* **20,** 145–151.

Borod, J. C. (1992). Interhemispheric and intrahemispheric control of emotion: A focus on unilateral brain damage. *Journal of Consulting and Clinical Psychology,* **60,** 339–348.

Bower, G. H. (1981). Mood and memory. *American Psychologist,* **36,** 129–148.

Bowlby, J. (1973). *Attachment and loss: Vol. 2. Separation: Anxiety and anger.* New York: Basic.

Bowlby, J. (1979). *The making and breaking of affectional bonds.* London: Tavistock.

Bowlby, J. (1980). *Attachment and loss: Vol. 3. Loss: Sadness and depression.* New York: Basic.

Bowlby, J. (1982). *Attachment and loss: Vol. 1. Attachment* (2d ed.). New York: Basic. (Original work published 1969)

Bradley, S. J. (1990). Affect regulation and psychopathology: Bridging the mind-body gap. *Canadian Journal of Psychiatry,* **35,** 540–547.

Brake, S. C., Shair, H. N., & Hofer, M. A. (1988). Exploiting the nursing niche: Infants' sucking and feeding behavior in the context of the mother-infant interaction. In E. Blass (Ed.), *Developmental psychobiology and behavioral ecology* (Vol. **9**). New York: Plenum.

Braungart, J. M., & Stifter, C. A. (1991). Regulation of negative reactivity during the Strange Situation: Temperament and attachment in 12-month-old infants. *Infant Behavior and Development,* **14,** 349–367.

Brazelton, T. B. (1984). *Neonatal Behavioral Assessment Scale* (2d ed.). Philadelphia: Lippincott.

Brazelton, T. B., Koslowski, B., & Main, M. (1974). Origins of reciprocity: The early mother-infant interaction. In M. Lewis & L. Rosenblum (Eds.), *The effects of the infant on its caregiver.* New York: Wiley.

Bretherton, I. (1985). Attachment theory: Retrospect and prospect. In I. Bretherton & E. Waters (Eds.), *Growing points of attachment theory and research. Monographs of the Society for Research in Child Development,* **50**(1–2, Serial No. 209).

Bretherton, I. (1987). New perspectives on attachment relations: Security, communication, and internal working models. In J. Osofsky (Ed.), *Handbook of infant development* (2d ed.). New York: Wiley.

Bretherton, I. (1990). Open communication and internal working models: Their role in the development of attachment relationships. In R. A. Thompson (Ed.), *Socioemotional development* (Nebraska Symposium on Motivation, Vol. **36**). Lincoln: University of Nebraska Press.

Bretherton, I., & Ainsworth, M. D. (1974). Responses of one-year-olds to a stranger in a Strange Situation. In M. Lewis & L. A. Rosenblum (Eds.), *The origins of fear*. New York: Wiley.

Bretherton, I., & Beeghly, M. (1982). Talking about internal states: The acquisition of an explicit theory of mind. *Developmental Psychology*, **18**, 906–921.

Bretherton, I., Fritz, J., Zahn-Waxler, C., & Ridgeway, D. (1986). Learning to talk about emotions: A functionalist perspective. *Child Development*, **57**, 529–548.

Brett, L., & Levine, S. (1979). Schedule-induced polydipsia reduces pituitary-adrenocortical activity in rats. *Journal of Comparative and Physiological Psychology*, **93**, 946–956.

Bridges, L. J., & Connell, J. P. (1991). Consistency and inconsistency in infant emotional and social interactive behavior across contexts and caregivers. *Infant Behavior and Development*, **14**, 471–487.

Brown, K., Covell, K., & Abramovitch, R. (1991). Time course and control of emotion: Age differences in understanding and recognition. *Merrill-Palmer Quarterly*, **37**, 273–287.

Bruner, J. (1983). *Child's talk: Learning to use language*. New York: Norton.

Bryden, M. P., & Ley, R. G. (1983). Right hemispheric involvement in the perception and expression of emotions in normal humans. In K. M. Heilman & P. Satz (Eds.), *Neuropsychology of human emotion*. New York: Guilford.

Buss, A. H., & Plomin, R. (1984). *Temperament: Early developing personality traits*. Hillsdale, NJ: Erlbaum.

Calkins, S. D., & Fox, N. A. (1992). The relations among infant temperament, security of attachment and behavioral inhibition at 24 months. *Child Development*, **63**, 1456–1472.

Calkins, S. D., Fox, N. A., & Marshall, T. R. (in press). Behavioral and physiological correlates of inhibition in infancy. *Child Development*.

Calkins, S. D., Fox, N. A., Rubin, K. H., Coplan, R. J., & Stewart, S. L. (1994). *Longitudinal outcomes of behavioral inhibition: Implications for behavior in a peer setting*. Unpublished manuscript.

Campos, J. J., & Barrett, K. C. (1984). Toward a new understanding of emotions and their development. In C. E. Izard, J. Kagan, & R. B. Zajonc (Eds.), *Emotions, cognition, and behavior*. Cambridge: Cambridge University Press.

Campos, J. J., Barrett, K. C., Lamb, M. E., Goldsmith, H. H., & Stenberg, C. R. (1983). Socioemotional development. In M. M. Haith & J. J. Campos (Eds.), P. H. Mussen (Series Ed.), *Handbook of child psychology: Vol. 2. Infancy and developmental psychobiology*. New York: Wiley.

Campos, J. J., Campos, R. G., & Barrett, K. C. (1989). Emergent themes in the study of emotional development and emotion regulation. *Developmental Psychology*, **25**, 394–402.

Campos, J. J., Kermoian, R., & Zumbahlen, M. R. (1992). Socioemotional transformations in the family system following infant crawling onset. In N. Eisenberg & R. A. Fabes (Eds.), *Emotion and its regulation in early development* (New Directions in Child Development, No. 55). San Francisco: Jossey-Bass.

Camras, L. A. (1982). Ethological approaches to nonverbal communication. In R. S. Feldman (Ed.), *Development of nonverbal behavior in children*. New York: Springer.

Cannon, W. B. (1927). The James-Lange theory of emotions: A critical examination and an alternative theory. *American Journal of Psychology*, **39**, 106–124.

Cantwell, D., Baker, L., & Mattison, R. (1979). The prevalence of psychiatric disorder in children with speech and language disorders: An epidemiological study. *Journal of the Academy of Adolescent and Child Psychiatry,* **18,** 450–461.

Carden, S. E., & Hofer, M. A. (1992). Effect of a social companion on the ultrasonic vocalizations and contact responses of 3 day old rat pups. *Behavioral Neuroscience,* **106,** 421–426.

Carey, W. B., & McDevitt, S. C. (1978). Revision of the Infant Temperament Questionnaire. *Pediatrics,* **61,** 735–739.

Carlson, V., Cicchetti, D., Barnett, D., & Braunwald, K. (1989). Disorganized/disoriented attachment relationships in maltreated infants. *Developmental Psychology,* **25,** 525–531.

Carlson, C. R., & Masters, J. C. (1986). Inoculation by emotion: Effects of positive emotional states on children's reactions to social comparison. *Developmental Psychology,* **22,** 760–765.

Carroll, B. J., Feinberg, M. F., Greden, J. F., Tarika, J., Albala, A. A., Haskett, R. F., et al. (1981). A specific laboratory test for the diagnosis of melancholia. *Archives of General Psychiatry,* **38,** 15–22.

Carstensen, L. L. (1991). Selectivity theory: Social activity in life-span context. In K. W. Schaie (Ed.), *Annual review of geriatrics and gerontology* (Vol. 11). New York: Springer.

Case, R., Hayward, S., Lewis, M., & Hurst, P. (1988). Toward a neo-Piagetian theory of cognitive and emotional development. *Developmental Review,* **8,** 1–51.

Cassidy, J. (1988). Child-mother attachment and the self in six-year-olds. *Child Development,* **59,** 121–134.

Cassidy, J. (1990). Theoretical and methodological considerations in the study of the self in young children. In M. T. Greenberg, D. Cicchetti, & E. M. Cummings (Eds.), *Attachment in the preschool years: Theory, research, and intervention.* Chicago: University of Chicago Press.

Cassidy, J., & Berlin, L. J. (in press). The insecure/ambivalent pattern of attachment: Theory and research. *Child Development.*

Cassidy, J., & Kobak, R. R. (1988). Avoidance and its relation to other defensive processes. In J. Belsky & T. Nezworski (Eds.), *Clinical implications of attachment.* Hillsdale, NJ: Erlbaum.

Chapple, E. D. (1970). Experimental production of transients in human interaction. *Nature,* **228,** 630–633.

Charlesworth, W. R. (1982). An ethological approach to research on facial expressions. In C. E. Izard (Ed.), *Measuring emotions in infants and children.* Cambridge: Cambridge University Press.

Chugani, H. T. (1994). Developmental aspects of regional brain glucose metabolism, behavior, and plasticity. In G. Dawson & K. Fischer (Eds.), *Human behavior and the developing brain.* New York: Guilford.

Cicchetti, D. (1989a). Developmental psychopathology: Past, present, and future. In D. Cicchetti (Ed.), *Emergence of a discipline: Rochester Symposium on Developmental Psychopathology* (Vol. 1). Hillsdale, NJ: Erlbaum.

Cicchetti, D. (1989b). How research on child maltreatment has informed the study of child development: Perspectives from developmental psychopathology. In D. Cicchetti & V. Carlson (Eds.), *Child maltreatment: Theory and research on the causes and consequences of child abuse and neglect.* Cambridge: Cambridge University Press.

Cicchetti, D. (1990). The organization and coherence of socioemotional, cognitive, and representational development: Illustrations through a developmental psychopathology perspective on Down syndrome and child maltreatment. In R. A. Thompson (Ed.), *Socioemotional development* (Nebraska Symposium on Motivation, Vol. **36**). Lincoln: University of Nebraska Press.

Cicchetti, D., & Beeghly, M. (Eds.). (1987). *Symbolic development in maltreated youngsters: An organizational perspective* (New Directions in Child Development, No. 36). San Francisco: Jossey-Bass.

Cicchetti, D., Ganiban, J., & Barnett, D. (1991). Contributions from the study of high-risk populations to understanding the development of emotion regulation. In J. Garber & K. A. Dodge (Eds.), *The development of emotion regulation and dysregulation.* New York: Cambridge University Press.

Coe, C. L., Mendoza, S. P., Smotherman, W. P., & Levine, S. (1978). Mother-infant attachment in the squirrel monkey: Adrenal response to separation. *Behavioral Biology,* **22,** 256–263.

Cohn, J. F., Matias, R., Tronick, E. Z., Connell, D., & Lyons-Ruth, D. (1986). Face-to-face interactions of depressed mothers and their infants. In E. Z. Tronick & T. Field (Eds.), *Maternal depression and infant disturbance.* San Francisco: Jossey-Bass.

Cole, P. M. (1985). Display rules and the socialization of affective displays. In G. Zivin (Ed.), *The development of expressive behavior: Biology-environment interactions.* New York: Academic.

Cole, P. M. (1986). Children's spontaneous expressive control of facial expression. *Child Development,* **57,** 1309–1321.

Cole, P. M., Barrett, K. C., & Zahn-Waxler, C. (1992). Emotional displays in toddlers during mishaps. *Child Development,* **63,** 314–324.

Cole, P. M., & Kaslow, N. J. (1988). Interactional and cognitive strategies for affect regulation: Developmental perspective on childhood depression. In L. B. Alloy (Ed.), *Cognitive processes in depression.* New York: Guilford.

Cole, P. M., & Putnam, F. W. (1992). The effect of incest on self and social functioning: A developmental psychopathology perspective. *Journal of Consulting and Clinical Psychology,* **60,** 174–184.

Cole, P. M., & Smith, K. D. (1993, March). *Preschoolers' behavioral difficulties and the self-regulation of negative emotion.* Paper presented at the meeting of the Society for Research in Child Development, New Orleans.

Connell, J. P., & Thompson, R. A. (1986). Emotion and social interaction in the Strange Situation: Consistencies and asymmetric influences in the second year. *Child Development,* **57,** 733–745.

Connor, R. L., Vernikos-Danellis, J., & Levine, S. (1971). Stress, fighting and neuroendocrine function. *Nature,* **234,** 561–566.

Coplan, R. J., Rubin, K. H., Fox, N. A., Calkins, S. D., & Stewart, S. (1994). Being alone, playing alone and acting alone: Distinguishing reticence and passive- and active-solitude in young children. *Child Development,* **65,** 129–137.

Coyne, J. C., & Downey, G. (1991). Social factors and psychopathology: Stress, social support, and coping processes. *Annual Review of Psychology,* **42,** 401–425.

Cramer, P. (1991). *The development of defense mechanisms: Theory, research, and assessment.* New York: Springer.

Crittenden, P. (1992). Attachment in the preschool years. *Development and Psychopathology,* **4,** 209–241.

Crockenberg, S. B. (1981). Infant irritability, mother responsiveness, and social support influences on the security of mother infant attachment. *Child Development,* **52,** 857–868.

Cummings, E. M. (1987). Coping with background anger in early childhood. *Child Development,* **58,** 976–984.

Cummings, E. M., Zahn-Waxler, C., & Radke-Yarrow, M. (1984). Developmental changes in children's reactions to anger in the home. *Journal of Child Psychology and Psychiatry,* **25,** 63–74.

Cummings, J. S., Pellegrini, D. S., Notarius, C. I., & Cummings, E. M. (1989). Children's responses to angry adult behavior as a function of marital distress and history of interparent hostility. *Child Development, 60,* 1035–1043.

Cutting, J. (1990). *The right cerebral hemisphere in psychiatric disorders.* New York: Oxford University Press.

Dahl, R., Ryan, N., Puig-Antich, J., Nguyen, N., Al-Shabbout, M., Meyer, V., & Perel, J. (1991). 24-hour cortisol measures in adolescents with major depression: A controlled study. *Biological Psychiatry, 30,* 25–36.

Darwin, C. (1965). *The expression of emotions in man and animals.* Chicago: University of Chicago Press. (Original work published 1872)

Davidson, R. J. (1984a). Affect, cognition and hemispheric specialization. In C. E. Izard, J. Kagan, & R. B. Zajonc (Eds.), *Emotion, cognition, and behavior.* Cambridge: Cambridge University Press.

Davidson, R. J. (1984b). Hemispheric asymmetry and emotion. In K. Scherer & P. Ekman (Eds.), *Approaches to emotion.* Hillsdale, NJ: Erlbaum.

Davidson, R. J. (1987). Cerebral asymmetry and the nature of emotion: Implications for the study of individual differences and psychopathology. In R. Takahashi, P. Flor-Henry, J. Gruzelier, & S. Niwa (Eds.), *Cerebral dynamics, laterality, and psychopathology.* New York: Elsevier.

Davidson, R. J., Ekman, P., Saron, C., Senulis, R., & Friesen, W. V. (1990). Approach-withdrawal and cerebral asymmetry: 1. Emotional expression and brain physiology. *Journal of Personality and Social Psychology, 58,* 33–341.

Davidson, R. J., & Fox, N. A. (1982). Asymmetrical brain activity discriminates between positive versus negative affective stimuli in human infants. *Science, 218,* 1235–1237.

Davidson, R. J., & Fox, N. A. (1988). Cerebral asymmetry and emotion: Development and individual differences. In D. L. Molfese & S. J. Segalowitz (Eds.), *Brain lateralization in children: Developmental implications.* New York: Guilford.

Davidson, R. J., & Fox, N. A. (1989). The relation between tonic EEG asymmetry and ten month old infant emotional responses to separation. *Journal of Abnormal Psychology, 98,* 127–131.

Davidson, R. J., Schaffer, C. E., & Saron, C. (1985). Effects of lateralized stimulus presentations on the self-report of emotion and EEG asymmetry in depressed and non-depressed subjects. *Psychophysiology, 22,* 353–364.

Davis, M., Hitchcock, J. M., & Rosen, J. B. (1987). Anxiety and the amygdala: Pharmacological and anatomical analysis of the fear potentiated startle paradigm. In G. H. Bower (Ed.), *The psychology of learning and motivation* (Vol. 21). New York: Academic.

Dawson, G., Grofer Klinger, L., Panagiotides, H., Hill, D., & Spieker, S. (1992). Frontal lobe activity and affective behavior of infants of mothers with depressive symptoms. *Child Development, 63,* 725–737.

Dawson, G., Grofer Klinger, L., Panagiotides, H., Spieker, S., & Frey, K. (1992). Infants of mothers with depressive symptoms: Electroencephalographic and behavioral findings related to attachment status. *Development and Psychopathology, 4,* 67–80.

Dawson, G., Panagiotides, H., Grofer, L., & Hill, D. (1991, March). *Individual differences in generalized frontal activity are related to intensity of infant emotional expression.* Paper presented at the meeting of the Society for Research in Child Development, Seattle.

Dawson, G., Panagiotides, H., Grofer Klinger, L., & Hill, D. (1992). The role of frontal lobe functioning in infant self-regulatory behavior. *Brain and Cognition, 20,* 152–175.

DeBary, H. A. (1879). *Die Erscheinung der Symbiose.* Strasbourg: Trubner.

DeGangi, G. A., DiPietro, J. A., Greenspan, S. I., & Porges, S. W. (1991). Psychophysiological characteristics of the regulatory disordered infant. *Infant Behavior and Development, 14,* 37–50.

de Kloet, E. R. (1991). Brain corticosteroid receptor balance and homeostatic control. *Frontiers in Neuroendocrinology,* **12**(2), 95–164.

Demos, V. (1986). Crying in early infancy: An illustration of the motivational function of affect. In T. B. Brazelton & M. Yogman (Eds.), *Affect and early infancy.* New York: Ablex.

Denenberg, V. H., & Whimbey, A. E. (1963). Behavior of adult rats is modified by experiences their mothers had as infants. *Science,* **142,** 1192–1193.

Denham, S. A., McKinley, M., Couchoud, E. A., & Holt, R. (1990). Emotional and behavioral predictors of preschool peer ratings. *Child Development,* **61,** 1145–1152.

DeVore, I. J. (1963). Mother-infant relations in free-ranging baboons. In H. Rheingold (Ed.), *Maternal behavior in mammals.* New York: Wiley.

Diamond, A. (1988). Abilities and neural mechanisms underlying $\overline{AB}$ performance. *Child Development,* **59,** 523–527.

Diamond, A. (1990). Developmental time course in human infants and infant monkeys, and the neural bases of, inhibitory control in reaching. In A. Diamond (Ed.), *The development of and neural bases of high cognitive functions. Annals of the New York Academy of Sciences,* **608,** 637–676.

Diamond, A., & Goldman-Rakic, P. S. (1989). Comparison of human infants and rhesus monkeys on Piaget's $\overline{AB}$ task: Evidence for dependence on dorsolateral prefrontal cortex. *Experimental Brain Research,* **74,** 24–40.

Dienstbier, R. A. (1989). Arousal and physiological toughness: Implications for mental and physical health. *Psychological Review,* **96,** 84–100.

DiPietro, J. A., Larson, S. K., & Porges, S. W. (1987). Behavioral and heart-rate pattern differences between breast-fed and bottle-fed neonates. *Developmental Psychology,* **23,** 467–474.

DiPietro, J. A., & Porges, S. W. (1991). Vagal responsiveness to gavage feeding as an index of preterm stress. *Pediatric Research,* **29,** 231–236.

Dix, T. (1991). The affective organization of parenting: Adaptive and maladaptive processes. *Psychological Bulletin,* **110,** 3–25.

Dodge, K. A. (1989). Coordinating responses to aversive stimuli: Introduction to special section on the development of emotion regulation. *Developmental Psychology,* **25,** 339–342.

Dodge, K. (1991a). Emotion and social information processing. In J. Garber & K. A. Dodge (Eds.), *The development of emotion regulation and dysregulation.* Cambridge: Cambridge University Press.

Dodge, K. (1991b). The structure and function of reactive and proactive aggression. In D. Pepler & K. H. Rubin (Eds.), *The development and treatment of childhood aggression.* Hillsdale, NJ: Erlbaum.

Dodge, K. A., & Garber, J. (1991). Domains of emotion regulation. In J. Garber & K. A. Dodge (Eds.), *The development of emotion regulation and dysregulation.* Cambridge: Cambridge University Press.

Dodge, K. A., Murphy, R. M., & Buchsbaum, K. (1984). The assessment of intention-cue detection skills in children: Implications for developmental psychopathology. *Child Development,* **55,** 163–173.

Dodge, K. A., & Somberg, D. R. (1987). Hostile attributional biases among aggressive boys are exacerbated under conditions of threats to the self. *Child Development,* **58,** 213–224.

Doussard-Roosevelt, J. A., Walker, P. S., Portales, A. L., Greenspan, S. I., & Porges, S. W. (1990). Vagal tone and the fussy infant: Atypical vagal reactivity in the difficult infant [Abstract]. *Infant Behavior and Development,* **13,** 352.

Dozier, M., & Kobak, R. R. (1992). Psychophysiology in adolescent attachment inter-

views: Converging evidence for repressing strategies. *Child Development,* **63,** 1473–1480.

Duffy, E. (1962). *Activation and behavior.* New York: Wiley.

Dunn, J. (1988). *The beginnings of social understanding.* Cambridge, MA: Harvard University Press.

Dunn, J., & Brown, J. (1991). Relationships, talk about feelings, and the development of affect regulation in early childhood. In J. Garber & K. A. Dodge (Eds.), *The development of emotional regulation and dysregulation.* Cambridge: Cambridge University Press.

Dunn, J., Kendrick, C., & MacNamee, R. (1981). The reaction of first-born children to the birth of a sibling: Mothers' reports. *Journal of Child Psychology and Psychiatry,* **22,** 1–18.

Egeland, B., & Farber, E. (1984). Infant-mother attachment: Factors related to its development and changes over time. *Child Development,* **55,** 753–771.

Egeland, B., Kalkoske, M., Gottesman, N., & Erickson, M. F. (1990). Preschool behavior problems: Stability and factors accounting for change. *Journal of Child Psychology and Psychiatry,* **31,** 891–909.

Eisenberg, N., & Fabes, R. A. (1992a). *Emotion and its regulation in early development.* San Francisco: Jossey-Bass.

Eisenberg, N., & Fabes, R. A. (1992b). Emotion, self-regulation, and social competence. In M. F. Clark (Ed.), *Review of personality and social psychology* (Vol. **14**). Newbury Park, CA: Sage.

Ekman, P. (1977). Biological and cultural contributions to body and facial movement. In J. Blacking (Ed.), *The anthropology of the body.* London: Academic.

Ekman, P. (1980). Biological and cultural contributions to body and facial movement in the expression of emotions. In A. O. Rorty (Ed.), *Explaining emotions.* Berkeley and Los Angeles: University of California Press.

Ekman, P., & Friesen, W. V. (1984). *EM-FACS coding manual.* San Francisco: Consulting Psychologists Press.

Ekman, P., Levenson, R. W., & Friesen, W. V. (1983). Autonomic nervous system activity distinguishes among emotions. *Science,* **221,** 1208–1210.

El-Sheikh, M., Cummings, E. M., & Goetsch, V. (1989). Coping with adults' angry behavior: Behavioral, physiological, and verbal responding in preschoolers. *Developmental Psychology,* **25,** 490–498.

Emde, R. N. (1980). Emotional availability. In P. M. Taylor (Ed.), *Parent-infant relationships.* New York: Grune & Stratton.

Emde, R. N., Biringen, Z., Clyman, R. B., & Oppenheim, D. (1991). The moral self of infancy: Affective core and procedural knowledge. *Developmental Review,* **11,** 251–270.

Emde, R. N., Gaensbauer, T. J., & Harmon, R. J. (1976). *Emotional expressions in infancy: A biobehavioral study* (Psychological Issues Monograph, Vol. **10,** No. 37). New York: International Universities Press.

Eppinger, H., & Hess, L. (1910). *Die Vagotonie* (Nervous and Mental Disease Monograph, No. 20). N.p.

Escher-Graeub, D., & Grossmann, K. E. (1983). *Attachment security in the second year of life: The Regensburg cross-sectional study* (Research report). Regensburg: University of Regensburg.

Fabes, R. A., & Eisenberg, N. (1991). Young children's coping with interpersonal anger. *Child Development,* **63,** 116–129.

Field, T. (1978). The three Rs of infant-adult interaction: Rhythms, repertoires, and responsivity. *Journal of Pediatric Psychology,* **3,** 131–136.

Field, T. (1984a). Early interactions between infants and their post-partum depressed mothers. *Infant Behavior and Development,* **7,** 517–522.

Field, T. (1984b). Separations of children attending new schools. *Developmental Psychology*, **20**, 786–792.

Field, T. (1985). Attachment as psychobiological attunement: Being on the same wavelength. In M. Reite & T. Field (Eds.), *Psychobiology of attachment and separation*. New York: Academic.

Field, T. (1987). Interaction and attachment in normal and atypical infants. *Journal of Consulting and Clinical Psychology*, **55**, 1–7.

Field, T. (1989). Infancy risk factors and risk taking: Comments on Rauh's paper. *European Journal of the Psychology of Education*, **4**, 175–177.

Field, T. (1991a). Psychobiological attunement in close relationships. In R. Lerner, D. L. Featherman, & M. Perlmutter (Eds.), *Life-span development and behavior*. Hillsdale, NJ: Erlbaum.

Field, T. (1991b). Young children's adaptations to repeated separations from their mothers. *Child Development*, **62**, 539–547.

Field, T., & Fogel, A. (Eds.). (1982). *Emotion and early interaction*. Hillsdale, NJ: Erlbaum.

Field, T., Healy, B., Goldstein, S., & Guthertz, M. (1990). Behavior-state matching and synchrony in mother-infant interactions of nondepressed versus depressed dyads. *Developmental Psychology*, **26**, 7–14.

Field, T., Healy, B., & LeBlanc, W. (1989). Matching and synchrony of behavior states and heartrate in mother-infant interactions of nondepressed versus depressed dyads. *Infant Behavior and Development*, **12**, 357–376.

Field, T., Lang, C., Pickens, J., & Yando, R. (1994). Longitudinal follow-up of infants of depressed mothers. Unpublished data.

Field, T., & Reite, M. (1984). Children's responses to separation from mother during the birth of another child. *Child Development*, **55**, 1308–1316.

Field, T., Stoller, S., Vega-Lahr, N., Scafidi, F., & Goldstein, S. (1986). Maternal unavailability effects on very young infants in homecare versus daycare. *Infant Mental Health Journal*, **7**, 274–280.

Field, T., Vega-Lahr, N., & Jagadish, S. (1984). Separation stress of nursery school infants and toddlers graduating to new classes. *Infant Behavior and Development*, **7**, 277–284.

Field, T., Woodson, R., Greenberg, R., & Cohen, D. (1982). Discrimination and imitation of facial expressions by neonates. *Science*, **218**, 179–181.

Finman, R., Davidson, R. J., Colton, M. B., Straus, A. M., & Kagan, J. (1989). Psychophysiological correlates of inhibition to the unfamiliar in children [Abstract]. *Psychophysiology*, **26**, S24.

Fogel, A. (1982a). Affective dynamics in early infancy: Affective tolerance. In T. Field & A. Fogel (Eds.), *Emotion and early interaction*. Hillsdale, NJ: Erlbaum.

Fogel, A. (1982b). Early adult-infant interaction: Expectable sequences of behavior. *Journal of Pediatric Psychology*, **7**, 1–22.

Fox, N. A. (1989). Psychophysiological correlates of emotional reactivity during the first year of life. *Developmental Psychology*, **25**, 364–372.

Fox, N. A. (1991). If it's not left, it's right: Electroencephalogram asymmetry and the development of emotion. *American Psychologist*, **46**, 863–872.

Fox, N. A., Bell, M. A., & Jones, N. A. (1992). Individual differences in response to stress and cerebral asymmetry. *Developmental Neuropsychology*, **8**, 161–184.

Fox, N. A., & Calkins, S. D. (1993). Pathways to aggression and social withdrawal: Interactions among temperament, attachment, and regulation. In K. H. Rubin & J. Asendorpf (Eds.), *Social withdrawal, inhibition and shyness in children*. Hillsdale, NJ: Erlbaum.

Fox, N. A., Calkins, S. D., Marshall, T. R., Rubin, K. H., Coplan, R. B., Porges, S. W., & Long, J. (in press). Frontal activation asymmetry and social competence at four years of age. *Child Development*.

Fox, N. A., & Davidson, R. J. (1984). Hemispheric substrates of affect: A developmental model. In N. A. Fox & R. J. Davidson (Eds.), *The psychobiology of affective development.* Hillsdale, NJ: Erlbaum.

Fox, N. A., & Davidson, R. J. (1986). Taste-elicited changes in facial signs of emotion and the asymmetry of brain electrical activity in human newborns. *Neuropsychologia,* **24,** 417–422.

Fox, N. A., & Davidson, R. J. (1987). Electroencephalogram asymmetry in response to the approach of a stranger and maternal separation. *Developmental Psychology,* **23,** 233–240.

Fox, N. A., & Davidson, R. J. (1988). Patterns of brain electrical activity during facial signs of emotion in 10-month-old infants. *Developmental Psychology,* **24,** 230–236.

Fox, N. A., & Davidson, R. J. (1991). Hemispheric asymmetry and attachment behaviors: Developmental processes and individual differences in separation protest. In J. L. Gewirtz & W. M. Kurtines (Eds.), *Intersections with attachment.* Hillsdale, NJ: Erlbaum.

Fox, N. A., & Fitzgerald, H. E. (1990). Autonomic function in infancy. *Merrill-Palmer Quarterly,* **36,** 27–51.

Fox, N. A., & Gelles, M. (1984). Face to face interaction in term and preterm infants. *Infant Mental Health Journal,* **5,** 192–205.

Fox, N. A., Kimmerly, N. L., & Schafer, W. D. (1991). Attachment to mother, attachment to father: A meta-analysis. *Child Development,* **62,** 210–225.

Fox, E. A., & Powley, T. L. (1985). Longitudinal columnar organization within the dorsal motor nucleus represents separate branches of the abdominal vagus. *Brain Research,* **341,** 269–282.

Fraiberg, S. (1980). *Clinical studies in infant mental health.* New York: Basic.

Frankenhaeuser, M. (1980). Psychobiological aspects of life stress. In S. Levine & H. Ursin (Eds.), *Coping and health.* New York: Plenum.

Frankenhaeuser, M., & Lundberg, U. (1985). Sympathetic-adrenal and pituitary-adrenal response to challenge. In P. Pichot, P. Berner, R. Wolf, & K. Thau (Eds.), *Psychiatry* (Vol. **2**). London: Plenum.

Frankenhaeuser, M., Lundberg, U., & Forsman, L. (1978). Dissociation between sympathetic-adrenal and pituitary-adrenal responses to an achievement situation characterized by high controllability: Comparison between type A and type B males and females. *Biological Psychology,* **10,** 79–91.

Frederickson, B. L., & Carstensen, L. L. (1990). Choosing social partners: How old age and anticipated endings make people more selective. *Psychology and Aging,* **5,** 335–347.

Fredrikson, M., Sundin, O., & Frankenhaeuser, M., (1985). Cortisol secretion during the defence reaction in humans. *Psychiatric Medicine,* **47,** 313–319.

Freud, A. (1966). *The ego and the mechanisms of defense.* New York: International Universities Press.

Freud, S. (1957). The unconscious. In J. Strachey (Ed.), *Standard edition of the complete psychological works of Sigmund Freud* (Vol. **14**). London: Hogarth. (Original work published 1915)

Frijda, N. H. (1986). *The emotions.* Cambridge: Cambridge University Press.

Frodi, A., & Thompson, R. A. (1985). Infants' affective responses in the Strange Situation: Effects of prematurity and of quality of attachment. *Child Development,* **56,** 1280–1290.

Fuster, J. M. (1989). *The prefrontal cortex: Anatomy, physiology, and neuropsychology of the frontal lobe.* New York: Raven.

Gable, S., & Isabella, R. (1992). Maternal contributions to infant regulation of arousal. *Infant Behavior and Development,* **15,** 95–107.

Gaensbauer, T. J., & Sands, K. (1979). Distorted affective communications in abused/

neglected infants and their potential impact on caretakers. *Journal of the American Academy of Child Psychiatry*, **18**, 238–250.

Garber, J., Braafladt, N., & Zeman, J. (1991). The regulation of sad affect: An information-processing perspective. In J. Garber & K. A. Dodge (Eds.), *The development of emotional regulation and dysregulation*. Cambridge: Cambridge University Press.

Garber, J., & Dodge, K. A. (Eds.). (1991). *The development of emotional regulation and dysregulation*. Cambridge: Cambridge University Press.

Garcia-Coll, C., Kagan, J., & Resnick, J. S. (1984). Behavioral inhibition in young children. *Child Development*, **55**, 1005–1019.

Gardner, G. G., & Olness, K. (1981). *Hypnosis and hypnotherapy with children*. New York: Grune & Stratton.

Garmezy, N., & Rutter, M. (1983). *Stress, coping, and development in children*. New York: McGraw-Hill.

Gekoski, M. J., Rovee-Collier, C. K., & Carulli-Rabinowitz, V. (1983). A longitudinal analysis of inhibition of infant distress: The origins of social expectations? *Infant Behavior and Development*, **6**, 339–351.

George, C., Kaplan, N., & Main, M. (1985). *The Berkeley Adult Attachment Interview*. Unpublished protocol, Department of Psychology, University of California, Berkeley.

Gianino, A., & Tronick, E. (1988). The mutual regulation model: The infant's self and interactive regulation and coping and defensive capacities. In T. Field, P. McCabe, & N. Schneiderman (Eds.), *Stress and coping* (Vol. 2). Hillsdale, NJ: Erlbaum.

Glass, D. C. (1977). *Behavior, patterns, stress, and coronary disease*. Hillsdale, NJ: Erlbaum.

Gnepp, J., & Hess, D. L. R. (1986). Children's understanding of verbal and facial display rules. *Developmental Psychology*, **22**, 103–108.

Goldman-Rakic, P. S. (1987). Circuitry of primate prefrontal cortex and regulation of behavior by representational memory. In F. Plum & V. Mountcastle (Eds.), *Handbook of physiology: Sec. 1. The nervous system: Vol. 5. Higher functions of the brain*. Bethesda, MD: American Physiological Society.

Goldsmith, H. H., & Alansky, J. A. (1987). Maternal and infant temperamental predictors of attachment: A meta-analytic review. *Journal of Consulting and Clinical Psychology*, **55**, 805–816.

Goldsmith, H. H., & Rothbart, M. (1990). *The Laboratory Temperament Assessment Battery* (Version 1.3; Locomotor Version). University of Oregon.

Gonzalez-Lima, F. (1989). Functional brain circuitry related to arousal and learning in rats. In J. Ewert & M. A. Arbib (Eds.), *Visuomotor coordination*. New York: Plenum.

Gonzalez-Lima, F., & Scheich, H. (1985). Ascending reticular activating system in the rat: A 2-deoxyglucose study. *Brain Research*, **344**, 70–88.

Goodenough, F. L. (1931). *Anger in young children*. Minneapolis: University of Minnesota Press.

Goodyer, I., Herbert, J., Moor, S., & Altham, P. (1991). Cortisol hypersecretion in depressed school-aged children and adolescents. *Psychiatry Research*, **37**, 237–244.

Gordon, S. L. (1989). The socialization of children's emotions: Emotional culture, competence, and exposure. In C. Saarni & P. Harris (Eds.), *Children's understanding of emotions*. Cambridge: Cambridge University Press.

Gorenstein, E. K., & Newman, J. P. (1980). Disinhibitory psychopathology: A new perspective and a model for research. *Psychological Review*, **87**, 301–315.

Gottman, J. M. (1981). *Time-series analysis: A comprehensive introduction for social scientists*. New York: Cambridge University Press.

Gottman, J. M. (1989). *Marital interaction: Experimental investigations*. New York: Academic.

Gottman, J., & Mettetal, G. (1986). Speculations about social and affective development: Friendship and acquaintanceship through adolescence. In J. M. Gottman & J. G. Parker (Eds.), *Conversations of friends: Speculations on affective development.* Cambridge: Cambridge University Press.

Gottman, J. M., Rose, F. T., & Mettetal, G. (1982). Time-series analysis of social-interaction data. In T. Field & A. Fogel (Eds.), *Emotion and early interaction.* Hillsdale, NJ: Erlbaum.

Graham, F. K., & Clifton, R. K. (1966). Heart rate change as a component of the orienting response. *Psychological Bulletin,* **65,** 305–320.

Graham, S., & Weiner, B. (1986). From an attributional theory of emotion to developmental psychology: A round-trip ticket? *Social Cognition,* **4,** 152–179.

Granger, D., Stansbury, K., & Henker, B. (1994). Preschoolers' behavioral and neuroendocrine responses to social challenge. *Merrill-Palmer Quarterly,* **40**(2), 190–211.

Gray, J. A. (1981). A critique of Eysenck's theory of personality. In H. J. Eysenck (Ed.), *A model of personality.* Berlin: Springer.

Greenberg, L. S., & Safran, J. D. (1987). *Emotion in psychotherapy.* New York: Guilford.

Greenspan, S. I. (1981). *The clinical interview of the child.* New York: McGraw-Hill.

Greenspan, S. I. (1991). *Infancy and early childhood: The practice of clinical assessment and intervention with emotional and developmental challenges.* Madison, CT: International Universities Press.

Grossmann, K. E., Grossmann, K., & Schwan, A. (1986). Capturing the wider view of attachment: A reanalysis of Ainsworth's Strange Situation. In C. E. Izard & P. B. Read (Eds.), *Measuring emotions in infants and children* (Vol. **2**). New York: Cambridge University Press.

Grossmann, K., Grossmann, K. E., Spangler, G., Suess, G., & Unzner, L. (1985). Maternal sensitivity and newborns' orientation responses as related to quality of attachment in northern Germany. In I. Bretherton & E. Waters (Eds.), *Growing points of attachment theory and research. Monographs of the Society for Research in Child Development,* **50**(1–2, Serial No. 209).

Groves, P. M., & Thompson, R. F. (1970). Habituation: A dual process theory. *Psychological Review,* **77,** 419–450.

Gunnar, M. (1980). Control, warning signals and distress in infancy. *Developmental Psychology,* **16**(4), 281–289.

Gunnar, M. (1986). Human developmental psychoneuroendocrinology: A review of research on neuroendocrine responses to challenge and threat in infancy and childhood. In M. Lamb, A. Brown, & B. Rogoff (Eds.), *Advances in developmental psychology* (Vol. **4**). Hillsdale, NJ: Erlbaum.

Gunnar, M. (1990). The psychobiology of infant temperament. In J. Columbo & J. Fagan (Eds.), *Individual differences in infancy.* Hillsdale, NJ: Erlbaum.

Gunnar, M. (1992, August). *Adrenocortical activity and the study of stress and coping in children.* Invited address presented to the 23d Congress of the International Society for Psychoneuroendocrinology, Madison, WI.

Gunnar, M., Connors, J., & Isensee, J. (1989). Lack of stability in neonatal adrenocortical reactivity because of rapid habituation of the adrenocortical response. *Developmental Psychobiology,* **22,** 221–233.

Gunnar, M., Gonzales, C., Goodlin, B., & Levine, S. (1981). Behavioral and pituitary-adrenal responses during a prolonged separation period in infant rhesus macaques. *Psychoneuroendocrinology,* **6**(1), 65–75.

Gunnar, M., Hertsgaard, L., Larson, M., & Rigatuso, J. (1992). Cortisol and behavioral responses to repeated stressors in the human newborn. *Developmental Psychobiology,* **24,** 487–505.

Gunnar, M., Larson, M., Hertsgaard, L., Harris, M., & Broderson, L. (1992). The stressfulness of separation among 9-month-old infants: Effects of social context variables and infant temperament. *Child Development, 63,* 290–303.

Gunnar, M., Malone, S., Vance, G., & Fisch, R. O. (1985). Coping with aversive stimulation in the neonatal periods: Quiet sleep and plasma cortisol levels during recovery from circumcision in newborns. *Child Development, 56,* 824–834.

Gunnar, M., Mangelsdorf, S., Larson, M., & Herstgaard, L. (1989). Attachment, temperament, and adrenocortical activity in infancy: A study of psychoendocrine regulation. *Developmental Psychology, 25,* 355–363.

Gunnar, M., Marvinney, D., Isensee, J., & Fisch, R. O. (1989). Coping with uncertainty: New models of the relations between hormonal behavioral and cognitive processes. In D. Palermo (Ed.), *Coping with uncertainty: Biological, behavioral, and developmental perspectives.* Hillsdale, NJ: Erlbaum.

Guthertz, M., & Field, T. (1989). Lab computer or on-line coding and data analysis for laboratory and field observation. *Infant Behavior and Development, 12,* 305–319.

Hachinski, V. C., Oppenheimer, S. M., Wilson, J. X., Guiraudon, C., & Cechetto, D. F. (1992). Asymmetry of sympathetic consequences of experimental stroke. *Archives of Neurology, 49,* 697–702.

Haft, W., & Slade, A. (1989). Affect attunement and maternal attachment: A pilot study. *Infant Mental Health Journal, 10,* 157–172.

Hamilton, N. G. (1988). *Self and others: Object relations theory in practice.* Northvale, NJ: Aronson.

Handlon, J., Wadeson, R., Fishman, J., Sachar, E., Hamburg, D., & Mason, J. (1962). Psychological factors lowering plasma 17-hydroxycorticostero concentrations. *Psychosomatic Medicine, 24,* 535–542.

Hanson, J. P., Larson, M. E., & Snowden, C. T. (1976). The effects of control over high intensity noise on plasma cortisol levels in rhesus monkeys. *Behavioral Biology, 16,* 333–340.

Harris, P. L. (1989). *Children and emotion: The development of psychological understanding.* Oxford: Blackwell.

Harris, P. L., & Gross, D. (1989). Children's understanding of real and apparent emotion. In J. W. Astington, P. L. Harris, & D. R. Olson (Eds.), *Developing theories of mind.* New York: Cambridge University Press.

Harris, P. L., Guz, G. R., Lipian, M. S., & Man-Shu, Z. (1985). Insight into the time course of emotion among Western and Chinese children. *Child Development, 56,* 972–988.

Harris, P. L., & Lipian, M. S. (1989). Understanding emotion and experiencing emotion. In C. Saarni & P. L. Harris (Eds.), *Children's understanding of emotion.* Cambridge: Cambridge University Press.

Harris, P. L., Olthof, L., & Meerum Terwogt, M. (1981). Children's knowledge of emotion. *Journal of Child Psychology and Psychiatry, 22,* 247–261.

Hart, J. (1983). *Modern eclectic therapy.* New York: Plenum.

Harter, S. (1977). A cognitive-developmental approach to children's expression of conflicting feelings and a technique to facilitate such expression in play therapy. *Journal of Consulting and Clinical Psychology, 45,* 417–432.

Harter, S. (1990). Self and identity development. In S. Feldman & G. R. Elliot (Eds.), *At the threshold: The developing adolescent.* Cambridge, MA: Harvard University Press.

Harter, S., & Monsour, A. (1992). Developmental analysis of conflict caused by opposing attributes in the adolescent self-portrait. *Developmental Psychology, 28,* 251–260.

Hazen, N., & Durrett, M. (1982). Relationship of security of attachment to exploration and cognitive mapping ability in two-year-olds. *Developmental Psychology, 18,* 751–759.

Heilman, K. M., Bowers, D., & Valenstein, E. (1985). Emotional disorders associated with neurological diseases. In K. M. Heilman & E. Valenstein (Eds.), *Neuropsychology*. New York: Oxford University Press.

Heilman, K. M., Schwartz, H. D., & Watson, R. T. (1978). Hypoarousal in patients with neglect syndrome and emotional indifference. *Neurology*, **28**, 229–233.

Heilman, K. M., & Van Den Abell, R. (1980). Right hemisphere dominance for attention: The mechanism underlying hemispheric asymmetries of inattention (neglect). *Neurology*, **30**, 327–330.

Heilman, K. M., Watson, R. T., Valenstein, E., & Goldberg, M. E. (1987). Attention: Behavior and neural mechanisms. *Handbook of physiology: Sec. 1. The nervous system: Vol. 5. Higher functions of the brain*. Bethesda, MD: American Physiological Society.

Heinicke, C. M., & Westheimer, T. (1965). *Brief separations*. New York: International Universities Press.

Henkin, R. I. (1970). The effects of corticosteroids and ACTH on sensory systems. *Progress in Brain Research*, **32**, 270–294.

Hennessy, J., & Levine, S. (1979). Stress, arousal and the pituitary-adrenal system: A psychoendocrine model. In J. Sprague & A. Epstein (Eds.), *Progress in psychobiological and physiological psychology* (Vol. **8**). New York: Academic.

Henriques, J. B., & Davidson, R. J. (1990). Regional brain electrical asymmetries discriminate between previously depressed and healthy control subjects. *Journal of Abnormal Psychology*, **99**, 22–31.

Henry, J. P., & Stephens, P. M. (1977). *Stress, health, and the social environment: A sociobiologic approach to medicine*. New York: Springer.

Hepper, P. G. (1986a). Kin recognition: Function and mechanisms. *Biological Review*, **61**, 63–93.

Hepper, P. G. (1986b). Parental recognition in the rat. *Quarterly Journal of Experimental Psychology*, **38B**, 151–160.

Hertsgaard, L., Gunnar, M., Larson, M., Brodersen, L., & Lehman, H. (1992). First time experiences in infancy: When they appear to be pleasant, do they activate the adrenocortical stress response. *Developmental Psychobiology*, **25**, 319–333.

Hesse, P., & Cicchetti, D. (Eds.). (1982). *Toward an integrative theory of emotional development* (New Directions in Child Development, No. 16). San Francisco: Jossey-Bass.

Hinshaw, S. P. (1987). On the distinction between attentional deficits/hyperactivity and conduct problems/aggression in child psychopathology. *Psychological Bulletin*, **101**(3), 443–463.

Hirshberg, L. M., & Svejda, M. (1990). When infants look to their parents: 1. Infants' social referencing of mothers compared to fathers. *Child Development*, **61**, 1175–1186.

Hirshfeld, D. R., Rosenbaum, J. F., Biederman, J., Bolduc, E. A., Faraone, S. V., Snidman, N., Reznick, J. S., & Kagan, J. (1992). Stable behavioral inhibition and its association with anxiety disorder. *Journal of the American Academy of Child and Adolescent Psychiatry*, **31**, 103–111.

Hofer, M. A. (1970). Physiological responses of infant rats to separation from their mothers. *Science*, **168**, 871–873.

Hofer, M. A. (1973a). The effects of brief maternal separations on behavior and heart rate of two week old rat pups. *Physiology and Behavior*, **10**, 423–427.

Hofer, M. A. (1973b). Maternal separation affects infant rats' behavior. *Behavioral Biology*, **9**, 629–633.

Hofer, M. A. (1973c). The role of nutrition in the physiological and behavioral effects of early maternal separation on infant rats. *Psychosomatic Medicine*, **35**, 350–359.

Hofer, M. A. (1975). Studies on how early maternal separation produces behavioral change in young rats. *Psychosomatic Medicine*, **37**, 245–264.

Hofer, M. A. (1976). The organization of sleep and wakefulness after maternal separation in young rats. *Developmental Psychobiology*, **9**, 189–205.

Hofer, M. A. (1980a). The effects of reserpine and amphetamine on the development of hyperactivity in maternally deprived rat pups. *Psychosomatic Medicine*, **42**, 513–520.

Hofer, M. A. (1980b). *The roots of human behavior*. San Francisco: Freedman.

Hofer, M. A. (1984). Relationships as regulators: A psychobiologic perspective on bereavement. *Psychosomatic Medicine*, **46**, 183–197.

Hofer, M. A. (1992). Developmental roles of timing in the mother-infant interaction. In G. Turkewitz & D. Devenny (Eds.), *Developmental time and timing*. Hillsdale, NJ: Erlbaum.

Hofer, M. A., & Shair, H. N. (1978). Ultrasonic vocalization during social interaction and isolation in 2-week old rats. *Developmental Psychobiology*, **11**, 495–504.

Hofer, M. A., & Shair, H. N. (1980). Sensory processes in the control of isolation-induced ultrasonic vocalizations by 2-week-old rats. *Journal of Comparative Physiology and Psychology*, **94**, 271–299.

Hofer, M. A., & Shair, H. N. (1982). Control of sleep-wake states in the infant rat by features of the mother-infant relationship. *Developmental Psychobiology*, **15**, 229–243.

Hofer, M. A., & Weiner, H. (1971). Development and mechanisms of cardiorespiratory responses to maternal deprivation in rat pups. *Psychosomatic Medicine*, **33**, 353–362.

Hofer, M. A., & Weiner, H. (1975). Physiological mechanisms for cardiac control by nutritional intake after early maternal separation in the young rat. *Psychosomatic Medicine*, **37**, 8–24.

Hoffman, L. (1981). *Foundations of family therapy*. New York: Basic.

Hoffman, M. L. (1982). Development of prosocial motivation: Empathy and guilt. In N. Eisenberg (Ed.), *The development of prosocial behavior*. New York: Academic.

Hopkins, D. A. (1987). The dorsal motor nucleus of the vagus nerve and the nucleus ambiguus: Structure and connections. In R. Hainsworth, P. N. McWilliams, & D. A. S. G. Mary (Eds.), *Cardiogenic reflexes*. Oxford: Oxford University Press.

Huffman, L. C., Bryan, Y. E., del Carmen, R., Pedersen, F. A., & Porges, S. W. (1992). *Autonomic correlates of reactivity and self-regulation at twelve weeks of age*. Unpublished manuscript, National Institute of Mental Health, Rockville, MD.

Huffman, L. C., Bryan, Y. E., Pedersen, F. A., & Porges, S. W. (1988). *Infant temperament: Relationships with heart rate variability*. Unpublished manuscript, National Institute of Mental Health, Rockville, MD.

Hugdahl, K., Franzon, M., Andersson, B., & Walldebo, G. (1983). Heart-rate responses (HRR) to lateralized visual stimuli. *Pavlovian Journal of Biological Science*, **18**, 186–198.

Huttenlocher, P. R. (1979). Synaptic density in human frontal cortex—developmental changes and effects of aging. *Brain Research*, **163**, 195–205.

Huttenlocher, P. R. (1994). Synaptogenesis in the human cerebral cortex. In G. Dawson & K. Fischer (Eds.), *Human behavior and the developing brain*. New York: Guilford.

Isabella, R., & Belsky, J. (1991). Interactional synchrony and the origins of infant-mother attachment: A replication study. *Child Development*, **62**, 373–384.

Isabella, R., Belsky, J., & von Eye, A. (1989). The origins of infant-mother attachment: An examination of interactional synchrony during the infant's first year. *Developmental Psychology*, **25**, 12–21.

Isen, A. M. (1984). Toward understanding the role of affect in cognition. In R. Wyler & T. Srule (Eds.), *Handbook of social cognition*. Hillside, NJ: Erlbaum.

Izard, C. E. (1977). *Human emotions*. New York: Plenum.

Izard, C. E., Hembree, E. A., Dougherty, L. M., & Spizzirri, C. L. (1983). Changes in facial expression of 2 to 19 month old infants following acute pain. *Developmental Psychology*, **19**, 418–426.

Izard, C. E., Porges, S. W., Simons, R. F., Haynes, O. M., Hyde, C., Parisi, M., & Cohen, B. (1991). Infant cardiac activity: Developmental changes and relations with attachment. *Developmental Psychology*, **27**, 432–439.

Jacobson, J. L., & Wille, D. E. (1986). The influence of attachment patterns on developmental changes in peer interaction from the toddler to the preschool period. *Child Development*, **57**, 338–347.

Jacobson, L., & Sapolsky, R. (1991). The role of the hippocampus in feedback regulation of the hypothalamic-pituitary-adrenalcortical axis. *Endocrine Reviews*, **12**, 118–134.

James, W. (1884). What is an emotion? *Mind*, **9**, 188–205.

Jones, B., & Mishkin, M. (1972). Limbic lesions and the problem of stimulus-reinforcement associations. *Experimental Neurology*, **36**, 362–377.

Kacsoh, B., Meyers, J. S., Crowley, W. R., & Grosvenor, C. E. (1990). Maternal modulation of growth hormone secretion in the neonatal rat: Involvement of mother-offspring interactions. *Journal of Endocrinology*, **124**, 233–240.

Kagan, J. (1976). Emergent themes in human development. *American Scientist*, **64**(2), 186–196.

Kagan, J. (1981). *The second year*. Cambridge, MA: Harvard University Press.

Kagan, J. (1984). *The nature of the child*. New York: Basic.

Kagan, J. (1994). *Galen's prophecy*. New York: Basic.

Kagan, J., Reznick, J. S., & Snidman, N. (1987). The physiology and psychology of behavioral inhibition in children. *Child Development*, **58**, 1459–1473.

Kagan, J., Reznick, J. S., & Snidman, N. (1988). Biological bases of childhood shyness. *Science*, **240**, 167–171.

Kagan, J., & Snidman, N. (1991a). Infant predictors of inhibited and uninhibited profiles. *Psychological Science*, **2**, 40–44.

Kagan, J., & Snidman, N. (1991b). Temperamental factors in human development. *American Psychologist*, **48**, 856–862.

Kalia, M. (1981). Brain stem localization of vagal preganglionic neurons. *Journal of the Autonomic Nervous System*, **3**, 451–481.

Kaplan, H. B., & Bloom, S. W. (1960). The use of sociological and social-psychological concepts in physiological research: A review of selected experimental studies. *Journal of Nervous and Mental Disease*, **131**, 128–142.

Kaplan, N., & Main, M. (1985, April). *Internal representations of attachment at six years as indicated by family drawings and verbal responses to imagined separations*. Paper presented at the meeting of the Society for Research in Child Development, Toronto.

Katz, L. F., & Gottman, J. M. (1991). Marital discord and child outcomes: A social psychophysiological approach. In J. Garber & K. A. Dodge (Eds.), *The development of emotion regulation and dysregulation*. Cambridge: Cambridge University Press.

Kaufman, I. C., & Rosenblum, L. A. (1969). Effects of separation from the mother on the emotional behavior of infant monkeys. *Annals of the New York Academy of Sciences*, **159**, 681–695.

Kaye, K., & Fogel, A. (1980). The temporal structure of face-to-face communication between mothers and infants. *Developmental Psychology*, **16**, 454–464.

Kelly, A. E., & Stinus, L. (1984). Neuroanatomical and neurochemical substrates of affective behavior. In N. A. Fox & R. J. Davidson (Eds.), *The psychobiology of affective behavior*. Hillsdale, NJ: Erlbaum.

Kinsbourne, M. (1978). Biological determinants of functional bisymmetry and asymmetry. In M. Kinsbourne (Ed.), *Asymmetrical function of the brain*. New York: Cambridge University Press.

Kinsbourne, M., & Bemporad, B. (1984). Lateralization of emotion: A model and the evidence. In N. A. Fox & R. J. Davidson (Eds.), *The psychobiology of affective development*. Hillsdale, NJ: Erlbaum.

Klinnert, M., Campos, J. J., Sorce, J. F., Emde, R. N., & Svejda, M. (1983). Emotions as behavior regulators: Social referencing in infancy. In R. Plutchik & H. Hellerman (Eds.), *Emotion: Theory, research and experience* (Vol. 2). New York: Academic.

Kluft, R. P. (1985). *Childhood antecedents of multiple personality*. Washington, DC: American Psychiatric Press.

Knight, R. B., Atkins, A., Eagle, C. J., Evans, N., Finkelstein, J. W., Fukushima, D., Katz, J., & Weiner, H. (1979). Psychological stress, ego defenses, and cortisol production in children hospitalized for elective surgery. *Psychosomatic Medicine, 41*(1), 40–49.

Kobak, R. R. (1985). *Attitudes towards attachment relationships and social competence among first-year college students*. Unpublished doctoral dissertation, University of Virginia, Charlottesville.

Kobak, R. R. (1987, April). Attachment, affect regulation, and defense. In J. Cassidy (Chair), *Attachment and defensive processes*. Symposium presented at the meeting of the Society for Research in Child Development, Baltimore.

Kobak, R. R., Cole, H. E., Ferenz-Gillies, R., & Fleming, W. S. (1993). Attachment and emotion regulation during mother-teen problem solving: A control theory analysis. *Child Development, 64*(1), 231–245.

Kobak, R. R., & Sceery, A. (1988). Attachment in late adolescence: Working models, affect regulation, and representations of self and others. *Child Development, 59,* 135–146.

Koenigsberg, H. W., & Handley, R. (1986). Expressed emotion: From predictive index to clinical construct. *American Journal of Psychiatry, 143,* 1361–1373.

Kopp, C. B. (1982). Antecedents of self-regulation: A developmental perspective. *Developmental Psychology, 18,* 199–214.

Kopp, C. B. (1989). Regulation of distress and negative emotions: A developmental view. *Developmental Psychology, 25*(3), 343–354.

Kopp, C. B. (1992). Emotional distress and control in young children. In N. Eisenberg & R. A. Fabes (Eds.), *Emotion and its regulation in early development* (New Directions in Child Development, No. 55). San Francisco: Jossey-Bass.

Kraemer, J. (1984). Effects of differences in early social experience on primate neurobiological behavioral development. In M. Reite & T. Field (Eds.), *Psychobiology of attachment*. New York: Academic.

Kuhn, C. M., Pauk, J., & Schanberg, S. M. (1990). Endocrine responses to mother infant separation in developing rats. *Developmental Psychobiology, 23,* 395–410.

Kuhn, C. M., & Schanberg, S. M. (1991). Stimulation in infancy and brain development. In B. J. Carroll & J. E. Barrett (Eds.), *Psychopathology and the brain*. New York: Raven.

Lacey, J. I. (1967). Somatic response patterning and stress: Some revisions of activation theory. In M. H. Appley & R. Trumbull (Eds.), *Psychological stress*. New York: Appleton-Century-Crofts.

Lamb, M. E., & Malkin, C. M. (1986). The development of social expectations in distress-relief sequences: A longitudinal study. *International Journal of Behavioral Development, 9,* 235–249.

Lamb, M. E., Thompson, R. A., Gardner, W., & Charnov, E. L. (1985). *Infant-mother attachment: The origins and developmental significance of individual differences in Strange Situation behavior*. Hillsdale, NJ: Erlbaum.

Lane, R., & Schwartz, G. (1987). Induction of lateralized sympathetic input to the heart by the CNS during emotional arousal: A possible neuro-physiologic trigger of sudden cardiac death. *Psychosomatic Medicine, 49,* 274–284.

Larsen, R. J., & Ketelaar, T. (1991). Personality and susceptibility to positive and negative emotional states. *Journal of Personality and Social Psychology, 61,* 132–140.

Larson, M., Gunnar, M., & Hertsgaard, L. (1991). The effects of morning naps, car trips, and maternal separation on adrenocortical activity in human infants. *Child Development*, **62**, 362–372.

Larson, S. K., & Porges, S. W. (1982). The ontogeny of heart period patterning in the rate. *Developmental Psychobiology*, **15**, 519–528.

Laudenslager, M. L., Reite, M., & Harbeck, R. J. (1982). Suppressed immune response in infant monkeys associated with maternal separation. *Behavioral and Neural Biology*, **36**, 40–48.

Lazarus, R. S. (1966). *Psychological stress and the coping process.* New York: McGraw-Hill.

Lazarus, R. S. (1991). *Emotion and adaptation.* New York: Oxford University Press.

Lazarus, R. S., & Folkman, S. (1984). *Stress, appraisal, and coping.* New York: Springer.

LeDoux, J. E. (1986). Sensory systems and emotion: A model of affective processing. *Integrative Psychiatry*, **4**, 237–248.

LeDoux, J. E. (1987). Emotion. In F. Plum (Ed.), *Handbook of Physiology: 1. The nervous system: Vol. 5. Higher functions of the brain.* Bethesda, MD: American Physiological Society.

LeDoux, J. E. (1989). Cognitive emotional interactions in the brain. *Cognition and Emotion*, **3**(4), 267–289.

LeDoux, J. E. (1991). Emotion and the brain. *Journal of NIH Research*, **3**, 49–51.

Lee, G. P., Loring, D. W., Meader, K. J., & Brooks, B. B. (1990). Hemispheric specialization for emotional expression: A reexamination of results from intracarotid administration of sodium amobarbital. *Brain and Cognition*, **12**, 267–280.

Leon, M. (1974). Maternal pheromone. *Physiology and Behavior*, **13**, 441–453.

Lerner, R. M., & Busch-Rossnagel, N. (1981). Individuals as producers of their development: Conceptual and empirical bases. In R. M. Lerner & N. Busch-Rossnagel (Eds.), *Individuals as producers of their development.* New York: Academic.

Lester, B., Hoffman, J., & Brazelton, T. B. (1985). The rhythmic structure of mother-infant interaction in term, and pre-term infants. *Child Development*, **56**, 15–27.

Lester, B. M., & Zeskind, P. S. (1982). A biobehavioral perspective on crying in early infancy. In H. E. Fitzgerald, B. M. Lester, & M. W. Youngman (Eds.), *Theory and research in behavioral pediatrics.* New York: Plenum.

Levine, S. A. (1970). The pituitary-adrenal system and the developing brain. In D. DeWied & J. A. W. M. Weijnen (Eds.), *Progress in brain research* (Vol. 32). Amsterdam: Elsevier Science.

Levine, S. A. (1983). *A psychobiological approach to the ontogeny of coping.* Unpublished manuscript, Stanford University.

Levine, S. A., & Coe, C. (1985). The use and abuse of cortisol as a measure of stress. In T. Field, P. McCabe, & N. Schneiderman (Eds.), *Stress and coping.* Hillsdale, NJ: Erlbaum.

Levine, S. A., Johnson, D. F., & Gonzales, C. A. (1985). Behavioral and hormonal responses to separation in infant rhesus monkeys and mothers. *Behavioral Neuroscience*, **99**(3), 399–410.

Levine, S. A., Wiener, S., Coe, C., Bayart, F., & Hayashi, K. (1987). Primate vocalizations: A psychobiological approach. *Child Development*, **58**, 1408–1419.

Levy, J. (1983). Individual differences in cerebral hemisphere asymmetry: Theoretical issues and experimental considerations. In J. B. Hellige (Ed.), *Cerebral hemisphere asymmetry: Method, theory, and application.* New York: Praeger.

Levy, J., Heller, W., Banich, M. T., & Burton, L. (1983). Are variations among right-handers in perceptual asymmetries caused by characteristic arousal differences in the hemispheres? *Journal of Experimental Psychology: Human Perception and Performance*, **9**, 329–359.

Lewis, M., & Feiring, C. (1989). Infant, mother, and mother-infant interaction behavior and subsequent attachment. *Child Development,* **60,** 831–837.

Lewis, M., & Michalson, L. (1983). *Children's emotions and moods: Developmental theory and measurement.* New York: Plenum.

Lewis, M., & Saarni, C. (1985). *The socialization of emotions.* New York: Plenum.

Lieberman, A. F., Weston, D. R., & Pawl, J. H. (1991). Preventive intervention and outcome with anxiously attached dyads. *Child Development,* **62,** 199–209.

Linnemeyer, S. A., & Porges, S. W. (1986). Recognition memory and cardiac vagal tone in 6-month-old infants. *Infant Behavior and Development,* **9,** 43–56.

Loewy, A. D., & Spyer, K. M. (1990). Vagal preganglionic neurons. In A. D. Loewy & K. M. Spyer (Eds.), *Central regulation of autonomic functions.* Oxford: Oxford University Press.

Luborsky, L. (1984). *Principles of psychoanalytic psychotherapy: A manual for supportive-expressive treatment.* New York: Basic.

Lundberg, U. (1986). Stress and type A behavior in children. *Journal of the American Academy of Child Psychiatry,* **25**(6), 771–778.

Luria, A. R. (1961). *The role of speech in the regulation of normal and abnormal behavior.* New York: Pergamon.

Lutkenhaus, P., Grossmann, K. E., & Grossmann, K. (1985). Infant-mother attachment at 12 months and style of interaction with a stranger at the age of three years. *Child Development,* **56,** 1538–1572.

Lyons-Ruth, K., Connell, D. B., & Grunebaum, H. (1990). Infants at social risk: Maternal depression and family support services as mediators of infant development and security of attachment. *Child Development,* **61,** 85–98.

Lyons-Ruth, K., Connell, D., Zoll, D., & Stahl, J. (in press). Infants' maltreatment, maternal behavior, and infant attachment behavior. *Developmental Psychology.*

Lyons-Ruth, K., Zoll, D., Connell, D., & Grunebaum, H. (1986). The depressed mother and her one-year-old infant: Environment, interaction, attachment and infant development. In E. Tronick & T. Field (Eds.), *Maternal depression and infant development.* San Francisco: Jossey-Bass.

MacLean, P. D. (1952). Some psychiatric implications of physiological studies on fronto-temporal portion of limbic system (visceral brain). *Electroencephalography and Clinical Neurophysiology,* **4,** 407–418.

Magnusson, D. (1988). *Individual development from an interactional perspective: A longitudinal study.* Hillsdale, NJ: Erlbaum.

Main, M. (1981). Avoidance in the service of attachment: A working paper. In K. Immelmann, G. W. Barlow, L. Petrinovich, & M. Main (Eds.), *Behavioral development: The Bielefeld Interdisciplinary Project.* Cambridge: Cambridge University Press.

Main, M. (1990). Cross-cultural studies of attachment organization: Recent studies, changing methodologies, and the concept of conditional strategies. *Human Development,* **33,** 48–61.

Main, M., & George, C. (1985). Response of abused and disadvantaged toddlers to distress in playmates: A study in the day care setting. *Developmental Psychology,* **21,** 407–412.

Main, M., & Goldwyn, R. (1984). Predicting rejection of her infant from mother's representations of her own experience: Implications for the abused-abusing intergenerational cycle. *Child Abuse and Neglect,* **8,** 203–217.

Main, M., & Goldwyn, R. (1994). *Interview-based adult attachment classifications: Related to infant-mother and infant-father attachment.* Unpublished manuscript, University of California, Berkeley, Department of Psychology.

Main, M., & Goldwyn, R. (in press). Adult attachment rating and classification systems.

In M. Main (Ed.), *A typology of human attachment organization assessed in discourse, drawings, and interviews*. New York: Cambridge University Press.

Main, M., & Hesse, E. (1989). *Interview-based assessments of a parent's unresolved trauma are related to infant "D" attachment status: Linking parental states of mind to infant behavior observed in a stressful situation*. Unpublished manuscript, University of California, Berkeley, Department of Psychology.

Main, M., & Hesse, E. (1990). Parents' unresolved traumatic experiences are related to infant disorganized attachment status: Is frightened and/or frightening parental behavior the linking mechanism? In M. Greenberg, D. Cicchetti, & E. M. Cummings (Eds.), *Attachment in the preschool years*. Chicago: University of Chicago Press.

Main, M., Kaplan, N., & Cassidy, J. (1985). Security in infancy, childhood, and adulthood: A move to the level of representation. In I. Bretherton & E. Waters (Eds.), *Growing points of attachment theory and research. Monographs of the Society for Research in Child Development*, **50**(1–2, Serial No. 209).

Main, M., & Solomon, J. (1986). Discovery of a new, insecure-disorganized/disoriented attachment pattern. In T. B. Brazelton & M. Yogman (Eds.), *Affective development in infancy*. Norwood, NJ: Ablex.

Main, M., & Solomon, J. (1990). Procedures for identifying infants as disorganized/disoriented during the Ainsworth Strange Situation. In M. T. Greenberg, D. Cicchetti, & E. M. Cummings (Eds.), *Attachment in the preschool years: Theory, research and intervention*. Chicago: University of Chicago Press.

Main, M., Tomasini, L., & Tolan, W. (1979). Differences among mothers of infants judged to differ in security. *Developmental Psychology*, **15**, 472–473.

Main, M., & Weston, D. (1981). The quality of the toddler's relationship to mother and father. *Child Development*, **52**, 932–940.

Malatesta, C. Z. (1990). The role of emotions in the development and organization of personality. In R. A. Thompson (Ed.), *Socioemotional development* (Nebraska Symposium on Motivation, Vol. **36**). Lincoln: University of Nebraska Press.

Malatesta-Magai, C. (1991). Development of emotion expression during infancy: General course and patterns of individual difference. In J. Garber & K. A. Dodge (Eds.), *The development of emotional regulation and dysregulation*. Cambridge: Cambridge University Press.

Malatesta, C. Z., Culver, C., Tesman, J. R., & Shepard, B. (1989). The development of emotion expression during the first two years of life. *Monographs of the Society for Research in Child Development*, **54**(1–2, Serial No. 219).

Malatesta, C. Z., & Haviland, J. M. (1982). Learning display rules: The socialization of emotion expression in infancy. *Child Development*, **53**, 991–1003.

Malatesta, C. Z., & Wilson, A. (1988). Emotion/cognition interaction in personality development: A discrete emotions, functionalist analysis. *British Journal of Social Psychology*, **27**, 91–112.

Mandler, G. (1982). The construction of emotion in the child. In C. E. Izard (Ed.), *Measuring emotion in infants and children*. New York: Cambridge University Press.

Mangelsdorf, S., Gunnar, M., Kestenbaum, R., Lang, S., & Andreas, D. (1990). Infant proneness-to-distress temperament, maternal personality, and mother-infant attachment: Associations and goodness-of-fit. *Child Development*, **61**, 820–831.

Marvin, R. S., & Stewart, R. (1990). A family systems framework for the study of attachment. In M. Greenberg, D. Cicchetti, & E. M. Cummings (Eds.), *Attachment in the preschool years*. Chicago: University of Chicago Press.

Mason, J. W. (1971). A re-evaluation of the concept of "non-specificity" in stress theory. *Journal of Psychiatry Research*, **8**, 323–333.

Mason, J. W. (1975). A historical view of the stress field. *Journal of Human Stress*, **1**, 22–36.

Mason, J. W., Sachar, E. J., Fishman, J. R., et al. (1965). Corticosteroid responses to hospital admission. *Archives of General Psychiatry, 13,* 1–8.

Masters, J. C. (1991). Strategies and mechanisms for the personal and social control of emotion. In J. Garber & K. A. Dodge (Eds.), *The development of emotional regulation and dysregulation.* Cambridge: Cambridge University Press.

Masters, J. C., Ford, M. E., & Arend, R. A. (1983). Children's strategies for controlling affective responses to aversive social experience. *Motivation and Emotion, 7,* 103–116.

Matas, L., Arend, R., & Sroufe, L. A. (1978). Continuity of adaptation in the second year of life: The relationship between quality of attachment and later competence. *Child Development, 49,* 547–556.

Matthews, K. A., & Angulo, J. (1980). Measurement of the type A behavior pattern in children: Assessment of children's competitiveness, impatience-anger, and aggression. *Child Development, 51,* 466–475.

Mattsson, A., Gross, S., & Hall, T. W. (1971). Psychoendocrine study of adaptation in young hemophiliacs. *Psychosomatic Medicine, 33*(3), 215–225.

Mayes, S. D. (1992). Eating disorders of infancy and early childhood. In S. R. Hooper, G. W. Hynd, & R. E. Mattison (Eds.), *Child psychopathology: Diagnostic criteria and clinical assessment.* Hillsdale, NJ: Erlbaum.

McBurnett, K. M., Lahey, B. B., Frick, P. J., Risch, C., Loeber, R., Hart, E. L., Christ, M. A. G., & Hanson, K. S. (1991). Anxiety, inhibition, and conduct disorder in children: 2. Relation to salivary cortisol. *Journal of the American Academy of Child and Adolescent Psychiatry, 30,* 192–196.

McCabe, P., & Schneiderman, N. (1985). Psychophysiological reactions to stress. In N. Schneiderman & J. Tapp (Eds.), *Behavioral medicine: The biopsychosocial approach.* Hillsdale, NJ: Erlbaum.

McCoy, C. L., & Masters, J. C. (1985). The development of children's strategies for the social control of emotion. *Child Development, 56,* 1214–1222.

McEwen, B. S., de Kloet, E. R., & Rostene, W. (1986). Adrenal steroid receptors and actions in the nervous system. *Physiological Review, 66,* 1121–1188.

Meaney, M. J., Aitken, D. H., Van Berkel, C., Bhatnager, S., & Sapolsky, R. M. (1988). Effect of neonatal handling on age related impairments associated with the hippocampus. *Science, 239,* 766–769.

Meerum Terwogt, M., Schene, J., & Harris, P. L. (1986). Self-control of emotional reactions by young children. *Journal of Child Psychology and Psychiatry, 27,* 357–366.

Mendelsohn, R. M. (1987). *The synthesis of self: Vol. 1. The I of consciousness: Development from birth to maturity.* New York: Plenum.

Mesulam, M. M. (1981). A cortical network for directed attention and unilateral neglect. *Annals of Neurology, 10,* 309–325.

Miller, P. J., & Sperry, L. L. (1987). The socialization of anger and aggression. *Merrill-Palmer Quarterly, 33,* 1–31.

Miller, S. M., & Green, M. L. (1985). Coping with stress and frustration: Origins, nature, and development. In M. Lewis & C. Saarni (Eds.), *The socialization of emotions.* New York: Plenum.

Mills, P. J., Berry, C. L., Dimsdale, J. E., Nelesen, R. A., & Ziegler, M. G. (1993). Temporal stability of task induced cardiovascular, adrenergic, and psychological responses. *Psychophysiology, 30,* 197–204.

Minuchin, P. (1985). Families and individual development: Provocations from the field of family therapy. *Child Development, 56,* 289–302.

Mischel, H. N., & Mischel, W. (1983). The development of children's knowledge of self-control strategies. *Child Development, 54,* 603–619.

Mishkin, M., & Aggleton, J. (1981). Multiple functional contributions of the amygdala in the monkey. In Y. Ben-Ari (Ed.), *The Amygdaloid Complex* (INSERM Symposium No. 20). Amsterdam: Elsevier, North-Holland Biomedical.

Miyake, K., Chen, S.-J., & Campos, J. J. (1985). Infant temperament, mother's mode of interaction, and attachment in Japan: An interim report. In I. Bretherton & E. Waters (Eds.), *Growing points of attachment theory and research. Monographs of the Society for Research in Child Development,* **50**(1–2, Serial No. 209).

Moffitt, T. E. (1990). Juvenile delinquency and attention deficit disorder: Boys' developmental trajectories from age 3 to age 15. *Child Development,* **61,** 893–910.

Moffitt, T. E., & Henry, B. (1989). Neuropsychological assessment of executive functions in self-reported delinquents. *Development and Psychopathology,* **1,** 105–118.

Molfese, D. L., & Betz, J. C. (1988). Electrophysiological indices of the early development of lateralization for language and cognition, and their implications for predicting later development. In D. L. Molfese & S. J. Segalowitz (Eds.), *Brain lateralization in children: Developmental implications.* New York: Guilford.

Molfese, D. L., & Segalowitz, S. J. (Eds.). (1988). *Brain lateralization in children: Developmental implications.* New York: Guilford.

Mora, G. (1980). Historical and theoretical trends in psychiatry. In H. I. Kaplan, A. M. Freedman, & B. J. Sadock (Eds.), *Comprehensive textbook of psychiatry* (Vol. 3). Baltimore: Williams & Wilkins.

Moruzzi, G., & Magoun, H. W. (1949). Brainstem reticular formation and activation of the EEG. *Electroencephalography and Clinical Neurophysiology,* **1,** 455–473.

Munck, A., Guyre, P. M., & Holbrook, N. J. (1984). Physiological functions of glucocorticoids in stress and their relations to pharmacologic actions. *Endocrine Review,* **5,** 25–44.

Myers, M. M., Brunelli, S. A., Shair, H. N., Squire, J. M., & Hofer, M. A. (1989). Relationships between maternal behavior of SHR and WKY dams and adult blood pressures of cross-fostered F1 pups. *Developmental Psychobiology,* **22,** 55–67.

Myers, M. M., Brunelli, S. A., Squire, J. M., Shindledecker, R., & Hofer, M. A. (1989). Maternal behavior of the SHR rat and its relationship to offspring blood pressures. *Developmental Psychobiology,* **22,** 29–53.

Nachmias, M., Gunnar, M., Mangelsdorf, S., Parritz, R. H., & Buss, K. (1993). *Behavioral inhibition and stress reactivity: Moderating role of attachment security.* Unpublished manuscript, University of Minnesota, Minneapolis.

Natelson, B. H., Ottenweller, J. E., Cook, J. A., Pitman, D. L., McCarthy, R., & Tapp, W. (1988). Effect of stressor intensity on habituation of the adrenocortical stress response. *Physiology and Behavior,* **43,** 41–46.

National Institute of Mental Health. (1992, November 30–December 1). *Developmental approaches to the assessment of psychopathology.* Rockville, MD.

Nauta, W. J. H. (1971). The problem of the frontal lobes: A reinterpretation. *Journal of Psychiatric Research,* **8,** 167–187.

Novaco, R. W. (1975). *Anger control: The development and evaluation of an experimental treatment.* Lexington, MA: Lexington.

Oswalt, G. L., & Meier, G. W. (1975). Olfactory, thermal and tactual influences on infantile ultrasonic vocalization in rats. *Developmental Psychobiology,* **8,** 129–135.

Pagani, F. D., Norman, W. P., & Gillis, R. A. (1988). Medullary parasympathetic projections innervate specific sites in the feline stomach. *Gastroenterology,* **95,** 277–288.

Palkovits, M. (1987). Organization of the stress response at the anatomical level. In E. R. de Kloet, V. M. Wiegant, & D. DeWied (Eds.), *Progress in Brain Research* (Vol. 72). Amsterdam: Elsevier Science.

Papez, J. W. (1937). A proposed mechanism of emotion. *Archives of Neurological Psychiatry,* **79,** 217–224.

Pastor, D. (1981). The quality of mother-infant attachment and its relationship to toddlers' initial sociability with peers. *Developmental Psychology*, **17**, 326–335.

Patterson, G. R. (1982). *A social learning approach: 3. Coercive family processes.* Eugene, OR: Castilia.

Patterson, G. R., DeBaryshe, B. D., & Ramsey, E. (1989). A developmental perspective on antisocial behavior. *American Psychologist*, **44**, 329–335.

Pennington, B. F. (1991). *Diagnosing learning disorders: A neuropsychological framework.* New York: Guilford.

Perria, L., Rosadini, G., & Rossi, G. F. (1961). Determination of side of cerebral dominance with amobarbital. *Archives of Neurology*, **4**, 173–181.

Petty, R. E., & Cacioppo, J. T. (1983). The role of bodily response in attitude measurement and change. In J. T. Cacioppo & R. E. Petty (Eds.), *Social psychophysiology: A sourcebook.* New York: Guilford.

Pimental, P. A., & Kingsbury, N. A. (1989). *Neuropsychological aspects of right brain injury.* Austin: Pro-Ed.

Plutchik, R. (1980). *Emotion: A psychoevolutionary synthesis.* New York: Harper & Row.

Porges, S. W. (1972). Heart rate variability and deceleration as indexes of reaction time. *Journal of Experimental Psychology*, **92**, 103–110.

Porges, S. W. (1973). Heart rate variability: An autonomic correlate of reaction time performance. *Bulletin of the Psychonomic Society*, **1**, 270–272.

Porges, S. W. (1983). Heart rate patterns in neonates: A potential diagnostic window to the brain. In T. Field & A. Sostek (Eds.), *Infants born at risk: Psychological, perceptual, and cognitive processes.* New York: Grune & Stratton.

Porges, S. W. (1985, April 16). Method and apparatus for evaluating rhythmic oscillations in aperiodic physiological response systems (U.S. Patent No. 4,510,944). Washington, DC.

Porges, S. W. (1986). Respiratory sinus arrhythmia: Physiological basis, quantitative methods, and clinical implications. In P. Grossman, K. Janssen, & D. Vaitl (Eds.), *Cardiorespiratory and cardiosomatic psychophysiology.* New York: Plenum.

Porges, S. W. (1991). Vagal tone: An autonomic mediator of affect. In J. Garber & K. A. Dodge (Eds.), *The development of emotional regulation and dysregulation.* Cambridge: Cambridge University Press.

Porges, S. W. (1992). Autonomic regulation and attention. In B. A. Campbell, H. Hayne, & R. Richardson (Eds.), *Attention and information processing in infants and adults.* Hillsdale, NJ: Erlbaum.

Porges, S. W., Arnold, W. R., & Forbes, E. J. (1973). Heart rate variability: An index of attentional responsivity in human newborns. *Developmental Psychology*, **8**, 85–92.

Porges, S. W., & Maiti, A. K. (1992). The smart and vegetative vagi: Implications for specialization and laterality of function [Abstract]. *Psychophysiology*, **29**, S7.

Porges, S. W., Stamps, L. E., & Walter, G. F. (1974). Heart rate variability and newborn heart rate responses to illumination changes. *Developmental Psychology*, **10**, 507–513.

Portales, A. L., Doussard-Roosevelt, J. A., Lee, H. B., & Porges, S. W. (1992). Infant vagal tone predicts 3-year child behavior problems [Abstract]. *Infant Behavior and Development*, **15**, 636.

Porter, F. L., & Porges, S. W. (1988). Neonatal cardiac responses to lumbar punctures [Abstract]. *Infant Behavior and Development*, **11**, 261.

Porter, F. L., Porges, S. W., & Marshall, R. E. (1988). Newborn pain cries and vagal tone: Parallel changes in response to circumcision. *Child Development*, **59**, 495–505.

Powell, G. F., Brasel, J. A., & Blizzard, R. M. (1967). Emotional deprivation and growth retardation simulating idiopathic hypopituitrism: 2. Endocrinologic evaluation of the syndrome. *New England Journal of Medicine*, **276**, 1279–1283.

Price, D. A., Close, G. C., & Fielding, B. A. (1983). Age of appearance of circadian rhythm in salivary cortisol values in infancy. *Archives of Disease in Childhood, 58,* 454–456.

Puig-Antich, J. (1982). Major depression and conduct disorder in pre-puberty. *Journal of the American Academy of Child Psychiatry, 21,* 118–128.

Putallaz, M., & Sheppard, B. H. (1992). Conflict management and the growth of social competence. In C. U. Shantz & W. W. Hartup (Eds.), *Conflict in child and adolescent development.* New York: Cambridge University Press.

Putnam, F. W. (1985). Dissociation as a response to extreme trauma. In R. P. Kluft (Ed.), *Childhood antecedents of multiple personality.* Washington, DC: American Psychiatric Press.

Randall, W. C., & Priola, D. V. (1965). In W. C. Randall (Ed.), *Nervous control of the heart.* Baltimore: Williams & Wilkins.

Randall, W. C., & Rohse, W. G. (1956). The augmenter action of the sympathetic cardiac nerves. *Circulation Research, 4,* 470–477.

Reeves, J. C., Werry, J. S., Elkind, G. S., & Zametkin, A. (1987). Attention deficit, conduct, oppositional, and anxiety disorders in children: 2. Clinical characteristics. *Journal of the American Academy of Child and Adolescent Psychiatry, 26,* 144–155.

Rehm, L. P. (1977). A self-control model of depression. *Behavior Therapy, 8,* 787–804.

Reite, M., & Capitanio, J. P. (1985). On the nature of social separation and social attachment. In M. Reite & T. Field (Eds.), *The psychobiology of attachment and separation.* New York: Academic.

Reite, M., Kaufman, I. C., Pauley, J. D., & Stynes, A. J. (1974). Depression in infant monkeys: Physiological correlates. *Psychosomatic Medicine, 36,* 363–367.

Reite, M., & Short, R. A. (1978). Nocturnal sleep in separated monkey infants. *Archives of General Psychiatry, 35,* 1247–1253.

Reite, M., Short, R., Seiler, C., & Pauley, J. D. (1981). Attachment, loss and depression. *Journal of Child Psychology and Psychiatry, 22,* 141–169.

Renken, B., Egeland, B., Marvinney, D., Mangelsdorf, S., & Sroufe, L. A. (1989). Early childhood antecedents of aggression and passive-withdrawal in early elementary school. *Journal of Personality, 57,* 257–282.

Renouf, A. G., & Harter, S. (1990). Low self-worth and anger as components of the depressive experience in young adolescents. *Development and Psychopathology, 2,* 293–310.

Richards, J. E. (1985). Respiratory sinus arrhythmia predicts heart rate and visual responses during visual attention in 14- and 20-week-old infants. *Psychophysiology, 22,* 101–109.

Richards, J. E. (1987). Infant visual sustained attention and respiratory sinus arrhythmia. *Child Development, 58,* 488–496.

Robins, L. N. (1966). *Deviant children grow up.* Baltimore: Williams & Wilkins.

Robins, L. N. (1986). The consequence of conduct disorder in girls. In D. Olweus, J. Block, & M. Radke-Yarrow (Eds.), *Development of antisocial and prosocial behavior: Research issues.* New York: Academic.

Robinson, R. G. (1985). Lateralized behavioral and neurochemical consequences of unilateral brain injury in rats. In S. D. Glick (Ed.), *Cerebral lateralization in nonhuman species.* New York: Academic.

Robinson, R. G., & Coyle, J. T. (1980). The differential effect of right versus left hemispheric cerebral infarction on catecholamines and behavior in the rat. *Brain Research, 188,* 63–78.

Robinson, R. G., Kubos, K. L., Starr, L. B., Rao, K., & Price, T. R. (1984). Mood disorders in stroke patients. *Brain, 107,* 81–93.

Robinson, R. G., & Szetela, B. (1981). Mood change following left hemispheric brain injury. *Annals of Neurology*, **9**, 447–453.

Rose, R. M. (1980). Endocrine responses to stressful psychological events: Advances in psychoneuroendocrinology. *Psychiatric Clinics of North America*, **3**(2), 251–276.

Rosenbaum, J. F., Biederman, J., Gersten, M., Hirschfield, D. R., Menninger, S. R., Herman, J. B., Kagan, J., Reznick, J. S., & Snidman, N. (1988). Behavioral inhibition in children of parents with panic disorder and agoraphobia: A controlled study. *Archives of General Psychiatry*, **45**, 463–470.

Rosenblatt, J. S. (1983). Olfaction mediates developmental transition in the altricial newborn of selected species of mammals. *Developmental Psychobiology*, **16**, 347–376.

Rosenfeld, P., Gutierrez, Y. A., Martin, A. M., Mallett, H. A., Alleva, E., & Levine, S. (1991). Maternal regulation of the adrenocortical response in preweanling rats. *Physiology and Behavior*, **50**, 661–671.

Rosenman, R. H., & Chesney, M. A. (1980). The relationship of type A behavior to coronary heart-disease. *Activitas Nervosa Superior*, **22**, 1–45.

Ross, E. D. (1981). The aprosodias: Functional-anatomic organization of the affect components of language in the right hemisphere. *Archives of Neurology*, **38**, 561–569.

Ross, E. D., & Mesulam, M. (1979). Dominant language functions of the right hemisphere? Prosody and emotional gesturing. *Archives of Neurology*, **36**, 144–148.

Roth, S., & Cohen, L. J. (1986). Approach, avoidance, and coping with stress. *American Psychologist*, **41**(7), 813–819.

Rothbart, M. K. (1981). Measurement of temperament in infancy. *Child Development*, **52**, 569–578.

Rothbart, M. K. (1988). Temperament and the development of the inhibited approach. *Child Development*, **59**, 1241–1250.

Rothbart, M. K. (1989). Temperament in childhood: A framework. In G. A. Kohnstamm, J. E. Bates, & M. K. Rothbart (Eds.), *Temperament in childhood*. Chichester: Wiley.

Rothbart, M. K., & Derryberry, D. (1981). Development of individual differences in temperament. In M. E. Lamb & A. L. Brown (Eds.), *Advances in developmental psychology* (Vol. 1). Hillsdale, NJ: Erlbaum.

Rothbart, M. K., & Derryberry, D. (1982). Theoretical issues in temperament. In M. Lewis & L. T. Taft (Eds.), *Developmental disabilities: Theory, assessment, and intervention*. New York: Spectrum.

Rothbart, M. K., & O'Boyle, C. G. (1992). Self-regulation and emotion in infancy. In N. Eisenberg & R. A. Fabes (Eds.), *Emotion and its regulation in early development* (New Directions in Child Development, No. 55). San Francisco: Jossey-Bass.

Rothbart, M. K., & Posner, M. I. (1985). Temperament and the development of self-regulation. In H. Hartlage & C. F. Telzrow (Eds.), *Neuropsychology of individual differences: A developmental perspective*. New York: Plenum.

Rothbart, M. K., Posner, M. I., & Boylan, A. (1990). Regulatory mechanisms in infant development. In J. T. Enns (Ed.), *The development of attention: Research and theory*. Dordrecht: Elsevier North-Holland.

Rothbart, M. K., Ziaie, H., & O'Boyle, C. G. (1992). Self-regulation and emotion in infancy. In N. Eisenberg & R. A. Fabes (Eds.), *Emotion and its regulation in early development* (New Directions in Child Development, No. 55). San Francisco: Jossey-Bass.

Rourke, B. P. (1989). *Nonverbal learning disabilities: The syndrome and the model*. New York: Guilford.

Rubin, K. H. (1989). *The Play Observation Scale*. Mimeograph, University of Waterloo, Waterloo, ON.

Rubin, K. H., & Lollis, S. P. (1988). Origins and consequences of social withdrawal. In

J. Belsky & T. Nezworski (Eds.), *Clinical implications of attachment*. Hillsdale, NJ: Erlbaum.

Rubin, K. H., Mills, R. S. L., & Rose-Krasnor, L. (1991). Conceptualizing different pathways to and from social isolation in childhood. In D. Cicchetti & S. Toth (Eds.), *Rochester Symposium on Developmental Psychopathology*. Hillsdale, NJ: Erlbaum.

Rubin, K. H., & Rose-Krasnor, L. (1986). Social-cognitive and social behavioral perspectives on problem solving. In M. Perlmutter (Ed.), *Cognitive perspectives on children's social and behavioral development* (Minnesota Symposium on Child Psychology, Vol. **18**). Hillsdale, NJ: Erlbaum.

Rutter, M. (1970). Sex differences in children's response to family stress. In E. J. Anthony & C. Koupernik (Eds.), *The child in his family*. New York: Wiley.

Rutter, M. (1983). Cognitive deficits in the pathogenesis of autism. *Journal of Child Psychology and Psychiatry*, **24**, 513–531.

Rutter, M. (1991). Age changes in depressive disorders: Some developmental considerations. In J. Garber & K. A. Dodge (Eds.), *The development of emotional regulation and dysregulation*. Cambridge: Cambridge University Press.

Rutter, M., & Garmezy, N. (1983). Developmental psychopathology. In E. M. Hetherington (Ed.), P. Mussen (Series Ed.), *Handbook of child psychology: Vol. 4. Socialization, personality, and social development*. New York: Wiley.

Ryan, N. D., & Dahl, R. E. (1993). The biology of depression in children and adolescents. In J. J. Mann & D. J. Kupfer (Eds.), *Biology of Depressive Disorders*. New York: Plenum.

Saarni, C. (1979). Children's understanding of display rules for expressive behavior. *Developmental Psychology*, **15**, 424–429.

Saarni, C. (1984). An observational study of children's attempts to monitor their expressive behavior. *Child Development*, **55**, 1504–1513.

Saarni, C. (1985). Indirect processes in affect socialization. In M. Lewis & C. Saarni (Eds.), *The socialization of emotions*. New York: Plenum.

Saarni, C. (1990). Emotional competence: How emotions and relationships become integrated. In R. A. Thompson (Ed.), *Socioemotional development* (Nebraska Symposium on Motivation, Vol. **36**). Lincoln: University of Nebraska Press.

Saarni, C. (1992). Children's emotional-expressive behaviors as regulators of others' happy and sad emotional states. In N. Eisenberg & R. A. Fabes (Eds.), *Emotion and its regulation in early development* (New Directions in Child Development, No. 55). San Francisco: Jossey-Bass.

Saarni, C., & Crowley, M. (1990). The development of emotion regulation: Effects on emotional state and expression. In E. A. Blechman (Ed.), *Emotions and the family: For better or for worse*. Hillsdale, NJ: Erlbaum.

Sachar, E. J., Fishman, J. R., & Mason, J. W. (1965). Influence of the hypnotic trance on plasma 17-hydroxycorticosteroid concentration. *Psychosomatic Medicine*, **27**(4), 330–341.

Sackeim, H. A., Greenberg, M., Weiman, A., Gur, R. C., Hungerbuhler, J. P., & Geschwind, N. (1982). Hemispheric asymmetry in the expression of positive and negative emotions: Neurological evidence. *Archives of Neurology*, **39**, 210–218.

Safran, J. D., & Greenberg, L. S. (1991). *Emotion, psychotherapy, and change*. New York: Guilford.

Sagi, A., Lamb, M. E., Lewkowicz, K. S., Shoham, R., Dvir, R., & Estes, D. (1985). Security of infant-mother, -father, and -metapelet attachments among kibbutz-reared Israeli children. In I. Bretherton & E. Waters (Eds.), *Growing points in attachment theory and research. Monographs of the Society for Research in Child Development*, **50**(1–2, Serial No. 209).

Sameroff, A. J., Seifer, R., & Elias, P. K. (1982). Sociocultural variability in infant temperament ratings. *Child Development, 53,* 164–171.

Sander, L. W. (1969). The longitudinal course of early mother-infant interaction: Cross-case comparisons in a sample of mother-child pairs. In B. Foss (Ed.), *Determinants of infant behavior.* London: Methuen.

Saper, C. B., Loewy, A. D., Swanson, L. W., & Cowan, W. M. (1976). Direct hypothalamo-autonomic connections. *Brain Research, 117,* 305–312.

Scaife, M., & Bruner, J. (1975). The capacity for joint visual attention in the infant. *Nature, 253,* 265–266.

Scanlan, J. M., Suomi, S. J., Higley, J. D., & Kraemer, G. (1982). *Stress and heredity in adrenocortical response in rhesus monkeys (Macaca mulatta).* Paper presented at the meeting of the Society for Neuroscience, Minneapolis.

Schachter, S. (1964). The interaction of cognitive and physiological determinants of emotional state. *Advances in Experimental Social Psychology, 1,* 49–80.

Schachter, S., & Singer, J. E. (1962). Cognitive, social, and physiological determinants of emotional state. *Psychological Review, 69,* 379–399.

Schanberg, S., & Field, T. (1987). Sensory deprivation stress and supplemental stimulation in the rat pup and preterm human neonate. *Child Development, 58,* 1431–1447.

Schneirla, T. C. (1959). An evolutionary and developmental theory of biphasic processes underlying approach and withdrawal. In M. R. Jones (Ed.), *Nebraska symposium on motivation* (Vol. 7). Lincoln: University of Nebraska Press.

Schwartz, G., Brown, S. L., & Ahern, G. L. (1980). Facial muscle patterning and subjective experience during affective imagery. *Psychophysiology, 17,* 75–82.

Selye, H. (1950). *Stress: The physiology and pathology of exposure to stress.* Montreal: Acta.

Serafetinides, E. A., Hoare, R. D., & Driver, M. V. (1965). Intracarotid sodium amylobarbitone and cerebral dominance for speech and consciousness. *Brain, 68,* 107–130.

Shantz, C. U., & Shantz, D. W. (1985). Conflict between children: Social-cognitive and sociometric correlates. In M. Berkowitz (Ed.), *Peer conflict and psychological growth* (New Directions in Child Development, Vol. 29). San Francisco: Jossey-Bass.

Shiller, V. M., Izard, C. E., & Hembree, E. A. (1986). Patterns of emotion expression during separation in the Strange Situation procedure. *Developmental Psychology, 22,* 378–382.

Silberman, E. K., & Weingartner, H. (1986). Hemispheric lateralization of functions related to emotion. *Brain and Cognition, 5,* 322–353.

Skinner, J. E., & Yingling, C. D. (1977). Central gating mechanisms that regulate event-related potentials and behavior—a neural model for attention. In J. E. Desmedt (Ed.), *Progress in clinical neurophysiology* (Vol. 1). New York: Karger.

Skolnick, N. J., Ackerman, S. H., Hofer, M. A., & Weiner, H. (1980). Vertical transmission of acquired ulcer susceptibility in the rat. *Science, 208,* 1161–1163.

Smith, P. B., & Pederson, D. R. (1988). Maternal sensitivity and patterns of infant-mother attachment. *Child Development, 59,* 1097–1101.

Smuts, B., & Levine, S. (1977). Limbic system regulation of ACTH. *Acta Physiologica Pololica, 28,* 93–108.

Snidman, N., & Kagan, J. (in press). Cardiac function and fear during infancy. *Psychophysiology.*

Solomon, J., George, C., & Ivins, B. (1987, April). *The relationship between mother-child interaction in the home and security of attachment at age six.* Paper presented at the meeting of the Society for Research in Child Development, Baltimore.

Spangler, G., & Grossmann, K. E. (1993). Biobehavioral organization in securely and insecurely attached infants. *Child Development, 64,* 1439–1450.

Spangler, G., Meindl, E., & Grossman, K. A. (1988, April). *Behavioral organization and adrenocortical activity in newborns and infants.* Poster presented at the 6th biennial International Conference on Infant Studies, Washington, DC.

Speltz, M. J., Greenberg, M. T., & DeKlyen, M. (1990). Attachment in preschoolers with disruptive behavior: A comparison of clinic-referred and nonproblem children. *Development and Psychopathology,* **2,** 31–46.

Spieker, S. J., & Booth, C. L. (1988). Maternal antecedents of attachment quality. In J. Belsky & T. Nezworski (Eds.), *Clinical implications of attachment.* Hillsdale, NJ: Erlbaum.

Spitz, R. (1965). *The first year of life: A psychoanalytic study of normal and deviant development of object relations.* New York: International Universities Press.

Sroufe, L. A. (1979). Socioemotional development. In J. Osofsky (Ed.), *Handbook of infant development.* New York: Wiley.

Sroufe, L. A. (1983). Infant-caregiver attachment and patterns of maladaptation in preschool: The roots of maladaptation and competence. In M. Perlmutter (Ed.), *Development and policy concerning children with special needs* (Minnesota Symposia on Child Psychology, Vol. **16**). Hillsdale, NJ: Erlbaum.

Sroufe, L. A. (1990). An organizational perspective on the self. In D. Cicchetti & M. Beeghly (Eds.), *The self in transition: Infancy to childhood.* Chicago: University of Chicago Press.

Sroufe, L. A., & Fleeson, J. (1986). Attachment and the construction of relationships. In W. Hartup & Z. Rubin (Eds.), *Relationships and development.* Hillsdale, NJ: Erlbaum.

Sroufe, L. A., Schork, E., Motti, F., Lawroski, N., & LaFreniere, P. (1984). The role of affect in social competence. In C. E. Izard, J. Kagan, & R. B. Zajonc (Eds.), *Emotions, cognition, and behavior.* Cambridge: Cambridge University Press.

Sroufe, L. A., & Waters, E. (1977). Attachment as an organizational construct. *Child Development,* **48,** 1184–1199.

Stamps, L. E., & Porges, S. W. (1975). Heart rate conditioning in newborn infants: Relationships among conditionality, heart rate variability, and sex. *Developmental Psychology,* **11,** 424–431.

Stansbury, K. (1991). *Developmental differences in emotion regulation: High- and low-risk preschoolers.* Poster presented at the convention of the American Psychological Society, Washington, DC.

Stanton, M. E., Gutierrez, Y. A., & Levine, S. (1988). Maternal deprivation potentiates pituitary-adrenal stress responses in infant rats. *Behavioral Neuroscience,* **102,** 692–700.

Stein, N. L., & Levine, L. J. (1989). The causal organization of emotional knowledge: A developmental study. *Cognition and Emotion,* **3,** 343–378.

Stein, N. L., & Trabasso, T. (1989). Children's understanding of changing emotional states. In C. Saarni & P. L. Harris (Eds.), *Children's understanding of emotion.* Cambridge: Cambridge University Press.

Steriade, M. (1980). State dependent changes in the activity of rostral reticular and thalamocortical elements. In J. A. Hobson & A. B. Scheibel (Eds.), *The brainstem core: Sensorimotor integration and behavioral state control.* Cambridge, MA: MIT Press.

Steriade, M. (1981). EEG desynchronization is associated with cellular events that are prerequisites for active behavioral states: Commentary on "Reticulo-cortical activity and behavior: A critique of the arousal theory and a new synthesis." *Behavioral and Brain Sciences,* **4,** 489–492.

Stern, D. N. (1974). Mother-infant play. In M. Lewis & L. Rosenblum (Eds.), *The effect of the infant on its caregiver.* New York: Wiley.

Stern, D. N. (1977). *The first relationship.* Cambridge, MA: Harvard University Press.

Stern, D. N. (1983). *The role and nature of empathy in mother-infant interaction.* Paper presented at the Second World Congress of Infant Psychiatry, Cannes.

Stern, D. N. (1985). *The interpersonal world of the infant: A view from psychoanalysis and developmental psychology.* New York: Basic.

Stiefel, G. S., Plunkett, J. W., & Meisels, S. J. (1987). Affective expression among preterm infants of varying levels of biological risk. *Infant Behavior and Development,* **10,** 151–164.

Stifter, C. A., & Fox, N. A. (1990). Infant reactivity: Physiological correlates of newborn and 5-month temperament. *Developmental Psychology,* **26,** 582–588.

Stifter, C. A., Fox, N. A., & Porges, S. W. (1989). Facial expressivity and vagal tone in five- and ten-month-old infants. *Infant Behavior and Development,* **12,** 127–137.

Stoller, S., & Field, T. (1982). Alteration of mother and infant behavior and heartrate during a still-face perturbation of face-to-face interaction. In T. Field & A. Fogel (Eds.), *Emotion and early interactions.* Hillsdale, NJ: Erlbaum.

Stone, E., Bonnet, K., & Hofer, M. A. (1976). Survival and development of maternally deprived rats: Role of body temperature. *Psychosomatic Medicine,* **33,** 242–249.

Stratton, P. (1982). Rhythmic functions in the newborn. In P. Stratton (Ed.), *The psychobiology of the human newborn.* New York: Wiley.

Strupp, H. H., & Binder, J. L. (1984). *Psychotherapy in a new key.* New York: Basic.

Stuss, D. T., & Benson, D. F. (1986). *The frontal lobes.* New York: Raven.

Stuss, D. T., Gow, C. A., & Hetherington, C. R. (1992). "No longer gage": Frontal lobe dysfunction and emotional changes. *Journal of Consulting and Clinical Psychology,* **60,** 349–359.

Suinn, R. M. (1990). *Anxiety management training.* New York: Plenum.

Tanaka, T., & Asahara, T. (1981). Synaptic actions of vagal afferents on facial motoneurons in the cat. *Brain Research,* **212,** 188–193.

Tellegen, A. (1982). *Brief manual for the Differential Personality Questionnaire.* Unpublished manuscript, University of Minnesota.

Tennes, K., Downey, K., & Vernadakis, A. (1977). Urinary cortisol exertion rates and anxiety in normal one-year-old infants. *Psychosomatic Medicine,* **39,** 178–187.

Tennes, K., & Kreye, M. (1985). Children's adrenocortical responses to classroom activities and tests in elementary school. *Psychosomatic Medicine,* **47,** 451–460.

Terrazian, H. (1964). Behavioral and EEG effects of intracarotid sodium amytal injection. *Acta Neurochirica,* **12,** 230–239.

Thoits, P. A. (1985). Self-labeling process in mental illness: The role of emotional deviance. *American Journal of Sociology,* **91,** 221–249.

Thomas, A., & Chess, S. (1977). *Temperament and development.* New York: Brunner/Mazel.

Thompson, M. E., Felsten, G., Yavorsky, J., & Natelson, B. H. (1987). Differential effect of stimulation of nucleus ambiguus on atrial and ventricular rates. *American Journal of Physiology,* **253,** R150–R157.

Thompson, R. A. (1987a). Development of children's inferences of the emotions of others. *Developmental Psychology,* **23,** 124–131.

Thompson, R. A. (1987b). Empathy and emotional understanding: The early development of empathy. In N. Eisenberg & J. Strayer (Eds.), *Empathy and its development.* Cambridge: Cambridge University Press.

Thompson, R. A. (1989). Causal attributions and children's emotional understanding. In C. Saarni & P. L. Harris (Eds.), *Children's understanding of emotion.* Cambridge: Cambridge University Press.

Thompson, R. A. (1990). Emotion and self-regulation. In R. A. Thompson (Ed.), *Socioemotional development* (Nebraska Symposium on Motivation, Vol. **36**). Lincoln: University of Nebraska Press.

Thompson, R. A. (1991). Construction and reconstruction of early attachments: Taking perspective on attachment theory and research. In D. P. Keating & H. Rosen (Eds.), *Constructivist perspectives on developmental psychopathology and atypical development*. Hillsdale, NJ: Erlbaum.

Thompson, R. A. (1992). *Social support and the prevention of child maltreatment*. Paper commissioned by the U.S. Advisory Board on Child Abuse and Neglect. (Available through the author at the University of Nebraska)

Thompson, R. A. (1993). Socioemotional development: Enduring issues and new challenges. *Developmental Review, 13*, 372–402.

Thompson, R. A., Cicchetti, D., Lamb, M. E., & Malkin, C. (1985). Emotional responses of Down syndrome and normal infants in the Strange Situation: The organization of affective behavior in infants. *Developmental Psychology, 21*, 828–841.

Thompson, R. A., Connell, J. P., & Bridges, L. (1988). Temperament, emotion, and social interactive behavior in the Strange Situation: A component process analysis of attachment system functioning. *Child Development, 59*, 1102–1110.

Thompson, R. A., Flood, M. F., & Lundquist, L. (in press). Emotional regulation and developmental psychopathology. In D. Cicchetti & S. Toth (Eds.), *Emotion, cognition, and representation* (Rochester Symposium on Developmental Psychopathology, Vol. 6). Rochester, NY: University of Rochester Press.

Thompson, R. A., & Lamb, M. E. (1983). Individual differences in dimensions of socioemotional development in infancy. In R. Plutchik & H. Kellerman (Eds.), *Emotion: Theory, research and experience: Vol. 2. Emotions in early development*. New York: Academic.

Thompson, R. A., & Lamb, M. E. (1984). Assessing qualitative dimensions of emotional responsiveness in infants: Separation reactions in the Strange Situation. *Infant Behavior and Development, 7*, 423–445.

Tomarken, A. J., Davidson, R. J., & Henriques, J. B. (1990). Resting frontal brain asymmetry predicts affective responses to films. *Journal of Personality and Social Psychology, 59*, 791–801.

Tomarken, A. J., Davidson, R. J., Wheeler, R. E., & Doss, R. C. (1992). Individual differences in anterior brain asymmetry and fundamental dimensions of emotion. *Journal of Personality and Social Psychology, 62*, 676–687.

Tomkins, S. (1962). *Affect, imagery, consciousness: Vol. 1. The positive affects*. New York: Springer.

Tomkins, S. (1963). *Affect, imagery, consciousness: Vol. 2. The negative affects*. New York: Springer.

Tomkins, S. S. (1984). Affect theory. In K. R. Scherer & P. Ekman (Eds.), *Approaches to emotion*. Hillsdale, NJ: Erlbaum.

Trevarthen, C. (1984). Emotions in infancy: Regulators of contact and relationships with persons. In K. R. Scherer & P. Ekman (Eds.), *Approaches to emotion*. Hillsdale, NJ: Erlbaum.

Trivers, J. (1974). Parent-offspring conflict. *American Zoologist, 14*, 249–264.

Tronick, E. Z. (1989). Emotions and emotional communication in infants. *American Psychologist, 44*, 112–119.

Tronick, E. Z., Als, H., Adamson, L., Wise, S., & Brazelton, T. B. (1978). The infant's response to entrapment between contradictory messages in face-to-face interaction. *Journal of Child Psychiatry, 17*, 1–13.

Tronick, E. Z., Als, H., & Brazelton, T. B. (1977). Mutuality in mother-infant interaction. *Journal of Communication, 27*, 74–79.

Tronick, E. Z., & Giannino, A. F. (1987). The transmission of maternal disturbance to the infant. In E. Z. Tronick & T. Field (Eds.), *Maternal depression and infant disturbance*. San Francisco: Jossey-Bass.

Truex, R. C., & Carpenter, M. B. (1969). *Human neuroanatomy.* Baltimore: Williams & Wilkins.

Tucker, D. M. (1981). Lateral brain function, emotion, and conceptualization. *Psychological Bulletin,* **89,** 19–46.

Tucker, D. M., & Frederick, S. L. (1989). Emotion and brain lateralization. In H. Wagner & T. Manstead (Eds.), *Handbook of psychophysiology: Emotion and social behavior.* New York: Wiley.

Tucker, D. M., & Williamson, P. A. (1984). Asymmetric neural control systems in human self-regulation. *Psychological Review,* **91,** 185–215.

Ursin, H., Baade, E., & Levine, S. (1978). *Psychobiology of stress.* New York: Academic.

van den Boom, D. C. (1989). Neonatal irritability and the development of attachment. In G. A. Kohnstamm, J. E. Bates, & M. K. Rothbart (Eds.), *Temperament in childhood.* New York: Wiley.

Vaughn, B. E., Kopp, C. B., Krakow, J. B., Johnson, B., & Schwartz, S. S. (1986). Process analyses of the behavior of very young children in delay tasks. *Developmental Psychology,* **22,** 752–759.

Vaughn, B. E., Lefever, G. B., Seifer, R., & Barglow, P. (1989). Attachment behavior, attachment security, and temperament during infancy. *Child Development,* **60,** 728–737.

Vaughn, B. E., Stevenson-Hinde, J., Waters, E., Kotsaftis, A., Lefever, G., Shouldice, A., Trudel, M., & Belsky, J. (1992). Attachment security and temperament in infancy and early childhood: Some conceptual clarifications. *Developmental Psychology,* **28**(3), 463–473.

Voeller, K. (1986). Right-hemisphere deficit syndrome in children. *American Journal of Psychiatry,* **143,** 1004–1009.

von Salisch, M. (1992). *The expression of contempt and disgust in peer negotiations.* Unpublished manuscript, Frei Universitaet, Berlin.

Vygotsky, L. (1987). Thinking and speech. In R. Rieber & A. Carton (Eds.), *The collected works of L. V. Vygotsky* (Vol. 1). New York: Plenum.

Wadeson, R. W., Mason, J. W., Hamburg, D. A., & Handlon, J. H. (1963). Plasma and urinary 17-OHCS responses to motion pictures. *Archives of General Psychiatry,* **9,** 146–156.

Wagner, H. L. (Ed.). (1988). *Social psychophysiology and emotion: Theory and clinical applications.* New York: Wiley.

Walden, T. A. (1991). Infant social referencing. In J. Garber & K. A. Dodge (Eds.), *The development of emotional regulation and dysregulation.* Cambridge: Cambridge University Press.

Walker, C. D., Rivest, R. W., Meaney, M. J., & Aubert, M. L. (1989). Differential activation of the pituitary-adrenocortical axis after stress in the rat: Use of two genetically selected lines (Roman low and high avoidance rats) as a model. *Journal of Endocrinology,* **123,** 477–485.

Ward, M. J., Botyanski, N. C., Plunket, S. W., & Carlson, E. (1991, April). *The concurrent and predictive validity of the Adult Attachment Interview for adolescent mothers.* Paper presented at the meeting of the Society for Research in Child Development, Seattle.

Warner, R. M. (1989). Periodic rhythms in conversational speech. *Language and Speech,* **22,** 381–396.

Waters, E. (1983). The stability of individual differences in infant attachment: Comments on the Thompson, Lamb, & Estes contribution. *Child Development,* **54,** 516–520.

Waters, E., Wippman, J., & Sroufe, L. A. (1979). Attachment, positive affect, and competence in the peer group: Two studies in construct validation. *Child Development,* **50,** 821–829.

Watson, D., & Clark, L. A. (1984). Negative affectivity: The disposition to experience aversive emotional states. *Psychological Bulletin*, **96**, 465–490.

Watson, J. S., & Ramey, C. T. (1972). Reactions to response-contingent stimulation in early infancy. *Merrill-Palmer Quarterly*, **18**, 219–227.

Weber, R. A., Levitt, M. J., & Clark, M. C. (1986). Individual variation in attachment security and Strange Situation behavior: The role of maternal and infant temperament. *Child Development*, **57**, 56–65.

Weiss, J. M. (1971). Effects of coping behavior with and without a feedback signal on stress pathology in rats. *Journal of Comparative and Physiological Psychology*, **77**, 22–30.

Weisz, J., Szilagyi, N., Lang, E., & Adam, G. (1992). The influence of monocular viewing on heart period variability. *International Journal of Psychophysiology*, **12**, 11–18.

Williams, P. (1989). *Gray's anatomy* (37th ed.). New York: Livingstone.

Williams, R., & Williams, V. (1993). *Anger kills.* New York: Random House.

Wilson, A. (1985). On silence and the Holocaust: A contribution to clinical theory. *Psychoanalytic Inquiry*, **5**, 63–84.

Winnicott, D. W. (1975). *Through paediatrics to psycho-analysis.* New York: Basic. (Original work published 1958)

Wolff, C. T. (1971). Dimensions and clusters of symptoms in disturbed children. *British Journal of Psychiatry*, **118**, 421–427.

Wolff, C. T., Friedman, S. B., Hofer, M. A., et al. (1964). Relationship between psychological defenses and mean urinary 17-OHCS excretion rates: A predictive study of parents of fatally ill children. *Psychosomatic Medicine*, **26**, 576–591.

Wolff, P. (1967). The role of biological rhythms in early psychological development. *Bulletin of the Menninger Clinic*, **311**, 197–217.

Wolff, P. H. (1987). *The development of behavioral states and the expression of emotions in early infancy.* Chicago: University of Chicago Press.

Wolkowitz, O. M., Breier, A., Doran, A., Rubinow, D., Berrettini, W., Coppola, R., Gold, P., & Pickar, D. (1988). Predisone-induced behavioral and biological changes in medically healthy volunteers. *Psychopharmacology Bulletin*, **24**(3), 492–494.

Wolpe, J. (1982). *The practice of behavior therapy* (3d ed.). New York: Pergamon.

Yanowitz, F., Preston, J., & Abildskov, J. (1966). Functional distribution of right and left stellate innervation to the ventricles: Production of neurogenic electrocardiographic changes by unilateral alterations of sympathetic tone. *Circulation Research*, **18**, 416–428.

Yokoyama, K., Jennings, R., Ackles, P., Hood, P., & Boller, F. (1987). Lack of heart rate changes during an attention-demanding task after right hemisphere lesions. *Neurology*, **37**, 624–630.

Young, E. A., Akana, S., & Dallman, M. (1990). Decreased sensitivity to glucocorticoid fast feedback in chronically stressed rats. *Neuroendocrinology*, **51**, 536–542.

Young, E. A., Haskett, R. F., Murphy-Weinberg, V., Watson, S. J., & Akil, H. (1991). Loss of glucocorticoid fast feedback in depression. *Archives of General Psychiatry*, **48**, 693–699.

Youngblade, L., & Belsky, J. (1990). Social and emotional consequences of child maltreatment. In R. T. Ammerman & M. Hersen (Eds.), *Children at risk.* New York: Plenum.

Zahn-Waxler, C., & Kochanska, G. (1990). The origins of guilt. In R. A. Thompson (Ed.), *Socioemotional development* (Nebraska Symposium on Motivation, Vol. **36**). Lincoln: University of Nebraska Press.

Zahn-Waxler, C., & Radke-Yarrow, M. (1982). The development of altruism: Alternative research strategies. In N. Eisenberg (Ed.), *The development of prosocial behavior.* New York: Academic.

Zahn-Waxler, C., Radke-Yarrow, M., Chapman, M., & Wagner, E. (1992). Development of concern for others. *Developmental Psychology, 28,* 126–136.
Zajonc, R. B. (1984). On the primacy of affect. *American Psychologist, 39*(2), 117–123.
Zivin, G. (1982). Watching the sands shift: Conceptualizing development of nonverbal mastery. In R. S. Feldman (Ed.), *Development of nonverbal behavior in children.* New York: Springer.
Zurif, E. G. (1974). Auditory lateralization: Prosodic and syntactic factors. *Brain and Language, 1,* 391–404.

A FUNCTIONALIST PERSPECTIVE ON THE NATURE OF EMOTION

Joseph J. Campos, Donna L. Mumme,
Rosanne Kermoian, and Rosemary G. Campos

The field of emotion is changing rapidly and, in the process, shifting its philosophical orientation. The changes are surprisingly broad, ranging from new conceptualizations of how physiological systems are related to emotion to new conceptualizations of how culture is related to emotion. They bring new theoretical vigor to the field and open up previously dormant areas of study. The changes bring about new ways of measuring emotions and create the need for a new lexicon to describe the nature of emotion. They lead to new criteria for what is a "basic" emotion and give new functions to well-studied processes. However, the most significant of all the changes is the incorporation of a new philosophical outlook on the nature of emotion: functionalism.

The functionalist approach to emotion is apparent in many of the essays in this *Monograph* (e.g., those by Cassidy, Cole et al., Fox, Kagan, and Thompson). More specifically, emotions are conceptualized as flexible, contextually bound, and goal directed. Within the context of functionalism, the essays in this volume reflect two themes at the forefront of theorizing about emotion in developmental psychology. Perhaps the most important theme is the notion that emotion subsumes two concepts: emotion as inherently regulatory and emotion as regulated (e.g., Cole et al., Thompson). Interestingly, contrary to the layperson's view of emotion regulation, much recent research, as reflected in this volume, is focused on how emotions are closely related to the regulation of actions and action tendencies, with less emphasis on the modulation of feeling or on the control of expression. A second theme in this *Monograph* is the importance of new methods of exploring the physiological control of emotion (e.g., Dawson, Field, Fox, Hofer, Porges et al., Stansbury & Gunnar).

Our overview of the field of emotion reveals at least eight new research directions. This Commentary will discuss (1) the new conceptualization that emotion is relational rather than intrapsychic; (2) the postulation of a close interrelation between emotion and an individual's goals; (3) the emphasis on emotion "expressions" as social signals, not merely outward signs of internal states; (4) the hypothesis that, far from involving only homeostasis and the internal milieu, the physiology of emotion can regulate and be regulated by social processes; (5) the restoration of neglected links between hedonic stimulation and emotion; (6) the emergence of empirical investigations of emotions, like shame and pride; (7) the interest in emotion regulation; and (8) the study of how emotion is shaped by culture.

Emotions: From the Intrapersonal to the Relational

Functionalism in emotion theory is concerned not with evolutionary survival value but rather with the link between emotion and what a person is *trying to do*. The functionalist approach is intrinsically relational (Lazarus, 1991): it postulates that one cannot understand emotion by examining either the person or environmental events as separate entities. Person and event constitute an indissociable whole. One's perception of an event is never free of the potential that it provides for action or its relevance to one's goal. Indeed, the event gains significance through the strivings of the individual, and thus both event and goal are intertwined (Lazarus, 1991). By analogy, person and environment are the warp and the woof that together form the fabric; each has a separate existence, but, when interrelated, both lose their separate identities.

Emotion can be succinctly defined from a functionalist perspective as the attempt by the person to establish, maintain, change, or terminate the relation between the person and the environment on matters of significance to the person (see, e.g., Campos, 1986; Campos, Campos, & Barrett, 1989; Frijda, 1986). This definition may initially appear to be odd, given the absence of any reference to the traditional elements found in the most prevalent definitions of *emotion*. There is no allusion to feeling, vegetative reactions, facial indices of internal states, or other intrapersonal criteria. Instead, emotion is synonymous with the significance of a person-event transaction.

What Makes Events Significant?

The functionalist approach to emotion is predicated on the assumption that only events that are significant to the person are emotional. It is therefore important to understand what makes events significant, as a basis for theorizing about emotion (see Fox's essay). Functionalists propose at least four ways that events become significant and serve to generate emotion: by virtue of their relation to one's goals, by the social signals of others, by their relation to hedonic stimulation, or by their evocation of schematic processes, specifically, memories of past encounters.

Goals and the generation of emotion.—Goals are a powerful source for the generation of emotion. Regardless of the specific goal, an individual who overcomes an obstacle to attain a goal experiences happiness, one who must relinquish a goal experiences sadness, and one who faces obstacles experiences anger or frustration. The specific nature of the goal can affect the experience of a given emotion. Avoidance of threat is linked to fear, desire to atone is linked to guilt, and the wish to escape the scrutiny of others following a transgression is linked to shame. Much of functionalist writing concerns listing and elaborating goal-emotion relations (e.g., Barrett, in press).

One of the most important theoretical advances in studying the link between goals and emotion is that of core relational themes (Lazarus, 1991). Such themes involve an appraisal of several factors related to the generation of quite specific emotion states. One of these factors is the goal relevance of an environmental encounter, which determines whether the transaction will be affective. A second is the congruence or incongruence of the event with one's goals, which makes the transaction pleasant or unpleasant. A third is the type of ego involvement of the person engaged in the transaction, which determines the specific type of positive or negative emotion one experiences, such as happiness, anger, pride, or shame. The concept of core relational themes permits the a priori identification of the quality and intensity of a person's emotion.

The work of Stein and Trabasso (e.g., Stein & Levine, 1987; Stein & Trabasso, 1989) provides a good illustration in developmental psychology of the significance of goals in accounting for emotion states. Using children's narratives to infer emotion, these researchers have discovered that children as young as 3 years construe their experiences of emotion in terms of how events affect goals. In addition to studying narratives, these researchers are also studying real-life events to determine whether children's reports are consistent with observations of their behavior.

Social signals and the generation of emotion.—Not all emotions are generated by the relation of events to goals. Social signals have powerful capacities to render person-environment transactions significant (Klinnert, Campos, Sorce, Emde, & Svejda, 1983). They do so in at least three ways. First, social signals can generate a contagious emotion and action readiness in the other (Hatfield, Cacioppo, & Rapson, 1994). Second, social signals can render present person-environment transactions significant by giving affective meaning to perceptions associated with the signal. Third, social signals can generate emotions such as pride, shame, and guilt through the enduring effects that they can have as accompaniments to the approval and disapproval of others.

Emotional contagion, the phenomenon whereby the face, voice, or gestures of another generate the same or a similar feeling and action readiness in the perceiver, is one means whereby social signals give events significance (Hatfield et al., 1994). Thus, the sight and sounds of joy can beget joy, those of fear can elicit fear, and so on. Indeed, even the perception of anger in another can lead to subsequent oppositionality, aggressive behavior, and anger-like emotion states, as the work of Cummings and his colleagues has shown (Cummings, Zahn-Waxler, & Radke-Yarrow, 1981). In developmental psychology, the work of Haviland and Lewicka (1987) suggests that affect contagion may appear as early as 10 weeks of age, while other studies show that affect contagion and related processes such as empathy have powerful effects on the generation of emotions in infants and children (Eisenberg & Strayer, 1987; Haviland & Lewicka, 1987; Stern, 1985; Zahn-Waxler, 1991).

Second, social signals can render person-environment transactions significant by regulating the behavior of the perceiver of the signal via nonverbal communication. Until the 1980s, the responses now designated as social signals served primarily as dependent variables in studies with both infants and adults. When so used, the signals were called *emotion expressions* because investigators wanted to make inferences about internal states. However, Fridlund (1991), Jones (1991), and others have proposed, as an alternative, that "expressive" variables are important primarily because the person uses them, intentionally or not, to influence the behavior of others. Two research approaches that reflect this reconceptualization are the investigation of "audience effects," in which the incidence and intensity of emotion expressions change when others are present (Fridlund, 1991; Jones, Collins, & Hong, 1991), and affect sharing, whereby the infant or adult deliberately targets an expressive display to another (Conrad, 1994).

Third, social signals can have a crucial and long-lasting role in the generation of emotions that depend on the approval and disapproval of others. There is little doubt that the self and self-conscious emotions such as shame and pride are strongly influenced by what Mead (1934) called the *reflected appraisals of others*. The blaming signals of the parent for a disapproved act or the praise signals of the parent for a highly desired accomplishment may elicit shame or pride in the infant. Research by Lewis (1992) and by Stipek (Stipek, Recchia, & McClintic, 1992) supports the relation between social signals and the ontogeny of self-conscious emotions.

Studies of social signaling are addressing several important issues: the identification of the contexts by which information about emotion contained in the face or voice regulates an infant's behavior; the determination of the age of onset of affect-generating and behavioral regulatory capacities of social signals; the identification of when the infant first learns what the object of the emotionally contagious social signal is (e.g., is the signal aimed at self or something else in the environment?); and the determination of how social signals create lasting emotion memories.

Hedonics and the generation of emotion.—The link between hedonic stimulation and emotion comes about when such stimulation is experienced and then becomes the object of one's striving (Frijda, 1986). Hedonic stimulation refers to the sights, sounds, smells, and tactile stimulations that intrinsically produce irreducible sensations of pleasure or of pain. Pleasure and pain are affectogenic in the following way: if, after experiences with pleasant stimulation, one wants to repeat the experience, the emotion of desire is generated; similarly, if one experiences pain and wants not to repeat the experience, an aversive emotion is created (Frijda, 1986).

Here, a clarification is in order between the terms *pleasure* and *pleasantness,* on the one hand, and *pain* and *unpleasantness,* on the other. Although in our language such terms are often used interchangeably, they are sharply differentiated in functionalist theories. Pleasantness and unpleasantness are complex conscious phenomena that are attributes of an emotion, accompanying the strivings of the person. The former occurs when functioning is unimpeded and encouraged socially, the latter when difficulties occur in one's strivings or with the social signals of others. Pleasantness and unpleasantness, then, accompany all emotion—whether real or imagined. On the other hand, pleasure and pain refer to a sensory quality analogous to the sight of color or the sensation of warmth. They are more stereotypical and less subject to contextual influences.

Although ignored recently as a topic of investigation, there are many reasons for studying hedonics as a generator of emotions, particularly those of desire (Young, 1975). There is an extraordinary prevalence in our society of problems related to the striving for pleasures and sensory delights. Indeed, more problems in our society are linked to the desire to obtain hedonic stimulation than to any other source of emotion, a point made repeatedly by L. Lipsitt (personal communication, June 28, 1985). The study of hedonics is not only an important frontier of research but one that is beginning to clarify the behavior regulatory and social functions of hedonic stimulation.

The consequences of pleasant and painful stimulation are also important in themselves and therefore deserve study. For instance, health care professionals are now rethinking the meaning of neonatal pain and the implications of pleasure as a way to minimize pain (Campos, 1988, 1989, in press). A number of painful and stressful medical procedures have traditionally been performed on newborns without analgesia or anesthesia because health care professionals have thought that newborns possess a high "stimulus barrier" to environmental stimulation and that neonatal mental processes are too immature for painful stimulation to have any long-lasting effects on memory. Recently, however, it has been shown that many medical procedures create unexpectedly high levels of stress in newborns (Campos, 1993). To reduce the stress of painful stimulation in the newborn, researchers are exploring how to use positive hedonic stimulation to regulate behavior. Blass and his associates, for example, have shown how the addition of sucrose can markedly prolong the soothing effects of pacifiers and can control infant colic (Blass & Hoffmeyer, 1991; Zeifman & Blass, 1994). Still other investigators are examining the effects of topical anesthesia for reducing the stress of painful procedures (Woolfson, McCafferty, & Boston, 1990).

Memory and the generation of emotion.—Memory of transactions from the past may make events significant and thereby generate emotion. Although all theories of emotion emphasize the importance of affect-laden memories in the generation of emotion, functionalist approaches emphasize the link between past experience and choice of present coping efforts. In developmental research, an excellent illustration of this link between past experience and choice of present coping strategy comes from the work of attachment theorists on the concept of working models (Bretherton, 1985).

Although infants whose attachment relationship is insecure-avoidant or insecure-ambivalent are similar in having a history of nonharmonious interactions with the parent, the specific nature of their interactions affects their working models of how to share their emotions with an attachment figure. As Cassidy points out, avoidantly attached infants typically have a history of interactions in which their attachment figure has ignored the infant's social signals, such as bids for comfort. When these bids are consistently rejected by the caregiver, the child is predisposed to muted affect during reunions with the caregiver. The past history of ignoring social bids makes the risk of present rejection too great. By contrast, infants who are classified as ambivalently attached have an attachment figure who has responded inconsistently to their social signals. When such children are reunited with the attachment figure following separation, they show exaggerated, rather than muted, emotional reactions. The function that such exaggeration serves, at least in part, is to ensure the parent's responsiveness and to avoid the parent's insensitivity. Thus, past experiences determine not only the precise nature of the emotion a child undergoes but also the manner by which the child responds to, or copes with, contemporary interactions with the parent.

Similar considerations apply to the *parents* of the children classified as ambivalently or avoidantly attached. The parents' behavior toward their children reflects the history of their interactions with their own parents.

Working models and memories of one's past transactions with caregivers and, in adulthood, with romantic figures (Hazan & Shaver, in press) thus influence the manifestation of emotion throughout the life span. Working models influence the nature of the emotion generated by an environmental transaction, the intensity of that emotion, and the specific way in which the emotion is shown in relationships.

Functionalist Reconceptualizations of Other Issues in Emotion

The functionalist approach to emotion makes it necessary to reconceptualize a number of different theoretical and methodological issues in emotion. In the following section, we briefly review the functionalist approach to the criteria for emotion, the study of the autonomic nervous system, feeling states, measurement, derived emotions, emotion regulation, and culture and emotion.

Criteria for Emotion

The functionalist approach to emotion proposes a major change in what constitutes the criteria for emotion. Because it assumes interweaving between the person and the environment, the functionalist approach differs from theories of emotion that are posed solely in terms of internal feeling states, autonomic nervous system patterns, facial or vocal expressive behaviors, or action tendencies (when strictly defined by EMG [electromyograph] or overt instrumental behaviors). Because almost any behavior can be in the service of any of a number of emotions, depending on context (Campos et al., 1989; Lazarus, 1991), functionalists propose that emotions are understood from inferences based on (1) the way that behavior is organized, (2) suppositions about what the organism is striving to accomplish, and (3) determination of whether the striving is progressing smoothly or with difficulty (Lazarus, 1991; Sroufe & Waters, 1977).

This change in view is reflected in the essays by Kagan and Thompson, which suggest that emotions are multifaceted, that they can be manifested in many ways, and that no single indicator can serve as the criterion for emotion. Kagan emphasizes a definition of *emotion* that is complex and contextually bound. His use of affect families to describe particular person-environment transactions complements a functionalist perspective. Emotion is manifested by physiology, cognition, and motor action, which, in combination, are linked to a particular incentive or goal. Thompson similarly argues that we are moving beyond a search for discrete emotions and proposes a methodological strategy that focuses on measuring emotion dynamics, which include the temporal and intensive features of emotion (see also

Thompson, 1993). The views of Kagan and Thompson clearly reflect the search for new ways of conceptualizing emotion.

Physiology as a Relational Process

Although functionalists use standard indices of emotion, these phenomena become important for different reasons than in prior approaches. For example, autonomic nervous system patterns are thought of not as "indices" of emotion, as traditionally described, but as action patterns with important functional consequences for transactions with the environment. These standard assessments of emotion are given new, relational, importance. For example, blushing, flushing and pallor, dry mouth and sweaty brows, pupillary dilation and cold hands, and patterns of respiration convey powerful messages to the perceiver (Fridlund, 1990). They can be important social signals, not mere reactions to environmental stressors.

As Porges, Doussard-Roosevelt, and Maiti point out, the vagus nerve in particular appears to serve relational functions in at least three ways. First, via connections to the larynx, the vagus nerve mediates vocal intonation and, thus, influences one critical means of signaling emotion to others. Second, via linkages to the facial nerve, the vagus influences facial movement patterns and, hence, both the signaling function of the face and the intake of sensory information affected by facial maneuvers. Third, vagal regulation of the heart also mediates metabolic output and, thus, influences the person's approach to and withdrawal from environmental events. Porges's model of vagal tone thus links an important component of the autonomic nervous system to the establishment or disruption of person-environment relations.

The relational function of the autonomic nervous system can also be seen in research on the influence of the mothers' responsiveness on infants' physiological states. For example, Field describes an extraordinary and unsuspected relational synchrony between the mother's physiological cycles and those of her infant. Moreover, these interpersonal physiological synchronies differ as a function of the mother's physical or emotional availability. Similarly, Hofer argues that the neural substrates of emotion in the rat mother and pup are mutually regulated by specific aspects of the mother-infant interaction. The warmth, nutrients, olfactory stimulation, and behavioral activity that the mother provides and the reciprocal reactions of the pup that maintain or induce the mother's behavior, or release it from inhibition, demonstrate an exquisite behavioral and physiological dyadic organization. This organization is so intertwined that Hofer calls it mother-infant *symbiosis*.

Another relational consequence of the autonomic nervous system is its differential patterning, depending on the person's goals in generating an environmental transaction. Lacey (1959) proposed that the specific autonomic pattern a person shows when encountering a stimulus depends on what the person is trying to do with that stimulus, not on the apparent affective content of the event. For example, when the person wants to relate attentively to the environment, heart rate slows, and skin conductance increases. However, when the person wants to buffer environmental inputs, a different pattern is shown: both heart rate and skin conductance increase.

Recent data examining endocrine function suggest that the endocrine system, like the autonomic nervous system, reflects the transactions of the person with the world. Stansbury and Gunnar, for example, describe how the relation between children who are classified as behaviorally inhibited and their HPA (hypothalamic-pituitary-adrenocortical) reactivity to stress may depend on the amount of social support available to the child. They describe how fearful toddlers who had social support, as measured by "secure attachment" to the parent who accompanied them, showed less cortisol elevation during testing with arousing novel stimuli than fearful toddlers who did not have social support.

Feeling States: Antecedents or Concomitants of Emotion?

Functionalists reinterpret how feelings originate, what role they serve in emotion, and what they signify for the individual. By doing so, they differ from traditional approaches in which feelings are the subject matter in emotion to be explained by theory and research (Izard, 1971, 1991; James, 1890). In most traditional theories, feelings are closely related to emotional behaviors, which are said to be motivated by and to follow the feeling state (Clore & Ortony, 1984). In still other theories (Izard, 1971; James, 1890; Laird, 1984), the quality and intensity of feelings are explained as the result of feedback from the periphery of the body (i.e., the face, body, and internal organs).

In contrast to traditional views, the functionalist rejects the role of feelings as the criterion for emotion. Instead, feelings are conceptualized as an indissociable but not antecedent facet of the total transaction between the person and the environment. Feelings function principally as signals that help one monitor the progress of person-environment relations (Frijda, 1986). However, for functionalists, feelings are not the most important part of the process of emotion generation or of the production of expressive and instrumental reactions (Solomon, 1993). Instead, functionalists typically focus on issues such as the fate of a person's goals (Lazarus, 1991).

The functionalist conceptualizes feelings as facets congruent in time and function with behavioral attempts by the person to affect the environment. Feeling is not the antecedent of emotional behavior. One experiences pleasantness at the precise moment when one forecasts progress toward attaining a goal, when one receives positive social signals, experiences pleasure, or remembers events favorable to oneself. One experiences unpleasantness when one notes impediments to the attainment of one's goals, when one is influenced by negative emotion signals, experiences pain, or recalls events unfavorable to oneself.

Functionalists postulate several means by which feelings are elicited. Each of these means of generating feelings is intrinsically tied to potential or real action. One way that feelings are generated is as an intrinsic conscious attribute of appraisals that involve an assessment of what one can do when faced with an event. One source of feelings, then, is the detection of the meaning underlying one's transactions with the environment. Moreover, as Dewey (1894, 1895) and later Gibson (1979) have pointed out, the perception and the meaning of an event are never independent of one's potential action toward it. Meaning, appraisal, action, and feeling are indissociable.

A second way that feelings are elicited stems from the registration in consciousness of the *efference* from one's goal-oriented motoric commands. Efference, unlike afference, is rarely linked to consciousness in psychological theories, yet efference plays a role in the perception of self-motion and object motion as well as in one's sense of "willing" a body movement to take place (Teuber, 1960). Functionalists add that efference in the service of important transactions with the environment can generate feeling. For a related point, see Ekman's discussion of affect programs and motor commands (Ekman, Levenson, & Friesen, 1983). This proposition about efference, action tendencies, and feeling indicates why it is inappropriate to make feeling precede emotional behavior. Feelings thus are coincident with motor commands.

The third way by which functionalists account for the generation of feeling is through feedback from one's body as a person attempts to adapt to an environmental demand. Such feedback from the body must be an important source of feeling because of the sheer frequency by which internal responses are used to describe emotions in a multiplicity of language families (Lakoff & Johnson, 1980). Peripheral feedback must be conditioned by the context in which such feedback is generated. The same felt heartbeat that pounds with fear can also pound in sexual arousal or in anger. The perception of peripheral feedback is thus context dependent. Moreover, because such feedback follows person-environment transactions, emotional behavior cannot be said to follow the generation of feeling states.

Emotion Measurement

The stress on what a person is trying to do may make it seem that the functionalist approach to emotion merely substitutes measures of action (e.g., muscular activity) for measures of the face, the autonomic nervous system, or feeling. However, the functionalist approach conceptualizes emotions as modes of adaptation of the person to the environment, modes that are often quite flexible, often unusual, but always in the service of a goal. Thus, what makes inference of an emotion possible for the observer witnessing such behavioral flexibility is the apparent goal that the person is trying to accomplish and the person's apparent relation to that goal, despite the fact that emotions may be manifested in flexible ways (see Kagan's discussion and also Barrett & Campos, 1987).

Flexible behavioral manifestation can even be observed in unlikely contexts. For example, in our own research on fear of heights as assessed using the visual cliff apparatus (Campos, Hiatt, Ramsay, Henderson, & Svejda, 1978), we have found two ways in which infants avoid the threat of falling. Some infants avoid crossing the deep side of the cliff; others cross but do so by detouring. They cross the deep side by holding on to the side wall of the apparatus. Both patterns of responding are in the service of fear.

By recognizing that a given emotion can be manifested in different ways (e.g., fear can result in either an approach or an avoidance response), functionalists raise new questions about links between emotion and physiology. For example, what frontal EEG patterns would detouring infants show? One might observe right hemisphere activation due to the action tendency of withdrawal typically associated with fear, or one might expect left hemisphere activation due to the fact that the infant is actually approaching the mother (Fox). On the other hand, the right and left frontal regions may be specialized for different kinds of coping strategies (Dawson).

In addition to raising questions about the link between emotion and physiology, the functionalist concern that a given emotion can be manifested in different ways raises methodological issues. One such problem is that of inferring emotions from the functional properties of a stream of behavior. This is one of the most difficult problems facing functionalist theories. An approach that begins to address this problem comes from attachment theory in developmental psychology as well as from ethology (Bischof, 1976; Waters, 1978).

Sroufe and Waters (1977) proposed that, for the study of infant-caregiver attachment, "proximity seeking" or "felt security" could not be adequately measured by reference to concrete behaviors like physical distance measurable in meters and, instead, suggested the importance of measuring such behavior by determining the functional equivalence of morphologically quite different behaviors. For instance, a child can manifest proximity seeking not only by physical approach measurable in actual distance but also by pickup bids, ease of soothing when distressed, or smiles of delight on reunion with the parent. The capacity of judges to make reliable inferences using a classification system that focuses on the flexibility and organization of behavior rather than by the measurement of discrete behavior (Bretherton & Waters, 1985) highlights a potentially successful functional method for the measurement of emotion.

"Basic" and "Derived" Emotions

Functionalists take a novel stance on what constitutes a "basic" emotion. At one time, theorists such as Izard (1972; Izard & Malatesta, 1987) proposed that the emotions identifiable from facial expressions were the "basic" or "fundamental" ones; all other emotions not so identifiable (e.g., guilt, pride, envy, and love) were "derived" or "secondary" emotions. These derived emotions were said to develop as blends or combinations of the fundamental emotions, together with the maturation of cognitive skills. These views led to considerable research on the basic emotions, especially their facial expressions, and the postponement of research on others.

For functionalists, the number of basic emotions corresponds to the number of adaptational demands, not to the more limited set of universally recognizable facial movement patterns. The implication of the functionalist view is that emotions like shame or guilt are as basic as fear or sadness, insofar as the functions of their behaviors can be identified. For example, guilt can be indexed by attempts at expiation or reparation and therefore is considered a basic emotion (Barrett, in press). Similar considerations apply to other emotions such as envy, love, and jealousy.

The emotions universally recognized from facial movement patterns thus constitute a subset of important emotions, as P. Ekman (personal communication, April 1991) suggests, but not the only "basic" ones. The consequence of this shift in the conceptualization of emotion is that emotions formerly little studied are now the topic of much important developmental research (see Fischer & Tangney, in press; Lewis, 1992).

Emotion Regulation

Most contributions to this *Monograph* allude to how emotions are both regulatory and regulated. Put another way, not only do people have emotions, but they manage them as well (Frijda, 1986). On first encountering this point, the reader might be somewhat perplexed by a distinction between emotion and emotion regulation. The functionalist approach to emotion, as described so far, highlights the flexibility of the manifestation of emotions, their exquisite sensitivity to both the social and the physical context of action, and their implicit dependence on processes that monitor their manifestation. These three features of the generation of emotion—behavioral flexibility, contextual appropriateness, and monitoring of progress toward a desirable outcome—appear to render emotion and the regulation of emotion as one and the same process. Why, then, make a distinction between the two?

For the functionalist, the distinction between emotion and emotion regulation arises because the manifestation of an emotion creates the setting for new person-environment transactions. Such transactions often require changes in the manifestation of the original emotion. The consequences of the original emotion can be social, such as when a child's anger elicits unwelcome and intense retaliation; they can be physical, such as when a child's anger results in breaking a toy; and they can be psychosomatic, such as when anger increases blood pressure. In each of these cases, the outcome is very different from the intended function of the initial manifestation of anger.

To deal with such consequences of emotion, infants and adults alike engage in *emotion regulation,* which Thompson defines as "the extrinsic and intrinsic processes responsible for monitoring, evaluating, and modifying emotional reactions, especially their intensive and temporal features, to accomplish one's goals" (pp. 27–28). In this definition, Thompson stresses the functionalist features of emotion regulation by highlighting emotion regulation as in the service of one's goals and the monitoring of the effect of one's behavior on the physical and social world.

Emotion regulation serves to avoid, displace, transform, minimize, inhibit, or intensify emotions (Calkins, Cole et al., and Thompson). Emotion regulation can involve forecasting encounters and predicting their implications for the self. Emotion regulation can reconcile conflicting emotions stemming from incompatible strivings. Moreover, emotion regulation involves selecting responses acceptable to the social group to which one belongs because emotions take place in a social context.

Emotion regulation can take place at three general loci: at the level of sensory receptors (input regulation), at central levels where information is processed and manipulated (central regulation), and at the level of response selection (output regulation). Emotion regulation is a powerful phenomenon—one that can range from the prevention of an emotion to the manifestation of the opposite emotion to the one elicited.

Input regulation is an unsuspectedly powerful means of regulating emotions. One way by which it occurs is through niche picking: by choice of environment, a person can avoid unwanted emotions. For example, a shy child can live in a way that entirely precludes threatening social encounters (Kagan). Input regulation can also occur through manipulations of one's attention. For instance, one can avert one's gaze to shut out noxious stimulation, as an infant does when turning away from an approaching stranger. Input regulation can take place through distraction, which is a powerful means for managing pain as well as the emotions of grief, shame, and guilt. Finally, input regulation can occur in perceptual denial—the defense mechanism whereby the stimulus input itself fails to register in consciousness, as in the subception phenomenon described by Lazarus and McCleary (1951).

Input regulation can also result in the opposite of avoiding the generation of an undesired emotion. It can increase the frequency and intensity of desired emotions. Niche picking serves not only to avoid encounters but also to make them likely. Directing attention can result in seeking out a person or an event. Hypervigilance can take place when one seeks a longed-for person or object. Input regulation thus powerfully regulates emotion. Curiously, it is an aspect of emotion regulation not often studied or discussed.

In addition to input regulation, emotions can also be regulated at the *central processing level*. For example, regulation can take place by what Thompson refers to as *interpretation* and Lazarus (1966) refers to as *defensive reappraisal*. The role of reappraisal in emotion regulation is typically that of changing the meaning of an encounter. Reappraisal is a process that can take place in many ways, perhaps the most prevalent of which is to relate an event to a different, more desirable, goal. For instance, when facing an anger-provoking encounter that will lead to unwanted consequences, one can treat the frustrating event as a challenge rather than an affront and thus change the nature of the emotion experience to a positive one. The meaning of an encounter can also change if one gives up on the goal toward which one is striving, thereby changing anger into sadness.

At this central level, emotion regulation can also transform, modify, minimize, and intensify an emotion. With the exception of intensification, these changes occur through the use of classic defense mechanisms. Thus, an emotion can become its opposite (as in reaction formation); it can also generate a new target for its expression (as in displacement); or it can be diminished by selective forgetting of the past encounters that create meaning for an event—repression if unconsciously motivated, "suppression" (see Gross, 1993) if consciously so. Intensification of an emotion can take place in at least two ways. One is by means of a deliberate enhancement of the emotion to maximize the chances of attaining one's end. The second is through the process of arousal transfer (Zillman, 1983)—the increase in level of arousal of a second emotion resulting from remaining arousal created by a previous but no longer present emotion.

Humor, a particularly effective means by which emotion regulation can take place, can influence emotion by all four central processes discussed so far. Although there are many explanations of how humor functions to regulate emotion, it appears to operate most often through two mechanisms: one is by rendering less serious one's concerns (hence, it is an instance of minimization of emotion), and the second is by adding a degree of pleasantness to what might otherwise be a uniquely unpleasant emotional encounter (hence, transforming an emotion).

Finally, emotion regulation involves *response selection and modification.* The most obvious way in which emotional responses are regulated is by their inhibition. In the face of powerful forces, one can hold completely in check one's tendency to act on an object or a person. Emotional responses can also be controlled so that they are not expressed overtly but are rather somehow leaked or expressed via another behavior, as happens when one lets out a sigh of exasperation. Emotional responses can also be masked, the posed expression serving as an overlay to the true emotion. Finally, emotional responses can be transformed, as when one calmly and coolly selects words that in themselves show no emotion but in context leave no doubt as to their true relational intent.

This treatment of emotion regulation is necessarily sketchy because an understanding of emotion regulation draws on the content of many fields of the behavioral sciences, including abnormal, social, and developmental psychology, perception, and the pragmatics of language. The treatment is incomplete also in focusing on emotion regulation from an intrapersonal vantage point. However, no treatment of emotion regulation from a functionalist perspective can avoid discussion of the social context that elicited the need for regulation in the first place and that specifies the rules of proper conduct.

Culture and Emotion

Those who take a functionalist approach are intrinsically interested in the many meanings that the same event can have, the behavioral flexibility with which humans show their emotions, and the multiplicity of ways humans cope with the problems posed by person-environment transactions. Functionalists believe that there are universal adaptational problems faced in all societies; hence, they believe in the universality of specific emotions (Lazarus, 1991). However, functionalists do not expect the same events to have the same meaning in different cultures or the same responses to be manifested when individuals encounter the same adaptational problem. This interest leads directly to a concern with culture and emotion, but a concern that is different from traditional theories.

For functionalists, culture determines what a person is exposed to and becomes familiar with, defines events for the person, constrains response options, and generates sets of social expectations in the child. These implicit definitions and meanings of transactions, the explicit constraints on specific actions, and the different histories of interaction are embedded in the person from the beginning of postnatal life and perhaps even during prenatal existence (DeCasper & Fifer, 1980). Culture is important, then, for illustrating human variation and how such variation comes about (Lutz & White, 1986).

Functionalists are also more interested in culture in itself than in cross-cultural comparisons. Cross-cultural work is deemed very difficult to conduct because, as work on the Strange Situation has shown (Miyake, Chen, & Campos, 1985), the same physical paradigm is very likely to have different meanings in different cultures. Moreover, the child is likely to have a different "adaptational level" of exposure to social signals in one culture than in another, generating different perceptual responses to the same display.

This position on culture and emotion thus differs from those that emphasize the search for universalities in single domains of behavior, such as the lexicon (Wierzbicka, 1992), appraisal patterns (Wallbott & Scherer, in press), or emotion expressions (e.g., Ekman, 1972, 1992; Ekman & Friesen, 1971). Functionalists agree that some of the most important research on emotion is the demonstration of universal recognition of facial displays across literate and preliterate cultures (Ekman, 1994). Most cross-cultural studies of emotion conducted to date depend heavily on lexical processes, such as matching a particular peak facial expression with emotion words (Russell, 1991, 1994). One concern, recently articulated by Campos (1994), is that prototypical facial affective displays are rare in real life and probably seen only when an emotion is extremely intense. Consequently, what is now needed are studies of what real people do in real-life settings communicating real, as opposed to exaggerated, displays. For example, studies of facial expression recognition should be followed by studies of infants and children with minimal socialization of display rules (Camras et al., 1994). Such studies are needed to determine whether facial displays are innate or resistant to the cultural pressures that exist from the beginning of pre- and postnatal life.

In sum, the ecological validity of cross-cultural work on emotion and its relevance for understanding the functions of emotion currently need verification. However, the verification of universality of expression is not the most important objective for functionalists studying culture and emotion. Functionalists emphasize the flexibility rather than the stereotypy of behavior and the identification of specific adaptational problems facing people in each culture. They observe how infants, children, and adults behave when pressed with adaptational demands and try to determine culture-specific rules of conduct. Furthermore, functionalists believe that cultures must be compared, not only in terms of expressions, but in terms of the many other facets that constitute an emotion.

For example, Shweder (1993) proposes a number of domains in terms of which cultures can be studied and perhaps compared to one another. These domains include the relative exposure of people to given events, the implications for the self drawn by people in a given culture, the relation of that event to the culture's value system, the choice of preferred responses, and the manner by which emotions are coded in the language and expressed in nonverbal behavior. Shweder's proposal thus permits the identification of the domains in which emotions are similar and those in which emotions differ. The functionalist approach to culture and emotion reflects an interest in culture's many influences, from the generation of values to the manifestation of emotional behaviors.

Final Comment

What preceded demonstrates some of the important ways in which a functionalist and relational approach to emotion is heuristic, pointing to new or neglected areas of emotion, reconceptualizing others, challenging orthodox interpretations, and generating exciting new hypotheses. Functionalism is gaining ground in other fields as well, notably perception and psycholinguistics, suggesting the emergence of a new zeitgeist in the social sciences.

Although the zeitgeist may be new, functionalism itself is not. The relational aspects of functionalism are already well established in biology, where the dependence of organisms for their existence on the presence of other organisms and the physical environment has repeatedly been demonstrated. In addition, the internal physiology of homeostatic systems is more open than was once believed. As Hofer notes, "the infant delegates a portion of the control of her *milieu interieur* to processes within her relationship with her mother. Likewise, the mother's lactational physiology and probably other aspects of her internal states are open to regulation by these same interactions" (p. 206). The new relational approach in the social sciences extends the notion of open systems to a more complex level—that of all person-environment interactions of significance to the person. Exploring the implications of this "symbiosis" of person and environment, we predict, will be a central topic in the study of emotion in the foreseeable future.

References

Barrett, K. (in press). Functionalist approach to shame and guilt. In J. P. Tangney & K. W. Fischer (Eds.), *Self-conscious emotions: Shame, guilt, embarrassment, and pride*. New York: Guilford.

Barrett, K., & Campos, J. (1987). Perspectives on emotional development: 2. A functionalist approach. In J. Osofsky (Ed.), *Handbook of infant development* (2d ed.). New York: Wiley.

Bischof, N. (1976). A systems approach toward the functional connections of attachment and fear. *Child Development,* **46,** 801–817.

Blass, E. M., & Hoffmeyer, L. D. (1991). Sucrose as an analgesic in newborn humans. *Pediatrics,* **87,** 215–218.

Bretherton, I. (1985). Attachment theory: Retrospect and prospect. In I. Bretherton & E. Waters (Eds.), *Growing points of attachment theory and research. Monographs of the Society for Research in Child Development,* **50**(1–2, Serial No. 209).

Bretherton, I., & Waters, E. (Eds). (1985). Growing points of attachment theory and research. *Monographs of the Society for Research in Child Development,* **50**(1–2, Serial No. 209).

Campos, J. (1986, April). Invited address presented to the International Conference for Infant Studies, Beverly Hills, CA.

Campos, J. (1994, June). *Past, present, and future in the studies of emotional expression.* Paper presented at an invited symposium at the meetings of the International Society for the Study of Behavioral Development, Beijing.

Campos, J., Campos, R., & Barrett, K. (1989). Emergent themes in the study of emotional development and emotion regulation. *Developmental Psychology,* **25,** 394–402.

Campos, J., Hiatt, S., Ramsay, D., Henderson, C., & Svejda, M. (1978). The emergence of fear of heights. In M. Lewis & L. Rosenblum (Eds.), *The development of affect.* New York: Plenum.

Campos, R. (1988). Comfort measures for infant pain. *Zero to Three,* **9,** 6–13.

Campos, R. (1989). Soothing pain-elicited distress in infants with swaddling and pacifiers. *Child Development,* **60,** 781–792.

Campos, R. (1993, Fall). Relieving infant pain with comforting techniques. *Society for Research in Child Development Newsletter.*

Campos, R. (in press). Rocking and pacifiers: Two comforting interventions for heelstick pain. *Research in Nursing and Health.*

Camras, L., Oster, H., Campos, J., Miyake, K., Campos, R., & Meng, Z. (1994, June). *Cross-cultural studies of infant facial expression.* Paper presented at an invited symposium at the meetings of the International Society for the Study of Behavioral Development, Beijing.

Clore, G., & Ortony, A. (1984). Some issues for a cognitive theory of emotion. *Cahiers de Psychologie Cognitive,* **4,** 53–57.

Conrad, R. (1994). *Infant affect sharing and its relation to maternal availability.* Unpublished doctoral dissertation, University of California, Berkeley.

Cummings, E. M., Zahn-Waxler, C., & Radke-Yarrow, M. (1981). Young children's responses to expressions of anger and affection by others in the family. *Child Development,* **52,** 1274–1282.

DeCasper, A., & Fifer, W. P. (1980). Of human bonding: Newborns prefer their mothers' voices. *Science,* **208,** 1174–1176.

Dewey, J. (1894). The theory of emotion: 1. Emotional attitudes. *Psychological Review,* **1,** 553–569.

Dewey, J. (1895). The theory of emotion: 2. The significance of emotions. *Psychological Review,* **2,** 13–32.

Eisenberg, N., & Strayer, J. (1987). *Empathy and its development.* New York: Cambridge University Press.

Ekman, P. (1972). Universals and cultural differences in facial expressions of emotion. In J. Cole (Ed.), *Nebraska Symposium on Motivation, 1971* (Vol. **19**). Lincoln: University of Nebraska Press.

Ekman, P. (1992) An argument for basic emotions. *Cognition and Emotion,* **6,** 169–200.

Ekman, P. (1994). Strong evidence for universals in facial expressions: A reply to Russell's mistaken critique. *Psychological Bulletin,* **115,** 68–87.

Ekman, P., & Friesen, W. (1971). Constants across cultures in the face and emotion. *Journal of Personality and Social Psychology,* **17,** 124–129.

Ekman, P., Levenson, R., & Friesen, W. (1983). Autonomic nervous system activity distinguishes among emotions. *Science,* **221,** 1208–1210.

Fischer, K., & Tangney, J. (in press). Self-conscious emotions and the affect revolution: Framework and introduction. In J. Tangney & K. Fischer (Eds.), *Self-conscious emotions: Shame, guilt, embarrassment, and pride.* New York: Guilford.

Fridlund, A. (1990). Evolution and facial action in reflex, social motive, and paralanguage. In P. Ackles, J. Jennings, & M. Coles (Eds.), *Advances in psychophysiology.* Greenwich, CT: JAI.

Fridlund, A. (1991). Sociality and solitary smiling: Potentiation by an implicit audience. *Journal of Personality and Social Psychology,* **60,** 229–240.

Frijda, N. (1986). *The emotions.* Cambridge: Cambridge University Press.

Gibson, J. (1979). *The ecological approach to visual perception.* Boston: Houghton Mifflin.

Gross, J. (1993). *Emotional suppression.* Unpublished doctoral dissertation, University of California, Berkeley.

Hatfield, E., Cacioppo, J., & Rapson, R. (1994). *Emotional contagion.* New York: Cambridge University Press.

Haviland, J. M., & Lewicka, M. (1987). The induced affect response: 10-week-olds' responses to three emotion expressions. *Developmental Psychology,* **23,** 97–104.

Hazan, C., & Shaver, P. (in press). Attachment theory and interpersonal relationships. *Psychological Inquiry.*

Izard, C. E. (1971). *The face of emotion.* New York: Appleton-Century-Crofts.

Izard, C. E. (1972). *Patterns of emotions: A new analysis of anxiety and depression.* New York: Academic.

Izard, C. E. (1991). *The psychology of emotions.* New York: Plenum.

Izard, C. E., & Malatesta, C. (1987). Perspectives on emotional development: 1. Differential emotions: Theory of early emotional development. In J. Osofsky (Ed.), *Handbook of infant development.* New York: Wiley.

James, W. (1890). *Principles of psychology.* New York: Holt.

Jones, S. S. (1991). An audience effect on smile production in 10-month-old infants. *Psychological Science,* **2,** 45–49.

Jones, S. S., Collins, K., & Hong, H. (1991). An audience effect on smile production in 10-month-old infants. *Psychological Science,* **2,** 45–49.

Klinnert, M., Campos, J., Sorce, J., Emde, R., & Svejda, M. (1983). Social referencing in infancy. In R. Plutchik & P. Kellerman (Eds.), *Theory, research, and experience* (Vol. 2). New York: Academic.

Lacey, J. (1959). Psychophysiological approaches to the evaluation of psychotherapeutic process and outcome. In E. Rubenstein & M. Parloff (Eds.), *Research in psychotherapy.* Washington, DC: American Psychological Association.

Laird, J. D. (1984). The real role of facial response in the experience of emotions: A reply to Tourangeau and Ellsworth and others. *Journal of Personality and Social Psychology,* **47,** 909–917.

Lakoff, G., & Johnson, M. (1980). *Metaphors we live by.* Chicago: University of Chicago Press.

Lazarus, R. S. (1966). *Psychological stress and the coping process.* New York: McGraw-Hill.

Lazarus, R. S. (1991). *Emotion and adaptation.* New York: Oxford University Press.

Lazarus, R. S., & McCleary, R. (1951). Autonomic discrimination without awareness: A study of subception. *Psychological Review, 58,* 113–122.

Lewis, M. (1992). *Shame: The exposed self.* New York: Free Press.

Lutz, C., & White, G. (1986). The anthropology of emotions. *Annual Review of Anthropology, 15,* 405–436.

Mead, G. (1934). *Mind, self, and society.* Chicago: University of Chicago Press.

Miyake, K., Chen, S., & Campos, J. (1985). Infant temperament, mother's mode of interaction, and attachment in Japan: An interim report. In I. Bretherton & E. Waters (Eds.), *Growing points of attachment theory and research. Monographs of the Society for Research in Child Development, 50*(1–2, Serial No. 209).

Russell, J. A. (1991). Culture and the categorization of emotions. *Psychological Bulletin, 110,* 426–450.

Russell, J. A. (1994). Is there universal recognition of emotion from facial expression? A review of the cross-cultural studies. *Psychological Bulletin, 115,* 102–141.

Shweder, R. (1993). Culture and the study of emotion. In M. Lewis & J. Haviland (Eds.), *Handbook of emotions.* New York: Guilford.

Solomon, R. (1993). *The passions: Emotions and the meaning of life.* Cambridge, MA: Hackett.

Sroufe, L. A., & Waters, E. B. (1977). Heart rate as a convergent measure in clinical and developmental research. *Merrill-Palmer Quarterly, 23,* 3–27.

Stein, N. L., & Levine, L. J. (1987). Thinking about feelings: The development and organization of emotional knowledge. In R. E. Snow & M. J. Farr (Eds.), *Aptitude, learning and instruction: Vol. 3. Cognitive and affective process analyses.* Hillsdale, NJ: Erlbaum.

Stein, N., & Trabasso, T. (1989). Children's understanding of changing emotion states. In C. Saarni & P. Harris (Eds.), *Children's understanding of emotion.* New York: Cambridge University Press.

Stern, R. (1985). *The interpersonal world of the infant.* New York: Basic.

Stipek, D., Recchia, S., & McClintic, S. (1992). Self-evaluation in young children. *Monographs of the Society for Research in Child Development, 57*(1, Serial No. 226).

Teuber, H.-L. (1960). Perception. In J. Field, H. W. Magoun, & V. E. Hall (Eds.), *Handbook of physiology: Sec. 1. Neurophysiology* (Vol. 3, Chap. 65). Washington, DC: American Physiological Society.

Thompson, R. A. (1993). Socioemotional development: Enduring issues and new challenges. *Developmental Review, 13,* 372–402.

Wallbott, H., & Scherer, K. (in press). Cultural determinants in experiencing shame and guilt. In J. Tangney & K. Fischer (Eds.), *Self-conscious emotions: Shame, guilt, embarrassment and pride.* New York: Guilford.

Waters, E. B. (1978). The stability of individual differences in infant-mother attachment. *Dissertation Abstracts International, 38,* 4996. (University Microfilms No. 10-13)

Wierzbicka, A. (1992). Talking about emotions: Semantics, culture, and cognition. *Cognition and Emotion, 6,* 285–319.

Woolfson, A. D., McCafferty, D. F., & Boston, V. (1990). Clinical experiences with a novel percutaneous amethocaine preparation: Prevention of pain due to venepuncture in children. *British Journal of Clinical Pharmacology, 30,* 273–279.

Young, P. T. (1975). *Understanding your feelings and emotions.* Englewood Cliffs, NJ: Prentice-Hall.

Zahn-Waxler, C. (1991). The case for empathy: A developmental perspective. *Psychological Inquiry, 2,* 155–158.

Zeifman, D., & Blass, E. (1994). *Sucrose calming in two- and four-week-old infants.* Manuscript submitted for publication.

Zillmann, D. (1983). Transfer of excitation in emotional behavior. In J. C. Cacioppo & R. Petty (Eds.), *Social psychophysiology: A sourcebook.* New York: Guilford.

CONTRIBUTORS

Susan D. Calkins (Ph.D. 1990, University of Maryland) is assistant professor of psychology at the University of North Carolina, Greensboro. Her research interests are in the areas of temperament and socioemotional development in infancy and early childhood.

Joseph J. Campos (Ph.D. 1966, Cornell University) is professor of psychology and director of the Institute of Human Development at the University of California, Berkeley. His interests are in infant development and emotion theory and research. His empirical research centers on the psychological correlates and consequences of experiences that follow the onset of crawling, walking, and propositional speech. He is also investigating the ontogeny of emotion in Japanese, Chinese, and American infants. He is the author (with Michael Lamb) of the text *Development in Infancy,* and editor (with Marshall Haith) the second volume of the 1983 edition of the *Handbook of Child Psychology.*

Rosemary G. Campos (Ph.D. 1987, University of Denver) is assistant research nurse at the University of California, San Francisco, as well as assistant research psychologist at the University of California, Berkeley. Her research interests center on infant pain and its soothing by behavioral and pharmacological methods. She is also conducting research on the development of emotion expression and emotion communication in Japan.

Jude Cassidy (Ph.D. 1986, University of Virginia) is associate professor of psychology at the Pennsylvania State University. Her research focuses on the socioemotional development of young children, principally within the family context.

Pamela M. Cole (Ph.D. 1980, Pennsylvania State University) is professor of psychology at the Pennsylvania State University. Her research interests include emotional development, developmental psychopathology, and cross-cultural issues.

Geraldine Dawson (Ph.D. 1979, University of Washington) is professor of psychology in the Department of Psychology, University of Washington, and currently associate editor of the *Journal of Autism and Developmental Disorders*. She has edited two books, *Autism: Nature, Diagnosis, and Treatment* and *Human Behavior and the Developing Brain* (with Kurt Fischer). Her research has focused on two areas, developmental psychopathology (autism and related disorders and children at risk for affective disorders) and developmental psychophysiology (psychobiological correlates of emotion expression and regulation in infants and young children).

Jane A. Doussard-Roosevelt (Ph.D. 1989, University of Maryland) is a faculty research associate in the Laboratory of Developmental Assessment and Intervention, Institute for Child Study, University of Maryland. Her research focuses on emotion regulation and attention in infants and young children, including the psychophysiological processes involved in these domains. Her current research (with Stephen Porges) examines the value of neonatal cardiac vagal tone measures in predicting the developmental outcome of high-risk preterm infants.

Tiffany Field (Ph.D. 1976, University of Massachusetts, Amherst) is professor of pediatrics, psychology, and psychiatry at the Touch Research Institute, University of Miami School of Medicine. Her recent research is focused on the emotional development of infants and children and the use of touch therapies as alternative medicine for people of all ages experiencing medical and psychiatric conditions. Recent related publications include *Infancy* and *Touch*.

Nathan A. Fox (Ph.D. 1975, Harvard University) is professor of human development and psychology at the University of Maryland, College Park. He is the coeditor of *The Psychological Effects of War and Violence on Children* (with Lewis A. Leavitt), *The Psychobiology of Affective Development* (with Richard J. Davidson), and *Infant Day Care* (with Greta Fein). He is associate editor of *Developmental Psychology* and past president of the International Society of Infant Studies. His research interests focus on the development of emotion, developmental psychophysiology, and the personality development of infants with different styles of temperament.

Megan R. Gunnar (Ph.D. 1978, Stanford University) is professor of psychology at the Institute of Child Development, the University of Minnesota. She received a Research Career Award from the National Institute of

Child Health and Development in 1985 and a Research Scientist Award from the National Institute of Mental Health in 1990. She is currently an associate editor of the *Psychological Bulletin*.

Myron A. Hofer (M.D. 1958, Harvard University) is professor of psychiatry and director of the Division of Developmental Psychobiology, College of Physicians and Surgeons, Columbia University. His interests have centered on the processes underlying development and in early attachment and separation from the mother. He has held a Research Scientist Award from the National Institute of Mental Health since 1978 and has been president of the American Psychosomatic Society and the International Society for Developmental Psychobiology. He is on the editorial boards of journals in these fields, is the author of *The Roots of Human Behavior* (1981), and the editor (with H. N. Shair and G. A. Barr) of *Developmental Psychobiology: New Methods and Changing Concepts* (1991). Recent research papers on separation distress vocalization and its regulation by social companions appear in *Behavioral Neuroscience* and *Developmental Psychobiology*.

Jerome Kagan (Ph.D. 1954, Yale University) is the Daniel and Amy Starch Professor of Psychology at Harvard University. His research interests include temperamental influences on development as well as cognitive and emotional development in infants and young children.

Rosanne Kermoian (Ph.D. 1982, Stanford University) is assistant director of the Institute of Human Development at the University of California, Berkeley. Her research interests concern processes of developmental transitions in infancy, with particular focus on the role of motoric acquisitions, such as reaching, creeping, and walking, on changes in emotionality, understanding of emotion communication, and socialization of emotion expression in different cultures.

Ajit K. Maiti (M.D. 1956, Ph.D. 1957, Calcutta University) is director of the Jivayan Institute for Human Living in Calcutta, India. His research interests focus on the influence of vestibular stimulation on cerebellar and autonomic function. He is a former recipient of the Shati Swarup Bhatnagar Award in Medicine and Physiology. He has also served as director of the Center for Neuroscience and head of the Department of Physiology at Calcutta University.

Margaret K. Michel (B.A. 1991, University of Virginia) is a graduate student in clinical psychology at the University of North Carolina, Chapel Hill. Her research is on children's testimony in sexual abuse cases.

Donna L. Mumme (Ph.D. 1993, Stanford University) is currently a NRSA postdoctoral fellow at the Institute of Human Development at the University of California, Berkeley. Her research focuses on the early development of emotion understanding, social referencing, and parent-infant interaction. She has a particular interest in infants' receptivity to emotion signals.

Stephen W. Porges (Ph.D. 1970, Michigan State University) is professor of human development in the Institute for Child Study and director of the Laboratory of Developmental Assessment and Intervention, University of Maryland. His research has focused on the use of physiological measures as indices of psychological state, individual differences, and health. He has been awarded a U.S. patent for his methods of calculating the vagal tone index. He is the editor of *Psychophysiology* (with Michael G. H. Coles, 1976) and of *Psychophysiology: Systems, Processes and Applications* (with Michael Coles and Emanuel Donchin, 1986). He is currently president of the Society for Psychophysiological Research.

Kathy Stansbury (Ph.D. 1990, University of California, Los Angeles) is assistant professor of psychology at the University of New Mexico, Albuquerque. Her research interests include the development of emotion regulation in normally developing and high-risk children and the role of psychoneuroendocrinology in this development.

Laureen O'Donnell Teti (M.S. 1994, University of Maryland, Baltimore County) is a graduate student in applied developmental psychology at the University of Maryland, Baltimore County. Her research focuses on socialization influences on emotional development in early childhood.

Ross A. Thompson (Ph.D. 1981, University of Michigan) is professor of psychology and associate director of the Center on Children, Families, and the Law at the University of Nebraska. His research interests include early emotional development, infant-parent attachment, and the applications of developmental psychology to law (child maltreatment, child custody, and grandparent visitation rights). He is the coauthor of *Infant-Mother Attachment* (1985) and the editor of *Socioemotional Development* and currently serves as associate editor of *Child Development*.

STATEMENT OF EDITORIAL POLICY

The *Monographs* series is intended as an outlet for major reports of developmental research that generate authoritative new findings and use these to foster a fresh and/or better-integrated perspective on some conceptually significant issue or controversy. Submissions from programmatic research projects are particularly welcome; these may consist of individually or group-authored reports of findings from some single large-scale investigation or of a sequence of experiments centering on some particular question. Multiauthored sets of independent studies that center on the same underlying question can also be appropriate; a critical requirement in such instances is that the various authors address common issues and that the contribution arising from the set as a whole be both unique and substantial. In essence, irrespective of how it may be framed, any work that contributes significant data and/or extends developmental thinking will be taken under editorial consideration.

Submissions should contain a minimum of 80 manuscript pages (including tables and references); the upper limit of 150–175 pages is much more flexible (please submit four copies; a copy of every submission and associated correspondence is deposited eventually in the archives of the SRCD). Neither membership in the Society for Research in Child Development nor affiliation with the academic discipline of psychology are relevant; the significance of the work in extending developmental theory and in contributing new empirical information is by far the most crucial consideration. Because the aim of the series is not only to advance knowledge on specialized topics but also to enhance cross-fertilization among disciplines or subfields, it is important that the links between the specific issues under study and larger questions relating to developmental processes emerge as clearly to the general reader as to specialists on the given topic.

Potential authors who may be unsure whether the manuscript they are planning would make an appropriate submission are invited to draft an outline of what they propose and send it to the Editor for assessment. This mechanism, as well as a more detailed description of all editorial policies, evaluation processes, and format requirements, is given in the "Guidelines for the Preparation of *Monographs* Submissions," which can be obtained by writing to the Editor designate, Rachel K. Clifton, Department of Psychology, University of Massachusetts, Amherst, MA 01003.